STUDIA PATRISTICA

VOL. CIII

STUDIA PATRISTICA

Editor:

Markus Vinzent, King's College London and Max Weber Centre,
University of Erfurt

STUDIA PATRISTICA

VOL. CIII

The Bible in the Patristic Period

Edited by
MARIUSZ SZRAM and MARCIN WYSOCKI

PEETERS
LEUVEN – PARIS – BRISTOL, CT
2021

Reviewers:
Bazyli DEGÓRSKI
Marcela ANDOKOVA

The publication and the conference are funded by the
Polish Ministry of Science and Higher Education within the program
"Regional Initiative of Excellence" in 2019-2022,
project number: 028/RID/2018/19

© Peeters Publishers — Louvain — Belgium 2021

D/2021/0602/47
ISBN: 978-90-429-4293-6
eISBN: 978-90-429-4294-3

A catalogue record for this book is available from the Library of Congress.

Printed in Belgium by Peeters, Leuven

Table of Contents

Abbreviations

AAA	Annals of Archaeology and Anthropology, Liverpool.
AC	L'Antiquité Classique, Brussels.
AnBib	Analecta biblica, Rome.
ANRW	Aufstieg und Niedergang der römischen Welt, Berlin.
ASE	Annali di Storia dell'Esegesi, Bologna.
BASOR	Bulletin of the American Schools of Oriental Research, Chicago.
BBBA	Berichte der Berlin-Brandenburgischen Akademie, Berlin.
BI	Biblical Interpretation, Leiden.
BIFAO	Bulletin de l'Institut Français d'Archéologie Orientale, Cairo.
BLE	Bulletin de Littérature Ecclésiastique, Toulouse.
CBQ	Catholic Biblical Quarterly, Washington, DC.
CCL	Corpus Christianorum. Series Latina, Turnhout.
CSCO	Corpus Scriptorum Christianorum Orientalium, Louvain.
CSEL	Corpus Scriptorum Ecclesiasticorum Latinorum, Vienna.
GCS	Die griechischen christlichen Schriftsteller der ersten drei Jahrhunderte, Leipzig/Berlin.
GCS NF	Die griechischen christlichen Schriftsteller. Neue Folge, Berlin.
HTR	Harvard Theological Review, Cambridge, MA.
ID	Impegno e Dialogo, Nola.
IJPT	International Journal of the Platonic Tradition, Leiden.
InvLuc	Invigilata lucernis, Bari.
JAJ	Journal of Ancient Judaism, Göttingen.
JBL	Journal of Biblical Literature, Philadelphia, PA et al.
JECS	Journal of Early Christian Studies, Baltimore, MD.
JGRChJ	Journal of Greco-Roman Christianity and Judaism, Hamilton, ON.
JHI	Journal of the History of Ideas, Philadelphia, PA.
JJP	Journal of Juristic Papyrology, Warsaw.
JNSL	Journal of Northwest Semitic Languages, Stellenbosch.
JPOS	Journal of the Palestine Oriental Society, Jerusalem.
JRp	Jahrbuch für Religionsphilosophie, Freiburg.
JRS	Journal of Roman Studies, Cambridge.
JSOT	Journal for the Study of the Old Testament, Newbury Park.
JTS	Journal of Theological Studies, London.
MSLCA	Miscellanea di Studi di Letteratura Cristiana Antica, Catania.
NT	Novum Testamentum, Leiden.
NTS	New Testament Studies, Cambridge.
ParOr	Parole de l'Orient, Kaslik.
PEQ	Palestine Exploration Quarterly, London.
PG	Patrologiae cursus completus. Series Graeca, Paris.
PGL	A Patristic Greek Lexicon, Oxford.
PLSuppl	Patrologiae cursus completus. Series Latina. Supplementum, Paris.
PO	Patrologia Orientalis, Paris.
RBen	Revue bénédictine, Maredsous.
RCCM	Rivista di cultura classica e medioevale, Pisa/Rome.

REAug	Revue des Études Augustiniennes et Patristiques, Paris.
RF	Roczniki Filozoficzne, Lublin.
RFN	Rivista di Filosofia Neo-Scolastica, Milan.
RSR	Recherches de Science Religieuse, Paris.
SACh SN	Studia Antiquitatis Christianae. Series nova, Katowice.
SCh	Sources Chrétiennes, Paris.
SCN	Studia Classica et Neolatina, Gdańsk.
SEA	Studia Ephemeridis "Augustinianum", Rome.
SJT	Scottish Journal of Theology, Edinburgh.
SPCh	Studia Philosophiae Christianae, Warsaw.
SPhiloA	Studia Philonica Annual, Atlanta, GA.
STAC	Studien und Texte zu Antike und Christentum, Tübingen.
StPatr	Studia Patristica, successively Berlin, Kalamazoo, Leuven.
SVF	Stoicorum Veterum Fragmenta, Leipzig.
TRE	Theologische Realenzyklopädie, Berlin.
TS	Theological Studies, New York et al., now Washington, DC.
VC	Vigiliae Christianae, Amsterdam.
VoxP	Vox Patrum, Lublin.
VT	Vetus Testamentum, Leiden.
ZAH	Zeitschrift für Althebraistik, Stuttgart et al.
ZAW	Zeitschrift für die Alttestamentliche Wissenschaft, Giessen/Berlin.

Introduction

Mariusz Szram, Marcin Wysocki
KUL, Lublin, Poland

The Patristic period in the history of theology can be termed, with no exaggeration, the time of the Bible. The Fathers of the Church and early Christian writers almost breathed the Holy Scriptures; they lived and thought with the Bible, they interpreted it, and they constantly invoked it. It was both the starting and end point of their philosophical and theological thought. It was not only a source of scientific commentaries and liturgical homilies, but also constituted the main reference point in works whose main purpose was not biblical exegesis. The authors of the Patristic era created the first translations of biblical books and developed methods for the interpretation of sacred texts, which were developing at that time in two directions: the literal and the allegorical. They emphasised the fact that scientific and spiritual readings of the Bible could not be separated, and that all of their interpretations of biblical texts had a spiritual orientation and primarily served the internal development of the believers. Each of these early Christian writers was, in a sense, a Biblical scholar. In the history of Patristic theology, however, there were unique individuals who have merited special recognition, especially in the field of Biblical studies. One such figure was unquestionably St. Jerome of Strydon, called the 'Father of Christian Biblical Studies', and the 1,600th anniversary of whose death was celebrated in the Christian world in 2019.

The Patristic Studies circle of the John Paul II Catholic University of Lublin, which has been one of the main Patristic centres in Poland for many years, joined in the celebration of this anniversary. From almost the very beginning of the history of the University of Lublin, founded in 1918, and which from 1928 has borne the title 'Catholic' in its name, patrology was present as a theological discipline, both taught and as a subject of academic research. Patrology as a subject first appeared in the course schedule of the Faculty of Theology at KUL in the academic year 1919/1920; it was only in 1923, however, that the Department of Patrology began to function. Its Head was Rev. Jan Czuj, the author of many academic publications, as well as a translator of many works by the Church Fathers, and a researcher into the doctrine of St. Augustine and St. Cyprian. After his departure in 1929 for the University of Warsaw, the Department was not formally staffed again until 1984. Renowned patrologists, however, continued to work there. Fulfilling the obligations of Head from 1967 to 1971 was Rev. Jan Maria Szymusiak SJ, a world-renowned expert on the theology of Athanasius the Great and Gregory of Nazianzus, and the author of a critical edition of the two apologies by Athanasius the Great, published in the series *Sources chrétiennes* (SC 56) in 1956. His successor was Rev. Andrzej Bober SJ, who taught patrology from 1971-1982. His area of interest was Celtic and Anglo-Saxon Patristics. In 1983 he was succeeded by Rev. Franciszek Drączkowski, a specialist on Clement of Alexandria and the author of a handbook on patrology which became very well-known throughout Poland, and who was appointed head of the Department in 1984 and who was still working up until 2011. Currently, the Department consists of four patrologists: Rev. Prof. Jerzy Pałucki (specialist in Ambrose of Milan and Paulinus of Nola), Rev. Prof. Mariusz Szram (main research area: Origen and Alexandrian Tradition), Rev. Prof. Marcin Wysocki (working on Tertullian, Cyprian, and Latin Christian Epistolography of the 4th and 5th century) and Most Rev. Dr hab. Piotr Turzyński (specialist in Augustine).

Last year's international Patristic conference, whose contributions we present in this volume, was the third such conference, and it took place on October 16-17, 2019. Current Patristic conferences refer to the symposia organised by the Inter-Faculty Institute for Research on Christian Antiquity, founded in 1969 by two professors from the Catholic University of Lublin: Rev. Jan Maria Szymusiak SJ and Ms. Leokadia Małunowiczówna, and headed until 2012 by Rev. Stanisław Longosz. The two previous international conferences were titled 'Between *religio licita* and *religio regalis*: the Church and Theology in a Time of Change on the 1,700th Anniversary of the Edict of Milan' (October 21-23, 2013) and 'The Fathers of the Church on Heresy' (May 17-19, 2016), and the papers delivered during them can be found in *Vox Patrum*, the oldest Patristic journal in Central and Eastern Europe, published under the editorship of three KUL professors: Rev. Stanisław Longosz (1981-2012), Rev. Piotr Szczur (2012-2018) and Rev. Marcin Wysocki (since 2018).

The conference in 2019, the fruit of which is this publication, was entitled 'The Bible in the Patristic Era –Translations and Spiritual Interpretation on the 1,600th Anniversary of the Death of St. Jerome'. It brought together a group of 17 academics from Italy, Poland and the USA, who raised in their talks a whole spectrum of issues related to the Bible, its translations and interpretation. Among the speakers were well-known scholars of Christian antiquity, including Prof. Ilaria Ramelli and Prof. Lorenzo Perrone. The different themes of the issues, namely the ancient centres of Biblical studies and early Christian authors (Origen, Jerome, Cyrillon, Philastrius of Brescia, Augustine, Paulinus of Nola, John Chrysostom and Sergius the Stylite) help us better understand what the Bible meant to early Christian writers, how they used it in their works and how they lived with it.

Between Ontologisation and Apophaticism:
On the Philosophical Interpretation of *Exodus* 3:14 in the Alexandrian Tradition (1ˢᵗ-3ʳᵈ century AD)

Damian Mʀᴜɢᴀʟsᴋɪ, Kraków, Poland

Aʙsᴛʀᴀᴄᴛ

In the patristic exegesis of the first three centuries AD, the Old Testament theophanies were usually considered as an argument for the pre-existence of the Logos, as well as for His Divine origin. Furthermore, according to Greek and Latin apologists, the phrase 'I am who I am' (*Exod.* 3:14) from the story of God's revelation on Mount Horeb was pronounced, not by the Father, but by the Son who was always working with the Father. The theologians of the Alexandrian tradition interpreted *Exod.* 3:14 in a slightly different way. Their attention was mainly attracted by the verb 'to be', or, more precisely, by the designation of God as 'being' (ὁ ὤν), since such a participle form appears in the Greek translation of the *Septuagint*. According to Philo, Clement and Origen of Alexandria, it is only God who is a true being, because, unlike other beings, He is eternal and immutable in His existence. On the other hand, the Alexandrian thinkers also claimed that the term 'being' (τὸ ὄν) could not be a proper name of God. As the Divine essence is transcendent and infinite, it cannot be embraced by any definition or name. The God of the Alexandrians, therefore, remains unknowable and unnameable. Although in Alexandrian exegesis apophatics takes precedence over the ontologisation of the name of God, the allegorical interpretation of the Scriptures proposed by Philo, Clement and Origen retains its philosophical character. In fact, in its background it appeals to numerous philosophical concepts, and especially to the Platonic and Middle Platonic theory of participation and the doctrine of the primary and supreme Principles.

1. An outline of the problem to be considered

Scholastic philosophy, while identifying the essence of God with His existence, often invoked the authority of St. Augustine. In fact, the latter, referring repeatedly to *Exod.* 3:14, where God says of Himself *ego sum qui sum*, stated that God is *verum esse*[1] or *summa essentia*.[2] Such an ontologisation of the biblical name of God, however, was not characteristic of the exegesis of the first three centuries AD. The interpretation of the Old Testament theophanies

---

[1] Augustinus Hipponensis, *Sermo* 7, 7.
[2] *Id., De Civitate Dei* 12, 2.

made by Christian apologists focused mostly on demonstrating the pre-existence and presence of the Logos in the history of salvation, yet before His
incarnation.[3] This also applies to the revelation of God on Mount Horeb
described in *Exodus*. According to Justin Martyr, it was obvious that it was not
God, 'the Creator of all things', who appeared to Moses in the flame of the
fiery bush, but his messenger, the Logos. However, the exceptional status of
this Messenger is evidenced by his words, namely that He is 'the God of Abraham, the God of Isaac and the God of Jacob' (*Exod.* 3:15).[4] Irenaeus of Lyon
also stated that it was not God the Father, but the Logos who said the words:
'I am who I am' (*Exod.* 3:14),[5] for 'He who is' reveals himself through the
Son 'who is in the Father, and has the Father in himself' (see *John* 14:10-1).[6]
A similar idea can be found in Tertullian, who noted that 'the Son has always
been working in the name of the Father', for He, like the Father, is 'the God,
who is, who was, and who is to come, the Almighty' (*Rev.* 1:8).[7] The expression 'I am who I am' (*Exod.* 3:14) is not, however, the proper name of the
Father, because, according to Tertullian, only the incarnate Logos, who came
in the name of the Father, revealed who really is 'He who is'.[8]

A similar interpretation of the Old Testament theophanies had already been
carried out in the exegesis of Hellenistic Judaism. Philo of Alexandria also
believed that the transcendent God could not appear anywhere on earth, and
the Jewish patriarchs had to do with the Logos, the angel, or with one or more
of God's powers. The Alexandrian tradition, however, paid particular attention
to the passage of *Exod.* 3:14, in which the Hebrew tetragrammaton YHWH
appears. In the *Septuagint*, it was translated as ἐγώ εἰμι ὁ ὤν ('I am He who

---

[3] It should be noted, however, that the earliest interpretations of the Old Testament theophanies (1st-2nd century AD) were associated with angelology and angelomorphic Christology.
However, over time, in the biblical theophanies the Fathers of the Church began to see the
presence of the Logos of God, and, later, even of the whole Trinity. For more on this topic, see
Charles A. Gieschen, *Angelomorphic Christology: Antecedents and Early Evidence*, Arbeiten
zur Geschichte des antiken Judentums und des Urchristentums 42 (Leiden, New York, Köln,
1998), 187-314; Leszek Misiarczyk, *Il midrash nel 'Dialogo con Trifone' di Giustino Martire*
(Płock, 1999), 71-112; Darrell D. Hannah, *Michael and Christ: Michael Traditions and Angel
Christology in Early Christianity*, Wissenschaftliche Untersuchungen zum Neuen Testament 2.
Reihe 109 (Tübingen, 1999), 163-220; Bogdan G. Bucur, 'The Early Christian Reception of
Genesis 18: From Theophany to Trinitarian Symbolism', *JECS* 23/2 (2015), 245-72. For more on
the bibliography on the patristic exegesis of the first three centuries AD, see Charles Kannen-
giesser, *Handbook of Patristic Exegesis*, The Bible in Ancient Christianity 1 (Leiden, Boston,
2006), 377-645.

[4] See Iustinus Martyr, *Dialogus cum Tryphone Iudaeo* 59, 1-60, 5; *Apologia I* 63, 6-17. See
also Bogdan G. Bucur, 'Justin Martyr's Exegesis of Biblical Theophanies and the Parting of the
Ways between Christianity and Judaism', *TS* 75 (2014), 34-51.

[5] See Irenaeus Lugdunensis, *Demonstratio praedicationis apostolicae* 2.

[6] See *id.*, *Adversus haereses* III 6, 1-2.

[7] See Tertullianus, *Adversus Praxean* 18, 1-5.

[8] See *id.*, *De oratione* 3.

is' or 'I am the being'), and it was precisely being 'the being' that attracted the attention of the Alexandrian exegetes. After all, the philosophically educated thinkers of Alexandria could not pass by the biblical statement in which God is declared to be being. However, the aim of this paper is to demonstrate that the Alexandrian tradition, although sometimes agreed to have considered God as being, was much more inclined towards apophatic theology, even when interpreting the passage of *Exod.* 3:14.[9]

2. Philo of Alexandria

The interpretation of *Exod.* 3:14, which we find in the works of Philo of Alexandria, develops in two different directions, which I would call the ontologising and the apophatic explanations of the text, respectively. When it comes to the former, the formula: ἐγώ εἰμι ὁ ὤν means, according to the Alexandrian thinker, that God is a true and real being. More than that, God alone subsists in being (ὁ θεὸς μόνος ἐν τῷ εἶναι ὑφέστηκεν):[10]

This is why Moses will say of Him as best he may in human speech, 'I am He who is' (*Exod.* 3:14), implying that others lesser than He have not being, as being indeed is (τῶν μετ' αὐτὸν οὐκ ὄντων κατὰ τὸ εἶναι), but exist in semblance (δόξῃ) only, and are conventionally said to exist.[11]

In this passage, Philo draws a clear Platonic distinction between true being, which, according to the philosopher of Athens, are ideas, and that which is always becoming and is never real.[12] The former is immutable and eternal, and as such it is an object of true knowledge, the latter constantly changing, so

---

[9] Although the bibliography on the patristic exegesis of the famous statement from *Exod.* 3:14 is quite extensive, not all authors note the tension between the apophatics and the ontologisation of God's name, which accompanied the allegorical interpretation of the Scripture as proposed by the Alexandrians. Nevertheless, a few recent publications on this topic deserve to be listed here. See Charles A. Gieschen, 'The Divine Name in Ante-Nicene Christology', *VC* 57 (2003), 115-58; Albert C. Geljon, 'Philo of Alexandria and Gregory of Nyssa on Moses at the Burning Bush', in George H. van Kooten (ed.), *The Revelation of the Name YHWH to Moses: Perspectives from Judaism, the Pagan Graeco-Roman World, and Early Christianity*, Themes in Biblical Narrative Jewish and Christian Traditions 9 (Leiden, Boston, 2006), 225-36; Cornelis den Hertog, *The Other Face of God: 'I am that I am' Reconsidered*, Hebrew Bible Monographs 32 (Sheffield, 2012), 155-224; Robert J. Wilkinson, *Tetragrammaton. Western Christians and the Hebrew Name of God: From the Beginnings to the Seventeenth Century*, Studies in the History of Christian Traditions 179 (Leiden, Boston, 2015), 123-54; Bogdan G. Bucur, *Scripture Re-envisioned: Christophanic Exegesis and the Making of a Christian Bible*, The Bible in Ancient Christianity 13 (Leiden, Boston, 2018), 71-118.

[10] Philo Alexandrinus, *Quod deterius* 160.

[11] *Ibid.*; trans. Francis H. Colson, George H. Whitaker, *Philo in Ten Volumes*, Loeb Classical Library 227 (Cambridge, MA, London, 1994), 309.

[12] See Plato, *Timaeus* 27d-28a.

knowledge of it is called a belief (δόξα).[13] In another place, Philo states that the expression ὁ ὤν, by which the Scriptures define the name of God, is the proper name of God (κυρίῳ ὀνόματι καλεῖται ὁ ὤν).[14] Furthermore, it should be stressed that the Alexandrian thinker, when speaking of God, frequently in his writings uses the neuter form of the present active participle of the verb εἰμί, preceded by the article τό.[15] In this manner, abandoning the linguistic tradition of the *Septuagint* and following the Platonic tradition, he calls God simply 'being' (τὸ ὄν), as if this philosophical term were His own name.[16] The distinction between true being and that which is in the process of becoming also appears in the treatise *De Vita Moysis*, where Philo reinterprets God's statement from the passage of *Exod.* 3:14 in the following way:

> God replied to Moses: "First tell them that I am He who is, that they may learn the difference between what is and what is not (ἵνα μαθόντες διαφορὰν ὄντος τε καὶ μὴ ὄντος), and also the further lesson that no name at all can properly be used of Me (οὐδὲν ὄνομα τὸ παράπαν ἐπ' ἐμοῦ κυριολογεῖται), to Whom alone existence belongs (ᾧ μόνῳ πρόσεστι τὸ εἶναι)".[17]

The first and last statements of the above passage confirm what has already been said. Thus, there is a difference between a true being and a non-being. And it is God alone who has veritable being, since His essence consists of being.[18] In the second part of the quoted text, however, Philo seems to contradict what he states elsewhere, when interpreting *Exod.* 3:14. Thus, the formula 'I am He who is' is no longer the proper name for God, since no name (οὐδὲν ὄνομα) can be properly attributed to God. As the existence of God is completely different to that of all other creatures, God is unknowable and unnameable.[19] Therefore, in another place the Alexandrian thinker states explicitly that God did not reveal His name to Moses, but by saying 'I am He who is' just declared 'My nature is to be, not to be spoken (ἴσον τῷ εἶναι πέφυκα, οὐ λέγεσθαι)'.[20] The ineffability and unknowability of God are related to the

---

[13] See Plato, *Respublica* 477a-b.

[14] Philo Alexandrinus, *De Abrahamo* 121.

[15] See, for instance, *id., De posteritate* 2-4; *Quod deterius* 154.161; *Quod Deus sit immutabilis* 55; *De mutatione nominum* 7; *De somniis* I 230; II 237.

[16] For more on the use of the term τὸ ὄν in Greek thought and on the possible philosophical influences on the doctrine of Philo, see Sean M. McDonough, *YHWH at Patmos: Rev. 1:4 in its Hellenistic and Early Jewish Setting*, Wissenschaftliche Untersuchungen zum Neuen Testament 2. Reihe 107 (Tübingen, 1999), 11-84.

[17] Philo Alexandrinus, *De Vita Moysis* I 75; trans. Francis H. Colson, *Philo in Ten Volumes*, Loeb Classical Library 289 (Cambridge, MA, London, 1984), 315.

[18] For more on the identification of God's essence with being in Philo, see A. Geljon, 'Philo of Alexandria' (2006), 226-31; C. den Hertog, *The Other Face of God* (2012), 160-5.

[19] See Philo Alexandrinus, *De posteritate* 15-6; *De confusione linguarum* 138-9; *De mutatione nominum* 7.15; *De somniis* I 67.

[20] *Id., De mutatione nominum* 11. See also *id., De somniis* I 230.

transcendence and infinity of His essence. There are no things in God which man can comprehend. 'For it is His existence (ὕπαρξις) which we apprehend,' Philo explicitly states, 'and of what lies outside that existence nothing (τῶν δέ γε χωρὶς ὑπάρξεως οὐδέν)'.[21]

At this point, the question arises as to whether the ontological interpretation of *Exod.* 3:14 contradicts the apophatic interpretation. In my opinion, it does not. For when Philo states that God is a true being, he means to say that, in contrast to other beings, He is immutable in His existence, and that any other existence originates from Him. But when he states that God is unknowable and ineffable, he speaks of the Divine essence which is absolutely transcendent and infinite. As infinite, it cannot be embraced by anything and, if so, it cannot have any definition or name. Thus, the term 'being' is not the proper name of God, because it does not describe what a transcendent God is, but merely indicates the difference between God and His creatures.

3. Clement of Alexandria

Clement of Alexandria refers directly to the passage of *Exod.* 3:14 only a few times, and almost every time he repeats what Philo claimed in his ontological interpretation of theophany on Mount Horeb.[22] He therefore states that the formula 'He who is' (ὁ ὤν) points to 'the only truly existing being (τὸν ὄντως μόνον ὄντα) who is, who was and who will be'.[23] Such a being should

[21] *Id., Quod Deus immutabilis sit* 62; trans. Francis H. Colson, George H. Whitaker, *Philo in Ten Volumes*, Loeb Classical Library 247 (Cambridge, MA, London, 1988), 41-3. See also *id., De posteritate* 169; *De somniis* I 230-1; *Quod deterius* 89. For more on the transcendence and ineffability of God in Philo, see Deirdre Carabine, *The Unknown God. Negative Theology in the Platonic Tradition: Plato to Eriugena*, Louvain Theological and Pastoral Monographs 19 (Leuven, 1995), 191-221; Roberto Radice, 'The Nameless Principle: From Philo to Plotinus an Outline of Research', in Francesca Calabi (ed.), *Italian Studies on Philo of Alexandria* (Boston, Leiden, 2003), 167-82; Francesca Calabi, 'Unknowability of God', in Francesca Calabi (ed.), *God's Acting, Man's Acting: Tradition and Philosophy in Philo of Alexandria* (Leiden, 2008), 39-56; Damian Mrugalski, *Il Dio trascendente nella filosofia alessandrina giudaica e cristiana: Filone e Clemente* (Roma, 2013), 63-144; Ilaria Ramelli, 'The Divine as Inaccessible Object of Knowledge in Ancient Platonism: A Common Philosophical Pattern across Religious Traditions', *JHI* 75/2 (2014), 167-88, 170-3.
[22] It is worth noting, however, that, apart from the phrase 'I am who I am' (*Exod.* 3:14), Clement's attention is drawn to some other details of theophany on Mount Horeb. For example, he sees an analogy between the thorns of the burning bush and the crown of thorns of Christ crucified (Clemens Alexandrinus, *Paedagogus* II 75, 1), or between the light coming out of the bush and the spiritual light of truth that emerges from the cross of Christ (*id., Stromata* I 164, 4). Such analogies are what the thinker of Alexandria calls 'a mystical interpretation'. For more on this topic, see Bogdan G. Bucur, 'Clement of Alexandria's Exegesis of Old Testament Theophanies', *Phronema* 29 (2014), 61-79.
[23] Clemens Alexandrinus, *Paedagogus* I 71, 2. See also *id., Stromata* V 34, 5-6; I 166, 4.

not be not be placed on an equal level with created or man-made things. In fact, the term 'being' refers in an appropriate way only to the uncreated being. Transferring God's name to that which is generated is not only incorrect, but also impious, since, according to Clement, the second commandment of the Decalogue forbids it.[24] The changeable creatures, in comparison with God, who is an eternal and immutable being, are as if they were non-beings. However, when man tries to talk about the essence of God, even the term 'being' becomes an inappropriate name. Therefore, Clement, just like Philo, develops this apophatic theology and insists on the radical unknowability and ineffability of the Divine essence:

> And if we give Him a name, either we call him the One or the Good or Mind or Being (αὐτὸ τὸ ὄν) or Father or God or the Demiurge or Lord, we do not do it in a correct way (οὐ κυρίως), and we do not talk as if conferring a name on Him. But because of our helplessness, we use nice names so that our mind may have these things to lean upon and not wander at random. For one by one they do not contain information about God, but all together they are indicative of the power of the Almighty.[25]

It follows from the above text that our author puts the term 'being' (τὸ ὄν) on an equal level not only with the other philosophical names of God, but also with these biblical ones. All of them are used improperly (οὐ κυρίως) in relation to God. What the human mind is able to comprehend about God concerns His power (δύναμις), not His essence (οὐσία). Divine power, in turn, indicates how God operates in the world, but not what He is.[26] Even the process of the abstraction and purification of notions regarding God, called the *via negativa*, does not ultimately provide knowledge of the essence of God. In fact, by abstracting all that belongs to bodies and things incorporeal, the human mind comes to a concept of unity (μονάς) which has no dimension of depth, nor of breadth, nor of length, nor even a position.[27] But God, according to Clement, is also beyond the One and above the Unity (ἐπέκεινα τοῦ ἑνὸς καὶ ὑπὲρ αὐτὴν μονάδα).[28] If God does not fall under any of the physical or metaphysical

---

[24] See *id., Stromata* VI 137, 3.

[25] *Id., Stromata* V 82, 1-2; trans. Henny F. Hägg, *Clement of Alexandria and the Beginnings of Christian Apophaticism* (Oxford, 2006), 156.

[26] See Clemens Alexandrinus, *Stromata* II 5, 4-5; VI 166, 1-3. See also H.F. Hägg, *Clement of Alexandria* (2006), 246-51.

[27] See Clemens Alexandrinus, *Stromata* V 71, 2-3. For more on the *via negativa* in Clement and its relationship to the doctrines of Middle Platonists, see Raoul Mortley, *From Word to Silence*, II: *The Way of Negation, Christian and Greek* (Bonn, 1986), 17-44; Michele Abbate, 'Non-dicibilità del "Primo Dio" e via remotionis nel cap. X del Didaskalikos', in Francesca Calabi (ed.), *Arrhetos Theos. L'ineffabilità del primo principionel medio platonismo* (Pisa, 2002), 55-75; Eric Osborn, *Clement of Alexandria* (Cambridge, 2005), 120-31; H.F. Hägg, *Clement of Alexandria* (2006), 217-27; Daniel Jugrin, 'The Way of ἀνάλυσις: Clement of Alexandria and the Platonic Tradition', *SPCh* 52 (2016), 72-94.

[28] Clemens Alexandrinus, *Paedagogus* I 71, 1.

categories, then the term 'being' is also used inappropriately in relation to Him. Moreover, according to Clement, all created beings have their limits, while God is eternal, incorporeal, indivisible and infinite.[29] And precisely because He has absolutely no boundaries or parts that can be distinguished in Him, God cannot be confined by any definition, or enclosed in any name.[30]

Clement also refers to the unknowability and ineffability of God when he alludes to the biblical tetragrammaton YHWH, which would express the name of God. In this regard, he states that not only God, but also His name, is above the whole world and even beyond the world of thought (ἐπέκεινα τοῦ νοη-τοῦ).[31] Although the Alexandrian thinker does not dedicate much space to an analysis of the theophany on Mount Horeb (from *Exod.* 3:14), referring to other revelations by God to Moses (those from *Exod.* 33:13 and *Exod.* 20:21), he states:

Moses, convinced that God will never be known to human wisdom, says, 'Reveal yourself to me' (*Exod.* 33:13), and finds himself forced to enter 'into the darkness' (*Exod.* 20:21) where the voice of God was present; in other words, into the unapproachable, imageless, intellectual concepts relating to ultimate reality. For God does not exist in darkness. He is not in space at all. He is beyond space and time and anything belonging to created beings. Similarly, He is not found in any section. He contains nothing. He is contained by nothing.[32]

The above interpretation of biblical theophany is an illustration of the theoretical distinction between the essence and power of God, which the Alexandrian thinker explains a bit earlier.[33] Thus, Moses, who witnesses the theophany, in fact remains surrounded by God's power. But he is not able to see or intellectually grasp God, because the uncreated essence of God cannot be embraced by what is created, as Clement explains.[34] God cannot be contained by anything, including the human mind, although the latter is incorporeal and capable of infinite growth in its knowledge of God.[35] In another place, the Alexandrian thinker states that not only the essence of God or His name, but also the Divine power, cannot be fully comprehended and uttered by man.[36]

---

[29] See *id.*, *Stromata* V 81, 6.

[30] See *ibid.*, II 5, 3; IV 156, 1.

[31] *Ibid.*, V 38, 6-7. See also *ibid.*, V 65, 2-3.

[32] *Ibid.*, II 6, 1-2; trans. John Ferguson: Clement of Alexandria, *Stromateis: Books One to Three* (Washington, DC, 2005), 160.

[33] See Clemens Alexandrinus, *Stromata* II 5, 3-5.

[34] See *ibid.*, II 5, 4; V 71, 5; V 78, 3; V 81, 4-5.

[35] See *ibid.*, II 134, 1. See also Arkadi Choufrine, *Gnosis, Theophany, Theosis; Studies in Clement of Alexandria's Appropriation of His Background* (New York, 2002), 178-86.

[36] See Clemens Alexandrinus, *Stromata* VI 166, 1-3. For more on the concept of God's transcendence in Clement and the negative theology that is associated with it, see Salvatore R.C. Lilla, *Clement of Alexandria: A Study in Christian Platonism and Gnosticism* (Eugene, OR, 2005), 212-26; E. Osborn, *Clement of Alexandria* (2005), 122-31; H.F. Hägg, *Clement of Alexandria* (2006),

To summarise, in Clement's allegorical interpretation of the Scripture, just as in Philo's case, one can note a similar tension between ontologisation and apophatics. On the one hand, the term 'being' is a proper name of God, or, rather, it can be applied in an appropriate manner only to God, for God alone is uncreated and immutable. On the other hand, the Christian thinker states that God is absolutely transcendent, unknowable and, therefore, unnameable. Even if he sometimes describes methods for gaining knowledge of God, he is ultimately aware that they lead to knowledge not of what God is, but of what He is not.[37] The term 'being' is, therefore, one of the inappropriate names attributed to God in theological language, since it only points to the difference between God and creatures. But it certainly does not indicate everything which God is in His infinite essence.

4. Origen of Alexandria

Origen, in his interpretation of *Exod.* 3:14, slightly departs from the theses put forward by Philo and Clement. Although the phrase 'I am He who is' means, according to him, that God is a true being, immutable and eternal, and although in Platonic terms he identifies a true being with the Good,[38] he seeks to give a moral interpretation of the passage of *Exodus*:

153-79, 207-51; Annewies van den Hoek, 'God beyond Knowing: Clement of Alexandria and Discourse on God', in Andrew B. McGowan, Brian E. Daley and Timothy J. Gaden (eds), *God in Early Christian Thought: Essays in Memory of Lloyd G. Patterson*, Vigiliae Christianae Supplement 94 (Leiden, Boston, 2009), 37-60; D. Mrugalski, *Il Dio trascendente* (2013), 199-274; Johannes A. Steenbuch, 'Negative Theology and Dialectics in Clement of Alexandria's Understanding of the Status and Function of Scripture', in Veronika Černušková, Judith L. Kovacs and Jana Plátová (eds), *Clement's Biblical Exegesis: Proceedings of the Second Colloquium on Clement of Alexandria (Olomouc, May 29–31, 2014)*, Vigiliae Christianae Supplement 139 (Leiden, Boston, 2016), 129-46; Tomasz Stępień and Karolina Kochańczyk-Bonińska, *Unknown God, Known in His Activities: Incomprehensibility of God during the Trinitarian Controversy of the 4th Century* (Berlin, 2018), 38-46.

[37] See Clemens Alexandrinus, *Stromata* V 71, 4; II 72, 4.

[38] As for the identification of God with the Good, apart from the passage quoted just below, see also Origenes, *De principiis* I 6, 2, where the Alexandrian thinker states that the Good exists substantially (*bonitas substantialiter inest*) only in the Trinity, while other beings participate in the Good. As for the identification of God with being, although the passage quoted above points out that, according to Origen, God is a true being, God is also beyond being. In fact, His transcendent, immutable and eternal essence differs from the essence of the created beings that originate in Him. In this statement, the Alexandrian thinker is obviously referring to the famous passage from Plato's *Republic* 509b. See Origenes, *Contra Celsum* 6, 64; *Commentarii in Iohannem* XIII 21, 123. For more on this issue see Damian Mrugalski, 'Metamorfozy Platońskiej "metafory słońca" (*Respublica* 509b) w hetero- i ortodoksyjnej teologii (I-III w.): Gnostycyzm, Klemens z Aleksandrii i Orygenes', *VoxP* 68 (2017), 21-58, 33-41. See also Manlio Simonetti, 'Dio (Padre)', in Adele Monaci Castagno (ed.), *Origene. Dizionario: La cultura, il pensiero, le opere* (Roma, 2000), 118-24; Ronald E. Heine, 'God', in John Anthony McGuckin (ed.), *The Westminster*

We can also introduce how the wicked are called 'those who are not' because of evil, from the name of God recorded in *Exodus*: "For the Lord said to Moses: «He who is, this is my name»" (*Exod.* 3:14). Now according to us who boast that we belong to the Church, it is the good God who speaks these words. This is the same God the Savior honors when he says: "No one is good except the one God, the Father" (*Mark* 10:18). "The one who is good", therefore, is the same as "the one who is". But evil or wickedness is opposite to the good, and "not being" is opposite to "being". It follows that wickedness and evil are "not being".[39]

The essence of God is immutable in its existence – that is why God is a true being. But non-being, according to Origen, is not what is changeable or corporeal, but what is evil and not holy. For God is not only good, but also holy, pure and perfect. Everyone who comes close to God and becomes one spirit with Him through a holy life and the practice of virtues participates more in true being. Everyone who moves away from God has no participation in Him, and by not participating in true being can rightly be called a non-being.[40] The lack of goodness, virtue or holiness, therefore, points to a lack of participation in the pure existence that the Giver of existence grants.

Origen links the notion of 'non-being' to the lack of goodness or holiness, and not to the ontological changeability or corporeality of the creatures, probably because, unlike his predecessors, he clearly advocates the doctrine of *creatio ex nihilo*.[41] According to him, non-being in the strict sense is an absolute nothing from which the whole world came into being by the power of God. Moreover, by constructing this argumentation, which is some form of theodicy, Origen wants to prove that God is not to be blamed for evil. If the Scriptures state that all that exists was made by the Logos of God, and without Him nothing was made (*John* 1:3), it follows that what does not exist, or 'non-being', was not made by God. Evil, in turn, can be identified with 'non-being' because it has no substantial existence. It is nothing more than the withdrawal of created beings from the good.[42] Thus, when it comes to corporeal and changeable beings, they cannot be called 'non-being', because their existence, however accidental, is good and originates in God. In fact, all creatures participate in

Handbook to Origen (Louisville, KY, London, 2004), 107-11; Claudio Moreschini, *Storia del pensiero cristiano tardo-antico* (Milano, 2013), 389-98.

[39] Origenes, *Commentarii in Iohannem* II 13, 95-96; trans. Ronald E. Heine: Origen, *Commentary on the Gospel according to John: Books 1-10* (Washington, DC, 1989), 119.

[40] See *id., In Epistulam ad Romanos libri* IV 5, 12.

[41] See *id., De principiis* I 3, 3; II 1, 4-5; *Commentarii in Iohannem* I 17, 103; *In Epistulam ad Romanos libri* IV 5, 13. Nevertheless, it is probable that Clement of Alexandria also believed that the world was created out of nothing. See Matteo Monfrinotti, *Creatore e creazione: Il pensiero di Clemente Alessandrino* (Roma, 2014), 178. In this respect, however, he was not as unequivocal as Origen. See Clemens Alexandrinus, *Stromata* II 74, 1; V 90, 1.

[42] See Origenes, *Commentarii in Iohannem* II 13, 91-9; *De principiis* II 9, 2. See also Adele Monaci Castagno, 'Male', in A. Monaci Castagno (ed.), *Origene* (2000), 256-7; C. Moreschini, *Storia del pensiero cristiano* (2013), 417-29.

God through their existence, both righteous and wicked. The latter thesis, in Origen's view, is also supported by the biblical statement of *Exod.* 3:14:

That the activity of the Father and the Son is to be found both in saints and in sinners is clear from the fact that all rational beings are partakers of the word of God, that is, of reason, and so have implanted within them some seeds, as it were, of wisdom and righteousness, which is Christ. And all things that exist derive their share of being from him who truly exists, who said through Moses, "I am that I am" (*Exod.* 3:14); which participation in God the Father extends to all, both righteous and sinners, rational and irrational creatures and absolutely everything that exists.[43]

Although the above text refers to the Stoic concept of the *logos spermatikos*, already present in the apologists,[44] our author still moves in the field of Platonic philosophy. Everything that exists participates in true being, and everything that exists is good because it ultimately originates from the supreme Good and was created in the image of the Good.[45] Just as rational beings can never lose their participation in the Logos, even if they do not listen to the Logos,[46] so none of the existing creatures is able to lose their participation in the true being that God is, even if they choose evil. In Origen's view, the changeability of rational beings, on the one hand, influences their departure, though never complete, from God; on the other hand, it enables them to reach ever greater degrees of perfection and holiness, and, through sanctification, to reach knowledge of God.[47] But what is the subject of this knowledge?

In the treatise *De principiis* Origen explicitly states that 'our mind is of itself unable to behold God as he is' (*mens nostra ipsum per seipsam deum sicut est non potest intueri*).[48] From the beauty of God's works and the comeliness of His creatures, the human mind is able to discover the existence of the Creator, but not to reach knowledge of the Divine essence.[49] Access to the latter is possible only through grace granted by God Himself. But even with the help of grace, as Origen states elsewhere, man will never reach full comprehension of

---

[43] Origenes, *De principiis* I 3, 6; trans. George W. Butterworth: Origen, *On First Principles* (Notre Dame, IN, 2013), 44.

[44] See Iustinus Martyr, *Apologia I* 46, 2-4; *Apologia II* 10, 2-4; 13, 3-5.

[45] For Plato, this highest Good is the Idea of the Good, which is the cause of the existence of all other ideas that are real beings (see Plato, *Respublica* 509b). The visible world is also good, not only because it is an image of the world of ideas, but also because it was created by a good God – the Demiurge. 'He was good,' as Plato directly states, 'and in the good no jealousy in any matter can ever arise. So, being without jealousy, he desired that all things should come as near as possible to being like himself' (Plato, *Timaeus* 29e).

[46] See Origenes, *Commentarii in Iohannem* II 15, 108-9.

[47] See *id., De principiis* I 3, 8.

[48] *Ibid.* I 1, 6; trans. G. Butterworth (2013), 13. See also *ibid.* II 6, 1.

[49] See *ibid.* I 1, 5, where Origen states that the nature of God cannot be understood or imagined by the human mind, even if it were the purest and clearest. See I. Ramelli, 'The Divine as Inaccessible Object' (2014), 179-81; T. Stępień and K. Kochańczyk-Bonińska, *Unknown God* (2018), 46-8.

the essence of God.[50] This is because Divine essence, just like Divine Wisdom and Power, is infinite.[51] The acquisition of knowledge of God by saints reveals further unsearchable and inscrutable depths of the riches and wisdom and knowledge of God.[52] Thus, according to Origen, just as according to Philo and Clement of Alexandria, the term 'being' neither defines nor adequately names God. What God is in His essence escapes any knowledge, any definition and any name. That is why the Alexandrian thinker, in his discussion with Celsus regarding the knowledge of God, states that 'we should accept the view that God has no characteristics of which we know'.[53] In fact, all that we can know is inferior to God as He really is.

5. Conclusions

It results from the above research that the interpretation of *Exod.* 3:14 as proposed by the Alexandrian thinkers differs from that given by the apologists of Rome, Asia Minor and Africa. The latter focused mainly on the pre-existence of the Logos in Old Testament times and, in some cases, even on proving that the Logos was not only the messenger of God, but also the God 'who is who was and will be'. Instead, the allegorical interpretation of Philo, Clement and Origen of Alexandria was aimed at demonstrating the transcendence of Divine nature. It sometimes led to the conclusion that the term 'being' is the proper name of God. However, by making such statements, Jewish and Christian thinkers were merely trying to emphasise the fact that God is a being totally different from those beings which are changeable creatures. After all, all being comes from God and exists by His power, while He remains uncreated, immutable, and eternal. But being different from what is created, mutable and

---

[50] See Origenes, *De principiis* IV 3, 14.

[51] See *id.*, *De oratione* 27, 16; *Contra Celsum* 3, 77; *In Numeros homiliae* 17, 4; *Philocalia* 23, 20. On the infinity and unknowability of God in Origen, see Damian Mrugalski, 'Nieskończoność Boga u Orygenesa: Przyczyna wielkiego nieporozumienia', *VoxP* 67 (2017), 437-75; *id.*, 'Potentia Dei absoluta et potentia Dei ordinata u Orygenesa? Nowa próba wyjaśnienia kontrowersyjnych fragmentów De principiis', *VoxP* 69 (2018), 493-526; *id.*, 'Agnostos Theos: Relacja między nieskończonością a niepoznawalnością Boga w doktrynach medioplatoników', *RF* 67 (2019), 44-8. See also Ilaria L.E. Ramelli, 'Divine Power in Origen of Alexandria: Sources and Aftermath', in Anna Marmodoro and Irini-Fotini Viltanioti (eds), *Divine Powers in Late Antiquity* (Oxford, 2017), 193-8; *id.*, 'Apokatastasis and Epektasis in *Cant* and Origen, in Giulio Maspero, Miguel Brugarolas and Ilaria Vigorelli (eds), *Gregory of Nyssa: "In Canticum Canticorum". Analytical and Supporting Studies. Proceedings of the 13th International Colloquium on Gregory of Nyssa (Rome, 17-20 September 2014)*, Vigiliae Christianae Supplement 150 (Leiden, Boston, 2018), 326-39.

[52] See *Rom.* 11:33. See also Origenes, *In Epistulam ad Romanos libri* VIII 13, 6; *De principiis* IV 3, 14.

[53] See Origenes, *Contra Celsum* 6, 62.

perishable does not necessarily imply being embraced by a definition or some specific metaphysical notion. Thus, paradoxically, the term 'being' was also considered by the Alexandrian thinkers to be an inappropriate name of God on a par with other names such as the Good, Creator, Lord and even God. Such statements always emerged in the context of examining the notion of God's absolute transcendence and infinity, from which the concept of the unknowability of Divine essence derives. Moreover, Philo, Clement and Origen of Alexandria devoted much more attention in their works to the apophatic theology postulating radical unknowability and unnameability of God than to a few mentions in which God is defined as being.

Although in the exegesis of *Exod.* 3:14 by the Alexandrian thinkers apophatics took precedence over the ontologisation of God's name, their allegorical interpretation retains its philosophical character. In fact, in its background it appeals to numerous philosophical concepts, and especially to the Platonic and Middle Platonic theory of participation and the doctrine of the primary and supreme Principles. The God of the Alexandrian thinkers is the supreme Principle of the whole of reality and remains 'beyond being'. Because of His transcendence, He cannot be defined as 'being', even if He is the source of the existence of all other beings.

Origen's Philosophical Exegesis of the Scripture Against the Backdrop of Ancient Philosophy (Stoicism, Platonism) and Hellenistic and Rabbinic Judaism[1]

Ilaria L.E. RAMELLI, Durham, USA / Cambridge University, UK / Sacred Heart University, Angelicum, Italy / Erfurt, MWK, Germany

ABSTRACT

Origen was the first professional Christian Scripture scholar we know of. This essay will address Origen's polemics against some 'pagan' intellectuals regarding the allegoresis of the Scripture, and will argue for the role of Origen's allegoresis as a philosophical task (besides being philological, rhetorical, historical, and so on), and how this relates to the notion of the Scripture as the embodiment of Christ-Logos. Structural continuities will be pointed out between Origen and the Stoic allegorical tradition, as well as the struggle with Middle-Platonic allegorists for the definition of which authoritative traditions were to be allegorized. Origen wished that, ideally, all Christians could ruminate on the Scripture and interpret it, and, relatedly, that all Christians could be philosophers (*Cels.* 1.9). This needed the philosophical exegesis of their authoritative text, the Scripture. Scriptural allegoresis was the heritage of Philo, although 'pagan' Platonists, such as Celsus and Porphyry, failed – or refused – to recognize this, while Origen, as will be pointed out, acknowledged his debt to the main Jewish Hellenistic allegorists. Indeed, it will be suggested that Origen's attitude toward Jewish exegesis was less ambivalent, or even hostile, than generally represented.

Introduction: What Will Be Argued

Origen was 'the first professional Christian Scripture scholar we know of'.[2] This essay will address Origen's polemics against some 'pagan' intellectuals about the allegoresis of the Scripture, and will argue for the role of Origen's allegoresis as a philosophical task (as it was in Stoicism and Middle Platonism), besides being philological, rhetorical, historical, and so on, and how this philosophical exegesis relates to the notion of the Scripture as the embodiment of Christ-Logos. Structural continuities will be pointed out between Origen and

---

[1] Many warm thanks to Fr Marcin Wysocki and KUL for the invitation to deliver the main lecture at the splendid 3rd International Patristic Conference, *The Bible in the Patristic Era – Translations and Spiritual Interpretation on the 1600th Anniversary of the Death of St. Jerome*, October 16-18, 2019, as well as for the discussion at the conference and to the audience.

[2] Brian Daley, *God Visible: Patristic Christology Reconsidered* (Oxford, 2018), 83.

Studia Patristica CIII, 13-58.

the Stoic allegorical tradition, as well as the struggle with Middle-Platonic allegorists over the definition of which authoritative traditions were to be allegorized.

Origen wished that, ideally, all Christians could ruminate on the Scripture and interpret it, and, relatedly, that all Christians could be philosophers.[3] This needed the philosophical exegesis of their authoritative text, the Scripture. Origen presented himself, not as a grammarian, nor as a philosopher – in the sense of a 'pagan' philosopher – but as a διδάσκαλος τοῦ λόγου, who teaches the Bible and the Logos that is Christ (we shall analyze this identity of the Scripture as one of the embodiments of the Logos). Since the Logos-Wisdom (the essence of philosophy) is Christ, Origen performs Christian exegesis and Christian philosophy together.

Origen's exegesis was philosophical (in addition to being philological and so on, as mentioned), and philosophy at that time was focusing more and more on commentaries, while Christian commentaries began to be produced in Origen's time. Commentaries in imperial and late antiquity became the predominant form of academic engagement with ancient, authoritative texts.[4] Even Plotinus' *Enneads*, which are formally not a commentary, were presented by him as an exegesis of Plato's dialogues.[5] Origen's *De Principiis*, which likewise is not a formal commentary, is structured as chunks of biblical commentaries throughout. Ancient commentaries were an integral part of reading and understanding literature and philosophy (and theology, as part and parcel of philosophy at that time). The gap between 'pagan' commentaries on poets, rhetoric, and philosophy vs. Christian commentaries on the Scripture was, in fact, blurred, as I have argued elsewhere: 'pagan' philosophers such as Numenius and Amelius commented on the Bible, and Christians such as Origen and (if Christian) Calcidius commented on Plato.[6]

Scriptural allegoresis was the heritage of Philo, although 'pagan' Platonists such as Celsus and Porphyry failed – or refused – to recognize this, while Origen, as will be pointed out, acknowledged his debt to Jewish Hellenistic allegorists. Indeed, it will be suggested that Origen's attitude toward Jewish exegesis was less ambivalent, or even hostile, than generally represented.

---

[3] Origenes, *Contra Celsum* I 9.

[4] Richard Sorabji, *The Philosophy of the Commentators: 200-600 AD*, I-III (Ithaca, 2005); the series Sorabji edits collects the translations of these commentators; Philippe Hoffmann, 'What Was Commentary in Late Antiquity?', in *A Companion to Ancient Philosophy*, ed. Mary-Louise Gill (London, 2006), 597-622.

[5] Plotinus is Plato's ἐξηγητής in *Treatise* 10 (5.1) 8, Περὶ τῶν τριῶν ἀρχικῶν ὑποστάσεων, titled after Origen by Porphyry according to Ilaria L.E. Ramelli, 'Origen, Greek Philosophy, and the Birth of the Trinitarian Meaning of Hypostasis', *HTR* 105 (2012), 302-50.

[6] 'Secular and Christian Commentaries in Late Antiquity', in *The Cambridge History of Later Latin Literature*, forthcoming.

Origen's Philosophical, Investigative ('Zetetic') Allegoresis: Plato, Paul, and the Meaning of the 'Spoils from Egypt'

Origen was 'the most influential exegete of the ancient Greek church',[7] as the *Suda* has already maintained: all subsequent theologians took their cue from his exegesis (182). The Scripture was his main authority,[8] but a Scripture to be interpreted *philosophically*: such a philosophical exegesis also removed problems and contradictions on the literal plane. Now, Origen's philosophical, allegorical interpretation is Platonic,[9] and often revealed that the Scripture taught the same truths as Plato. Similarly, the Bible had also been 'Philo's *explanandum*, and what the *explanatio* to a large degree consist of are *Platonic* expressions and ideas as well as their Platonist developments'.[10]

Significantly, Origen parallels the deeper interpretation that Plato's dialogues required in order to attain their 'more sacred, more divine' level with the deeper interpretation required by Scripture for the same reason.[11] In *Commentary on the Song of Songs*,[12] Origen Platonically posits two ontological levels of reality, the physical and the metaphysical, which he, like the Bible and Plato respectively,[13] calls 'visible-invisible', 'corporeal-incorporeal' and 'earthly-heavenly'. From these two interrelated ontological levels, he deduces two interrelated Scriptural exegetical levels: the literal and the spiritual.[14] Hence, Origen's allegorical exegesis and the search for noetic/spiritual meanings in Scripture, inspired by Paul's statement that 'the letter kills, the Spirit vivifies' (2*Cor.* 3:16). According to Origen, Paul's words here refer to spiritual exegesis,[15] *i.e.* that inspired

---

[7] Judith Kovacs, 'Servant of Christ and Steward of the Mysteries', in Paul Blowers *et al.* (eds), *In Dominico Eloquio* (Grand Rapids, 2002), 147-71: 147.

[8] On scriptural authority: Stefan Schorch, 'The Authority of the Torah', in Tobias Nicklas (ed.), *Scriptural Authority in Early Judaism and Ancient Christianity* (Berlin, 2013), 1-15; Benjamin Wright, 'Pseudonymous Authorship and Structures of Authority in Aristeas', in Tobias Nicklas (ed.), *Scriptural Authority in Early Judaism and Ancient Christianity* (Berlin, 2013), 43-61; Guy G. Stroumsa, *The Scriptural Universe of Ancient Christianity* (Cambridge, 2016), with my review in *JRS* 108 (2018), 295-7.

[9] That Origen employed Platonism to interpret the Scripture is recognized by most scholars; see also the revised dissertation by Vito Limone, *Origene e la filosofia greca* (Brescia, 2018), a thorough work on Origen bringing to light many examples of this.

[10] Sami Yli-Karjanmaa, 'Philo of Alexandria', in Harold Tarrant, Dirk Baltzly, Danielle A. Layne and François Renaud (eds), *Brill's Companion to the Reception of Plato in Antiquity* (Leiden, 2018), 115-29.

[11] See Origenes, *Contra Celsum* VI 6.

[12] See *id.*, *Libri X in Canticum canticorum* III 13, 9-16; 27.

[13] Plato (*Res Publica* 509D) posits visible (ὁρατόν) in opposition to intelligible (νοητόν); *Phaedo* 85E; Apuleius (*De Platone et dogmate eius* 1, 5) quotes Plato that God is invisible (ἀόρατος): the 'visible/invisible' language is not only scriptural, as Origen remarks, but also Platonic.

[14] See Origenes, *Libri X in Canticum canticorum* III 13, 28.

[15] See *id.*, *Contra Celsum* VII 20.

by the Spirit (*secundum spiritum intelligat*) and able to attain spiritual hidden meanings (*spiritalia mysteria*),[16] tracing 'hints of a spiritual, rational interpretation' (*indicia spiritualis uerbi et interpretationis rationabilis*).[17] In *Commentary on John*, he clarifies 2*Cor.* 3:16 as bringing about real death (sin, which separates people from God): 'The letter kills and brings about death, not as a separation of the soul from the body, but of the soul from God, its Lord, and the Holy Spirit'.[18]

Origen's *Letter to Gregory/Theodore* exhorts the disciple to take what he has learnt from Greek philosophy and the liberal arts at Origen's school as preparation (προπαιδεύματα) for Christianity, Χριστιανισμόν.[19] The liberal arts are useful (χρήσιμος) for the interpretation of the Scripture: they are the helpmates of philosophy, which, in turn, is crowned by theology – a structure that most Platonists would have agreed with. Here, Origen's use of the 'spoils from Egypt' allegory (*Exod.* 12:35-6) may suggest an antagonism to Greek *paideia*, but this depends on the context, Origen's source – Philo,[20] extremely influential on Origen's exegesis, as we shall see – and the genre.

Indeed, in this letter Origen is addressing a student who must choose whether to become a lawyer, a professional philosopher in a 'pagan' school, or an exegete-theologian. In this context of opposite choices, it is normal to use the 'spoils from Egypt' image, which can be explained away easily. Origen derived this metaphor from Philo, but what Origen suggests is a strong assimilation of Greek *philosophy*, without which the disciple could not pursue *theology*. As philosophy is the pinnacle of *paideia*, so is theology the pinnacle of philosophy. Origen is using Plato's own terminology when stating that the liberal arts are the assistants/fellow-workers (συνέριθοι) of philosophy, and that the latter is the συνέριθος of Christian theology.[21] Philo, with whom Origen was well acquainted, had already posited the same hierarchy of liberal arts, philosophy, and theology, which probably inspired Origen.[22] Philo here remarks that the liberal arts (τὰ ἐγκύκλια) contribute to the acquisition of philosophy, and philosophy to that of wisdom (σοφία). For philosophy, etymologically, seeks wisdom (φιλο-σο-φία), and wisdom is 'the knowledge of things divine and human and their causes'. The liberal arts, Philo concludes, serve philosophy, but 'philosophy is a slave [δούλη] of theology' (this anticipates the Mediaeval motto, *philosophia ancilla theologiae*). Basically, what Philo here calls wisdom and what Origen

---

[16] *Id., Libri X in Canticum canticorum* III 1, 4.
[17] *Ibid.* II 8, 23.
[18] See *id., Commentarii in Ioannem* XIII 21, 140.
[19] *Id., Epistula ad Gregorium Thaumaturgum* 1.
[20] J.S. Allen, *The Despoliation of Egypt in Pre-Rabbinic, Rabbinic, and Patristic Traditions* (Leiden, 2008), 91-117 on Philo.
[21] See Plato, *Respublica* 7, 533D; *De legibus* 899D.
[22] See Philo Alexandrinus, *De Congressu Eruditionis Gratia* 78-80.

calls epoptics is theology.[23] This is clear not only from our analysis of Plato's epoptics, but also from the last part of Philo's passage, where he compares philosophy, which teaches self-control, to theology, which elevates philosophy: 'Philosophy teaches self-control [ἐγκράτεια] of the belly, of the parts below it, and of the tongue. These acts of control are to be chosen [αἱρετά] by themselves, but they appear more venerable if practiced for the glory and pleasure of God'. Philo uses, as usual, Stoic terminology here (ἐγκράτεια, αἱρετά, etc.), and he also follows the Stoic line when he values the liberal arts.

This valuing of the liberal arts as the basis for philosophy and theology is one of the reasons why Origen dismissed the Middle Platonist Celsus qua 'Epicurean',[24] since Epicureans, unlike Plato and the Stoics, devalued the liberal arts. As Origen often remarks, whatever was said by philosophers well and reasonably, wisely and knowingly, must be appropriated, as Justin and Clement also maintained.[25] Not every philosophy is useful – Epicureanism was dismissed by Origen, Platonism was retained – and within what is good, some doctrines are better than others. While the 'Egyptians', *i.e.* the 'pagans', misused their own *paideia* and philosophy, because they put it into the service of a false religion, the Hebrews, *i.e.* the Christians, used it properly, to support the true religion.[26] This perspective will be further developed in the *Letters* of the Christian Platonist Ps.Dionysius.

Origen's *Letter to Gregory/Theodore* appears more hostile to 'Gnostics' than to philosophers. 'Gnostics' are unmasked as false Christians who, instead of using philosophy for Christian theology, were lured by 'paganism' and interpreted the Scripture according to their 'inventions' (ἀναπλάσματα) and 'heretical thoughts' (αἱρετικὰ νοήματα). Origen often attributes myths and inventions to them. As Origen recommends at the end of the letter, Christian theology must be firmly grounded in biblical exegesis, which had to be anti-'heretical',[27] but the 'zetetic' exegesis theorized and practiced by Origen was philosophical. Only this could attain the spiritual meanings of the Scripture. Clement's *Letter to Theodore* about the 'spiritual Gospel of Mark' is now deemed not to be a forgery, and has been reattributed to Origen by Michael Zeddies.[28] If this is the

---

[23] See my 'Epopteia, epoptics in Platonism, "pagan" and Christian', in Harold Tarrant (ed.), *The language of Inspiration or Divine Diction in the Platonic Tradition* (forthcoming).

[24] Origenes, *Contra Celsum* III 49.

[25] See *id.*, *In Leviticum homiliae XVI* 7, 6, 7.

[26] Significantly, Frances Young's 'Towards a Christian *paideia*', in Margaret Mitchell and Frances Young (eds), *The Cambridge History of Christianity I* (Cambridge, 2006), 485-500, is dominated by Origen; her 'Biblical Interpretation', in *Brill Encyclopedia of Early Christianity* online (print Leiden 2021), 19-25 has a brief overview of Origen's (only scriptural) exegesis (20-22).

[27] Alain le Boulluec, 'L'écriture comme norme hérésiologique dans les controverses des IIᵉ et IIIᵉ siècles (domaine grec)', in Georg Schöllgen and Clemens Scholten (eds), *Stimuli. FS Dassmann*, (Münster, 1996), 66-76.

[28] Michael Zeddies, 'Did Origen Write the Letter to Theodore?', *JECS* 25 (2017), 55-87; *id.* 'An Origenian Background for the Letter to Theodore', *HTR* 112/3 (2019), 376-406. Cautiously

case (although there is no certainty whatsoever), the recipient, Theodore, a disciple of the author's, might be Gregory Thaumaturgus; what is more, the Gospel's spiritual nature (πνευματικώτερον) and its being composed for the 'perfect'[29] would fit well with Origen's spiritual exegesis, which addresses the perfect (as we shall see). Origen never mentions the 'mystical Mark', at least in his extant works, but was acquainted with the Carpocratians.[30] This would also fit well with the oath of secrecy that Origen took at Ammonius' school, if we assume that this was 'our' Origen.

Origen's philosophical exegesis was already theorized by Plato, who related hermeneutics (ἑρμηνευτική) to the royal or divine art because of its directive power,[31] and described Apollo as an 'ancestral ἐξηγητής' who guides, indicates, and signifies.[32] In his *Laws*, Plato prescribed the institution of exegetes to the interpretation of the Delphic oracles. Likewise, Plotinus viewed Plato's texts as oracles to be interpreted[33] – exactly as Origen viewed the Scripture: this was further stressed by Origen's follower, Dionysius the Areopagite, who repeatedly called the Scripture 'oracles' (λόγια).[34] Remarkably, the very fact that Origen theorized about biblical exegesis within his *philosophical* master-piece (in Book IV of *First Principles*), rather than in exegetical works, further reveals that scriptural hermeneutics was, for Origen, a *philosophical* task, exactly as it was for Plato, most Stoics, and the 'Middle Platonists', as will be pointed out below.

Indeed, Origen applied the terminology and method of philosophical 'zetesis' to Scriptural interpretation. Thus, he suggested that, whereas every Scriptural passage has a *spiritual* sense, the few passages deprived of *literal* meaning,[35] because of logical absurdities (ἄλογα), paradoxes (παράδοξα) or material impossibilities (ἀδύνατα),[36] such as anthropomorphisms applied to God,[37] point to the necessity of seeking deeper meanings.[38] Interestingly, anthropomorphisms

---

favorable to the authenticity of the letter (as Clement's), rather than a forgery by Morton Smith, is Ilaria L.E. Ramelli, 'The Birth of the Rome-Alexandria Connection: The Early Sources on Mark and Philo, and the Petrine Tradition', *The Studia Philonica Annual* 23 (2011), 69-95, and Annewies van den Hoek therein.

[29] Examined in Ramelli, 'Rome-Alexandria Connection' (2011).

[30] See Origenes, *Contra Celsum* V 62.

[31] Plato, *Politicus* 260DE.

[32] *Id.*, *Respublica* 4, 42BC.

[33] A. Eon, 'La notion plotinienne d'exégèse', *Revue Internationale de Philosophie* 92 (1970), 276.

[34] I argue this, and Dionysius' Origenian legacy in 'Origen, Evagrius and Dionysios', in *Oxford Handbook to Dionysius the Areopagite* (Oxford, forthcoming), Ch. 5.

[35] Origenes, *De Principiis* IV 2, 5; 9.

[36] *Ibid.* IV 3, 1-4.

[37] On which see Mark Sheridan, *Language for God in the Patristic Tradition: Wrestling with Biblical Anthropomorphism* (Downers Grove, 2015).

[38] Origenes, *De Principiis* II 9 (analysed below).

ascribed to deities were one of the main reasons which, in ancient Greece, first led to the allegoresis of myths, in that anthropomorphisms represented the deities in an unworthy way that called for an explanation,[39] and Stoicism, in particular, allegorized all anthropomorphisms, especially the attribution of passions to the divine.

Now, we shall see that Origen, albeit disagreeing with Stoic materialism and immanentism (already rejected by Justin), drew on Stoic allegoresis, and prominently on that of anthropomorphisms, as well as on Philo's biblical allegoresis, for his own allegorical/noetic/spiritual exegesis of the Scripture. Origen criticized Celsus for failing to understand that biblical anthropomorphisms, such as passions, are due to God's condescension – an aspect he emphasizes in *Homilies on Jeremiah* and elsewhere, and which was emphasized by Philo beforehand, and later by John Chrysostom[40] – but must be interpreted allegorically.[41] He applied to them primarily his principle of seeking meanings that are worthy of God: theological anthropomorphisms 'must be understood in a manner worthy of God'; for instance, 'God's heart should be interpreted as God's intellectual and purposeful power concerning the universe'.[42]

The Scripture and Christ-Logos: Unity and Philosophical Hermeneutics inspired by the Logos

The Scripture is the revelation of Christ-Logos[43] and the body of the Logos, who assumed the human body in Mary and assumes the body of the *littera* in Scripture.[44] Being an incarnation of Christ-Logos, its meditation is sacramental, a Eucharistic manducation. Indeed, the Eucharistic bread is the material representation of the flesh that is perceptible by spiritual senses.[45]

In *Commentariorum series in Matthaeum* 27, Origen observes that, as Christ came hidden in a body in order to appear as a simple human to carnal humans, and as God only to spiritual humans, so is the Scripture hidden in its literal sense as in a body, that mediocre readers may understand the literal sense only,

---

[39] Ilaria L.E. Ramelli, *Allegoria, I, L'età classica* (Milan, 2004), Ch. 1.

[40] See Ilaria Ramelli, 'Origen's Exegesis of Jeremiah: Resurrection Announced throughout the Bible and its Twofold Conception', *Augustinianum* 48 (2008), 59-78; Ioannes Chrysostomus, *In Ioannem homiliae* 27, 1: God's συγκατάβασις, due to our frailness. Philo (*Quod Deus Sit Immutabilis* 63-4; *cf.* 52) preceded Origen when stating that, by condescension, God 'tells beneficial lies [in Scripture] for the slower and the dull'.

[41] Origenes, *Contra Celsum* IV 71.

[42] *Id., Commentarii in Ioannem* 1, 38, 281-2.

[43] See *id., De Principiis* I 3, 2.

[44] See, for instance, Origenes, *In Leviticum homiliae* 1, 1; *Contra Celsum* VI 77; *Commentariorum series in Matthaeum* 27. See also Annewies van den Hoek, 'The concept of σῶμα τῶν Γραφῶν in Alexandrian theology', *StPatr* 19 (1989), 250-4.

[45] Origenes, *De Pascha* 18, 11-9.

and spiritual readers the spiritual sense. In *De Pascha*, Origen reflects that 'if the Paschal Lamb is Christ and Christ is *the Logos*, what is then the flesh *of the divine Words/Logoi, if not the Holy Scripture?* […] Its flesh and blood […] are the divine Scripture: when we manducate it, we possess Christ'.[46] Meditating on the Scripture is tantamount to eating the Eucharistic body of Christ-Logos. Not accidentally, the Philocalists in Chapter 15 associated the language of the Scripture with the flesh of Christ, which are both manifestations ('bodies') of the same Logos.[47]

Thus, being an exegesis of the Logos, the exegesis of the Scripture is philosophical. The structure of the Bible, with the Spirit dwelling in the Scripture's literal body, parallels the structure of Christ, with the divine dwelling in a human body. This is revealed by the 'second cycle' of *First Principles*, focused on the Incarnation/Inhumanation. Indeed, in his philosophical masterpiece Origen seems to move from theories that were in continuity with Greek philosophy, in the first cycle, to those more difficult to accept for Greek philosophy, such as the Incarnation,[48] in the second cycle.[49] Therefore, literalism (to the exclusion of noetic-spiritual meanings), according to Jordan Wood, is not only a hermeneutical, but also a Christologico-metaphysical, error by Origen.[50]

As anticipated, the Scripture is a form of incarnation or embodiment of the Logos. This has only *one* body, the OT and NT together,[51] 'one book',[52] 'one loaf',[53] 'one and the same book', because the Scripture has one content,

---

[46] *Ibid.* 26, 5-8; 33, 20-32.

[47] This last point was noted by Andrew Blaski, 'The *Philocalia of Origen*: A Crude or Creative Composition?', *VC* 73/2 (2019), 174-89.

[48] Origenes, *De Principiis* II 6.

[49] On the structure of *First Principles* and its cycles, see Samuel Fernández,'The Pedagogical Structure of Origen's *De principiis*', in Ilaria Ramelli, Kevin Corrigan and Monica Tobon (eds), *Evagrius between Origen, the Cappadocians, and Neoplatonism* (Leuven, 2017), 15-22; John Behr, *Origen: On First Principles*, I (Oxford, 2017), XXX-XXXVI; also Brian Daley ('Origen's *De Principiis*: A Guide to the Principles of Christian Scriptural Interpretation', in John Petruccione [ed.], *Nova et Vetera* [Washington, 1998], 3-21). Ryan Haecker ('Triadic Circles: On the Trinity as the Systematic Structure of Origen's *On First Principles*', paper, Oxford Patristics Conference, August 2019, forthcoming) thinks of a triadic structure, and concurs with me that its title refers to the three ἀρχαί, the Trinity.

[50] Jordan Wood, 'Origen's Polemics in *Princ.* 4.2.4', *VC* 69 (2015), 30-69; Elizabeth Dively Lauro, *The Soul and Spirit of Scripture within Origen's Exegesis* (Atlanta, 2005), on the interplay between the somatic-historical level, the psychic on vice and virtue, and the pneumatic which reveals God's plan for salvation through Christ. Frances Young, 'Interpretation of Scripture', in *Oxford Handbook of Early Christian Studies* (Oxford, 2008); DOI:10.1093/oxfordhb/9780199271566.003.0042, emphasizes the societal and liturgical context of scriptural exegesis in patristics.

[51] Origenes, *De Principiis* prol. 1.

[52] *Id., Commentarii in Ioannem* 5, 5.

[53] *Id., In Leviticum homiliae* 13, 4.

Christ.[54] As an *ecclesiasticus*, Origen stresses the unity of the OT and NT, looking for the same Logos in both.[55] The Gospels etymologically announce good things, which are, again, Jesus.[56] The injunction of *Exod.* 12:9b to eat wholly the Passover lamb reminds us that the whole Scripture is *one* body.[57] This is a major tenet of Origen's ubiquitous anti-Marcionite and anti-Gnostic perspective (an integrative biblical perspective held also by Irenaeus and Clement in a similar anti-'heretic' function). Consequently, reading or listening to the Scripture – the body of Christ-Logos – is a Eucharistic act.

Origen often speaks of the Scripture's harmony, consequentiality, peace (ἁρμονία, ἀκολουθία, συμφωνία, εἱρμός, εἰρήνη), and of the affinity (συγγένεια) of its various exegetical readings to one another, between the OT and NT, the Law and the prophets, the Gospels, and the apostolic writings.[58] Origen speaks of 'extremely strong, robust connections', which link all parts of the Scripture, and create 'the harmony of the whole compound'; therefore, in all of the Scripture, the unity of πνεῦμα, the Spirit/inspiration, is unbroken;[59] here we can detect a Stoic derivation: a πνεῦμα and τόνος ('tension') that permeate everything.[60] Both notions were accepted in imperial Platonism. Origen's description of the Scripture as 'God's harmonious instrument, which from various sounds produces one saving melody'[61] inspired Gregory Nyssen's musical metaphors which he applied to the Scripture, to the world – both incarnations of Christ-Logos, the one-and-many – and to soteriology.[62] The identification of the Scripture as the body of the Logos is the reason why Origen, after exhorting his flock to come to church and listen to the Scripture every day, states that Christians 'manducate daily the Lamb's flesh, that is, eat daily the flesh of the Logos, God's Word [*carnes Uerbi*]'.[63] Of this, Origen represented himself as the "teacher" (διδάσκαλος) and interpreter, an exegete.[64]

---

[54] *Id., Philocalia* 5, 4-7.

[55] See *id., In Lucam homiliae* XVI 6: *aequalem et in veteri et in nova lege quaero rationem.*

[56] *Id., Commentarii in Ioannem* 1, 10.

[57] *Ibid.* 10, 103.

[58] See *id., Philocalia* 6, 1; 1, 30.

[59] *Id., Commentarii in Ioannem* 10, 18, 107.

[60] See *Stoicorum veterum fragmenta* 2, 439-62.

[61] Origenes, *Philocalia* 6, 2,

[62] See Ilaria Ramelli, 'Harmony between *arkhē* and *telos* in Patristic Platonism and the Imagery of Astronomical Harmony Applied to the Apokatastasis Theory', *IJPT* 7 (2013), 1-49. On the *akolouthia* of Scripture in Origen, see also Sébastien Morlet, *Symphonia. La concorde des textes et des doctrines dans la littérature grecque jusqu'à Origène* (Paris, 2019).

[63] Origenes, *In Genesim homiliae* 10, 3; my 'Origene: la Scrittura come incarnazione di Cristo-Logos', in Ennio Innocenti (ed.), *Rivelazione e Storia* (Vatican City, 2014), 154-72; Wood, 'Polemics' (2015); Hans Boersma, *Scripture as a Real Presence* (Grand Rapids, 2017), esp. Ch. 8 on Origen on Canticles.

[64] See Ilaria L.E. Ramelli, 'Autobiographical Self-Fashioning in Origen', in Maren Niehoff and Joshua Levinson (eds), *Self, Self-Fashioning and Individuality in Late Antiquity: New Perspectives* (Tübingen, 2019), 271-88.

Stoic allegorists were aware of the principle of interpreting Homer with Homer,[65] which Clement and Origen (but also Valentinus and Heracleon)[66] applied to the Scripture: interpreting the Scripture with the Scripture. Clement had already maintained that each point in the Scripture can be clarified thanks to similar points.[67] In *Philocalia* 2, from the commentary on *Psalm* 1 (see also chs. 1-7), Origen equates God's Providence and *dynamis,* permeating everything, to the divine inspiration pervading all of the Scripture down to the smallest details: 'traces' and 'hints' of God's Wisdom are to be found everywhere, spread 'in each letter'; for, as the Jewish masters asserted, the Scripture's words have been calculated 'with the utmost accuracy'; not even a single word is superfluous.[68]

The same Logos which inspired the Scripture – Moses, the prophets, the apostles – and likewise inspired Greek philosophers, especially Plato, is that which is incarnate in the Scripture, and became incarnate in Jesus, and is also the Logos which inspires the philosophical exegete. Likewise, Clement had deemed the same Logos, which inspired the Scripture, to also be its true 'exegete', by whom the interpreter is illuminated.[69] The Logos guarantees the unity of the Scripture and the coherence of its interpretation. This is why Origen, when philosophically interpreting the Scripture, which is a 'zetetic' work, feels inspired by the Logos as both philosopher and exegete. Christ-Logos-Wisdom, indeed, illuminates the exegete's and philosopher-theologian's intellect.[70] Origen describes the toil of the exegete – primarily himself – as helped by the Logos: if 'one has done everything in one's own power, and has exercised one's senses to distinguish good and evil', then God takes away the veil of allegory.[71]

The Bodies of Christ: Human, Rational, Scriptural, and Cosmic

For Origen, Christ's body is the *Scripture*, as has been said; a *human* body, that of Jesus, but also of all humanity, which he assumed, and, relatedly, the Church, which, at the eventual apokatastasis will coincide with all humanity;

---

[65] Christoph Schäublin, 'Homerum ex Homero', *Museum Helveticum* 34 (1977), 221-7; Jaap Mansfeld, *Prolegomena: Questions to Be Settled before the Study of an Author or a Text* (Leiden, 2005), 204-5.

[66] As shown by Carl Johan Berglund, 'Literary Criticism in Early Christianity: How Heracleon and Valentinus Use One Passage to Interpret Another', *JECS* 27/1 (2019), 27-53.

[67] Clemens Alexandrinus, *Stromata* VII 16, 96, 2-4.

[68] See Origenes, *Philocalia* 6; *Commentarii in Matthaeum* 16, 2; *Commentorium series in Matthaeum* 89; *In Numeros homiliae XXVIII* 3, 2; 27, 1; *In Iesum Nave homiliae XXVI* 15, 3; *Commentarii in Ioannem* 19, 40, 89.

[69] Clemens Alexandrinus, *Stromata* I 26, 169.

[70] See Origenes, *Homiliae in Ieremiam* 19, 11; *Libri X in Canticum canticorum* 3, 11, 17-9: *Verbum illuminat mentem*; 1, 1, 14; *In Canticum canticorum homiliae* 1, 7.

[71] *Id., Contra Celsum* IV 50.

all rational creatures or *logika*, since Christ is the Logos; and the *cosmos* – all of creation.[72] Therefore, Origen sometimes sets aside the Scripture to argue philosophically from reality and reason. This is clear, for instance, in one of the recently discovered Munich homilies: faith should be based 'not so much on the Scripture as on a proof clearer than the Scripture [ἐναργεστέρα ἀπόδειξις]; and the proof that is clearer than the Scripture is heaven, earth and all that is in it' (§2 fol.216r/353).[73] This is the cosmos, which is one of the incarnations of Christ.

This notion of the cosmic Christ is already clearly attested to in the Christian Middle Platonist Bardaisan, as I have shown elsewhere,[74] and is anticipated by Philo: one temple of God is the cosmos, and another the rational soul.[75] Origen likens the universe to 'an immense organism kept together by God's Logos and Dynamis [*virtute dei ac ratione*] as by a soul'.[76] Origen thereby likens Christ-Logos, and possibly the Spirit, to the Platonic and Stoic world soul,[77] which Middle-Platonically distributed the Forms to matter.[78] Alcinous identified the world soul with its Intellect/Nous,[79] which worked very well with Origen's notion of Christ-Logos-Nous, the Mind of God, and also cosmic Christ. In contrast to the transcendence of God's essence (πόρρω μὲν κατ' οὐσίαν), Clement stresses that 'God's power is always present, fastened onto our power of inspection, beneficence, and instruction'.[80] The idea that God's Dynamis permeates (διήκει) and keeps together the world, just as the intellectual soul does with the body, was taken over by Gregory Nyssen. *Nous* is the one power (μία τίς

---

[72] Origenes, *H.2Ps*.36.

[73] Origenes, *H.1Ps*.77.

[74] In Ilaria Ramelli, *Bardaiṣan of Edessa: A Reassessment of the Evidence and a New Interpretation. Also in the Light of Origen and the Porphyrian Fragments from De India*, Eastern Christian Studies 22 (Piscataway, 2009); *ead.*, 'Bardaisan of Edessa, Origen, and Imperial Philosophy: A Middle Platonic Context?', *Aram* 30 (2018), 1-26.

[75] Philo Alexandrinus, *De Somniis* 1, 215.

[76] Origenes, *De Principiis* II 1, 3.

[77] Heinrich Dörrie (*Der Platonismus in der Antike*, I [Stuttgart, 1987], 32) and Christoph Markschies ('Die Seele als Bild der Welt', *BBBA* 14 [2009], 9-24) argued that a world soul is absent in the Patristic era. Of a different opinion are Charlotte Köckert, *Christliche Kosmologie und kaiserzeitliche Philosophie. Die Auslegung des Schöpfungsberichtes bei Origenes, Basilius und Gregor von Nyssa vor dem Hintergrund kaiserzeitlicher Timaeus-Interpretationen*, STAC 56 (Tübingen, 2009), 245-7 (with my review in *Augustinianum* 52 [2012], 550-2) and especially Johannes Zachhuber, https://www.academia.edu/5977922/The_world_soul_in_ early_Christian_ thought. On the world soul in Origen: Christian Hengstermann, 'Christliche Natur- und Geschichtsphilosophie: Die Weltseele bei Origenes', in Alfons Fürst (ed.), *Origenes und sein Erbe* (Münster, 2011), 43-75.

[78] 'Engendered in matter as a necessary first step towards its imitation of the forms'. See George Boys-Stones, *Platonist Philosophy 80BC to AD250: An Introduction and Collection of Sources in Translation* (Cambridge, 2018), 218; see all Ch. 8.

[79] Rightly so, according to Carl O'Brien, 'Alcinous' Reception of Plato', in *Brill's Companion to the Reception of Plato* (2018), 171-82, 176.

[80] Clemens Alexandrinus, *Stromata* II 5, 5.

ἐστι δύναμις) that permeates all of the sensory organs and enables perception.[81] The same expression was already found in Numenius, with whose ideas Origen was familiar.[82]

This concept was along the same lines as the *De mundo* ascribed to Aristotle and known to Aristobulus and Philo: the transcendent deity is immanent in the world due to its *dynamis*; 'it is nobler and worthier of the divinity to dwell in the highest place, while its power [δύναμιν] permeates the whole cosmos'.[83] The idea that Christ-Logos keeps the world together like a soul was also adopted by Athanasius,[84] and is consistent with Origen's idea of the cosmos as one incarnation of Christ: not only all of humanity (*omne hominum genus*), but even all of creation is his body (*totius creaturae universitas*).[85] As Origen himself remarks, while for the immanentistic Stoics the world is the first God, for the Platonists it is the second, or – with reference to Numenius – the third.[86]

The unitary exegesis of the Scripture practiced and promoted by Origen, grounded in the conviction that Scripture is the body, soul and spirit/nous of Christ and is, in fact, all about Christ, interestingly parallels the Neoplatonic – and especially Procline – unitary exegesis of Plato's dialogues. According to Proclus, each dialogue of Plato has one focus or target (σκοπός), but can be read on several levels; for instance, the Atlantis myth in the *Timaeus* can be read on both the historical plane and at the allegorical level (as Origen also interpreted this myth by Plato). Each dialogue's σκοπός is usually explained in Proclus' prologue to the commentary on the given dialogue: for instance,

---

[81] Gregorius Nyssenus, *De opificio hominis* 138D. In *Dialogus de anima et resurrectione* (32AB), Macrina cites and approves of the Pythagorean-Platonic principle that 'what sees and what hears is the intellect', and Gregory insists on the same principle, that *nous* works through sense-perception, in *De opificio hominis* pref.10. Macrina may be referring to Porphyry (*Vita Pythagorae* 46), who attributes this maxim to Pythagoras. This is a tenet of Platonism, which Macrina develops at length and demonstrates with examples in *De anima*, and which Gregory endorses. The Middle Platonist popular philosopher Maximus of Tyre (*Dissertationes* 11, 9), probably known to Origen, attributed this maxim to 'the Syracusan', Epicharmus (B12 DK). It was quoted by other Middle- and Neo-Platonists. Gregory was acquainted not only with Origen's ideas, but also with those of Plotinus and Porphyry. Plotinus had spoken at length about the soul's powers/faculties, through which the soul operates in the body. These δυνάμεις enable the body to sustain itself, operate, reproduce, and perceive. In this way, Plotinus could avoid positing a soul that descended completely into a body. See 'Divine Power in Origen of Alexandria: Sources and Aftermath', in Anna Marmodoro and Irini Fotini Viltanioti (eds), *Divine Powers in Late Antiquity* (Oxford, 2017), 177-98; 'Gregory of Nyssa on the Soul (and the Restoration): From Plato to Origen', in Anna Marmodoro and Neil McLynn (eds), *Exploring Gregory of Nyssa: Historical and Philosophical Perspectives* (Oxford, 2018), 110-41.

[82] F4b27DP: διήκουσα δι' ὅλου τοῦ σώματος.

[83] Aristoteles, *De mundo* 397b23-30, 398b7-11 and 20-22; quotation from 398b7-9. See my 'Divine Power' (2017).

[84] See Athanasius Alexandrinus, *De incarnatione Verbi* 41.

[85] Origenes, *H.2Ps.*36.

[86] *Id., Contra Celsum* V 7.

the σκοπός of *Alcibiades I* is knowledge of ourselves or of our essence.[87] Likewise, for Origen the Scripture has one focus or target, Christ-Logos, but can be interpreted at different levels, from the literal to the allegorical. Therefore, this is an overarching structural parallel.

If the body of Christ, in Origen's view, is both a human body and the cosmos and the Scripture, the same philosophy that studies the cosmos and anthropology must also study the Scripture. The aforementioned theorization of biblical exegesis in Book IV of *First Principles*, within Origen's philosophical-theological (and not formally exegetical) masterpiece, means that allegoresis for him was part and parcel of philosophy – just as it was for the Stoics and Middle Platonists.[88] The few biblical passages that have a spiritual meaning alone, since their literal meaning is impossible, were meant by God 'to induce even one, stupid like a beast and so asleep as to snore, to see that it is necessary to abandon the literal meaning and ascend to spiritual interpretations'[89] (note Origen's ascription of idiocy to those who cannot rise beyond literal meanings, repeated *e.g.* in *Contra Celsum*: only 'a blockhead' cannot understand the allegorical meaning of some biblical passages[90] – the same contempt is shown towards the 'Philistines', a category, analysed below, of literalists and enemies of Origen's own allegorical exegesis).

Origen explains that such passages, endowed with an exclusively spiritual meaning, were meant 'for those who are *more expert* and particularly *fond of investigation* [ἐντρεχεστέρους, ζητητικωτέρους], so that, applying themselves to the toil of the *examination* [ἐξετάσεως] of the Scriptures, they might be *persuaded by reason* [πεῖσμα ἀξιόλογον] that in the Scriptures it is necessary to *research* [ζητεῖν] a meaning worthy of God'.[91] The last point, that of finding meanings worthy of God, was a pivotal tenet for Origen and a guiding light for all of his exegesis and theology. Origen applies here the terminology of philosophical investigation or 'zetesis', examination, and persuasion by reason, to scriptural exegesis, because, in his view, as in that of Philo, most Stoics and most Middle Platonists, allegoresis is part and parcel of philosophy, whose apex is, in turn, theology. In connection with this, in fact, Philo spoke of Mosaic 'philosophy'.

In *Stromateis*, Clement had already postulated the biblical necessity of expressing the highest truths figuratively, that they may be accessible only to those who pursue true knowledge-gnosis by means of investigation: 'Scriptures hide their meaning for many reasons: (1) in order for us to *learn how to*

---

[87] Proclus, *In Platonis Alcibiadem I* 5, 15-10, 23 Segonds.
[88] As I argued in *Allegoria*, I (2004) and 'The Philosophical Stance of Allegory in Stoicism and its Reception in Platonism', *IJCT* 18 (2011), 335-71; for more, see 'Allegorising and Philosophising', in *Oxford Handbook of Graeco-Roman Mythography* (Oxford, 2021).
[89] Origenes, *H.3Ps*.36.7.
[90] *Id.*, *Contra Celsum* VII 34.
[91] *Id.*, *De Principiis* IV 2, 9.

investigate and to be always alert, that we may find the words of salvation;
(2) since understanding these truths would not even have been expedient to the
totality of humans, that they might not suffer damage by interpreting wrongly
what the Holy Spirit had said for our salvation. This is why the spiritual meanings of the prophecies, reserved as they are for selected people, among those
who are admitted from faith to knowledge [γνῶσις], are enveloped in the veil
of the parables'.[92]

The Philosophical Function of Stoic and Middle Platonic Allegoresis: Structural Links with Origen

Stoic allegorists – *i.e.* many Stoics, prominently Chrysippus, although not
all of them – viewed allegoresis as an essential aspect and tool of philosophy,
far from being a mere etymologizing or literary/rhetorical device (σχῆμα).
Rather, allegoresis was philosophical in its value, since the objects of physics
and theology were coextensive in Stoic immanentism, and allegoresis showed
precisely this nexus, by identifying deities with physical elements – or the
pneuma that extended through physical elements – or properties.[93]

a. *The Philosophical Function of Allegoresis in Ancient, Middle, and Roman Stoicism*

Since the beginning of Stoicism, allegoresis was used from Zeno's commentaries on Homer and Hesiod to Cleanthes' allegorical interpretation of
archaic poetry, in which he even proposed textual emendations that supported
his own allegories, and two important systematic statements.[94] But it was especially Chrysippus who both used allegoresis in his exegesis of Orpheus, Homer,
and Hesiod in *On Divinities* 2, and also *theorized* on allegoresis in Book 1 of
the same work.[95] Here, he posited the relationship between allegoresis and
theology, as expressed in poetry, rituals, and tradition in general, including
visual representations. He claimed that the truth (the Logos, later also identified
by Origen with Truth qua Christ) is expressed by philosophers, poets, and
'legislators', or institutors of norms and customs, including rituals. Poetry, the
main expression of myth, and cultic traditions must therefore be allegorized, in
order to detect the truth hidden in them, and since the truth/Logos is one, this

---

[92] Clemens Alexandrinus, *Stromata* VI 15, 126, 2.
[93] See Ilaria Ramelli, 'The Philosophical Role of Allegoresis as a Mediator', *JRp* 12 (2013),
9-26; the examination in *Allegoria* I (2004), Chs 1-2; texts and commentaries in *Allegoristi
dell'età classica*, Il Pensiero Occidentale (Milan, 2007).
[94] SVF I 486; I 538.
[95] SVF II 1009.

will be at one with the philosophical truth of Stoicism. Allegory was, for Chrysippus, the main modality of the study of theology; he connected it with physics and ethics, so that allegoresis became an important instrument of cultural unity. This need must have been sorely felt by Chrysippus, given his broad cultural interests.[96]

The allegoresis of myths was carried out by many exponents of Stoicism afterwards, such as Diogenes in *Athena,* Apollodorus in *On Divinities*, in a work on etymology, and in a Homeric commentary full of allegorico-etymological interpretations, and Crates of Mallus, the author of systematic commentaries on Homer. Crates put his own philosophical and philological skills to the service of his interpretation of Homer, viewed as a poet steeped in many disciplines. He was a 'critic' (κριτικός, his own self-designation), versed in philology, grammar, linguistics, and literature, all of this framed within one philosophical system: the Stoic one.

Annaeus Cornutus – a contemporary of Nero and a victim of his, as he exiled Cornutus – was influenced by Chrysippus and Apollodorus, and was contemporary with another Stoic allegorist, Chaeremon of Alexandria.[97] In his handbook of allegoresis applied to Greek deities, for each divinity he provides an allegorico-etymological interpretation of his or her names and epithets, attributes, iconography, and aspects of myths and rituals. Physical allegory – Zeus represents ether, Hera air, Poseidon water, etc. – prevails, but there are also ethical and historical exegeses. In the conclusion, in section 35, Cornutus declares the ancients 'able to understand the nature of the cosmos and well capable of expressing philosophical truths on it through symbols and allusions'. Under such riddles, allegoresis finds the philosophical truth: this is why it belongs to philosophy. That Cornutus' and Chaeremon's allegoresis influenced Origen's biblical allegoresis was highlighted, although polemically, by Porphyry, as we shall see shortly.

b. *Reasons for the Philosophical Function of Allegoresis in Stoicism, Platonism, and Origen*

The Stoics attached philosophical prominence to allegory. This did not simply mean for them to support Stoic philosophy in an 'apologetical' fashion,

---

[96] See Ramelli, 'Philosophical Stance' (2011) and further arguments in 'Valuing Antiquity in Antiquity by Means of Allegoresis', in James Ker and Christoph Pieper (eds), *Valuing the Past in the Greco-Roman World. Proceedings of the Penn-Leiden Colloquium on Ancient Values VII, Leiden 14-16 June 2012* (Leiden, 2014), 485-507.

[97] See my *Allegoria I* (2004), Ch. 7; *Anneo Cornuto* (Milan, 2003), with reviews by Roberto Radice, *Aevum* 79 (2005), 220 and Franco Ferrari, *Athenaeum* 95 (2007), 550-51; 'Cornutus and the Stoic Allegorical Tradition', *Aitia* 8 (2018). Critical edition: Lucius Annaeus Cornutus, *Compendium de Graecae theologiae traditionibus*, ed. José Torres (Berlin, 2018); George Boys-Stones, *Annaeus Cornutus: The Greek Theology, Fragments, and Testimonia* (Atlanta, 2018).

given the Stoics' apparently growing interest in allegoresis and allegorical production. In such a structured philosophical system, the support of Homeric
allegoresis and other mythological and cultic traditions would have proved too
episodic to be fruitful. I suspect that Stoicism rather intended to serve the interpretation of theological poems and aimed at integrating the traditional expressions of theology – poetic, cultic, iconographic, etc. – into its own philosophical system for the creation of a broad cultural synthesis, including traditional
heritage, but one philosophically legitimized after rationalistic attacks, such as
those against the abovementioned anthropomorphisms in theological myths.
The Stoics, interested as they were in linguistics, etymology, poetry and literature, intended to validate poetry and other expressions of theology by means of
allegoresis, so as to construct an organic cultural unity based on the Logos.

Indeed, the whole Stoic allegorical discourse revolves around the Logos-
Pneuma, of which deities are partial manifestations: the Logos inspired poets
and creators of myths and rituals, as well as the 'natural' language which etymology (closely related to Stoic allegoresis) tends to reveal in order to find the
truth in the words (in Origen, this Logos will become the transcendent/imma-
nent Christ-Logos). The Stoics, from Zeno to Heraclitus the Rhetor and *De vita
et poësi Homeri*, insisted so much on Homer as the possessor of the truths of
various disciplines, from geography to physics, because they aimed at projecting
their own ideal of cultural unity grounded in the Logos onto cultural origins
('Homer'). This ideal, transformed and centered around Christ-Logos, will still
be pivotal in Origen's thought. In his view, all disciplines, philosophical theology, and exegesis focus on Christ-Logos, which is the pivot of the whole of
Origen's cultural enterprise.

The view of allegoresis as a prominent part of philosophy, promoted by
Stoicism, returned in Middle- and Neo-Platonism, which incorporated significant
Stoic elements, but within a Platonic framework, on both the 'pagan' and the
Christian side.[98] An example of 'pagan' imperial Platonism comes from Plutarch,
who in *Isis and Osiris* theorized about the allegorical interpretation of the myth
of Isis and Osiris, warning against its literal reading:[99] it rather had to be
handled 'in a holy and *philosophical* manner'.[100] This indicates the philosophical
nature of allegoresis: the myth (μῦθος) reflects a rational, *philosophical discourse*
(λόγος), which turns the mind of the reader to higher realities.[101] This is why
Plutarch often speaks of μυθολογία in connection with allegoresis, since
philosophical allegoresis turns the myth into a *logos* that makes sense philosophically. He also allegorized non-Greek myths, such as Egyptian ones, *e.g.*

---

[98] Ramelli, 'Allegorising and Philosophising' (Oxford, 2021).
[99] Plutarch, *De Iside et Osiride* 355B.
[100] *Ibid.* 355D.
[101] *Ibid.* 359A.

in *Isis and Osiris*, just as Philo allegorized the Bible through Platonic lenses, and also as Numenius and Amelius allegorized the Bible.[102]

Origen, who relied on the classical commentary tradition[103] and, as noted above, included his theorization of biblical allegoresis in his philosophical masterpiece and used philosophical 'zetesis' as an exegetical methodology, considered allegoresis to be an integral part of philosophy, just as the Stoic and Middle-Platonic allegorizers did. The question of the aim of Origen's allegorical hermeneutics (that is, was Origen using the Scripture in defence of his Platonizing metaphysical system, or was he using Platonizing metaphysics to provide a philosophical basis for the Scripture?) is structurally the same as the question of the purpose of Stoic allegoresis: did Stoic allegorizers use myth in defence of their own philosophical system, or did they deploy philosophical allegoresis in defence of mythical and ritual traditions, integrating them into a unitary philosophical system? I support the latter alternative for both Stoicism and Origen. This is, as previously mentioned, a structural, methodological parallel, beyond the obvious metaphysical differences, between immanentistic Stoicism and Origen's transcendental, Platonizing system.

c. *Origen's Debt to Stoic Allegoresis and Porphyry's 'Reductionism'*

Well acquainted as he was with both Stoic allegoresis and Origen's allegoresis, Porphyry emphasizes the link between Origen's and the Stoics' allegoresis. Porphyry remarks that Cornutus and Chaeremon were among Origen's favourite readings (together with Plato, Neopythagoreans, and the 'Middle Platonistis'): structurally, both of them supported, like Origen, the function of allegoresis as part and parcel of philosophy:

Some, out of a desire to get free from the ineptitude of Jewish Scripture, but without simply abandoning it, turned to incoherent exegeses, not fitting the texts [...] they pretend, boastfully, that the things Moses clearly said are enigmata, and proclaim they are oracles full of recondite mysteries [...] then they develop their exegeses [...]. This method, odd as it is, derives from a man whom I also met when I was still quite young, who gained great renown and is still well known thanks to the writings he left: Origen, whose fame is widespread among the masters of these doctrines [...] He availed himself "of the books of the Stoics Chaeremon and Cornutus, from which he learnt the allegorical method of the Greek mysteries, which he applied, then, to the Jewish Scriptures".[104]

---

[102] See briefly below. On the parallel between Plutarch and Philo in their interest not only in Plato, but also in Eastern myths, see G. Sterling, 'When East and West Meet: Eastern Religions and Western Philosophy in Philo of Alexandria and Plutarch of Chaeronea', *SPhiloA* 28 (2016), 137-50.

[103] G. Kennedy, *Cambridge History of Literary Criticism* (Cambridge, 1989), I 29-35; Ch. Schäublin, 'Zur pagan Prägung der christlichen Exegese', in Johannes van Oort (ed.), *Christliche Exegese zwischen Nicaea und Chalcedon* (Kampen, 1992), 148-73.

[104] Porphyrius, *Contra Christianos* F39. Analysis in 'Origen, Greek Philosophy' (2012); 'Origen and the Platonic Tradition' (2017).

Origen, according to Porphyry, transferred allegoresis from traditional 'pagan' myths – allegorized by both Stoics and 'Middle Platonists' – to the Scripture. Porphyry takes into account neither Clement, who was familiar with Stoic allegoresis, including that of Chaeremon,[105] and applied it to the Scripture, nor Philo or other Jewish allegorical exegetes of the Scripture. We shall ask shortly why Porphyry, like Celsus, omitted scriptural allegoresis prior to Origen. Celsus and Porphyry deemed Origen's transfer of allegoresis from Greek myths to the Bible illegitimate, but Porphyry leveled a similar charge – namely, misappropriating the allegorical method – at the 'pagan' Neopythagorean/Middle Platonist Cronius.[106] Therefore, these polemics were at work within an intra-Platonist debate. Porphyry, like Origen and unlike Cronius and other extreme allegorists whom he attacked in *De Styge*, embraced a multi-layered allegoresis, both literal and allegorical, against the mere allegorizers. Only, he applied it to Homer, while Origen applied it to the Scripture (and Plato). Porphyry read Homer through a Platonist lens, just as Origen read the Scripture through a Platonist lens (and Plato mostly allegorically, as several Platonists did).

Indeed, Origen was well acquainted with Cornutus and Chaeremon.[107] He may have derived the expression 'seminal *logoi*' directly from him: according to Simplicius, it was Cornutus who called the Stoic 'natural *logoi*' σπερματικοί.[108] Origen then applied this notion to Christ. The method suggested by Cornutus to find philosophical truths hidden in myths was a comparison with other peoples' mythological and cultic traditions, and Chaeremon allegorized Egyptian mythology and the symbolic value of hieroglyphics. Origen was very likely thinking of Chaeremon, already known to Clement, when praising 'Egyptian sages' who 'studied their traditional writings, giving profound philosophical interpretations of what they deem divine'.[109] Origen sometimes shows reminiscences of Stoic etymologizing and Stoic allegoresis of myths. He expressly mentions the Stoics' etymological principles based on their conception of language 'by nature' (φύσει), places it in opposition to Aristotle's view, and distinguishes it from that of Epicurus.[110] In *De Principiis*, 'soul' ψυχή, is said to derive from 'cooling' ψῦχος/ψῦξις,[111] according to an old Stoic etymology.[112] This is a central point in Origen's concept of the soul and its fall, seen as a

---

[105] Clemens Alexandrinus, *Stromata* V 4, 20 (on the symbolical, tropic-metaphorical, and allegorical-enigmatic usage of hieroglyphics), parallel to Porphyry *ap.* Eusebius (*Historia Ecclesiastica* VI 19, 4-8) seems to come from Chaeremon's *Hieroglyphics* (*cf.* Clemens Alexandrinus, *Stromata* V 4, 19).

[106] Porphyrius, *De Styge* F372.

[107] As detailed in I. Ramelli, 'Origen and the Stoic Allegorical Tradition: Continuity and Innovation', *InvLuc* 28 (2006), 195-226.

[108] Simplicius, *In Aristotelis Categorias commentarium* 351.

[109] Origenes, *Contra Celsum* I 13.

[110] *Ibid.* I 24.

[111] *Id., De Principiis* II 8, 2-3.

[112] SVF II 222-3.

cooling down from the ardent love of God. Moreover, in Origen's extant writings there are allegorical interpretations of Greek mythical figures recalling the Stoic ones; for instance, Origen's allegoresis of Athena as 'intelligence'[113] is Stoic. But Origen denied that Athena had an individual substance, as God's Logos has, with reference to the crucial notion of hypostasis,[114] so central to Origen's theology, and criticized Stoic allegoresis and its derivates as merely physical: Isis and Osiris, even allegorized, teach people to worship inanimate water and earth.[115] The Stoic exegesis of Hades as tenebrous air enveloping the Earth (attested to in Cornutus' *Compendium of Greek Theology* on the basis of earlier Stoic traditions[116]) is also present in Origen's *De Principiis*: the dead descend to Hades, that is, this world, because they are judged deserving of occupying the region around the Earth.[117] But Numenius, well known to Origen, in F32DP had already interpreted Hades as the contiguous region we call our world. Origen might have drawn this interpretation from both.

Allegoresis in Numenius, Celsus, Amelius, and Origen: Intra-Platonic Polemics on Original Philosophy and Authoritative Texts

The Middle Platonist-Neopythagorean Numenius, a 'pagan' as far as we know, was held in high esteem by Plotinus and Origen. He was not only listed by Porphyry among Origen's frequent readings, but explicitly praised by Origen for his exegesis, not only of Greek myths, but also of the Scripture, including some passages of what became the New Testament.[118] Numenius, 'in his desire for learning, wanted to examine our Scriptures, too, and was interested in them as being susceptible to allegorical interpretation [τροπολογουμένων], and not full of odd ideas'.[119]

Numenius, 'the Pythagorean philosopher, a man who expounded Plato much better [than Celsus], and studied the Pythagorean doctrines in depth, in many passages of his works quotes Moses' and the prophets' writings, and offers likely allegoreses [τροπολογοῦντα] of them, for example in *Hoopoe*, *On Numbers*, and *On Place*. In the third book *On Good*, he also cites a story concerning Jesus, without mentioning his name, and interprets it allegorically [τροπολογεῖ]'.[120]

---

[113] Origenes, *Contra Celsum* VIII 67.
[114] I point out in 'Hypostasis' its importance and novelty in Origen's thought.
[115] Origenes, *Contra Celsum* V 38.
[116] See Lucius Annaeus Cornutus, *Theologiae Graecae compendium* 35.
[117] Origenes, *De Principiis* IV 3, 10.
[118] Origen quotes him four times: *Contra Celsum* I 5 (F1b); IV 51 (F10a); V 38 (F53); V 57 (F29).
[119] Origenes, *Contra Celsum* IV 51.
[120] *Ibid.* IV 51.

Numenius, describing Plato as 'Atticizing Moses' or 'Moses speaking Greek',[121] and whose philosophy went back to Pythagoras and 'barbarians' such as the Jews, Egyptians, and the like (F1a), parallels Justin's and Origen's claim that Moses preceded Plato. This point was then taken over by the Origenian Eusebius to support the agreement between the Scripture and Greek philosophy, especially Platonism:[122] Eusebius even referred to the 'pagan' authoritative commentators of Plato.[123] Origen was, in fact, using Plato's point that the Greeks, unlike the Egyptians, are recent[124] and Origen's very operation of reconstructing the 'original philosophy' was intra-Platonic and common to Numenius, Ammonius Saccas, and Porphyry. According to Celsus, however, this ἀρχαῖος λόγος or 'original philosophy' was common to the Egyptians, Chaldaeans, Magi, Persians, Indians, etc.,[125] but *not* to Jews or Christians, who distorted it.[126] This is why he identified the 'true Logos' (ἀληθὴς λόγος) with the ἀρχαῖος λόγος, and not Christ-Logos.

Instead, Numenius intended to recover Plato's philosophy, torn apart by skeptical Academics, Stoics, and Aristotle (F24DP), without prejudice against 'barbarian' philosophies. In *On Good* 1, Numenius included the Jews among those nations who deemed God incorporeal and allegorized the sayings of the prophets.[127] His 'investigation' of the Scripture (βασανίσας, *ibidem*) corresponds to Origen's 'zetetic' method in exegesis and philosophical theology. Indeed, Numenius inspired Origen both exegetically and theologically.[128] His allegorical reading of the Scripture parallels his exegesis of Plato: for example, he associated the myth of Er with Homer's representation of the underworld in the *Odyssey*. Similarly, Origen paralleled Plato's myths with the Scripture's myths,

---

[121] F8.13 = Clemens, *Stromata* I 22, 150, 4; Eusebius, *Preparatio evangelica* 11, 10, 14; 9, 6, 9; Theodoretus Cyri, *Graecarum affectionum curatio* 2, 114. Gregory Sterling ('The Theft of Philosophy: Philo of Alexandria and Numenius', *SPhiloA* 27 [2015], 71-86, 84) prudently hypothesizes that Numenius knew some of Philo's works, being interested in finding a bridge between East and West through his reconstruction of Platonism.

[122] Eusebius, *Preparatio evangelica* 11 pref.; 15, 1, 5.

[123] *Ibid.* 11 pref.; 3, 4.

[124] See Plato, *Timaeus* 22AC.

[125] Origenes, *Contra Celsum* I 14; VI 80.

[126] *Ibid.* III 16; IV 21; IV 41-42; VI 80; VII 58. On the concept of 'ancient wisdom' in Middle Platonism, see also Boys-Stones, *Platonist Philosophy* (2018), Ch. 1; also Guy Stroumsa, *Philosophy of the Barbarians*, in Hubert Cancik *et al.* (eds), *Geschichte-Tradition-Reflexion: FS Martin Hengels* (Tübingen, 1996), II, 339-68; Matthias Baltes, 'Der Platonismus und die Weisheit der Barbaren', in Matthias Baltes, *Epinoêmata* (München, 2005), 1-29. On the non-Christian allegoresis of the Christian Scripture, see my '"Revelation" for Christians and Pagans and their Philosophical Allegoresis: Intersections within Imperial Platonism', an invited lecture given at the international conference, *Ancient Revelation*, in Durham University, 25-27 June 2019, forthcoming.

[127] Origenes, *Contra Celsum* I 15.

[128] See Ramelli, 'Origen, Patristic Philosophy'.

with the difference that the Greek myths had no historical truth, while biblical myths, for Origen, have.[129]

Instead, for Celsus, as previously mentioned, the 'original philosophy' or 'old Logos', which contained truths to be discovered allegorically, was common to all ancient peoples, apart from the Jews. Therefore, the Scripture should *not* be interpreted in a philosophico-allegorical way:

The more reasonable ones among Jews and Christians interpret these stories *allegorically* [...] They have recourse to allegory because they are ashamed of them [...] try to allegorize these stories someway; yet, they are *not susceptible to any allegorical interpretation*, but, on the contrary, are bare myths, of the most stupid kind [...] However, the allegories that appear to be written on these myths are far more shameful and unlikely than the myths themselves, since, with astonishing and totally senseless madness, they link together things that are absolutely and completely incompatible with one another.[130]

Since 'in the Law and prophets there is no deeper doctrine beyond the literal sense of the words',[131] so philosophical allegoresis could not be applied.

Siding with Numenius, Origen contested Celsus' point and even likened biblical myths to Plato's myths. If Plato's myths are allegorized, biblical myths should be allegorized as well:

Those who run into this myth, imitating Celsus' malignity, will deride it and tease Plato, so great as he is. But be this far from Christians! Or if they *investigate philosophically the contents that are expressed mythically*, and are thereby able to find what Plato meant, they will see how he could hide *under mythical appearance those doctrines which seemed to him particularly sublime*, because of the majority, while revealing them, as appropriate, to those who know how to ferret out from myths what the author meant concerning the truth.[132]

Celsus' claim that the Scripture 'cannot be interpreted allegorically' since 'there is no profounder meaning beyond the literal level' is rejected by Origen.[133] This was a crucial point in the controversy over which texts were worthy of allegoresis. Origen again attacks Celsus' statement that Christians 'took refuge in allegory' to defend the Scripture; Origen retorts and refers to 'outrageous' allegorisations of mythical stories by Chrysippus (referring to Zeus' and Hera's intercourse, whose description and iconographical representation Chrysippus famously allegorized). What is more, Origen states that he is following Plato, *Philebus* 12BC, regarding his reverence for divine names, as a loading star for allegoresis, and *Respublica* (377-8) regarding the rejection of myths which may

---

[129] Origenes, *Contra Celsum* VIII 47.
[130] *Ibid.* IV 48-51.
[131] *Ibid.* VII 18.
[132] *Ibid.* IV 39.
[133] *Ibid.* IV 49; VII 18.

harm the young.[134] Origen, overall, makes it clear that his allegorical method follows Plato – just as the allegoresis of 'pagan' imperial Platonists did. For instance, Origen connects the flood narrated in Genesis with Plato's reference to the gods purifying the earth.[135]

Christian Polemics on Biblical Allegoresis. Allegory, History, and Philology in Origen's Holistic and 'Laborious' Exegesis

a. *Exegetical and Theological Polemics Throughout Origen's Life*

Origen's hermeneutical treatment in Book IV of *First Principles* was likely addressed to those who taught the Scripture in the Church, allegorists, including those outside the Church, and 'literalists', who are here the main target of Origen's criticism. Origen programmatically denounces 'many methodological mistakes' in scriptural exegesis.[136] 'Jews', 'heretics' who separate the God of the OT from that of the NT, especially Marcionites,[137] and those 'too simple' (ἀκεραιότεροι) within the Church itself, all stick to 'bare literalism' (ψιλὸν γράμμα) instead of spiritual exegesis (κατὰ τὰ πνευματικά).[138] These exegetes 'interpret the Scripture in an earthly, carnal sense' and deceive others.[139] In the late phase of his life, Origen was still polemicizing against Marcion, as is clear, for example, from the late Munich homilies. Here, in *Homilia* 1 *in Ps*. 77, Origen criticizes Marcion's unrestrained emendation (διόρθωσις) of the Scripture, whereby he 'removed essential things [τὰ ἀναγκαῖα] from the foundations of the Gospels – the Saviour's birth and countless other things, including visions, prophecies, and essential parts [τὰ ἀναγκαῖα] of the Apostle's teaching' (§1, fol. 215v/352). Indeed, Origen engaged in New Testament philology, like his teacher Ammonius, and especially criticized Marcion's edition (both his Gospel and the edition of the Pauline letters: *Euangelion* and *Apostolikon*) for athetizing many passages, both from Paul and from the Gospel, such as those concerning Jesus' birth by Mary,[140] prophecies, etc.; Marcion did so in order to 'emend the Scripture'.[141]

---

[134] *Ibid*. IV 48.

[135] Plato, *Timaeus* 22D; Origenes, *Contra Celsum* VI 58.

[136] Origenes, *De principiis* IV 2, 1.

[137] Marcionites are also criticized for their literalism in *Commentarii in Matthaeum* 15, 3; *Commentarii in Epistulam ad Romanos* 2, 13, and (against the two deities) in *De Principiis* II 5, 1.

[138] Origenes, *De principiis* IV 2, 2.

[139] *Id.*, *Libri X in Canticum canticorum* IV 3, 19.

[140] This also relates to Marcion's alleged Docetism, a charge that David Wilhite, in *The Gospel according to Heretics: Discovering Orthodoxy through Early Christological Conflicts* (Grand Rapids, 2015) deems incorrect. So also his 'Was Marcion a Docetist? The Body of Evidence vs. Tertullian's Argument', *VC* 71 (2017), 1-37.

[141] Origenes, *Homiliae in Psalmum* 77 I 1, fol. 21v-216r: διορθοῦν τὴν γραφήν. See also *Commentarii in Ioannem* 2, 6, 24; *Contra Celsum* II 27; *Commentarii in Matthaeum* 1, 3. Susan

b. *The Importance of History and the Telos*

Richard P.C. Hanson has deemed Origen's allegoresis to be arbitrary and lacking in historical perspective: 'In history as event, in history as the field of God's self-revelation par excellence, Origen is not in the least interested'.[142] Tzamalikos and I have extensively shown that this is hardly the case,[143] especially from the viewpoints of philosophy or history and of its orientation towards the *telos*. The centrality of Christ's historical coming and sacrifice in Origen's thought is hard to overestimate, so I agree with Brian Daley that Origen was 'one of the most strongly incarnational thinkers of the early Church'.[144] And Origen's whole philosophical theology is oriented toward the *telos* (which coincides with the apokatastasis). This is also the main difference between Origen's own doctrine of apokatastasis and those of the Stoics and (later) the Neoplatonists, which entailed an infinite repetition of aeons without end, without a *telos* at the end of all aeons.

According to Origen, Christ's Cross, which happened once in history, has a universal and eternal validity, for all rational creatures, in all aeons.[145] Jesus' resurrection and miracles really took place, although they also signify spiritual resurrection and miracles, while the Neoplatonic exegetes of myths deemed myths only 'allegories of eternal truths'.[146]

c. *Philology in the Service of Exegesis*

The *littera*, the literal level of the Scripture, which Origen addressed by means of classical philological techniques,[147] is useful to 'edify' those who cannot understand the Scripture more profoundly,[148] in the same way, indeed, that the body is the vehicle of the soul's recovery or restoration of its former status as *nous*,[149] and the world, created by God and governed by God's Logos,

Docherty ('New Testament Scriptural Interpretation in its Early Jewish Context', *NT* 57 [2015], 1-19) highlights the plurality of textual forms before the adoption of the masoretic text in the second century – just before Origen's time.

[142] Richard P.C. Hanson, *Allegory and Event* (Richmond, 1959), 276.

[143] Panayiotis Tzamalikos, *Origen: Philosophy of History and Eschatology* (Leiden, Boston, 2007), with my review in *RFN* 100/2 (2008), 453-8; Ilaria L.E. Ramelli, *Apokatastasis; Tempo ed Eternità in Età Antica e Patristica* (Assisi, 2015).

[144] Brian Daley, *God Visible* (2018), 89.

[145] See my 'The Universal and Eternal Validity of Jesus's High-Priestly Sacrifice. The Epistle to the Hebrews in Support of Origen's Theory of Apokatastasis', in Richard J. Bauckham, Daniel R. Driver, Trevor A. Hart and Nathan MacDonald (eds), *A Cloud of Witnesses: The Theology of Hebrews in Its Ancient Contexts*, Library of New Testament Studies 387 (London, 2008), 210-21.

[146] So the Neoplatonic allegorist Secundus Salustius, Περὶ θεῶν καὶ κόσμου 4, 9.

[147] *E.g.* Bernhard Neuschäfer, *Origenes als Philologe*, I-II (Basel, 1987); Lorenzo Perrone, 'Rediscovering Origen Today', *StPatr* 66 (2013), 103-22; Dieter Lau, *Origenes' tropologische Hermeneutik* (Frankfurt, 2016).

[148] Origenes, *De Principiis* IV 2, 6; 8-9.

[149] *Ibid.* II 8, 3.

favors the restoration of all *logika*.[150] Likewise, the *littera* of the Bible, too, is a preparation for apokatastasis. Origen's monumental philological effort in the *Hexapla* (τὰ Ἑξαπλᾶ),[151] shows his attention to the *littera* of the Scripture: it is a list of parallel columns, including the Hebrew, the Septuagint, and later Greek versions by Aquilas, Symmachus, and Theodotion, plus a fifth, sixth, and seventh translation.[152]

Ammonius, Origen's teacher, drawing on Alexandrian textual scholarship, composed a Gospel harmony (*Diatessaron Gospel*, similar to the title of Tatian's *Diatessaron*) with similar parallel passages, which inspired Origen's *Hexapla* and Eusebius' Gospel Canons. Eusebius, in his preface, reports that Ammonius of Alexandria put Matthew and the parallel pericopes from the other Gospels in four parallel columns.[153] Origen did not include texts from what became the New Testament in his biblical philological masterpiece, although he did comment on many New Testament books with textual discussions, and offers rich evidence for the critical editions of John, Matthew, etc., and, by establishing the four Gospels as 'non-controversial'[154] and much else, contributed to the formation of the NT canon,[155] a process that lasted from the end of the first century until the middle of the fourth.[156]

Origen studied Hebrew to some extent.[157] He added to his *Hexapla* a column with the transliteration of Hebrew letters into Greek letters and was helped in the *Hexapla* by someone who knew Hebrew better – we do not know whether Origen read the Gospel of the Hebrews in Aramaic/Hebrew, as Jerome implies.[158] The Septuagint, which was deemed inspired, was central to Origen's

---

[150] *Ibid.* II 1, 1-3.

[151] Eusebius, *Historia Ecclesiastica* VI 16, 4.

[152] *E.g.* Antonio Cacciari, 'Nuova luce sull'officina origeniana. I LXX e "gli altri"', *Adamantius* 20 (2014), 217-25.

[153] Anthony Grafton and Megan Williams, *Christianity and the Transformation of the Book* (Cambridge, 2006), 86-132; 178-245; my review in *Adamantius* 14 (2008), 637-41, and (although at times flawed) Matthew Crawford, 'Ammonius of Alexandria, Eusebius of Caesarea, and the Origins of Gospels Scholarship', *NTS* 61 (2015), 1-29.

[154] Eusebius, *Historia Ecclesiastica* VI 25: ἀναντίρρητα.

[155] See Ilaria Ramelli, 'Fonti note e meno note sulle origini dei Vangeli: osservazioni per una valutazione dei dati della tradizione', *Aevum* 81 (2007), 171-85 and 'The Birth of the Rome-Alexandria Connection' (2011). Origen, in translation, distinguished the four Gospels that became canonical from the others, written by 'heretics' such as those of the Egyptians, of the Twelve Apostles, of Basilides, Thomas, Matthias, etc. (*In Lucam homiliae* 1, 1). Elsewhere (*e.g. Commentarii in Ioannem* 2, 12; *Commentarii in Matthaeum* 10, 17) he cites the Gospels according to the Hebrews and to Peter, without criticizing them.

[156] Jens Schröter, 'The Formation of the New Testament Canon and Early Christian Apocrypha', in Andrew Gregory and Christopher Tuckett (eds), *The Oxford Handbook of Early Christian Apocrypha* (Oxford, 2015), 167-84, 167.

[157] See Eusebius, *Historia Ecclesiastica* VI 16, 1.

[158] Hieronymus, *De viris illustribus* s.v. *James the Just*: the *Gospel according to the Hebrews* was translated by Jerome into Greek and Latin, but, beforehand, 'Origen used it'. Pamphilus 'copied' the 'Hebrew' Gospel believed to have been composed by Matthew, probably from a

Hexapla, both physically and axiologically.[159] Origen's masterpiece of biblical philology was in the service of his exegesis: he himself explains that, to emend the faulty manuscripts of the Bible of the Church, that is, the LXX, ratified by the Letter of Aristeas,[160] a comparison with the other versions[161] was necessary. Moreover, he wanted to establish the Septuagint's critical text with an indication of the passages that were present there, but absent from the Hebrew, or present in the Hebrew but absent from the Septuagint.[162] Indeed, in discussions with Jews, Origen could not adduce any passages present in the Septuagint but absent from the Hebrew (as he himself attests in *Epistula ad Iulium Africanum* 9). Therefore, a careful comparative edition was in order, for both his debates and his exegesis. Indeed, in his commentaries Origen abundantly used the *Hexapla*, which enlarged his exegetical spectrum, since different variants offered a basis for different interpretations. This was a real goldmine for Origen's 'zetetic', heuristic scriptural interpratation.

The exegetical and theological implications of such comparative readings were huge. Origen often refers to his hard work on the manuscripts, checking the Hebrew and other versions.[163] He also remarks upon this in his late Munich homilies: 'God knows how much I labored in comparative examinations of Hebrew texts and editions, to see how to emend errors!'.[164] He stresses that the interpretations he offers are 'laborious',[165] and observes that biblical allegorists subject themselves to 'hard work' (πόνος),[166] a term repeated by Origen everywhere.

Consistently, Origen often applies the language of 'zetesis' to his philological endeavors: his careful scrutiny (συνεξετάζειν) of both the Hebrew and the other versions (τὰ Ἑβραϊκὰ καὶ αἱ ἐκδόσεις) was aimed at the correction of errors (ἡ διόρθωσις τῶν σφαλμάτων); through his extensive investigation (πολλὴ ἐξέτασις) of these readings in all recensions, Origen maintains, he discovered that one of the two was an interpolation (παραγέγραπται, Munich *H*.1 *Ps*.77). But the whole exegetical task is hard work – the hallmark of

manuscript in Origen's library; Pamphilus' Hebrew manuscript was still preserved in the Caesarea library in Jerome's day (*ibid.* s.v. *Matthew*).

[159] See Ilaria L.E. Ramelli, 'Making the Bible World Literature: The Vulgate and Ancient Versions', in Ilaria L.E. Ramelli and Wiebke Denecke (eds), *The Wiley-Blackwell Companion to World Literature*, I (Oxford, 2020), 267-79.

[160] See *e.g.* Michael White and Anthony Keddy, *Jewish Fictional Letters from Hellenistic Egypt* (Atlanta, 2018), 1-273.

[161] See Sébastien Morlet, 'L'utilisation des revisions juives de la Septante', in Rémi Gounelle and Jan Joosten (eds), *La Bible juive dans l'Antiquité* (Prahins, 2014), 117-40; Nicholas deLange, *Greek Bible Translations in Byzantine Judaism* (Tübingen, 2015).

[162] Origenes, *Commentarii in Matthaeum* 15, 14.

[163] See *id.*, *Epistula ad quosdam caros suos in Alexandria*; *Epistula ad Iulium Africanum* 6.

[164] *Id.*, *Homiliae in Psalmum* 77 I 1, fol. 215r.

[165] *Id.*, *Commentarii in Matthaeum* 13, 17.

[166] *Id.*, *Contra Celsum* VII 10.

Origen's own intellectual activity – and very few Christians undertake it, 'devoting their whole life to "searching [ἐρευνᾶτε] the Scriptures" and laboring to study their meaning'.[167] Jesus' imperative, 'search [ἐρευνᾶτε] the Scriptures' (*John* 5:39), is repeated by Origen everywhere, for example in *De Principiis* (IV 3, 5), *Contra Celsum* (III 33), and *Commentarii in epistulam ad Romanos* (7, 17, 4), where this exhortation refers to the activity of investigation into the Scriptures, extending even into night vigils. This was, again, an autobiographical point.[168]

It is possible to find Origen's philological exactitude throughout, for example when he observes that some words appear only in the Gospels and nowhere else in previous literature: 'First of all we must know that the expression ἐπιούσιον is never mentioned by any of the Greeks, nor the learned/philosophers [τῶν σοφῶν], is not in common linguistic use, but seems to have been created by the evangelists [ἔοικε πεπλάσθαι ὑπὸ τῶν εὐαγγελιστῶν]'.[169] But, as usual in his exegesis, he looks for a parallel in the whole Bible, and finds it in the Septuagint: λαὸς περιούσιος ἀπὸ πάντων τῶν ἐθνῶν (*Exod.* 19:5).[170] Both words, Origen notes, come from *ousia*: '*epiousios* bread designates bread provided for the sake of subsistence [εἰς τὴν οὐσίαν]; *periousios* people indicates a people that is the property [οὐσίαν] of God, and takes part in it'.[171] The subsistence/existence that Origen means in the case of the bread is eternal life, the life given by God. So, the bread of the prayer is 'the living bread, which has descended from heaven' (*John* 6:51), Christ being this bread, which 'offers to those who eat it participation in its immorality, since God's Logos is immortal'.[172] This bread is Christ-Logos. For we must ask God for 'heavenly, great gifts'.[173] Indeed, Origen identifies the *epiousios* bread with God's Wisdom, 'by which the angels too are nourished'.[174] The motif of the bread of angels also appears in one of the newly discovered Munich homilies: angels 'eat food that is not corporeal [τροφῇ οὐ σαρκικῇ]' but is 'heavenly, given to them for the subsistence of their own substance [οὐρανίῳ, ἀναδιδομένη εἰς τὴν σύστασιν τῆς οὐσίας αὐτῶν]'.[175] As happens often, here Origen proposes alternative exegeses, based on the etymology of *epiousios*, not from *ousia* this time, but from ἐπιέναι, 'to come upon/after': this bread is 'the bread that is typical of the next world' (οἰκεῖον τοῦ μέλλοντος αἰῶνος).[176] It was common for Origen

---

[167] *Ibid.* VI 37.
[168] See Ramelli, 'Self' (2019).
[169] Origenes, *De oratione* 27, 7.
[170] *Ibid.*
[171] *Ibid.*
[172] *Ibid.* 27, 9.
[173] *Ibid.* 27, 1.
[174] *Ibid.* 27, 11.
[175] *Id., Homiliae in Psalmum 77* IV 10, GCS n.F. 19, 404.1-5.
[176] *Id., De oratione* 27, 13.

to interpret references to food and bread in the Bible as references to the spiritual bread or the nourishment of the soul. For instance, in *Contra Celsum* he comments on *Proverbs* 13:25: 'A righteous man eats and fills his soul, but the souls of the impious are in need'. Origen remarks: 'it is the food of the soul that is indicated in the blessing in the Law. It is not the composite human being – body and soul – who is filled by this food, but the soul alone'.[177] In this way, Origen can reconcile the OT blessing about food and Jesus' asceticizing exhortation not to think about what one will eat or drink in *Matt.* 6:25-8. Origen proposes two interpretations, one profound, the other simple. The former is not explained here; the latter amounts to an exhortation to practice a simple life. This was imperative for the ascetic Origen, who linked asceticism with justice.[178]

Origen and 'Judaic' Exegesis between Rhetoric, Dialogue, and Indebtedness: Philo, Plato, Origen's Exegesis of Plato, and the Rabbis

a. *The Meaning of 'Judaizing' Exegesis*

Origen's ubiquitous rhetoric against 'Judaizing' exegesis, paralleled with literal/'carnal' exegesis, is traditional: Justin had already accused the 'Jews' of interpreting the Scripture 'in a mean way' (ταπεινῶς) without scrutinising (ἐξετάζειν) the power of the words (δύναμις).[179] Such rhetoric, especially in Origen's *Commentary on John*, just as happened with Justin,[180] targeted less contemporary Jews than Origen's Christian opponents, who were primarily literalist exegetes and Christians who literally observed the precepts of the Law.[181] Origen refers to them, for instance, in *Commentarii in Matthaeum* (12, 5); *In Leviticum homiliae XVI* (5, 8); *Homiliae in Psalmum 73* II, and *Homiliae in Psalmum 77* I, where women who followed Jewish unleavening and fast observances were expelled from the church.

---

[177] *Id., Contra Celsum* VII 24.

[178] As pointed out by Ilaria L.E. Ramelli, *Social Justice and the Legitimacy of Slavery: The Role of Philosophical Asceticism from Ancient Judaism to Late Antiquity* (Oxford, 2016), in the chapter on Origen.

[179] Iustinus Martyr, *Dialogus cum Tryphone Iudaeo* 112, 1. See Origenes, *De Principiis* IV 3, 2; *Commentarii in Ioannem* 10, 291; *Contra Celsum* II 3; *Commentarii in Epistulam ad Romanos* 9, 1, 1. See also Susanna Drake, 'Images of Jewishness in Origen's *Letter to Africanus*', *StPatr* 46 (2010), 253-66; *Slandering the Jew* (Philadelphia, 2013), Chs 2-3. On Justin's attitude towards Judaizers and Marcionism, see Benjamin White, 'Justin between Paul and the Heretics', *JECS* 26/2 (2018), 163-89.

[180] This move in Justin's *Dialogue* is argued for by Matthijs DenDulk, *Between Jews and Heretics: Refiguring Justin Martyr's Dialogue with Trypho* (London, 2018).

[181] On this, see also Michael Azar, *Exegeting the Jews: The Early Reception of the Johannine 'Jews'* (Leiden, 2016), esp. Ch. 2.

For this reason, Origen etymologically calls the Ebionites 'poor', since they continue to observe the Law, but with a poor (literal) understanding of the Law.[182] Since the Law is, instead, spiritual – a Pauline tenet that Origen repeats everywhere – Christians, in Origen's view, must observe it *spiritually* and not literally.

b. *Christian 'Literalists', Marcionites, Gnostics, and 'Philistines'*

Thus, 'Jews' were far from being the only, or even the primary target, of Origen's criticism. Origen was aware that 'literalists' also existed among Christians, and, conversely, knew that Jewish exegesis was also allegorical. Christian 'literalists' were actually Origen's own antagonists, as is clear, for example, from his *De Principiis* against literalists,[183] Jews, and the heterodox, and especially from the 5th *Homily on Psalm* 36 against the distinction between God the creator and a superior good God, as advanced by the Marcionites and Gnostics, 'because they interpret the Law exclusively literally, ignoring that it is spiritual'.[184] Here, Jewish literalists are not even mentioned.

Origen dubs Christian literalists (and his critics) 'Philistines' in his *Homilies on Genesis*. In one of them, Origen calls 'Philistines' those Christians who did not want him to investigate the causes for the choice of Jacob over Esau (causes which, to Origen's mind, lie in the fall of rational creatures, to be reversed by the eventual apokatastasis): 'some Philistines', Origen denounces, 'will immediately attack and slander me while I am going to explain the causes for Jacob being chosen'.[185] These Christian literalists criticized Origen's allegoresis and consequent theological doctrines, opposing his spiritual interpretation, represented by the notion of 'digging deep' to find living water, that is, the hidden meaning of Scripture, which requires a profound interpretation. The 'Philistines', those Christian literal exegetes,

limit the Scripture's interpretation to the earthly and fleshly law, precluding the spiritual, mystical exegesis [...] If I attempt to find out the spiritual sense of the Scripture, to remove the veil of the Law and show that what is written is allegorical, I dig wells, but immediately the friends of literal exegesis will calumniate and ambush me, instantly machinating, with hostilities and persecutions, claiming that truth cannot be found but on earth.[186]

Although in his late Munich homily on *Psalm* 76 Origen claims, certainly with auto-apologetical intent, that he is more circumspect about 'flights towards the tropological',[187] nevertheless his *Homilies on Genesis* were also composed

---

[182] Origenes, *Contra Celsum* II 1.
[183] See *id., De Principiis* IV 2, 2.
[184] *Id., Homiliae in Psalmum 36* V 5.
[185] *Id., In Genesim homiliae XVI* 13, 4.
[186] *Ibid.* 13, 2-3.
[187] *Id., H.76Ps.3.2*

in his advanced years (in the 240s), and yet, here too, he sticks to allegoresis against his literalist opponents. Thus, we cannot simply trace a chronological parable from allegoresis to literal exegesis in Origen, all the more so, since the best places to develop complex allegoresis were his commentaries, although there is a great deal of allegoresis in his 'simpler' homilies as well. This means that allegoresis was deeply engrained in Origen's method of interpretation.

c. *Jewish Allegoresis: Philo's Platonizing Approach*

Origen knew not only that literalist exegetes were also to be found among Christians (and were his main opponents), and not just among the Jews, but was also well aware that Jewish exegesis was allegorical as well, not just literal. Philo of Alexandria and Aristobulus are the most conspicuous examples, and Origen overtly claimed them as his predecessors,[188] although allegoresis did not work in the same way in all of Philo's treatises, and his primary task was the exegesis of the Scripture.[189]

Philo's impact on Origen's exegesis – and thereby on later Christian exegesis – is structural, but often it also extends to exegetical details.[190] Origen's explicit appeals to Philo always occur in connection with fundamental exegetical strategies.[191] Allegoresis allowed Philo to interpret the Scripture in the light

---

[188] As I argued in 'Philo as Origen's Declared Model. Allegorical and Historical Exegesis of Scripture', *Studies in Christian-Jewish Relations* 7 (2012), 1-17; 'Philo as One of the Main Inspirers of Early Christian Hermeneutics and Apophatic Theology', *Adamantius* 24 (2018), 53-70. An almost complete catalogue of Origen's passages based on Philo is to be found in Annewies van den Hoek, 'Philo and Origen: A Descriptive Catalogue', *StPhiloA* 12 (2000), 44-121. On Philo I give no bibliography, only referring the reader to my 'Philo's Dialectics of Apophatic Theology, His Strategy of Differentiation, and His Impact on Patristic Exegesis and Theology', *Philosophy* 3 (2019), 36-92. On Aristobulus see Carl R. Holladay, *Fragments from Hellenistic Jewish Authors, III: Aristobulus* (Atlanta, 1995); Markus Mülke, *Aristobulos in Alexandria* (Berlin, 2018).

[189] Rightly noted – along the lines of Valentin Nikiprowetzky, David Winston, and David Runia – by Jerome Moreau, 'A Noocentric Exegesis: The Function of Allegory in Philo of Alexandria and Its Hermeneutical Implications', *SPhiloA* 29 (2017), 61-80: allegory is a tool used to show that the law of nature and the law of Moses are identical ('noocentric exegesis'). I note that, structurally, Stoic exegesis had a parallel aim: to show that theology and the philosophy of nature are coextensive (see Ramelli, *Allegoria* [2004]; 'Stoic Cosmo-Theology Disguised as Zoroastrianism in Dio's *Borystheniticus*? The Philosophical Role of Allegoresis as a Mediator between *Physikē* and *Theologia*', *JRp* 12 [2013], 9-26).

[190] Case studies in Ramelli, 'Philosophical Allegoresis of Scripture; Philo as One of the Main Inspirers of Early Christian Hermeneutics and Apophatic Theology', *Adamantius* 24 (2018), 276-92.

[191] As I pointed out in detail in 'Philosophical Allegoresis of Scripture in Philo and Its Legacy in Gregory of Nyssa', *SPhiloA* 20 (2018), 55-99 and 'Philo and Origen: Allegorical Exegesis of Scripture', *Studies in Christian-Jewish Relations* 7 (2012), 1-17. Jennifer Otto, *Philo of Alexandria and the Construction of Jewishness in Early Christian Writings* (Oxford, 2018), deems Origen's appeals to Philo as an effort to define the continuities and distinctive features of Christian beliefs and practices vs. those of the Jews. This could surely be a component of Origen's references to Philo, but does not erase the value of Origen's appeals to Philo as an authoritative antecedent,

of *Platonism*, especially 'Middle Platonism', Stoicism – although, metaphysi-
cally, Philo, like Origen, rejected Stoic immanentism – and Pythagoreanism.
These are the same philosophical lines (in addition to some Aristotelian concepts) in whose light Origen read the Scripture. Philo was so convinced that
the Scripture and Platonism were inspired by the same Logos as to insist that
the Scripture expounded the Platonic doctrine of the Ideas.[192] Indeed, Philo
viewed the Scripture as an allegorical exposition of Platonic doctrines, and this
is because, as previously mentioned, allegoresis enabled him to read the Scripture in the light of *Platonism*. Origen was more interested in Philo's *Allegorical
Commentary*, which shows Platonic features and is an earlier text,[193] and less
in his later *Exposition of the Law*, which is more centered on Stoicism, addresses
a broader audience, and is more apologetic of Judaism within the Roman
Empire.

d. *Philo and Origen vs. Exclusive Allegoresis. Paul's Role and the Lexical
    Problem*

Origen, like Philo, allegorized the Bible in order to interpret it philosophically, but, again like Philo, dismissed a mere allegorization of the Scripture,
which always rejected the literal level. This exclusively allegorical exegesis
was practiced by pre-Philonic Jewish allegorizers, by 'Gnostic' Christian allegorizers, and by Stoic and 'pagan' Middle-/Neo-platonic allegorizers.

Origen rarely used ἀλληγορία, ἀλληγορέω and related words, since he
deemed this terminology too closely linked to 'pagan' allegoresis. Thus, he
employed it almost only in his treatise against the 'pagan' Platonist Celsus, and
a few other times in his *Commentary on John, First Principles*, and *Commentary on Matthew*,[194] mostly in reference to St Paul's use of ἀλληγορούμενα
within his own interpretation of the story of Hagar and Sarah in *Gal.* 4:22-31.

which is explicit, including in *Contra Celsum*, and significant, since – as I have argued – it
appears in connection with fundamental exegetical strategies, which Origen appropriated and
came originally from Philo. This is also confirmed by the attempt, on the part of 'pagan' Platonists such as Celsus and Porphyry, to sever Origen's allegoresis of the Scripture from its most
important Biblical antecedent, Philo, and rather connect it exclusively to Stoic allegoresis, of
which Origen would be a deformation, applied as it was to a 'spurious' book such as the Bible
(Porphyry). Origen's move in his appeal to Philo as his antecedent – Otto herself calls Philo a
'predecessor', according to Origen – should be viewed against the backdrop of his anti-Marcionite
polemic. See also my review of Otto in *SPhiloA* 31 (2019), 325-9.
    [192] *Exod.* 33:18 (*Spec.* 1.41.45-8); *Exod.* 25:40 (*QE* 2.82; *Mos.* 2.74-6).
    [193] At least according to Maren Niehoff, *Philo of Alexandria: An Intellectual Biography* (New
Haven, 2018).
    [194] Origenes, *Commentarii in Ioannem* 1, 180; 3, 131; 20, 74; 166; 329; *De Principiis* IV 2, 6;
Commentarii in Matthaeum 17, 35. On the relativization of the typology-allegory distinction, see
e.g. Jean-Noël Guinot, 'La frontière entre allégorie et typologie', *RSR* 99 (2011), 303-24; Bogdan
Bucur, 'The Early Christian Reception of Genesis 18', *JECS* 23 (2015), 245-71, esp. 265.

This and 2*Cor*. 3:6, 'the letter kills, the Spirit vivifies', were foundational texts for biblical allegoresis: Origen had recourse to them at least fifty and eighty-two times respectively.[195]

Origen regularly adduced Paul as a justification for biblical allegoresis[196] and calls Paul's exegeses ἀλληγορίαι and typological interpretations (τυπικῶς).[197] In his commentary on John, Origen engaged in a debate with the Valentinian Heracleon's allegorical interpretation, reporting 48 fragments from him or testimonies about him. Origen did not criticize Heracleon's use of allegoresis per se, but he attacked Heracleon because his allegoresis led to questionable doctrines,[198] such as the Valentinian tripartition of rational creatures considered to be evil or good by nature, which clashed with Origen's theology of freedom. Origen describes Heracleon as 'a disciple of Valentinus', whose exegesis sometimes proved 'exceedingly forced'.[199]

Origen criticized not allegoresis, but an *exclusively* allegorical interpretation of the Scripture. In his view, the spiritual sense of the Scripture absorbed both its soul and its body, without destroying them. Such a composite perspective of the absorption of each level of reality or the Scripture into higher levels (body into soul and soul into intellect/spirit) was developed especially by Nyssen and Evagrius, both faithful followers of Origen. Evagrius was also a follower of Gregory of Nyssa, as I hope to have demonstrated.[200]

Origen highlights the close relationship between the spiritual and the material levels of reality, as well as that between *littera* and allegoresis as far as exegesis is concerned.[201] Origen even includes spiritual or noetic (intellectual) senses under allegoresis, as opposed to physical senses under the *littera*.[202] Even in the *Dialogue with Heraclides*, in which he addresses people who are not philosophical experts, Origen both theorizes on the spiritual/interior senses (16-20) and insists on the Scripture's spiritual meaning: μυστικόν,

---

[195] There are even more occurrences than those listed in *Biblia Patristica*.

[196] See Origenes, *Contra Celsum* IV 44, etc.

[197] *Id.*, *De Principiis* IV 2, 6. See Ilaria L.E. Ramelli, 'The Role of Allegory, Allegoresis, and Metaphor in Paul and Origen', *JGRChJ* 14 (2018), 130-57.

[198] See Jeffrey Trumbower, 'The Struggle with Heracleon over the Idea of Fixed Natures', *VC* 43 (1989), 138-54; Bart Ehrman, 'Heracleon, Origen, and the Text of the Fourth Gospel', *VC* 47 (1993), 105-18; Ansgar Wucherpfennig, *Heracleon Philologus* (Tübingen, 2002); Einar Thomassen, 'Heracleon', in Tuomas Rasimus (ed.), *The Legacy of John* (Leiden, 2010), 173-210; Carl Johan Berglund, 'Origen's Vacillating Stances toward his Valentinian colleague Heracleon', *VC* 71 (2017), 541-69.

[199] Origenes, *Commentarii in Ioannem* 2, 100-1.

[200] See my 'Gregory Nyssen's and Evagrius' Relations: Origen's Heritage and Neoplatonism', in *StPatr* 84 (2017), 165-231.

[201] See Origenes, *De Principiis* IV 2, 9; III 4, 6; *Commentarii in Matthaeum* 10, 14-5; 15, 1; etc.

[202] On Origen's spiritual senses (*sensus mentis*, *De Principiis* I 1, 7) see Mark McInroy, *Origen*, in Paul Gavrilyuk and Sarah Coakley (eds), *The Spiritual Senses* (Cambridge, 2012), 20-35.

πνευματικόν (15). This is why he 'anguishes' about speaking or not speaking: he wants to speak for those who are worthy (ἀξίους, again this important exegetical and theological category for Origen) of the spiritual meaning, but not for those unworthy.

e. *The Special Status of the Accounts of the Beginning and the End, and Plato's Influence*

According to both Philo and Origen, most of the Scripture had both literal and allegorical meanings, as Origen explained in his own theory of exegesis in *De Principiis* 4 and elsewhere, including *Contra Celsum* (V 56) on the New Testament as involving historical events charged with allegorical meanings.

However, both Philo and Origen thought – unlike subsequent Rabbinic and Christian exegetes – that, for example, the Genesis account of creation had a special status and was required to be interpreted *only* allegorically. I suspect a Platonic influence on this concept. As I shall briefly explain, the narratives concerning the *arkhē* and the *telos* have special hermeneutical rules, both in Plato, who treated them as myths (the *Timaeus*, the myth of Poros, and the eschatological myths), and in the Scripture. Origen himself noted the parallels between Plato and the Scripture – although he also 'corrected' Plato's myths regarding some souls' 'incurability'[203] and the pre-existence of matter.[204]

As for the biblical narratives about the *telos*, Origen and the Origenian tradition were suspicious of literal interpretations of the Apocalypse of John or Revelations, which produced millenarianism, but Origen accepted Revelations as belonging to the Scripture, commented on it, and cited it, but interpreting it in an exclusively allegorical way.[205] In the prologue to his *Commentary on the Song of Songs*, Origen refers to the Jewish tradition that ascribed a peculiar standing to the beginning of *Genesis,* which ought to be studied after all the rest, just like the *Song of Songs.* For, as Origen explained, these biblical books are the δευτερώσεις, 'second/subsequent objects of study', because they should come *after* all the other biblical books and be exclusively allegorized – not interpreted both literally and allegorically, but exclusively allegorically. Now, Origen claims that the *Jewish tradition* had chosen these δευτερώσεις. The Greek δευτέρωσις reflects the Hebrew *mishnah*, literally 'repetition', *e.g.* in Jerome's *Letter* 121.[206] Indeed, in the Mishnah – stemming roughly from Origen's

---

[203] Origenes, *De Principiis* III 6, 5.

[204] Id., *In Genesim homiliae XVI* 14, 3; *De Principiis* II 4, 3.

[205] See Ilaria Ramelli, 'Origen's Interpretation of Violence in the Apocalypse', in Joseph Verheyden *et al.* (eds), *Ancient Christian Interpretations of Violent Texts in the Apocalypse* (Göttingen, 2011), 46-62.

[206] From *shnh,* 'repeat'. Ancient Christian authors used δευτέρωσις to designate the exegesis of contemporary Rabbis (Eusebius, *Commentarii in Isaiam* 1, 21-22; *Demonstratio evangelica* VI

time, like the Tosefta[207] – Genesis 'may not be expounded by two, nor the *merkabah* by one, unless he is a scholar and has understood on his own' (*m.Ḥagigah* 2.1). Philo not only practiced scriptural allegoresis, but also attests to the regular practice of scriptural allegoresis among Essenes and Therapeutae (*Quod omnis probus liber sit* 75ff.; *De vita contemplativa*) and informs us, for instance, that the story of Joseph in Egypt was interpreted allegorically by other exegetes before him (*De Iosepho* 151).

Both Origen and Philo were probably inspired, I suspect, by Plato's philosophical myths regarding the exclusively allegorical interpretation of the creation story. Origen explicitly appreciated them as the only way of speaking of what is impossible to expound theoretically, so as to conceal the truth from 'the majority' and to reveal it only to 'those who know', *i.e.* those able to interpret Plato's myths allegorically.[208] Origen was aware that Plato could only use mythical (and therefore allegorical) language, and not theoretical, when he dealt with the origin of the world and the soul – especially in the *Timaeus* – and in his eschatological myths. Likewise, for Origen, *arkhē* and *telos* were left unclarified by the teaching of the Church[209] and were unknown even to angels.[210] Another biblical passage, *Isa.* 6:2, according to Origen, expresses the same notion that *arkhē* and *telos* are unknowable historically and are expressible only allegorically: the Seraphim, who cover God's head and feet (*Isa.* 6:2), indicate allegorically the unknowability of the *arkhē* and *telos*.[211]

It appears significant that, when Origen speaks of spiritual things, which are reserved for those to whom the Spirit communicates meanings 'no longer through letters, but through living words',[212] he echoes Plato's 'living speech' in *Phaedrus* 276A. As in so many other cases, Origen is reading the Scripture through the lens of Plato. Like Proclus later (*Theologia Platonica* 1, 4; *In Platonis Parmenidem commentaria* I 646, 16-647, 18 Steel), Origen was aware that Plato had many ways to deal with theology: not only dialectical or scientific, to be read in a literal way, but also symbolic or mythical, to be read allegorically.

18, 36); Azzan Yadin-Israel, 'Tradition and Transmission in Papias and the Early Rabbis', *JECS* 23 (2015), 337-62, 339.

[207] *E.g.* Richard Kalmin, 'Mishnah, Midrash, Talmud', in *Companion to World Literature* 1; Martin Goodman, 'Mishnah', *OCD* July 2015, DOI:10.1093/acrefore/9780199381135.013.4222; *id.*, 'Tosefta', *OCD* March 2016, DOI:10.1093/acrefore/9780199381135.013.6988.

[208] Origenes, *Contra Celsum* IV 39. Ilaria L.E. Ramelli, 'Origen's Allegoresis of Plato's and Scripture's Myths', in Nathaniel Desrosiers and Lily Vuong (eds), *Religious Competition in the Greco-Roman World* (Atlanta, 2016), 85-106; 'Proclus'. That there were connections between Biblical (OT and NT) myths and 'pagan' myths is now stressed, independently of Origen, by Bruce Louden, *Greek Myth and the Bible* (London, 2018).

[209] Origenes, *De Principiis*, prol. 7.

[210] See Origenes, *De Principiis* IV 3, 14; Pamphilus Caesariensis, *Apologia pro Origene* 82.

[211] Origenes, *De Principiis* IV 3, 14; *In Isaiam homiliae* XXXII 1, 2; 4, 1; *H.4Ps.76.5*.

[212] *Id.*, *De Principiis* IV 2, 4.

f. *Origen's Linking of Plato's Myths to those of the Scripture*

Origen read *Genesis* with Plato at the back of his mind. This seems to be confirmed by the fact that he explicitly linked Plato's myth of Poros to the *Genesis* account of creation, both in *Contra Celsum* (IV 39) and in his lost *Commentary on Genesis*. The *Genesis* story of the creation of humanity and its fall, and Plato's myths of Poros and Penia and the soul's fall, according to Origen, expressed the same content symbolically, and both of those mythical accounts, in the Bible and in Plato, had to be interpreted *only* allegorically. In *Contra Celsum*, Origen declares that the *Genesis* story of the protoplasts' sin and their envelopment in 'skin tunics' (which represents mortal, heavy corporeality) is not literal, but has a 'mystical and secret meaning', which Origen links to the symbolic meaning of Plato's myth of the soul's descent after the loss of its wings.[213] The biblical story 'has a kind of secret and mystical meaning [ἀπόρρητον, μυστικὸν λόγον], even more than Plato's myth of the descent of soul, when it loses its wings [πτερορρυούσης] and falls down, until it becomes attached to something solid'. The echoes of Plato are evident in Origen's words – primarily in the key word πτερορρυούσης – as well as the parallels between Plato and the Scripture.

According to Origen, Plato's reference to a pure earth (*Phaedrus* 109AB) was anticipated by Moses (*Exod.* 3:8), meaning not Judaea, but the heavenly Jerusalem.[214] Plato's idea of precious stones in his image of the stones in the better land (*Phaedrus* 110DE) parallels *Isa.* 54:11-2 and the City of God. Origen even treats myths, such as those of Hesiod about the initial unity of gods and humans together,[215] as symbolic expressions of the truth of the prelapsarian harmony.[216] Another parallel is between Hesiod's Pandora myth and the biblical myths in *Contra Celsum*: since Hesiod's myth has allegorical meanings, biblical myths should also be considered to have them, as Origen argues.[217]

Plato and Origen exclusively allegorized the mythical and biblical accounts of protology (the ἀρχή). Likewise, Philo provided an *exclusively allegorical* exegesis of the biblical Paradise as virtue and Eden as luxury,[218] Adam as the mind and Eve as the senses. In *De Principiis*, Origen explicitly included the account of Paradise and the *Genesis* story of creation among the scriptural passages deprived of any literal meaning: 'these things *indicate symbolic truths in an allegorical way*, by means of what *looks like a historical account*, and yet has *never happened corporeally*'.[219] Adam's story never happened historically,

---

[213] *Id., Contra Celsum* IV 40.
[214] *Ibid.* VII 28.
[215] Hesiod, fr. 82 (216) Rzach.
[216] Origenes, *Contra Celsum* IV 79, where Origen inserts a reminiscence of Plato, *Leges* 677B.
[217] See Origenes, *Contra Celsum* IV 38.
[218] See Philo, *Legum allegoriae* I 45.
[219] Origenes, *De Principiis* IV 3, 1.

but must be interpreted allegorically, because it encompasses 'mysteries' and symbols. *Gen.* 2:7, with God's insufflation of the Spirit into Adam, 'is meant allegorically and needs an explanation, showing that God imparted a share of incorruptible Spirit to the human'.[220] Similarly, the biblical description of God walking in Paradise in the protological account (*Gen.* 3:8) must not be taken literally, but it means that God was moved by the protoplasts who had sinned.[221] Adam's story must be interpreted 'philosophically', since Adam means 'human' and his story expresses 'the nature of humanity […] the whole race', and the serpent's story has 'a remarkable allegorical meaning'.[222] Many examples of the allegorical exegesis of creation and Paradise, the scriptural narrative about the ἀρχή, can be found in Origen's own exegetical production.[223] Origen, like Philo, allegorized the account of creation, and attributed to it an epistemological standing similar to that of Plato's creation myth, that is, exclusively allegorical and not literal-historical. Indeed, such accounts do not belong to human history.

g. *Plato's Acquaintance with Jewish 'Philosophy': Jews (and Christians) as Philosophers*

The way in which Origen explains the similarities that emerge between Plato's myth and *Genesis'* myth is similar to that which is found in Jewish Hellenistic apologetics: 'It is not quite clear whether the Poros myth occurred to Plato's mind by chance or, as some believe, during his sojourn in Egypt Plato also encountered people who adhered to *the Jews' philosophy*'.[224]

Note that Origen speaks here of Jewish *philosophy*, and not of the Jewish religion or cult, not only because 'religion' in the modern sense was a word lacking in the ancient world,[225] but also because the Jews worshipped the true

---

[220] *Id., Contra Celsum* IV 37.

[221] *Ibid.* VI 64.

[222] *Ibid.* IV 40.

[223] Among the many examples are: the etymology of Eden as ἤδη, 'once upon a time', to signify a primeval state (*Fragmenta in Genesim* 236; D15 Metzler); 'intelligible trees' (*In Genesim homiliae XVI* 2, 4), 'intelligible rivers' and 'intelligible woody valleys' in Paradise (*Selecta in Numeros* PG 12, 581B). The whole of the first *Homily on Genesis* bristles with passages from the creation story of which only an allegorical explanation is given. From *H.1Ps.36* it is clear that the creation account must be allegorized.

[224] Origenes, *Contra Celsum* IV 39.

[225] Carlin Barton and Daniel Boyarin, *Imagine No Religion: How Modern Abstractions Hide Ancient Realities* (New York, 2016), not only emphasize the fact that *religio* and θρησκεία cannot be translated as 'religion' in modern terms (on which see also John Scheid, 'Religion, Roman, terms relating to', in *OCD*, online Mar 2016, DOI:10.1093/acrefore/9780199381135.013.5549 and Emily Kearns, 'Religion, Greek', *ibid.*, DOI:10.1093/acrefore/9780199381135.013.5537), but also argue that 'religion' did not exist in antiquity as a standalone entity, as private religion. There exists no word for 'religion' in Greek, Latin, or Hebrew, and the concept is elusive in ancient Jewish, Greek, and Roman culture: see Jörg Rüpke, *Religion of the Romans* (Cambridge, 2007), 5-12; Brent Nongbri, *Before Religion* (New Haven, 2013). *Inreligiositas* has more to do with wrong cults,

God, and therefore their 'whole nation philosophized'[226] – as Origen would
have liked all Christians to do,[227] as previously mentioned – and because the
noetic/symbolic interpretation of the Scripture is, in Origen's view, again, a
philosophical task: this had already been performed by Jewish authors, such as
Philo and Aristobulus. Origen underlined this point. Indeed, in *Contra Celsum*,
after reporting Celsus' declarations against any allegoresis of the Scripture,
Origen remarks that those claims are not only an attack on the Christian allegoresis of the Scripture, but also on the *Jewish* allegoresis: 'He gives the
impression of saying so concerning the treatises of Philo or of those even more
ancient exegetes, such as Aristobulus. I suppose that Celsus had not even read
those books!'.[228] Origen is thereby claiming a non-Christian and pre-Christian
ancestry in the philosophical allegoresis of the Scripture: a Hellenistic Jewish
philosophical allegoresis, as well as Plato.

It is not accidental that he explicitly praised Philo as an intelligent exegete.
In *Contra Celsum*, referring to *De Somniis* (1, 133-88), Origen states that Jacob's
vision of the ladder in *Gen.* 28, with angels going up and down, was 'interpreted
in a small book by Philo, which deserves the close and intelligent scrutiny of
those who love the truth [ἄξιον φρονίμου καὶ συνετῆς ἐξετάσεως παρὰ τοῖς
φιλαλήθεσιν]'.[229] The symbology of the ladder, indeed, was, for Origen, important and Christological: he found the same image in Plato's ladder of love and
in Jacob's ladder, both leading to the divine.[230]

h. *Philo's Composite Exegesis as Antecedent: Philo Claimed as Predecessor in Points Crucial to Allegoresis*

According to Origen, the scriptural passages that are literally true are '*much
more numerous* than those which have 'bare spiritual meanings'', which are
not wrapped up in a literal sense as by a body or robe.[231] The stories of the

---

or lack thereof, than wrong beliefs. Tertullian turns this anti-Christian charge against traditional
Greco-Roman religion, which committed the crime *verae inreligiositatis* (*Apologeticum* 24, 2).

[226] Origenes, *Contra Celsum* IV 31, echoing Philo, *De Specialibus Legibus* 2, 62.

[227] Origenes, *Contra Celsum* I 9.

[228] *Ibid.* IV 51.

[229] *Ibid.* VI 21.

[230] He also posited Christ as the staircase of the Temple, leading to God: Christ is all the steps,
from humanity to the angelic level, that of the other powers, to the Divinity (*cf.* Origenes, *Commentarii in Ioannem* 19, 6, 38-9).

[231] Pamphilus Caesariensis, *Apologia pro Origene* 123. Origen's γυμνὰ πνευματικά was likely
inspired by Philo (*De migratione Abrahami* 89), the 'naked truth' (ἀλήθεια γυμνή) sought by
extreme allegorists who read the Scripture *only* spiritually: on them, see David Hay, 'References
to Other Exegetes', in David Hay (ed.), *Both Literal and Allegorical: Studies in Philo of Alexandria's Questions and Answers of Genesis and Exodus* (Atlanta, 1991), 81-97. Consistently, Philo
criticized them for neglecting the body (*De Specialibus Legibus* 2, 64-67). Likewise, Origen valued
the body as well, and used both allegoresis and literal exegesis.

Patriarchs and the miracle of Joshua happened historically.[232] Philo would have agreed with Origen. Likewise, Jesus' miracles were both physical and spiritual. In most scriptural passages, 'their spiritual sense must be received only after maintaining their historical truth'.[233] The historicity of the Scripture is unquestionable for both Origen and Philo, but both postulate spiritual/allegorical meanings in addition to the historical level. Origen praised precisely Philo when he referred to those Jews who interpreted the Law both literally and 'allegorically',[234] according to the ecclesiastical doctrine that the Scripture teaches 'forms of certain mysteries, images of divine things; here the whole church entertains one opinion: all the Law is in fact spiritual'.[235] For Origen, Philo the Jew, who stuck to both the historical and the allegorical meaning of the Scripture, was a better exegete than Christian 'heretics' were. Origen's attitude toward Philo as his predecessor in Scriptural allegoresis is perhaps less ambivalent than commonly assumed. Origen tends to refer to Philo expressly as a predecessor, *precisely in points that are crucial to his scriptural allegorical method.* This suggests that Philo inspired not only Origen's philosophical theology, which is true in many ways, but primarily Origen's technique of philosophical allegoresis of the Bible.[236]

i. *Threefold Christology, Three Moral Levels, and Threefold Exegesis*

Origen drew on Philo especially with regard to the moral interpretation of the Scripture, in reference to the moral choices of the soul between good and evil.[237] This level is the 'soul' of the Bible, while the *littera* is its 'body' and the spiritual meaning its 'spirit'. The moral level, the 'soul', is useful for those who are making moral progress, as opposed to the 'too simple' (*simpliciores*), the target of the *littera*, and the perfect, who reach the spiritual level. Origen, in *De Principiis*, relies on *Prov.* 22:20, interpreted as an invitation to read the Scripture 'in three ways'. Indeed, the aim of exegesis is the salvation of the human being in its three components and phases of development,

that the *simpler person* may be edified by the *flesh*, so to say, of the Scripture, its most obvious meaning; the *person somewhat advanced* may be edified by its *soul*, as it were, and the *perfect* [...] by *the spiritual law*, which includes in itself the shadow of future goods. For, as the human consists of *body, soul, and spirit*, so also does the Scripture.[238]

---

[232] Pamphilus Caesariensis, *Apologia pro Origene* 125.

[233] *Ibid.* 113.

[234] Origenes, *Contra Celsum* VII 20.

[235] *Id., De Principiis* I prol. 8, with reference to *Rom.* 7:14.

[236] As argued in 'Philo as Origen's Declared Model'.

[237] Origenes, *In Numeros homiliae XXVIII* 9, 7: *Moralis doctrina vel ratio*; id., *In Genesim homiliae XVI* 2, 6: *moralis interpretatio, moralis locus.*

[238] Origenes, *De Principiis* IV 2, 4 = *Philocalia* 1, 11.

The sense-perceptible level of reality – Christ's human nature and the *littera* of the Scripture – parallel, in Origen's view, the intelligible level of reality, Christ's divine nature and the spiritual sense of the Scripture.[239] Not all of the Scripture has a literal meaning, but all of the Scripture has an allegorical, spiritual meaning:

'Do you think these are myths? Do you think the Holy Spirit in the Scriptures just tells stories? This is rather teaching for souls, spiritual instruction […] All that is written in the Scripture is mysteries', that is, allegories, noetic/spiritual senses.[240]

As we read the Bible, Origen notes, based on his own practice of assiduously reading and meditating on the Scripture, 'a heap of symbolic meanings increases before us […] such an immense sea of mysteries!'.[241]

j. *Jewish Priests' Allegoresis and Celsus' and Porphyry's Omission of Jewish Antecedents*

As has been pointed out, Origen was well aware of Jewish allegorical interpretations of the Scripture, and knew that 'Jewish' exegesis was not only 'literal' and 'carnal', as much rhetoric had it. He even claims that Jewish priests, 'in secret', researched and discussed the symbolic meaning of the Law.[242] Among such priests there might have been Philo, who was 'of priestly descent' according to Jerome,[243] or other priests such as the teachers of St. Paul – an allegorist himself, and in whose letters Origen constantly sought a Scriptural justification for his own biblical allegoresis, as I have pointed out above. Perhaps among those 'priests' there might even have been the early Rabbis.

Origen, indeed, linked his own allegorical exegesis of the Scripture to a similar Judaic practice. Whereas 'pagan' allegorists such as Porphyry accused him of arbitrarily transferring allegoresis from Stoic philosophy (which applied it to classical myths) to a 'barbarian' text such as the Bible, Origen stressed that he owed scriptural allegoresis to Philo, Aristobulus, and 'the Jewish priests' – besides, of course, Plato himself. He claimed that the Jews were superior even to philosophers, since they worshipped the true God.[244]

Celsus and Porphyry omitted – intentionally, I suspect – the Hellenistic Jewish antecedents to the Christian philosophical allegoresis of the Scripture, as Origen himself denounced in the case of Celsus. The latter was unwilling to admit that Jewish Hellenistic exegetes, such as Aristobulus, Philo, and others,

---

[239] See *id., In Leviticum homiliae XVI* 1, 1; *Commentariorum series in Matthaeum* 27.

[240] *Id., In Genesim homiliae XVI* 10, 2.

[241] *Ibid.* 9, 1.

[242] *Id., Contra Celsum* V 44.

[243] Hieronymus, *De viris illustribus* 11. See the analysis in 'Rome-Alexandria Connection' (2011).

[244] Origenes, *Contra Celsum* V 43.

had inaugurated the philosophical allegoresis of the Bible. Origen, instead, proudly cited these Jewish precursors of his own allegoresis.

Celsus significantly omitted not only Philo, but also Paul,[245] as though he intended to silence the 'Hellenistic' side of Christianity and all Jewish allegorizers of the Scripture. Indeed, his 'Jew', the polemicist whom Celsus used as a mouthpiece, addressed not Gentile, but Jewish Christians.[246] Like Philo, Paul also promoted biblical allegoresis, as Origen stresses throughout. For instance, he adduces *Gal.* 4:21-4 and *1Cor.* 9:8-10 in defence of allegorical hermeneutics,[247] and cites *1Cor.* 9:9-10; *Eph.* 5:31-2, and *1Cor.* 10:1-4 in *Contra Celsum*.[248] And in many other passages, Paul grounds not only Origen's philosophical allegoresis, but many points of his theology as well, including his soteriology and eschatology and, pertaining to these, his doctrine of apokatastasis.[249]

This seems to have been the main reason why Celsus, who did not admit that allegorical exegesis applied to the Scripture, which, in his view, could not contain philosophical truths, silenced both Philo and Paul as the antecedents of Origen's scriptural allegoresis. He thus chose to mention only the imperial Stoic allegorizers Cornutus and Chaeremon as Origen's source of inspiration, in order to charge Origen with the undue transfer of their philosophico-allegorical tools to the wrong object.

k. *From Exegetical to Theological Errors*

Origen, in his allegorization of the Bible, countered, as has been mentioned, the 'Gnostic' and Marcionite claims that the Old Testament was separate from the New as a product of an inferior God or an evil demiurge, and consequently contained no philosophical truths to be decoded by allegoresis. The Marcionites and Gnostics 'do not respect the expositive symphony [συμφωνία] of the Scripture from the beginning to the end';[250] they fail to offer 'the *whole* theology'.[251] Origen, instead, aimed to offer a 'full' philosophical theology, by interpreting the Old and New Testament as a single whole.

Origen explains that the distinction between God the creator and a superior, good God, typical of the Marcionites and of some 'Gnostics', arises from their failure to read the Old Testament *allegorically*: 'they are so mistaken in their thoughts because they interpret the Law *exclusively literally*, and ignore the fact

[245] *Ibid.* I 63.
[246] *Ibid.* II 1.
[247] *Ibid.* II 4.
[248] *Ibid.* IV 49.
[249] See my 'Paul on Apokatastasis: 1 Cor 15:24-28 and the Use of Scripture', in Stanley Porter and Christopher Land (eds), *Paul and Scripture* (Leiden, 2019), 212-32.
[250] Origenes, *Commentarii in Ioannem* 10, 42, 290.
[251] *Id., Commentarii in Ephesios* 2, 27: πᾶσαν.

that *the Law is spiritual*.[252] This is, once again, Paul's declaration, on which Origen based his allegoresis: indeed, according to Origen, at the Transfiguration Moses represents not historical Law, but 'spiritual Law'.[253] By denying the spiritual nature of the Law, the Marcionites and 'Gnostics' found in the Old Testament anthropomorphisms and details unworthy of God, and concluded, as a consequence, that the Hebrew Bible, and the material world, were the products of an evil demiurge. It is clear that exegetical and theological mistakes are closely intertwined in Origen's view.

In the passage above, indeed, it emerges that an exegetical error brings about a serious theological one. If these 'heretics' had read the Old Testament allegorically, like Philo, they would have found it 'worthy of God', as Origen himself always required. As a consequence, Philo was a better exegete, and thereby a better theologian, than Christian 'heretics' were. As Origen realized, Philo was aware of what Paul, his contemporary, claimed: that the Law has a spiritual meaning.[254] Paul, Origen surmises, learnt this from his teacher, Rabbi Gamaliel, who was, perhaps, included amongst the Jewish priests whom Origen mentioned as interpreting the Scripture allegorically 'in secret'. However, Origen, like Philo,[255] criticized extreme allegorists of the Scripture, who refused to admit the historicity of the Bible or of parts thereof, as though the whole of the Bible were a myth, deprived of historical value. Origen, instead, drawing inspiration from both Plato and Philo, as pointed out above, treated only a few parts of the Scripture as merely mythical, without a historico-literal substratum.

l. *Origen's Lost Exegesis and Engagement with Contemporary Jewish Exegesis: Learning as Worship and the Rejection of Philo's Logos Theology as Experienced by Origen*

Much of Origen's exegetical production is unfortunately lost (notwithstanding the abundance of what is extant), primarily his *Commentary on Genesis*. This is the main work that could illuminate even better Origen's indebtedness to Philo. Part of Origen's lost exegesis of *Genesis* is to be found in Eusebius' *Eclogae propheticae*, in which he reproduced, paraphrased, or abridged passages from Origen's *Contra Celsum* and commentaries.[256] Here, Eusebius calls Origen 'that marvellous man',[257] 'the most laborious [φιλοπονώτατος] exegete of holy

---

[252] *Id., H.*5 *Ps.*36.5.

[253] *Id., Contra Celsum* VI 68.

[254] *Rom.* 7:14: see above.

[255] Philo Alexandrinus, *De migratione Abrahami* 89-93.

[256] Sébastien Morlet, 'Origen as an Exegetical Source in Eusebius' *Prophetic Extracts*', in Aaron Johnson and Jeremy Schott (eds), *Eusebius of Caesarea: Traditions and Innovations* (Cambridge, 2013), 207-37.

[257] Eusebius, *Eclogae propheticae* 4, 7.

scriptures'[258] – with a superlative that Athanasius also used to characterize Origen – who offered 'an extremely complete exegesis', a 'fullest clarification' of the Bible.[259]

Origen was aware not only of Philo's and Aristobulus' exegesis, but also of contemporary Jewish biblical exegesis and often referred to such interpretations.[260] For instance, he mentions a Judaic exegesis reported by a convert from Judaism,[261] the interpretation of Susannah's story provided by a wise Hebrew,[262] and the exegesis offered by 'patriarch Ioullos and another of the wisest Jews'.[263] Based on the Hebrew tradition, Origen imagined the Bible as a house composed of rooms, of which the keys are exchanged and interchangeable:[264] this stressed, again, the unity of the Scripture and of its interpretation, a point that was very dear to Origen, as well as to Clement.

The exegesis of the Hebrew Bible by both the Rabbis and Origen developed in an awareness of the other side's interpretation, which implied interactions, influences, and polemics. Origen also held a public debate with wise Jews before 'many people',[265] and other discussions.[266] Origen's relations with contemporary Jews were probably richer in Caesarea than in Alexandria.[267] The 'emphasis on learning as a form of worship' shown by the Rabbis[268] is remarkably similar to the approach of Origen, their contemporary, who – as has been pointed out above in the section on the various 'bodies' of Christ – regarded the Scripture as the incarnation of the Logos, and its study as a Eucharistic act. Indeed, Origen also emphasized the idea of learning as a form of worship, exactly as the Rabbis did.

In Palestine, Origen met Jews who did not accept Philo's Logos theology – perhaps also in the awareness that this had been promoted by Christians – but not all Rabbis did so, as we shall see in a moment.[269] The 'Jew' in Celsus' *True*

[258] *Ibid.* 3, 6.

[259] *Ibid.* 2, 2; 3, 6.

[260] Origenes, *Commentarii in Ioannem* 6, 83; *Contra Celsum* I 45; I 55; II 31; *In Ezechielem homiliae XIV* 4, 8; *Libri in Psalmos* 11, 352.

[261] *Id., Homiliae in Ieremiam* 20, 2.

[262] *Id., Epistula ad Iulium Africanum* 11 [7]; *Stromata* 10, PG 11, 101BC.

[263] *Id., Libri in Psalmos* PG 12, 1056B. The Hebrew mentioned more than once by Origen (*C.Ps.*1; *De Principiis* I 3, 4; *Selecta in Ezechielem* 9, 2) seems to have been a Jew from Palestine, the son of a rabbi, who embraced Christianity and migrated to Egypt.

[264] *Id., Philocalia* 2, 3.

[265] *Id., Contra Celsum* I 45.

[266] *Ibid.* I 49: debates with Jews on the title 'God's Child'; *ibid.* I 55: debate with a learned Jew on *Isaiah* 52-53; *ibid.* II 31: meetings with many wise Jews.

[267] On the legacy of Origen's thought in Caesarea, see Brouria Bitton-Ashkelony *et al.* (eds), *Origeniana Duodecima. Origen's Legacy in the Holy Land* (Leuven, 2019).

[268] Martin Goodman, 'Religion, Jewish', *OCD* March 2016, DOI:10.1093/acrefore/9780199938 1135.013.5540; 'Rabbis', *ibid.*, DOI:10.1093/acrefore/9780199381135.013.5493.

[269] On which see Daniel Boyarin, *Border Lines. The Partition of Judaeo-Christianity* (Philadelphia, 2004), Chs 5-6. On Origen's relationship to Hellenistic Judaism: Robert Berchman, *From*

Logos observed that the identification of the Logos with the Child of God was accepted by Christians and Jews alike. Origen, for his part, remarks that he met with many wise Jews, but none of them accepted such identification of the Logos as the Child of God.[270]

Unlike the Jews whom Origen met later, Philo identified the Logos with the Child of God.[271] Origen was well familiar with Philo's Logos theology, and used it in his own Trinitarian theology and Christology, but in *Contra Celsum* he rather speaks of the Rabbis he met in Palestine in his day, who rejected Logos theology as the heresy of 'the two powers in heaven',[272] probably also because of the Christian overtones that this theory was meanwhile assuming. Yet, it must be observed that there is some Logos theology in Rabbinics.[273] Origen himself reports on the exegesis of *Isa.* 6:3 by a 'Hebrew master', in which the two seraphim who sing the Trisagion are 'the only-begotten Son of God and the Holy Spirit'.[274] Origen obviously viewed in this image a Trinitarian representation.

The time of the Tannaim, the most authoritative of the Rabbis, lasted until around the 250s, when Origen died. Thus, Origen's lifespan was contemporary with the Tannaim. Later Rabbis attributed to them a high authority. Among the Rabbis, Tannaitic Rabbis especially raised the study of the Scripture to the status of a divine service, as Origen did ('a form of worship', as previously mentioned). Precisely because of their abovementioned polemic against Logos theology, they replaced the Logos/Memra with the Torah. This is also why they thought that creation was not performed by the Logos – as Philo, John and Origen maintained – but by the Torah itself.[275] Both they and Origen claimed authority as exegetes of the Bible at the same time, and in competition with one another.[276]

Philo To Origen: Middle Platonism in Transition (Chico, CA, 1984); David Runia, *Philo in Early Christian Literature* (Assen, 1993), 157-83.

[270] Origenes, *Contra Celsum* II 32.

[271] Philo Alexandrinus, *De Agricultura* 51; *De Confusione Linguarum* 146.

[272] Origenes, *Contra Celsum* II 32.

[273] Hans Bietenhard, 'Logos-Theologie im Rabbinat. Ein Beitrag zur Lehre vom Worte Gottes im rabbinischen Schrifttum', *ANRW* II, 19, 2 (1979), 580-618, on Dibbur as Word, word of God, and Hypostasis in Rabbinics, with some discussion of the work on Origen (609-11).

[274] Origenes, *De Principiis* I 3, 4.

[275] Tzvi Novick, 'Creator, Text, and Law: Torah as Independent Power in Rabbinic Judaism', in Gary Anderson and Markus Bockmuehl (eds), *Creation 'Ex Nihilo'* (Notre Dame, IN, 2018).

[276] Nicholas de Lange, *Origen and the Jews* (Cambridge, 1976); *id.*, 'Jewish Influence on Origen', in Henri Crouzel (ed.), *Origeniana* (Bari, 1975), 225-42; John McGuckin, 'Origen on the Jews', in Daniel Wood (ed.), *Christianity and Judaism* (Oxford, 1992), 1-13; Anna Tzvetkova-Glaser, *Pentateuchauslegung bei Origenes und den frühen Rabbinen* (Frankfurt, 2010); Paul Blowers, 'Origen, the Rabbis, and the Bible', in Charles Kannengiesser (ed.), *Origen of Alexandria: His World and His Legacy* (Notre Dame, IN, 1988), 96-116; R. Brooks, 'The Appropriate Jewish Background for the Study of Origen', in Charles Kannengiesser (ed.), *Origen of Alexandria: His World and His Legacy* (Notre Dame, IN, 1988), 63-95; William Horbury, 'Origen and the Jews',

Indeed, both Rabbis and Christians competed for the exclusive right to interpret the Bible.[277] Origen's etymologies of biblical names find parallels in Rabbinic literature,[278] and Maren Niehoff argued that Origen knew and mostly, although not always, rejected the exegetical traditions preserved in *Genesis Rabbah*, which, composed in Caesarea, developed in dialogue with Origen's own commentary on *Genesis*.[279] The closeness between Isaac carrying the wood as a cross for his own sacrifice in *Genesis Rabbah* (56:3) and Origen's Christological reading of Isaac carrying the wood as a figure of Christ to be crucified in *Commentarii in Genesim* (*F*54) was noted by Anna Tzvetkova-Glaser.[280] I pointed out further parallels in my review, with a focus on Isaac: the cross element, Isaac's willingness to be sacrificed, and the date itself of his sacrifice on 15 Nisan are strikingly close to the circumstances of Jesus' death.[281]

The same debate with Origen and early Christian theology seems to have happened around the Rabbinic rejection of Logos theology. In both cases, Rabbinic exegetical and theological choices were dictated by their confrontations with the exegesis and theology of Origen and other early Christians.[282] There was a relationship of reception, interaction, and reaction between the two poles of Rabbinic exegesis and Origen's (and his followers') exegesis.

m. *Other Parallels to Rabbinic Exegesis: the Scripture's Unity and the Pervasiveness of Inspiration*

Origen employed an intra-biblical comparative method, exactly as the early Rabbis did: in order for him to explain a passage, he drew inspiration from other relevant biblical passages. According to him, as has been pointed out above, just as in the opinion of Philo and the early Rabbis, the Bible forms a coherent unity. The difference lies in the fact that Philo and Origen privileged

in James Aitken and James Carleton Paget (eds), *The Jewish-Greek Tradition in Antiquity and the Byzantine Empire* (Cambridge, 2014), 79-91; Robert Chazan, *From Anti-Judaism to Anti-Semitism* (Cambridge, New York, 2016), Ch. 3.

[277] Jonathan Bourgel, *La communauté judéo-chrétienne de Jérusalem* (Paris, 2015), Ch. 5. *Cf.* Emmanouela Grypeou and Helen Spurling (eds), *The Exegetical Encounter between Jews and Christians in Late Antiquity* (Leiden, 2009), especially Philip Alexandre, 'In the Beginning: Rabbinic and Patristic Exegesis of Genesis 1:1', p. 1-29, and Marc Hirschman, 'Origen's View of "Jewish Fables" in Genesis', p. 245-54. On Jews in Origen's time: Daniel Schwartz, *Judaeans and Jews* (Toronto, 2015).

[278] De Lange, *Origen* (1976), 16-7.

[279] 'Origen's Commentary on Genesis as a key to *Genesis Rabbah*', in Peter Schäfer *et al.* (eds), *Genesis Rabbah in Text and Context* (Tübingen, 2016), 129-53.

[280] Glaser, *Pentateuchauslegung* (2010), 186-202, not mentioned by Niehoff in *Origen's Commentary* (2016).

[281] See my review of Glaser, *Pentateuchauslegung* (2010), BMCR 2011.05.50.

[282] This is also confirmed by Isaac Kalimi, *Fighting Over the Bible: Jewish Interpretation, Sectarianism and Polemic from Temple to Talmud and Beyond* (Leiden, 2017), 90-124, although he focuses mostly on Medieval times.

allegorical hermeneutics, while the Rabbis refrained from using this. In their allegoresis, both Philo and Origen tended not to consider isolated allegorical points, but a whole passage in its allegorical system. In support of his practice, Origen in *Contra Celsum* cited once again St. Paul, 1*Cor.* 2:13, with its exhortation to compare spiritual realities with other spiritual realities.[283] This is a strategy that, to a certain extent, Philo had already employed.

To the same effect, Origen linked divine providential power, which pervades everything, to the divine inspiration that pervades all of the Scripture, down to the smallest details.[284] 'Traces' and 'hints' of God's Wisdom are 'in each letter' of the Bible, since, 'as *the Jewish masters* asserted', the Scripture's words have been calculated with the utmost accuracy.[285] This was maintained by the Rabbis as well.

Origen was not reluctant to base his own exegesis on the authority of Jewish (both Hellenistic and Rabbinic) exegetes: the accuracy of each word and letter of the Scripture is a tenet that both Philo and the Rabbis shared, and Origen continued with it. The comparative hermeneutical method suggested and practiced by Origen on the basis of Jewish exegesis brought together the allegorical meaning of one Scriptural passage with those of other passages, from both the Old and the New Testament,[286] and served him well in his polemic against the Marcionite (and 'Gnostic') severing of the two Testaments. The latter are explicitly criticized by Origen because 'they do not respect the expositive harmonic interconnection of Scripture from beginning to end'.[287] In this respect, according to Origen, both Philo and the Rabbis did better than Christian 'heretics', whose bad exegesis resulted in theological errors.

Origen's Platonic and Apophatic Allegoresis

We can consider Origen's exegesis to be educative of his public (when his homilies and debates took place) and of his readers (when his commentaries and homilies were read). It brought them closer to God and facilitated their assimilation with God, both a Platonic and a Christian ideal. Plato's dialogues were also educative and elevated their readers towards the divine and the assimilation with God.[288]

---

[283] Origenes, *Contra Celsum* IV 71

[284] *Id., Philocalia* 2.

[285] *Id., Philocalia* 6; *Commentarii in Ioannem* 19, 40, 89; *Commentarii in Matthaeum* 16, 2; *Commentariorum series in Matthaeum* 89; *In Numeros homiliae XXVIII* 3, 2; 27, 1.

[286] E.g. *id., Commentarii in Matthaeum* 10, 15; *In Leviticum homiliae XVI* 1, 7.

[287] *Id., Commentarii in Ioannem* 10, 42, 290.

[288] See A.K. Cotton, *Platonic Dialogue and the Education of the Reader* (Oxford, 2014), who reinterprets Plato's 'early', 'middle', and 'late' dialogues as targeting people at different philosophical stages.

Not accidentally, as I have pointed out, Origen explicitly claimed Plato as an authoritative antecedent for his own allegorical exegesis. Further instances come to mind; for example, while explaining exactly the core feature of his biblical hermeneutics, Origen cites Plato: biblical allegorists 'dig wells,[289] endeavoring to find the inner fountainhead and origin of good refreshment'.[290] This is an obvious reference to *Phaedr.* 243D, which Origen uses in connection with the allegoresis of the Scripture. Such a direct citation of Plato within a methodological exegetical passage squares well with the fact that Origen's scriptural allegoresis was Platonic. Origen's apophatic theology was also inspired by Plato's words on the difficult knowledge and expression of God in his *Timaeus.*[291]

On the basis of his apophaticism, which has both Platonic and biblical bases, Origen remarks that even the Scripture does not contain 'some of the more majestic and divine aspects of God's mysteries', being just 'the most elementary and short introduction' to 'the totality of knowledge'.[292] Likewise, Plato did not express everything in his dialogues, but, given his distrust of writing, also had higher, 'unwritten doctrines' on protology. Origen clearly alludes to these unwritten doctrines: 'Plato had something more sacred and divine than the teachings he wrote down and transmitted'.[293] This is one of the many parallels that Origen saw between Plato and the Scripture. We have also seen above how he endeavored to account for them.

Origen, consistently with his apophatic reading of the Scripture, maintains that the αἰώνιον Gospel mentioned in *Rev.* 14:6 will be delivered in another aeon (αἰών), the promised land, where there are 'the real and living paradigms' (Ideas/Logoi) of the Mosaic Law. There, the saints will be 'instructed with the rules of the true Law, that of the other aeon [...] the perfect teachings of heaven. This will truly consist of what is called the "αἰώνιον Gospel" and the "ever new" Testament, which will never grow old'.[294] In the same way the Platonic Forms/Ideas, the metaphysical paradigms of everything (and which Origen viewed as part of the Christ-Logos-Wisdom of the Middle-Platonic noetic cosmos in the mind of God, and called Forms and *logoi*), never grow old, since they are adiastematic: they transcend the dimensions of space and time of this world.[295] This will be the perfect, eternal Scripture, the αἰώνιον Gospel.

---

[289] See above on this metaphor based on Jacob's wells, often used by Origen for allegoresis.

[290] Origenes, *Contra Celsum* IV 44.

[291] See 'The Divine as an Inaccessible Object of Knowledge in Ancient Platonism: A Common Philosophical Pattern across Religious Traditions', *JHI* 75.2 (2014), 167-88.

[292] Origenes, *Commentarii in Ioannem* 13, 5, 27-30.

[293] *Id., Contra Celsum* VI 6, possibly related to Ammonius' secrecy oath.

[294] *Id., De Principiis* III 6, 7.

[295] Here, Origen clearly conflated the Biblical and the Platonic meaning of αἰώνιος: the Gospel is such because it belongs to the other world and is absolutely eternal in that it transcends time. For both meanings, see Ilaria Ramelli and David Konstan, *Terms for Eternity. Αἰώνιος and*

Brief Conclusions

This essay has thus examined Origen's polemics against 'pagan' intellectuals about the allegoresis of the Scripture, and has argued for the role of Origen's allegoresis as a philosophical task, as it was in Stoicism and imperial Platonism. I have endeavored to show how, for Origen, this approach relates to the notion of the Scripture as one of the embodiments of Christ-Logos. Structural continuities have been pointed out between Origen and the Stoic allegorical tradition, as well as the controversy with Middle-Platonic allegorists about the definition of which authoritative traditions were to be allegorized. Origen's Scriptural allegoresis was the legacy of Philo, although 'pagan' Platonists such as Celsus and Porphyry refused to recognize this debt, while Origen, as has been argued, acknowledged his debt to the Jewish Hellenistic allegorists. Indeed, I have suggested that Origen's attitude toward Jewish exegesis was less ambivalent, or even hostile, than generally represented. Origen's exegesis, I finally pointed out, was apophatic and referred to the αἰώνιον Gospel, in the other aeon, which is – like the Platonic Ideas/Forms – an adiastematic, and therefore super-temporal, eternal paradigm.

ἀίδιος *in Classical and Christian Authors* (Piscataway, 2007; second edition 2013), and the reviews by Carl O'Brien, *CR* 60/2 (2010), 390-1, and Danilo Ghira, *Maia* 61 (2009), 732-4.

Mysteria in psalmis:
Origen and Jerome as Interpreters of the Psalter

Lorenzo PERRONE, Bologna, Italy

*Mysteria sunt quae dicuntur
in psalmis et figuris plena sunt omnia.*
Hieronymus, *Tractatus in Psalmos* 89, 14 (s.a.)

ABSTRACT

A comparative analysis of Origen's *Homilies on the Psalms* and Jerome's *Tractatus in Psalmos* proves that Jerome does not substantially plagiarise the Alexandrian. Although partially acquainted with Origen's interpretation, Jerome introduces into his own exegesis a personal agenda and distinct sensitivities. We could even say that, in spite of his mostly cursory and, at first sight, simple-looking comments, the learned biblical scholar is, to some extent, more present in the preaching of Jerome, thanks especially to his frequent recourse to the Hebrew text, his propensity for etymologies and his display of historical erudition nurtured by the Bible. Moreover, the fact that Jerome does not rely on Origen alone, but now and then has recourse to other commentators of the Psalter, is additional proof of independence. Among these interpreters, one should point in particular to Eusebius of Caesarea and Didymus. Moreover, we are allowed to surmise the influence of other mediators of the eastern patristic exegesis to the Latin world, such as Hilary of Poitiers, Eusebius of Vercelli and Ambrose.

1. Introduction: the shadow of Origen on Jerome's exegesis of the Psalms

Jerome, acclaimed as the translator of the Bible, has not enjoyed a corresponding reputation as its interpreter, especially with regard to his exegesis of the Psalter. Over the last three decades, the *Tractatus in Psalmos*, the homilies he gave in Bethlehem at the beginning of the 5th century, has not attracted much attention since the controversial hypothesis of Vittorio Peri on their Origenian authorship was dismissed by critics.[1] The renowned *scriptor* of the Vatican Library found some authoritative supporters during the eighties, among whom the most outstanding was Marie-Josèphe Rondeau. In fact, her two volumes on

---

[1] Vittorio Peri, *Omelie origeniane sui Salmi. Contributo all'identificazione del testo latino*, Studi e Testi 289 (Città del Vaticano, 1980). For a brief presentation of the current state of research, see Alessandro Capone, '*Folia vero in verbis sunt*: parola divina e lingua umana nei *Tractatus in psalmos* attribuiti a Gerolamo', *Adamantius* 19 (2013), 437-40.

the patristic commentators of the Psalms from the third to the fifth centuries are still unsurpassed as a comprehensive overview.[2] The French scholar devoted a separate treatment to the *Tractatus*, regarding them, likewise, as an adaptation by Jerome of homilies originally preached by Origen.[3] In his review of Peri's book, Jean Gribomont, the famous Benedictine scholar who enjoyed humour, summarised its results as follows: 'À part quelques épices, toute la pâte est origénienne' ('Apart from a few spices, all the dough is Origen's').[4] Though reacting favourably to Peri, Gribomont wondered why Jerome had contented himself with a mere reworking of Origen, instead of embarking on a more creative exegesis of the Psalms: did he perhaps feel unable to face the complexities of the Psalter, or did he more simply prefer to deal with the Prophets?[5] It was, therefore, a specialist on Jerome's exegesis of Isaiah, Pierre Jay, who chiefly contributed to the abandonment of the attribution of the *Tractatus* to Origen. In the wake of his critique, as I hinted, a certain lack of interest seems to have surrounded it until recently, even if Jay himself recognised the influence of Origen on Jerome and invited us to uncover the Origenian materials in the *Tractatus* through new studies.[6]

Our evidence of Origen's interpretation of the Psalter was substantially modified and enriched in 2012 thanks to the discovery by Marina Molin Pradel of twenty-nine Greek homilies in a Munich codex.[7] It goes without saying that this discovery has also reopened the problem of the *Tractatus*, inasmuch as many of the new texts deal with the same psalms on which Jerome preached (*Ps.* 15; 67; 74; 75; 76; 77; 80; 81). At present, we only have preliminary studies, but these have already shown that Jerome was certainly acquainted

---

[2] Marie-Josèphe Rondeau, *Les commentaires patristiques du Psautier (IIIe-Ve siècles)*. I: *Les travaux des Pères grecs et latins sur le Psautier. Recherches et bilan*, Orientalia Christiana Analecta 219 (Roma, 1982); *Les commentaires patristiques du Psautier (IIIe-Ve siècles)*. II: *Exégèse prosopologique et théologie*, Orientalia Christiana Analecta 220 (Roma, 1985).

[3] M.-J. Rondeau, *Les commentaires patristiques* (1982), 54-5, 158-61; (1985), 137-67.

[4] Jean Gribomont, 'Review of V. Peri, *Omelie origeniane* (1980)', *Cristianesimo nella Storia* 2 (1981), 526.

[5] *Ibid.* 526: 'Reste une observation sur les programmes exégétiques de l'érudit. Lui, qui avait traduit, à plusieurs reprises, le Psautier, et qui possédait dans sa bibliothèque des commentaires sur ce livre important, s'abstient de mettre en chantier une étude originale; même au temps où il ne voudrait plus passer pour un traducteur d'Origène, il se contente d'adapter superficiellement l'œuvre de celui-ci. Se sentait-il incapable d'affronter la complexité des Psaumes? Accordait-il, plus simplement, une priorité aux Prophètes?'

[6] Pierre Jay, 'Jérôme à Bethléem. Les *Tractatus in Psalmos*', in Yves-Marie Duval (ed.), *Jérôme entre l'Occident et l'Orient* (Paris, 1988), 380: 'Toutefois restituer au prédicateur de Bethléem [...] la pleine responsabilité de ces *Tractatus*, ce n'est pas les retirer totalement à Origène. Leur dépendance origénienne apparaît en effet assez étroite pour qu'on puisse espérer dégager grâce à eux quelques matériaux sur l'exégèse des psaumes de l'Alexandrin'.

[7] On this new collection, see my introduction in Origenes, *Die neuen Psalmenhomilien. Eine kritische Edition des Codex Monacensis Graecus 314*, ed. Lorenzo Perrone, Marina Molin Pradel, Emanuela Prinzivalli and Antonio Cacciari, GCS NF 19, Origenes Werke 13 (Berlin, 2015), 1-34.

with the new homilies, although he apparently went along with his own interpretation.[8] However, a synoptic analysis of both series is not an easy, or pressing,
task for several reasons. On the one hand, Jerome does not always follow
Origen's text for his own interpretation of the same psalm, but is led to use
materials taken from the homilies while commenting on another psalm. On the
other, the appropriate method for examining the specific profile of Jerome's
exegesis of the Psalter would demand that we take into account, as far as possible, the developments of patristic interpretation from the middle of the third
century to the beginning of the fifth. In spite of the influential role played by
the Alexandrian on Jerome, we should not forget that he was familiar with other
commentators on the Psalms, such as Eusebius of Caesarea, Hilary of Poitiers
and Didymus the Blind, to mention just the most important, and whose writings
ad hoc the monk of Bethlehem recorded first in the *De uiris inlustribus* (393),[9]
and subsequently in *Letter 112* to Augustine (404).[10] Jerome was a well-read
scholar, and we should not isolate the Origenian inprint on his exegesis to the
exclusion of other influences. Last, but not least, Jerome was also acquainted with
Jewish interpretive traditions that were unknown to Origen.[11] Such a demanding
approach, as partially illustrated by some of the most recent investigations, is

---

[8] See, especially, Elena Orlandi, 'Aspetti della rielaborazione delle omelie origeniane sui
Salmi (*Cod. Mon. Graec.* 314) nei *Tractatus in Psalmos* di Gerolamo', in Élie Ayroulet and Aline
Canellis (eds), *L'exégèse de saint Jérôme* (Saint-Étienne, 2018), 101-13; 'Esegesi e omiletica nei
Tractatus in Psalmos. Il salmo 15 dal *Codex Monacensis Graecus* 314 alla rielaborazione di
Gerolamo', in Daniele Tripaldi (ed.), *La lira di Davide. Esegesi e riscritture dei Salmi dall'
Antichità al Medioevo* (Roma, 2018), 283-305.

[9] Hieronymus, *De uiris inlustribus*, ed. Aldo Ceresa-Gastaldo, Biblioteca Patristica (Firenze,
1988), capp. 81 (Eusebius of Caesarea): *edidit infinita uolumina, de quibus haec sunt:* [...] *et 'In
centum quinquaginta Psalmos' eruditissimi commentarii*; 90 (Theodore of Heraclea): *elegantis
apertique sermonis et magis historicae intelligentiae edidit sub Constantio principe 'Commentarios
in Matthaeum' et 'Iohannem' et 'In Apostolum' et 'In Psalterium'*; 94 (Asterius): *scripsit, regnante
Constantio,* [...] *et 'In psalmos commentarios' et multa alia quae a suae partis hominibus studio-
sissime leguntur*; 96 (Eusebius of Vercelli): *sub Iuliano imperatore ad ecclesiam reuersus edidit
'In psalmos commentarios' Eusebii Caesariensis, quos de Graeco in Latinum uerterat*; 100 (Hilary
of Poitiers): *confecit* [...] *et 'In psalmos commentarios', primum uidelicet et secundum et a quin-
quagesimo primo usque ad sexagesimum secundum et a centesimo octauo decimo usque ad
extremum, in quo opere imitatus Origenem nonnulla etiam de suo addidit*; 109 (Didymus the Blind):
Hic plurima nobiliaque conscripsit: 'Commentarios in Psalmos' omnes'.

[10] *Id., Epistula* 112, 20, ed. Isidorus Hilberg, CSEL 55 (Vindobonae, 1918): *maxime in expla-
natione Psalmorum quos apud Graecos interpretati sunt multis uoluminibus, primus Origenes,
secundus Eusebius Caesariensis, tertius Theodorus Heracleotes, quartus Asterius Scythopolitanus,
quintus Apollinaris Laodicenus, sextus Didymus Alexandrinus. Feruntur et diuersorum in paucos
psalmos opuscula; sed nunc de integro Psalmorum corpore dicimus. Apud Latinos autem Hilarius
Pictauiensis et Eusebius Vercelensis episcopus, Origenem et Eusebium transtulerunt: quorum
priorem et noster Ambrosius in quibusdam secutus est.*

[11] Sandro Leanza, 'Gerolamo e la tradizione ebraica', in Claudio Moreschini and Giovanni
Menestrina (eds), *Motivi letterari ed esegetici in Gerolamo* (Brescia, 1997), 18-38.

not always able to trace a clear genealogical picture;[12] in any case, it points to a more complex stratigraphy of the *Tractatus*, one going beyond the simple relationship between Jerome and Origen.

2. A preliminary picture: affinities and discrepancies between the two commentators of the Psalms

Having said that, a preliminary overview of the main affinities and distinctions between Origen and Jerome as commentators of the Psalms will prove useful, before we engage more closely in a synoptic treatment of some of their respective homilies. Both authors fully realised the special tasks a commentator of the Psalms has to face, as paradigmatically illustrated, first of all, by Origen, for the subsequent exegetes with regard to 'the titles' and 'the person speaking' in the Psalms.[13] However, their literary activity on the biblical book is comparable only to a certain extent: one should never forget the diversity of the output, greater by far in the case of Origen, notwithstanding the heavy losses his writings went through in the course of history.[14] However, the fragmented heritage of the Alexandrian includes several significant portions of his copious *tomoi* and the commentary volumes on the Psalms, mainly thanks to the selections made for the *Philocalia*,[15] in addition to a larger amount of extracts and *scholia* of more or less reliable authenticity[16] preserved in the *catenae*, and a

---

[12] A good example of this approach in recent studies on Hieronymus, *Tractatus in Psalmus*, is Daniela Scardia, '*Melius dicitur graece*: termini greci ed esegesi nei *Tractatus in Psalmos* di Gerolamo', in Paolo B. Cipolla, Carmelo Crimi, Renata Gentile, Lisania Giordano and Arianna Rotondo (eds), *Spazi e tempi delle emozioni. Dai primi secoli all'età bizantina* (Acireale, Roma, 2018), 231-69. See also Franz-Xaver Risch, 'Zur lateinischen Rezeption der *Scholia in Psalmos* von Origenes', in Anders Christian Jacobsen (ed.), *Origeniana Undecima. Origen and Origenism in the History of Western Thought*, Bibliotheca Ephemeridum Theologicarum Lovaniensium 279 (Leuven, 2016), 295-7.

[13] Lorenzo Perrone, 'Origen Reading the Psalms: The Challenge of a Christian Interpretation', in Moshe Blidstein, Serge Ruzer and Daniel Stökl Ben Ezra (eds), *Scriptures, Sacred Traditions, and Strategies of Religious Subversion. Studies in Discourse with the Work of Guy G. Stroumsa*, Studien und Texte zu Antike und Christentum 112 (Tübingen, 2018), 138-47.

[14] See Ronald E. Heine, 'Restringing Origen's Broken Harp. Some Suggestions Concerning the Prologue to the Caesarean *Commentary on the Psalms*', in Brian E. Daley S.J. and Paul R. Kolbet (eds), *The Harp of the Prophecy. Early Christian Interpretation of the Psalms* (Notre Dame, IN, 2015), 47-74.

[15] Lorenzo Perrone, 'I commenti di Origene ai Salmi nella *Filocalia*: il primato dell'ermeneutica spirituale e della grazia divina' (forthcoming).

[16] The list of the sources is as follows: Origène, *Philocalie 1-20: Sur les Écritures*, ed. Marguerite Harl, SCh 302 (Paris, 1983); Origène, *Philocalie 21-27: Sur le libre arbitre*, ed. Éric Junod, SCh 226 (Paris 1976) = Origenes, *Philocalia* (1, 29; 2-3; 26); *La chaîne palestinienne sur le Psaume 118 (Origène, Eusèbe, Didyme, Apollinaire, Athanase, Théodoret)*, ed. Marguerite Harl and Gilles Dorival, SCh 189-190 (Paris 1972) = *Catenae in Psalmum 118*; Origenis, *Scholia in*

considerable *corpus* of homilies in Greek and Latin (29 and 9, respectively).[17] These impressive remains attest to the longstanding activity of Origen as an interpreter of the Psalter, the primary occupation among his many works, starting in Alexandria and continuing in Caesarea until his final years.[18] Due to the exceptional amount of them, Origen's writings on the Psalms from the very beginning met with the difficulty of being preserved and transmitted.[19]

When compared with the huge *corpus* of the Alexandrian, the works of Jerome on the Psalter appear more limited: beyond the two series of *Tractatus* (59 and 15 homilies, respectively), we have only the *Commentarioli in Psalmos*, composed some time before them and expressly presented by the author as a reworking of Origen's *Enchiridion* on the Psalter.[20] Here, we find *in nuce* many remarks and formulations that are generally more expanded upon, if not revised, in the Bethlehem homilies.

These short notes mainly combine a philological approach to the Psalms (by also pointing to the Hebrew) with a christological interpretation of their content.[21]

Psalmos, PG 12, 1053-685; Origenes, *Excerpta in Psalmos*, PG 17, 105-40; *Origenes in Psalmos*, in Jean Baptiste Pitra, *Analecta Sacra* II (Tusculum, 1884), 395-483; III (Venice, 1883), 1-522 = *Fragmenta in Psalmos*.

[17] See, respectively, Origenes Werke 13 and Origene, *Omelie sui Salmi, Homiliae in Psalmos XXXVI – XXXVII – XXXVIII*, ed. Emanuela Prinzivalli, Biblioteca Patristica (Firenze, 1991). Only of *Homiliae in Psalmum 36* I-IV do we have both the Greek and Latin texts.

[18] On the many-sided literary production on the Psalms, see Pierre Nautin, *Origène. Sa vie et son œuvre* (Paris, 1977), 261-92; M.-J. Rondeau, *Les commentaires patristiques* (1982), 44-51.

[19] V. Peri, *Omelie origeniane* (1980), 12-3 stresses this problem for the homilies, but the commentaries were not unaffected by it: 'Probabilmente già al tempo di Panfilo ed anche prima chi avesse voluto prendere conoscenza dell'intera opera omiletica di Origene sul salterio non sarebbe stato in grado di procurarsela, per la vastità e la dispersione della materia in un numero ridotto di copie manoscritte'.

[20] According to the preface, Jerome wished to complete the concise 'map-like' digest of the *Enchiridion* with the help of other writings by Origen. See Hieronymus, *Commentarioli in Psalmos*, ed. Germain Morin, CCL 72 (Turnhout, 1959), 177-8: *et (quod solent ii facere, qui in breui tabella terrarum et urbium situs pingunt, et latissimas regiones in modico spatio conantur ostendere) ita in psalterii opere latissimo quasi praeteriens aliqua perstringerem, ut ex paucis quae tetigissem, intellegantur et cetera, quae omissa sunt, quam uim habeant et rationem. Non quo putem a me posse dici quae ille praeteriit: sed quod ea quae in tomis uel in omiliis ipse disseruit, uel ego digna arbitror lectione, in hunc angustum commentariolum referam.* On Origen's *Enchiridion*, see Franz-Xaver Risch, 'Das Handbuch des Origenes zu den Psalmen. Zur Bedeutung der zweiten Randkatene im *Codex Vindobonensis theologicus graecus* 8', *Adamantius* 20 (2014), 36-48.

[21] Colette Estin, *Les Psautiers de Jérôme à la lumière des traductions juives antérieures*, Collectanea Biblica Latina 15 (Roma, 1984), 31: 'L'ouvrage se présente sous forme de notations brèves, voire parfois quasi télégraphiques, dont le contenu est essentiellement philologique. Jérôme y rapporte de nombreuses leçons hexaplaires et quelquefois, mais relativement peu souvent, il discute le texte en recourant à l'hébreu. Il a, par ailleurs, à cœur de donner pour la majorité des psaumes une "clef": la plupart du temps, il s'agit d'une interprétation christologique, formulée de façon globale pour tout le psaume ou détaillée sur plusieurs versets'. See also Hieronymus, *Commentarioli in Psalmos*, ed. Siegfried Risse, Fontes Christiani 79 (Turnhout, 2005), 40-65.

Contrary to the *Commentarioli*, which refer laudably to Origen,[22] the *Tractatus*
do not mention the Alexandrian anymore, so that, according to Germain Morin,
their discoverer at the end of the nineteenth century, we should situate the
homilies in the aftermath of the Origenist controversy (*i.e.* between 401 and
410). There are, nevertheless, some clues to support the idea that Jerome's
homilies reflect a much longer period, ranging from 389 to 410.[23] In any case,
the *Commentarioli* and *Tractatus* do not represent the only evidence of Jerome's
work on the Psalter. They are framed by his early revision of the Latin Psalter,
then by the *Psalterium Gallicanum*, a further revision of the Old Latin translation of the Septuagint Psalter on the basis of the *Hexapla* (*ca.* 389-392 or even
earlier) and, finally, by the *Psalterium iuxta Hebraicum*, a subsequent translation from the Hebrew (*ca.* 393 or a few years later).[24] In addition, the monk of
Bethlehem deals with the Psalms in several of his letters which provide further
relevant comments.[25]

If Jerome cannot compete with Origen as regards the volume of exegetical
production on the Psalms, both converge in the recognition of the correct hermeneutics required by them. In this sense, they approach the biblical text in a
similar way, taking into account the complex nature of the Psalter (as did most
of the Christian interpreters in Late Antiquity); that is, not only as a 'spiritual'
or 'moral' book, but also as a 'prophetic' and 'mystical' one, which gives voice
to God, Christ, the Church as his mystical body, and the faithful as members
of this. For both exegetes, an interpretation of this kind is made possible by
the adoption of allegory and recourse to analogous 'technicalities' in its wake,
the most momentous of which is the introductory explanation of the 'titles' (or

---

[22] Jerome mostly relies on the Alexandrian, according to S. Risse, *Commentarioli* (2005),
29-30.

[23] See Alessandro Capone, 'Scomposizione e composizione dei *Tractatus in psalmos* di
Gerolamo', in É. Ayroulet and A. Canellis (eds), *L'exégèse de saint Jérôme* (2018), 148: 'La data-
zione proposta da Morin (401-410) non regge di fronte all'esame dei rinvii interni ai *Tractatus*
e dei riscontri con il resto della produzione geronimiana. I *Tr. in Ps.* sono stati composti in un
arco temporale molto più ampio, che è ragionevole far iniziare dal 389 circa e concludere dopo
il 410'.

[24] See *Biblia Sacra iuxta Vulgatam Versionem*, ed. Bonifaz Fischer and Jean Gribomont,
Editio Tertia Emendata (Stuttgart, 1983), 770-955; Eva Schulz-Flügel, 'Hieronymus, Feind und
Überwinder der Septuaginta? Untersuchungen anhand der Arbeiten an den Psalmen', in Anneli
Aejmelaeus and Udo Quast (eds), *Der Septuaginta-Psalter und seine Tochterübersetzungen. Symposium
in Göttingen 1997* (Göttingen, 2000), 33-50; Alfons Fürst, *Hieronymus. Askese und Wissenschaft
in der Spätantike* (Freiburg, Basel, Wien, 2003, 2016²), 107-25; S. Risse, *Commentarioli* (2005),
7-18.

[25] Among them, the most notable are *Epistula* 28 (*De diapsalmate*); *Epistula* 65 (*In Ps.* 44);
Epistula 106 (*Ad Sunniam et Fretelam*); *Epistula* 140 (*In Ps.* 89). See C. Estin, *Les Psautiers de
Jérôme* (1984), 28-34; Aline Canellis, 'Saint Jérôme et l'exégèse du Psaume 89 (d'après l'*Epistula*
140 à Cyprien, les *Tractatus* et les *Commentarioli*)', in É. Ayroulet and A. Canellis (eds), *L'exégèse
de saint Jérôme* (2018), 115-29.

rubrics) as a key to understanding the Psalms,[26] and, even more so, the identification of 'the person who speaks' (τὸ πρόσωπον τὸ λέγον) in them.[27]

This does not imply that Origen and Jerome always delivered the same explanation. The monk of Bethlehem can occasionally exhibit a solution different to those of the Alexandrian (and of other interpreters as well), as we see, for example, in his exegesis of the title of *Ps.* 7. Here, he distinguishes the person of 'Chousi son of Iemeni' (*Ps.* 7:1 = *Chush ben-Yemini*) from 'Chousi the Arachi, friend of David' (*2Kgs.* 15:32.37; 16:16-8; 17:5-8.14-5), thus rejecting the historical connection of the psalm with the rebellion of Abessalom against his father.[28] On the contrary, the title has to do with Saul's persecution of David, as he explained in the *Commentarioli*, perhaps depending upon a Jewish interpretive tradition.[29] This case illustrates the propensity of Jerome for historical erudition concerning the Bible, which might also be regarded as one of his distinctive traits. Moreover, since the prosopological approach of Jerome mirrors the christological debates of the fourth century as a reaction to Arianism and Apollinarianism, we notice in him a different awareness of the human component in the mystery of the Incarnate.[30]

Further distinctive aspects may surface within a substantial continuity: Jerome, initially a faithful disciple of Origen as a commentator of the Bible (and whom he will still appreciate even after becoming an anti-Origenist, in

---

[26] For example, in Hieronymus, *Tractatus siue Homiliae in Psalmos*, ed. Germain Morin, CCL 78 (Turnhout, 1958) see *Tractatus in Psalmos* 1, 1: *Quidam putant istius psalmi clauem super Xpisti domini nostri persona esse referendam* (3, 10-2). Like Origen, Jerome links the image of the 'key' to *Luke* 11:52, as in *Tractatus in Psalmos* 82, 12: *Legunt hoc philosophi et inrident; legunt rhetores et nunc putant esse deleramenta. Non solum autem rhetores, sed et Iudaei: non habent 'clauem scientiae'* (*Luke* 11:52), *quoniam uelamen positum est ante oculos eorum* (*2Cor* 3:13-6) (94, 125-8). For a vindication of the methodical principle, see *Tractatus in Psalmos* 93, 1: *Semper de titulo disputamus, ut ex titulo intellegatur et psalmus* (142, 1-2). Thus, Jerome revises the opposite opinion he expressed in *Commentarioli in Psalmos* 93: *Et iste apud Hebraeos non habet inscriptionem: unde superfluum est de titulo disputare* (225, 1-2).

[27] M.-J. Rondeau, *Les commentaires patristiques* (1985).

[28] Hieronymus, *Tractatus in Psalmos* 7, 1: *Deinde ille Chusi per aliam litteram scribitur in Regnorum: ibi Chusi per 'samech' scribitur, hic autem Chusi per 'sin' litteram scribitur. Deinde ille Chusi filius Arachi; unde multi Graecorum nescientes legunt: 'Chusi amicus Dauid'. Non ita habet in hebraeo, sed ita habet scriptum: 'Chusi filius Arachi, amicus Dauid'. Videte ergo quoniam et in lectione errant Graeci* (21, 56-62). According to Alessandro Capone (ed.), Girolamo, *59 Omelie sui Salmi (1-115). Omelia sul Salmo 41 ai neofiti* (Roma, 2018), 89 n. 17, Jerome rejects the interpretation of Eusebius, Didymus and others, going back perhaps to Origen himself.

[29] Hieronymus, *Commentarioli in Psalmos* 7, 1: *Plerique, et maxime ii qui hebraici sermonis scientiam non habent, hunc psalmum arbitrantur eo tempore esse cantatum, quo Chusi filius Arachi amicus Dauid destruxit consilium Achitofel, et ad eum nuntios misit, ne in eremo ultra resideret, sed procul fugeret, ne obprimeretur a filio. Vero sciendum est vehementer errare* [...]. *Sciendum itaque Chusi interpretari Aethiopem et totum psalmum contra Saul esse conscriptum* (188, 2-189, 18). See S. Risse, *Commentarioli* (2005), 31-2.

[30] Lorenzo Perrone, '"Four Gospels, Four Councils" – One Lord Jesus Christ. The Patristic Developments of Christology within the Church of Palestine', *Liber Annuus* 49 (1999), 377-83.

contrast to the condemned 'dogmatician'), has constant recourse to the exegetical terminology of the Alexandrian. However, in the *Tractatus* (and to a lesser
extent in the *Commentarioli*) he does so, as it were, in a more schematic and
repetitive way than his model.[31] Jerome invariably signals the plurality of the
scriptural senses with formulaic expressions, such as *secundum historiam* or
secundum litteram, to indicate the literal meaning as distinguished from the
allegorical one.[32] As for the latter, he introduces it mostly with the words *secundum spiritalem intellegentiam* (or simply *secundum intellegentiam*), but frequently by the standard formula *secundum trophologiam*.[33] Interestingly, while
the formulae κατὰ τὴν ἱστορίαν (or κατὰ τὸ ῥητόν) and κατὰ τὴν τροπολογίαν occur in a few passages of the homilies of Origen, τροπολογία is given
moderate prominence compared to the other terms the preacher uses for the
spiritual interpretation, such as ἀναγωγή or ἀλληγορία.[34] Clearly, Jerome shares
the same preference for τροπολογία, but he generalises its use to the detriment
of *anagoge* and *allegoria*.[35]

---

[31] On the terminological features in *Homiliae in Psalmos*, see Manlio Simonetti, 'Leggendo
le *Omelie sui Salmi* di Origene', *Adamantius* 22 (2016), 473-4.

[32] For a few examples, see Hieronymus, *Tractatus in Psalmos* 7, 3: *nobis curae est, non solum
secundum historiam, sed secundum spiritalem intellegentiam interpretari* (23, 124-6); *ibid.* 76,
17: *Interim dicamus secundum litteram; haereamus terrae propter simpliciores* (59, 136-7); *ibid.*
76, 18: *Videtis quomodo adhuc in terra haeream et loquar secundum litteram occidentem* (59,
146-7); *ibid.* 76, 20: *Hoc secundum litteram quomodo intellegis? Propter simpliciores secundum
litteram diximus; reuertamur ergo ad intellegentiam spiritalem* (60, 151-3); *ibid.* 76, 21: *Hoc
secundum litteram intellegamus de Moyse et Aaron* (62, 234-5); *ibid.* 133, 3: *Hoc interim secundum
litteram. Ceterum secundum intellegentiam spiritali quomodo dicitur peccatori 'Terra es et in
terram ibis'* (*Gen.* 3:19), *sic et sancto dicitur: caelum es et in caelum ibis* (291, 246-9). Analogous
to this is the picture offered by *id.*, *Commentarioli in Psalmos* 103, 6-7: *Haec omnia possunt stare
et iuxta historiam: quo scilicet in similitudinem montium fluctus maris adtollantur, et rursus instar
uallis unda desidat. Sed et iuxta allegoriam sequitur intellectus* (228, 6-9); *ibid.* 103, 10: *Locus iste
secundum historiam manifestus est* [...] *Potest autem et iuxta anagogen de saeculis huius nocte
cantari* (228, 10-4).

[33] *Id.*, *Tractatus in Psalmos* 89, 10 includes much of the terminology under examination: *Hoc
interim diximus secundum historiam; ceterum dicamus secundum anagogen. Et omnis quidem
psalmus recipit tropologiam; et poteram nunc per singulos uersiculus currere, et spiritalem intellegentiam in singulis dicere, sed hora excludimur* (123, 116-20). See also *ibid.* 149, 6: *Gladium
ancipitem: et secundum historiam et secundum allegoriam, et secundum litteram et secundum
spiritum* (351, 88-90).

[34] In addition, M. Simonetti, 'Leggendo le *Omelie*' (2016), 473 also records the use of σύμβο-
λον. We find the expression κατὰ τὴν τροπολογίαν in only four passages: Origenes, *Homiliae in
Psalmum 36* III, 6 (147, 6-7); *Homiliae in Psalmum 73* III, 3 (255, 17); *Homiliae in Psalmum 77*
IV, 8 (399, 14); *ibid.* IX, 5 (474, 4). As for the formula κατὰ τὴν ἱστορίαν, see *Homiliae in
Psalmum 36* III, 10 (152, 9); *Homiliae in Psalmum 73* II, 8 (250, 15); *Homiliae in Psalmum 77*
IV, 5 (395, 5); *Homiliae in Psalmum 80* I, 8 (494, 14-5). For the equivalent expression κατὰ τὸ
ῥητόν, see *Homiliae in Psalmum 73* I, 1 (225, 19); *ibid.* I, 8 (234, 13-4); *Homiliae in Psalmum 76*
III, 2 (330, 8); *Homiliae in Psalmum 77* II, 1 (368, 16); *ibid.* IV, 8 (399, 12).

[35] The term appears in Greek in Hieronymus, *Tractatus in Psalmos* 66, 8: *Secundum* τροπολογίαν *autem omnes fines terrae* [...] *non illi qui in terra sunt media, sed qui in fine terrae sunt,*

Another feature seems to be characteristic of Jerome: the references to the Hebrew text (as well as to the hexaplaric readings of the Greek Psalter) are more frequent and specific than is the case with Origen, even though his *Homilies on the Psalms* offer richer evidence for such an approach.[36] Jerome apparently profits both from his revision of the LXX Psalter and from the ongoing work for its translation from the Hebrew. Beyond the similarity with the Alexandrian, as far as the philological method is concerned, he also unveils his preference for the *Hebraica ueritas*, even if he does not vindicate it polemically as in his other writings.[37] Thus, in the *Tractatus* on *Ps.* 86 Jerome explains v. 5a first according to the *textus receptus* of the Septuagint (Μήτηρ Σιὼν ἐρεῖ ἄνθρωπος, 'Mother Sion will say: man'), and then according to the *Hebraica ueritas*. In fact, the Hebrew text, for him, corresponds to the original reading of the Septuagint (Μήτι [= μὴ τῇ] Σιὼν ἐρεῖ ἄνθρωπος), which he also followed in the *Psalterium Gallicanum* (*Numquid Sion dicet homo*). Notwithstanding this, Jerome feels obliged to comment initially upon the common text, though interpolated, without actually dismissing it.[38] Moreover, on *Ps.* 115:11 (Ἐγὼ εἶπα ἐν τῇ ἐκστάσει μου· Πᾶς ἄνθρωπος ψεύστης, 'I said in my alarm, "Every person is a liar"') the monk of Bethlehem is led to pay homage to the

qui relinquunt terram, et ad caelum ire festinant (39, 169-72). But the Latin form is mainly *trophologia*. Cf., for instance, *ibid*. 75, 3: *secundum trophologiam non est umbraculum Domini, nisi ubi pax est.* [...] *Secundum litteram possumus dicere de Hierusalem et Sion, quoniam ibi fuit templum: secundum trophologiam uero et anagogen dicimus quia in Sion habitatio Dei sit* (50, 19-28). See also *id.*, *Commentarioli in Psalmos* 9: *Totus igitur psalmus per tropologiam ad Xpisti pertinet sacramentum* (191, 4-5). Jean-Louis Gourdain, 'L'exégèse de Jérôme prédicateur', in É. Ayroulet and A. Canellis (eds), *L'exégèse de saint Jérôme* (2018), 196 has noted the preminence of τροπολογία in *Tractatus in Psalmos*: 'Si dans les *Tractatus in Psalmos*, on trouve encore de nombreux *tropologia*, mais pratiquement toujours dans l'expression figée, *secundum tropologiam* (13 fois sur 14), ou quelques autres termes, comme *anagoge* (3 fois) ou *allegoria* (3 fois), pour désigner le sens spirituel, ce sont quand même les expressions *intellegentia spiritalis / spiritaliter intellegere*, fondées sur l'opposition paulinienne entre "la lettre qui tue" et "l'esprit qui donne la vie" (2*Cor.* 3:6), qui l'emportent avec 26 emplois'.

[36] Antonio Cacciari, 'Nuova luce sull'officina origeniana. I LXX e "gli altri"', *Adamantius* 20 (2014), 217-25; Lorenzo Perrone, 'The Find of the Munich Codex. A Collection of 29 Homilies of Origen on the Psalms', in A.C. Jacobsen (ed.), *Origeniana Undecima* (Leuven, 2016), 209-20.

[37] For claims of the *Hebraica ueritas*, see Hieronymus, *Tractatus in Psalmos* 76, 21: *Non enim dicitur secundum hebraicam ueritatem Ause, sed Osee, hoc est saluator* (63, 264-6).

[38] *Ibid.* 86, 5a: *Dicamus ergo primum secundum quod uulgo dicitur (neque enim debemus et illam interpretationem dimittere)* [...] *Dicamus et secundum Hebraicam ueritatem* (115, 165-73). V. Peri, *Omelie origeniane* (1980), 89 exploits this passage for his thesis, but we have no evidence of the comments of Origen on *Ps.* 86:5a (the excerpt in PG 12, 1546D-1547A and Pitra, 150 is a *scholion* of Evagrius). See also Hieronymus, *Commentarioli in Psalmos* 86, 5a: *'Mater Sion, dicet homo'. Pro 'mater Sion', Septuaginta interpretes transtulerunt: 'Numquid Sion dicet homo?' Quod homo Xpistus natus sit in ea: sed uitiose RO littera graeca addita fecit errorem* (222, 16-9). Jerome does not quote the hexaplaric readings: Ἀ. Καὶ τῇ Σιὼν λεχθήσεται; Σ. Περὶ τῇ Σιὼν λεχθήσεται; Θ. Καὶ τῇ Σιὼν ῥηθήσεται (see *Origenis Hexaplorum quae supersunt*, ed. Frederick Field, II [Oxonii, 1875], 238-9, which I shall abbreviate as Field).

text of the Church, after following the reading of the Hebrew: 'Every person is a lie' (*'Omnis homo mendacium', quod dicitur 'zecam'*).[39]

Mendacium hic dixit, quasi umbram, quasi imaginem; quemadmodum dicitur et in alio loco: 'Verumtamen in imagine pertransit homo' (Ps. 38:7). Eadem intelligentia et nunc dicitur: 'Omnis homo mendacium', hoc est omnis homo umbra. Hoc autem dicimus secundum hebraicam ueritatem. Loquamur autem et secundum septuaginta interpretes. Dicat enim aliquis: Quid ad me, quid habet in hebraico? Ego ecclesiam sequor: 'Ego dixi in excessu meo: Omnis homo mendax' (Ps. 115:11).	'Here it says "lie" with the meaning of "shadow", of "phantom", as is said elsewhere: "In fact, a person passes through as a phantom" (*Ps.* 38:7). Also, now it says with the same meaning: "Every person is a lie", that is, "every man is a shadow". Yet we say this according to the Hebrew truth. But we should speak also according to the seventy translators. Somebody indeed could object: Does it matter me what we have in Hebrew? I follow the Church: "I said in my alarm, Every person is a liar" (*Ps.* 115:11)'.

Although abstaining from a tone that is too polemical, now and then Jerome does not hesitate to appreciate the Hebrew text as being better than the Greek one, that is, the text of the Septuagint, since he supports the claim of the superiority of the Hebrew by referring to the other Greek translators.[40] Moreover, when commenting on the title of *Ps.* 9 (Εἰς τὸ τέλος, ὑπὲρ τῶν κρυφίων, 'Regarding completion. Over the secrets of the son') he points again (as in the *Commentarioli* or in the *Prefaces* to the *Vulgata*)[41] to the apologetic tradition,

---

[39] Hieronymus, *Tractatus in Psalmos* 115, 11: '*Ego autem dixi in excessu meo: Omnis homo mendax'. In hebraico aliter habet: 'Ego dixi in excessu meo: Omnis homo mendacium', quod dicitur 'zecam'* (240, 16-8). *Id.*, *Commentarioli in Psalmos* 115, 2 (11) presents a different form of the Hebrew: '*Ego dixi in excessu mentis meae: omnis homo mendax'. Ubi nos legimus 'mendax', ibi in hebraeo positum est KIVZHB: quod interpretatur Symmachus 'mendacium', quinta uero editio 'deficit'* (234, 3-6). For the English translation of the Septuaginta, I shall follow Albert Pietersma and Benjamin G. Wright (eds), *A New English Translation of the Septuagint and the Other Greek Translations Traditionally Included under That Title* (Oxford, 2007).

[40] See, for instance, Hieronymus, *Tractatus in Psalmos* 5, 10: *Melius habet in hebraeo: 'Cor eorum* ἐπίβουλον' (16, 159-60). Here, Jerome follows Aquila: ἔντερον αὐτῶν ἐπίβουλον (Field, 92), which renders the Hebrew *kirbam hawot* (the LXX has ἡ καρδία αὐτῶν ματαία). For a brief mention of a mistake in the Septuagint, see *id.*, *Tractatus in Psalmos* 74, 1: *In hebraeo non habet 'in finem' sed habet 'uictori'. Et Septuaginta interpretes non ualde errauerunt: siquidem uictoria perfecta est* (48, 1-2).

[41] *Id.*, *Commentarioli in Psalmos* 9: *Vnde et Septuaginta interpretes Xpisti passionem et resurrectionem, quae ignota prius mundo fuit, per uerbum absconsionis celare uoluerunt, ne a gentibus illo tempore facile nosceretur* (191, 6-9). See also the *Prologus in Pentateuchum* (400) on the reservations regarding the doctrine of the Trinity: *Denique ubicumque sacratum aliquid Scriptura testatur de Patre et Filio et Spiritu Sancto, aut aliter interpretati sunt aut omnino tacuerunt, ut et regi satisfacerent et arcanum fidei non vulgarent* (Vulg. 3, 23-5). The same preface offers a historico-doctrinal explanation for the lack of the *testimonia*, meant to prevent King Ptolemy, who was well disposed towards Judaism because of his Platonism, from discovering a second God among the Jews (*Iudaei prudenti factum dicunt esse consilio, ne Ptolemeus, unius dei cultor, etiam*

according to which the seventy translators applied self-censorship or a sort of *arcani disciplina* in their work, by hiding overly explicit formulations of Christ's message out of religious-political caution towards King Ptolemy and the pagan milieu of Alexandria.[42]

As has already been hinted at, in order to overcome these limitations of the Septuagint, Jerome exploits the other *ekdoseis* of the Hexapla, even though he names the translators only in the second series (*series altera*) of the *Tractatus*, a group of fifteen homilies which seem, at least partially, to go back to a written text. An interesting case here is the treatment of *Ps.* 67:7a (Ὁ Θεὸς κατοικίζει μονοτρόπους ἐν οἴκῳ, 'God settles solitary ones into a home'), a passage on which we have Origen's comments, thanks to his *2ⁿᵈ Homily on Psalm 67*. After explaining the Latin rendering of the Septuagint (*Deus inhabitare facit unius moris in domo*) in a way that clearly echoes Origen's interpretation (the sinner constantly 'changes' according to his sin, whereas the righteous never changes), he adds a reference to the Hebrew.[43] The rendering of *yechidim* with *monachi* mirrors the translation of Symmachus and Theodotion, whereas in the *Psalterium iuxta Hebraicum* Jerome will opt for *solitarii*.[44] But here and elsewhere, where the *Tractatus* addresses the same psalms commented on by Origen, we can observe that the Alexandrian avoids referring to the hexaplaric readings in his preaching (even if he certainly knew of them).[45]

---

apud Hebraeos duplicem diuinitatem deprehenderet, quos maxime idcirco faciebat, quia in Platonis dogma cadere uidebantur (Vulg. 3, 21-3).

[42] *Id., Tractatus in Psalmos* 9, 1: *In hebraico enim habet 'Alamoth', quod interpretatur, pro morte* [...] *Pro morte* ergo filii *in hebraeo scriptum est. Videte igitur Septuaginta interpretes, quoniam Ptolomeo gentili regi interpretabantur, et durum erat dicere* mortem filii, occultum *interpretati sunt. Non dixerunt: 'Pro morte filii', sciebant enim quod de filio Dei diceretur. Videbant scriptum esse, et tamen timebant Dei filium dicere esse moriturum* (28, 19-29, 27). The title of *Ps.* 9 is the crown witness for Jerome's thesis, as he repeats in *Tractatus in Psalmos* 15 (series altera): *Post haec quaeritur, cur Septuaginta intepretes aliter quam in hebraeo et apud ceteras editiones est transferre uoluerunt. Quod et de multis aliis locis, sed maxime de praescriptione noni psalmi intellegi potest. Qui cum apud hebraeos praenotetur* LAMANASSE ALMUTH LABEN, *quod interpretatur Symmachus 'triumphus adolescentiae filii', Septuaginta interpretes, nolentes tam aperte Ptolomaeo regi et gentibus passionem et resurrectionem prodere Saluatoris, transtulerunt 'In finem pro occultis filii'* (365, 49-366, 58).

[43] *Id., Tractatus in Psalmos* 67, 7: *In hebraeo autem habet: 'Dominus inhabitare facit monachos in domo'; id est in quibus non cohabitat peccatum* (41, 37-39).

[44] Σ. Δίδωσιν οἰκεῖν μοναχοῖς οἰκίαν. Θ. Κατοικίζει μοναχοὺς ἐν οἴκῳ (Field, 200).

[45] On the contrary, see Hieronymus, *Tractatus in Psalmos* 75, 3a: *'Et factus est in pace locus eius': quod dicitur hebraice 'in Salem'.* [...] *In hebraico habet: 'Et factum est in Salem umbraculum eius'* (49, 5-50, 18). The most eloquent case is *ibid.*, 76, 3: *'Manibus meis nocte contra eum: et non sum deceptus'. In hebraico aliter habet: 'Manus mea nocte extenditur, et non quiescit. Manibus meis nocte contra eum'* (55, 19-21); 76, 4: *In hebraico aliter habet: 'Memor fui Dei, et conturbatus sum'.* [...] *In hebraeo melius habet: 'Loquebar in memetipso, et defecit spiritus meus'* (56, 49-53); *ibid.* 76, 5: *In hebraeo aliter habet: 'Prohibebam suspectum oculorum meorum, constupebam et non loquebar'.* [...] *Hoc iuxta hebraicum* (56, 56-57, 61); *ibid.* 76, 11: *In hebraeo aliter habet: 'Et dixi: Inbecillitas mea'* (58, 93-4); *ibid.* 76, 18: *'Discusserunt nubes aquas'*

In the light of what we have seen so far, Jerome appears to be a diligent disciple of Origen's, eager to apply the same methods even more faithfully than the Alexandrian master himself did. This impression is further corroborated by the use that the monk of Bethlehem makes of two additional 'technicalities' of patristic exegesis: the numerological and the etymological interpretation.[46] The former has a particularly interesting application within the Psalter regarding the fifteen 'Odes of the steps' (*Cantica graduum*) (*Ps.* 119-133). This number, referring in ancient sources to the fifteen steps of the Temple, results from the sum of seven and eight, as Origen briefly observes in his 'General introduction to the Psalms' (the so called *Catholica*, according to its recent editors), probably echoing *Ezek.* 40.[47] However, we lack a numerological explanation by the Alexandrian, apart from a short remark in a catena fragment on *John* 11:18 (the fifteen stadia between Bethany and Jerusalem), in which he relates number 7 to the sabbath and number 8 to circumcision.[48] As for Jerome, in the *Commentarioli* he abstains from giving his own interpretation, as he says, because of the abundant exegetical tradition already existing on the *Graduum psalmi*.[49] Presumably, he has Hilary of Poitiers in mind, if not also Origen and other interpreters.[50] On the contrary, in the

---

habet in hebraeo (59, 141); *ibid.*, 76, 21: *Non enim dicitur secundum hebraicam ueritatem* (63, 264-5). No comparable remarks appear in the four homilies of Origen on *Ps.* 76, about which see Lorenzo Perrone, 'Scrittura e cosmo nelle nuove Omelie di Origene sui Salmi: L'interpretazione del Salmo 76', in José Carlos Caamaño and Hernán Giudice (eds), *Patrística, Biblia y Teología. Caminos de diálogo* (Buenos Aires, 2017), 45-72. For other examples, absent in Origenes, *Homiliae in Psalmos*, see Hieronymus, *Tractatus in Psalmos* 77, 13: *In hebraico non habet 'utrem', sed 'aceruum'* (72, 249-50); *ibid.* 80, 16: *In hebraico melius habet: 'Inimici Domini negabunt eum', hoc est Iudaei inimici ipsius negabunt eum* (81, 180-2).

[46] For numerology, see Alessandro Capone, 'Numeri e simboli nell'esegesi geronimiana dei Salmi', *RCCM* 59 (2017), 172-81.

[47] Origenes, *Catholica*, in *Die Prologtexte zu den Psalmen von Origenes und Eusebius*, ed. Cordula Bandt, Franz-Xaver Risch and Barbara Villani (Berlin, 2019), 4, 18-9: 'τῶν ἀναβαθμῶν ᾠδαί', τὸν ἀριθμὸν πεντεκαίδεκα, ὅσοι καὶ οἱ ἀναβαθμοὶ τοῦ ναοῦ, τάχα δηλοῦσαι τὰς ἀναβάσεις περιέχεσθαι ἐν τῷ ἑβδόμῳ καὶ ὀγδόῳ ἀριθμῷ. See Franz-Xaver Risch, 'Die Stufen des Tempels. Zur Auslegung der Gradualpsalmen bei Origenes', in Brouria Bitton-Ashkelony (ed.), *Origeniana XII: Origen's Legacy in the Holy Land – A Tale of Three Cities: Jerusalem, Caesarea and Bethlehem*, Bibliotheca Ephemeridum Theologicarum Lovaniensium 302 (Leuven, 2019), 254-5: 'in den *Catholica* fügt er über jüdische Tradition und mögliche Realsituationen hinaus die Vermutung hinzu, daß mit der Zahl Fünfzehn eine Gliederung in Sieben und Acht angedeutet werde. [...] Im vorausgehenden Kontext der *Catholica* hat Origenes Bemerkungen zur Sabbattheologie gemacht; ihr folgt diese Arithmetik in scheinbar freier Spekulation'.

[48] Origenes, *Fragmenta in Iohannem* 80 on *John* 11:18, ed. Erwin Preuschen, GCS 4 (Leipzig, 1903), 547: γειτνιᾷ τοίνυν ἐν μέσῳ σταδίων ιε΄, ὅσοι καὶ τοῦ ναοῦ ἀναβαθμοί. Διαιρεῖται δὲ ὁ ιε΄ἀριθμὸς εἰς τὸν ζ΄τοῦ σαββάτου καὶ τὸν η΄τῆς περιτομῆς, οἷς μόνον μερίδα διδόναι ὁ Ἐκκλησιαστὴς παραινεῖ· 'Δὸς μερίδα, λέγων, τοῖς ἑπτὰ καί γε τοῖς ὀκτώ' (*Eccl.* 11:2).

[49] Hieronymus, *Commentarioli in Psalmos* 119: *Et quia a plerisque super his latissime disputatum est, stultum est parua dicere uelle pro magnis* (235, 1-236, 5).

[50] Hilarius Pictaviensis, *Tractatus in Psalmos*, ed. Anton Zingerle, CSEL 22 (Vindobonae, 1891), 547-8.

Tractatus on *Ps*. 119 he exploits the mention of the number 15 in *Gal*. 1:18: Paul spent fifteen days in Jerusalem together with Peter to 'confront' (*conferre*) the Old and the New Testament, symbolically equivalent to the numbers 7 and 8, respectively.[51] This interpretation is not attested to in Origen, but the numerological distinction of 7 and 8 in relation to the Old and New Testament finds a parallel in Didymus.[52] Moreover, Jerome, in the same *Tractatus*, appears to be a unique patristic witness to a rabbinic tradition, according to which the fifteen steps of the Temple (whose ruins he was still able to see) were not square, but shaped as a semicircle.[53]

The difference to Origen is even more perceptible concerning the recourse to etymological interpretation, the main tool for allegorical exegesis in the Alexandrian tradition from Philo onwards. Jerome, who not incidentally translated the *Onomasticon* of Eusebius and who himself wrote a book on the Hebrew names of the Bible (*Liber interpretationis hebraicorum nominum*),[54] is particularly fond of explaining the symbolic meaning of the biblical names of places or persons:[55]

---

[51] Hieronymus, *Tractatus in Psalmos* 119: *Interim nunc dicamus de primo graduum, relinquentes mysterium quare quindecim sint gradus: eadem enim frequenter dicere, taedium est audientibus. Vnde et apostolus, quindecim dies fecisse apud Petrum in Hierosolyma, ut conferret utrumque testamentum, et septenarium et octonarium* (246, 24-247, 2).

[52] F.-X. Risch, 'Die Stufen des Tempels' (2019), 257 thinks, nevertheless, that Jerome and Didymus may depend upon Origen: 'Man verschafft sich einen Sinn, wenn man die Zahl von Sabbat und Beschneidung als Epoche der jüdischen Religion und der nunmehr metaphorischen Beschneidung im Christen liest [...] Daß es ungefähr so zu verstehen ist, bezeugen Didymus und Hieronymus, deren Exegese nicht selten Motive entwickelt, die Origenes bereitgestellt hatte. [...] Das Geben der Sieben bedeutet für beide die Anerkennung des Alten Testamentes ... das Geben der Acht die Anerkennung des Neuen Testamentes ... Einzig die Christen anerkennen beide Testamente und erfüllen so die Fünfzehnzahl'. For another numerological interpretation establishing a connection between the Gospel (= 4) and the Law (= 10), see Hieronymus, *Tractatus in Psalmos* 93, 1: *Videtis igitur quoniam dies quarta, hoc est quarta sabbati, ex utroque latere duplici trinitate firmatur. Simulque considerandum, quia quartus numerus uirtute decimus est. Quomodo? Si enim conputes et ordinem facias, unum, duo, tres, quattuor, decimus numerus efficitur. Videtis igitur quoniam quartus numerus effecit decimum et considerate ex hoc quia quattuor euangelia in decalogo conputantur, ut quodcumque dicebatur in decalogo, hoc conpleatur in quattuor euangelia, ut non dissentiat lex uetus ab euangelica dignitate* (142, 7-16). Furthermore, see the symbolism of number 10 as elaborated on in *Tractatus in Psalmos* 10 (*s.a.*) (355, 3-15).

[53] Hieronymus, *Tractatus in Psalmos* 119: *Hoc igitur templum in circuitu quindecim gradus habuit* (247, 37). See F.-X. Risch, 'Die Stufen des Tempels' (2019), 262: 'Die [...] Mischna *Middot* erwähnt, ohne ersichtlichen Grund, daß die Stufen "nicht eckig waren, sondern wie ein Halbkreis". [...] Der lateinische Exeget kann der Rundung keine Bedeutung abgewinnen, vielleicht auch weil Origenes hierzu möglicherweise nichts gesagt hat'.

[54] See Hieronymus, *Liber interpretationis hebraicorum nominum*, ed. Paul de Lagarde, CCL 72 (Turnhout, 1959), 57-161.

[55] See, for instance, *id.*, *Tractatus in Psalmos* 82, 6: *Videte nominum sacramenta* (91, 36-7); *id.*, *Commentarioli in Psalmos* 107, 10b: *Idumaea autem aut 'terrena' interpretatur, aut 'sanguinaria'. Et totus psalmus secundum sensum duplicem aut ad David refertur, quod super has gentes Deo se adiuuante regnauerit: aut ad Xpistum, ut secundum interpretationem nominum hebraeorum diuersas ecclesiae reputemus esse uirtutes* (231, 4-8).

for him, the names conceal 'mysteries' (*sacramenta*).[56] It is such a frequent feature in the *Tractatus* that there is no need to insist on it. However, it is again interesting to check it against Origen's practice of etymology in the *Homilies on the Psalms*. The Alexandrian does not ignore it – as we also know from his other writings – but his use is generally more sober when compared to Jerome's and, occasionally, may lead to a different outcome. Both hint, for instance, at the meaning of place names such as Edom or Bosor when quoting the christologically crucial passage of *Isa.* 63:1 ('Who is this that comes from Edom, a redness of garments from Bosor?'), but they explain it in a partially different way: while the Alexandrian, in the *2ⁿᵈ Homily on Psalm 15*, proposes the two symbolic correspondences 'Edom' = 'earthly (things)' and 'Bosor' = 'flesh',[57] the *Tractatus* on *Ps.* 67 has only the second of them. Instead, 'Edom' means, for Jerome, 'blood'.[58] He therefore revises his own previous interpretation in the *Commentarioli*, where he gave to 'Edom' the meaning of 'earthly' or 'deficient'.[59] In fact, as proved elsewhere by his writings, Jerome strives to provide a more correct etymology for both Edom and Bosor, whereby he expressly criticises those who, like Origen, interpret 'Bosor' as 'flesh', instead of reading the Hebrew word for Bosra.[60] Even if a larger amount of the etymologies attested to by Jerome probably goes back to Origen, we should not overlook his efforts at elaborating on his own opinions, thanks to his familiarity with the Hebrew and knowledge of Eusebius and other commentators. Proof of this is *Epistula* 78 to Fabiola, his 'response' to the famous *27ᵗʰ Homily on Numbers* by Origen on the forty-two mansions of Israel in the desert (*Num.* 33:1-49), in

---

[56] *Id., Tractatus in Psalmos* 82, 9: *Videtis quia difficillima loca sunt, uidetis quia obscura sunt, et in singulis sermonibus magna sunt sacramenta, et necessitate conpellimur in uerbis hebraicis et plenis mysteriis diutius immorari. Neque enim nunc rhetoricum locum euentilamus, sed id quod ab Spiritu sancto dictum est, interpretari nitimur. Nisi enim sic interpretemur ut diximus, quid prodest ecclesiis Christi legere tarbernacula Idumaeorum et Ismahelitae et cetera nomina?* (93, 86-93).

[57] Origenes, *Homiliae in Psalmum* 15 II, 8: Ξενίζονται γοῦν αἱ δυνάμεις ἐπὶ τῇ καινῇ ἱστορίᾳ, ὅτι βλέπουσι σάρκα ἀναβεβηκυῖαν εἰς οὐρανὸν καὶ λέγουσι· 'τίς οὗτος ὁ παραγενόμενος ἐξ Ἐδώμ', τουτέστι τῶν γηΐνων, 'ἐρύθημα ἱματίων' (*Isa.* 63:1a); Βλέπουσι τὰ ἴχνη τοῦ αἵματος καὶ τῶν τραυμάτων· 'ἐκ Βοσόρ', τῆς σαρκός, 'οὕτως ὡραῖος ἐν στολῇ βίᾳ μετὰ ἰσχύος; ἐγὼ διαλέγομαι' (*Isa.* 63:1bc) (105, 19-106, 3).

[58] Hieronymus, *Tractatus in Psalmos* 67, 24: *Edom interpretatur sanguis, Bosor caro: ipsum significat Dominum nostrum crucifixum* (45, 160-1).

[59] *Id., Commentarioli in Psalmos* 136, 7a: *Quia uero Edom 'terrenus' siue 'deficiens' interpretatur, intellege contrarias inimicasque uirtutes semper hoc agere, ut nihil in ecclesia, nihil in Ierusalem remaneat* (242, 22-4).

[60] *Id., Commentarii in Esaiam* 10, 34, 1-7 in *Commentaires sur le Prophète Isaïe. Livres VIII-XI*, ed. Véronique Somers, Roger Gryson *et al.* (Freiburg im Breisgau, 1996): *Et nonnulli existimant, quia Bosor caro dicitur, per uictimam Domini in Bosra, tormenta omnium in carne monstrari, qui pio labuntur errore. In praesenti enim loco non per* Sin *litteram, quae in Bosor, hoc est in carne, ponitur, sed per* Sade *scribitur, et Bosra appellatur, quae iuxta Iesum et Hieremiam non in Edom, id est, Idumaea, sed in terra Moab inuenitur* (420, 81-7). See also *ibid.* 17, 63, 1ab (721, 53-63). For other occurrences, see Girolamo, *59 Omelie sui Salmi*, ed. A. Capone (2018), 148 n. 38.

which Jerome shares the numerological explanation of the Alexandrian, but modifies in several places the list of the toponyms and their interpretation.[61] On the other hand, Jerome, despite his strong interest in etymology, may sacrifice it when following more closely in the footsteps of Origen. The Alexandrian is actually surprisingly silent on the names which play an important role in his spiritual explanation of the Psalter, as we can see with the names of Ephraim and Manasse in the *Homilies on Psalm 77*, although he displays their etymology elsewhere: Ephraim = 'fructification', Manasse = 'oblivion'. Jerome is, indeed, acquainted with both in the *Tractatus*, but he does not mention them either when preaching on *Ps. 77*.[62]

3. Jerome's preaching on the same psalms as Origen: a free 'counterpoint' to the Alexandrian?

The affinities and diversities that we have noted between Jerome and Origen lend support to the idea that the former inclines to develop, so to say, a free 'counterpoint' to the latter. To what extent this might be true ought to be further verified by a synoptic treatment of the homilies that the two authors devoted to the same psalms. However, since a detailed examination of their respective *corpus* would demand a more thorough investigation than is possible at present, I shall again sketch an overview based on some exemplary cases as a prelude to future study.

Leaving aside the two *Homilies on Psalm 15*, which undoubtedly offer the most conspicuous evidence for Jerome's acquaintance with the texts of the Alexandrian,[63] let us first of all briefly evoke the interpretation given by the two preachers on *Ps. 67*. This difficult psalm demanded from Origen seven homilies, two of which survive in the Munich collection. Originally, then, it

---

[61] Aline Canellis, 'L'exégèse de Nombres 33, 1-49: d'Origène à saint Jérôme (*Epist.* 78 à Fabiola)', dans Emanuela Prinzivalli, Françoise Vinel and Michele Cutino (eds), *Transmission et réception des Pères grecs dans l'Occident, de l'Antiquité tardive à la Renaissance. Entre philologie, herméneutique et théologie* (Paris, 2016), 57-79. As observed by Antonio Cacciari, 'Omelia XXVII: Ascesa e tappe', in Mario Maritano and Enrico dal Covolo (eds), *Omelie sui Numeri. Lettura origeniana* (Roma, 2004), 130-1: 'all'interpretazione aritmologica [...] sono affidate alcune funzioni di grande rilievo: anzitutto, di saldare le vicende del cammino d'Israele verso le "promesse" al cammino di Cristo nella storia; poi, di riaffermare l'unità dell'Antico e del Nuovo Testamento; infine, di conseguenza, di dare la chiave di lettura complessiva di questo passo e dell'intero contesto di *Nm* altrimenti destinato al rifiuto'.

[62] Hieronymus, *Tractatus in Psalmos* 107, 9: *Manasses interpretatur 'ex obliuione'* [...] *Et Efraim interpretatur 'fructifer'* (204, 112-7). See Origenes, *Commentarii in Iohannem* XXVIII, 24, 213, ed. Erwin Preuschen, GCS 10 (Leipzig, 1903), 420, 16-8: Ἑρμηνεύεται δὲ Ἐφραῖμ καρποφορία, ἀδελφὸς ὢν Μανασσῆς, πρεσβυτέρου τοῦ ʽἀπὸ λήθης' (*Gen.* 41:51-2) λαοῦ.

[63] As has been proved by Elena Orlandi, 'Esegesi e omiletica nei *Tractatus in Psalmos*. Il salmo 15 dal *Codex Monacensis Graecus* 314 alla rielaborazione di Gerolamo', in Daniele Tripaldi (ed.), *La lira di Davide. Esegesi e riscritture dei Salmi dall' Antichità al Medioevo* (Roma, 2018), 283-305.

was the second largest series after the nine sermons on *Ps.* 77. Although a closer comparison with the *Tractatus* is limited only to vv. 2-7, extensively commented on by Origen, but mainly the object of short 'glosses' by Jerome – who proceeds in the same manner until the end (v. 36) – it is, nevertheless, possible to detect some points of similarity.

The first aspect that deserves attention is the identification of the *prosopon*: for the Alexandrian, v. 2ab ('Let God rise up and let his enemies be scattered') initially means God (the Father), and only subsequently the Lord (as the resurrected Christ).[64] On the contrary, Jerome (like Hilary of Poitiers) applies the verse, in particular, to Christ in his passion and resurrection[65] and, in a more general sense, to the faithful who experience tribulations and beg for God's help.[66] He thus omits the long and brilliant developments of the *1st Homily on Psalm 67* on the biblical anthropomorphisms of God, but he exploits, like Origen, the same quotation from *Ps.* 43.[67] Jerome combines it with *Matt.* 8:25 (the appeal to Jesus by his disciples for the stilling of the storm) to express the urgent call to the Lord in a situation of distress, without discussing in what sense the Scriptures speak of God as 'sleeping' or 'awaking'. However, he manifestly reuses these passages of the *1st Homily on Psalm 67* in another occasion, when he illustrates the different scriptural *schemata* of God in the *Tractatus* on *Ps.* 81.

Here, Jerome is more didactic and orderly than Origen, but his list of the 'four different forms' of the behaviour of God (*quattuor schematibus Dei*) – actually, there are five – essentially corresponds to Origen's discussion of *Ps.* 67:2a, although in a slightly different order: (God is namely said by the Scriptures) 1) 'to stand' (*stare* = ἑστηκέναι), 2) 'to walk' (*ambulare* = περιπατεῖν), 3) 'to sit' (*sedere* = καθέζεσθαι), 4) 'to sleep' (*dormire* = ὑπνοῦν), and 5) 'to wake up' / 'to rise up' (*euigilare* / *consurgere* = ἀνίστασθαι). In any case, the scriptural quotations for the changing states of God in relation to humankind do not differ in either author, although Origen inserts, as

---

[64] For the transition to the christological interpretation, see Origenes, *Homiliae in Psalmum 67* I, 4 (185, 14-6).

[65] Hilarius Pictaviensis, *Tractatus in Psalmos* 67: *Est autem ipse totus sacramentis legis euangeliorumque contextus magnaque et ex praeteritis et ex futuris allegoricorum dictorum interpretatione confertus: qui et legis latae in se doctrinam contineat et adsumptae a domino carnis adferat notionem et impietatem populi anterioris exprobret et futurae cognitionis nostrae fidem nuntiet et domini super caelos conplectitur ascensum et futuri regni eius gloriam conprehendat* (276, 22-277, 5).

[66] Hieronymus, *Tractatus in Psalmos* 67, 2: *Et specialiter intellegitur iste psalmus, et generaliter. Specialiter in ipsum Dominum, ut resurgat a mortuis, et disperdat inimicos suos, hoc est diabolum et exercitum suum, aut Iudaeos. Generaliter autem, quando in tribulatione sumus et angustia, et dicimus: 'Exsurge, ut quid dormitas Domine? ed adiuua nos'* (Ps. 43:24.27) (40, 1-6).

[67] Respectively, vv. 24a.25 in Origen and 24a.27 in Jerome.

usual, more references.[68] In turn, Jerome makes the frame of 'sinner / saint', in relation to the different *schemata*, more explicit than is the case with the Alexandrian.[69]

[68] *Cf.* Origenes, *Homiliae in Psalmum 67* I, 3 (180, 2-184, 2) with Hieronymus, *Tractatus in Psalmos* 81, 1 (82, 1-83, 23; 83, 37-84, 48; 84, 49-52).

Ζητητέον γὰρ ὁ θεὸς πότε μὲν ἀνίσταται, πότε δὲ ὑπνοῖ· τοιαῦτα γάρ τινα ἐν τῇ κοινῇ ἐκδοχῇ λέγουσι περὶ αὐτοῦ αἱ θεῖαι γραφαί, νοῆσαι δὲ δεῖ πῶς ταῦτα ἀναγέγραπται. Περὶ μὲν γὰρ τοῦ ὑπνοῦν αὐτόν φησί τις ἐν ψαλμοῖς εὐχόμενος· ᾽ἀνάστηθι, ἵνα τί ὑπνοῖς, κύριε; ἵνα τί τὸ πρόσωπόν σου ἀποστρέφεις; ἐπιλανθάνῃ τῆς πτωχείας ἡμῶν καὶ τῆς θλίψεως ἡμῶν᾽ (*Ps.* 43: 24a.25); Περὶ δὲ τοῦ καθέζεσθαι· ᾽ὁ καθήμενος ἐπὶ τῶν χερουβὶμ ἐμφάνηθι, ἐναντίον Ἐφραῖμ καὶ Βενιαμὶν καὶ Μανασσῆ᾽ (*Ps.* 79:2c-3a). Περὶ δὲ τοῦ ἑστηκέναι θεόν, αὐτὸς τῷ Μωϋσῇ λέγει· ᾽σὺ δὲ αὐτοῦ στῆθι μετ᾽ ἐμοῦ᾽ (*Deut.* 5:31). Καὶ περὶ τοῦ περιπατεῖν, ἐν τῇ Γενέσει ἀναγέγραπται, ὅτι μετὰ τὴν παράβασιν ἤκουσεν ὁ Ἀδὰμ ᾽κυρίου τοῦ θεοῦ περιπατοῦντος ἐν τῷ παραδείσῳ τὸ δειλινόν᾽ (*Gen.* 3:8). [...] Οὕτως οὖν ὡς πρὸς μὲν τὸ ἀληθὲς ἄτρεπτος καὶ ἀναλλοίωτος ὁ θεός· δι᾽ ἡμᾶς δέ, ὅτε μὲν καθέζεσθαι λέγεται, τῷ δέ τινι καθεζόμενος οἷον τῷ κρινομένῳ. Μὴ γὰρ εἴη αὐτὸν ἑστηκέναι τῷ κρινομένῳ!· ᾽βίβλοι γὰρ ἠνεῴχθησαν καὶ κριτήριον ἐκάθισεν᾽ (*Dan.* 7:10), καὶ καθέζεται ὅτε κρίνει. Τῷ δὲ ἁγίῳ καὶ μακαρίῳ, ᾧ ἁρμόζει τὸ ᾽ὁ πιστεύων εἰς ἐμὲ οὐ κρίνεται᾽ (*John* 3:18), οὐ καθέζεται ἀλλὰ ἕστηκεν. Διὸ λέγει ὁ ἑστηκὼς τῷ ἤδη ἀξίῳ ἑστηκέναι μετὰ τοῦ θεοῦ· ᾽σὺ δὲ αὐτοῦ στῆθι μετ᾽ ἐμοῦ᾽ (*Deut.* 5:31). Ὁτὲ δὲ τῷ ἐπισκόπῳ τῷ ἀναξίῳ προνοίας καὶ χάριτος τοῦ θεοῦ ᾽ὁ μὴ νυστάζων, ὁ μὴ ὑπνώττων ὅταν φυλάττῃ τὸν Ἰσραήλ᾽, ὑπνοῖ· κἂν μετανοήσῃ ἐκεῖνος, ᾧ ὑπνοῖ ὁ θεός, λέγεται· ᾽ἐξηγέρθη ὡς ὁ ὑπνῶν κύριος, ὡς δυνατὸς καὶ κεκραιπαληκὼς ἐξ οἴνου᾽ (*Ps.* 77:65)· οὕτω δὲ καὶ ἀνίσταται.

Multa sunt schemata. Frequenter enim sedemus, interdum stamus, interdum iacemus, interdum currimus, interdum ambulamus. Ita et Deus describitur pro uarietate hominum, et status ipsius diuersus inducitur. Si sancti sumus, et sumus similes Moysi, dicitur ad nos: 'Tu uero hic sta mecum' (Deut. 5:31). Hoc enim dicit Deus ad Moysen. Stabat enim Moyses super petram: propterea et Deus stabat illi. Si uero sancti prius fuerimus, et postea peccatores, iam non nobis stat Deus, sed ambulat: hoc est, mouetur de loco suo, qui nobis ante steterat. Postquam nos moti fuerimus, et ipse nobiscum pariter commouetur. Denique et Adam quamdiu in paradiso fuit, et legem seruabat, stabat ei Deus. Postquam uero transgressus est, audiuit uocem Dei ambulantis in paradiso. Vis scire quia ambulat ei Deus? Quid ei dixit? Adam, ubi es (Gen. 3:9)? Qui ante stantem Deum non fugerat, postea ambulantem fugit.
Diximus de stante, diximus de ambulante: dicamus de sedente. Quandocumque sedens inducitur Deus, dupliciter inducitur: aut quasi rex, aut quasi iudex. [...] Quando uero quasi iudex inducitur: 'Throni positi sunt et libri aperti sunt' (Dan. 7:9.10). [...] Diximus de Deo quod aliis stet, aliis ambulet, aliis uero sedeat aut quasi rex aut quasi iudex: aliis uero dormit. Si quando nos derelinquit temptationibus: licet simus sancti, tamen relinquimur temptationibus, ut probemur: eo tempore nobis dormit Dominus. Denique quid dicit et psalmista? 'Exsurge, utquid dormitas Domine' (Ps. 43:24a)? Et apostoli quando erant in naui, et nauis fluctibus tundebatur. [...] Denique excitant eum, et euigilat, et statim tempestas quiescit. Diximus de quattuor schematibus Dei, quia aliis stat, aliis ambulat, aliis sedet, aliis quasi dormit, aliis uero euigilat et consurgit. [...] In qua ipsa synagoga nostra diuersa deus habet schemata; aliis stat, aliis sedet, aliis ambulat, aliis dormit. Cum ipse sit immutabilis, pro nostra uarietate mutatur. Vide hominis dignitatem.

[69] For a similar argument, partially resting on the same quotations (*Gen.* 3:8; *Deut.* 5:31; *Dan.* 7:10.9), see Hieronymus, *Tractatus in Psalmos* 98, 1c.

Origenes, *Homilia in Psalmum 67* I, 3

ὑπνοῦν: *Ps.* 43:24a.25
καθέζεσθαι: *Ps.* 79:2c-3a / *Dan.* 7:10
ἑστηκέναι: *Deut.* 5:31 (twice) / *Dan.* 7:10 /
    John 3:18
περιπατεῖν: *Gen.* 3:8
ἀνίστασθαι: *Ps.* 77:65

Hieronymus, *Tractatus in Psalmos* 81, 1

stare: *Deut.* 5:31
ambulare: *Gen.* 3:9
sedere: *Dan.* 7:9.10
dormire: *Ps.* 43:24a
euigilare / consurgere: *Ps.* 43:24a

Not only does Jerome feel free to adapt and better arrange the exegesis of Origen, he also extrapolates important motifs from it by retelling them in his own way. While the Alexandrian deals in a long section of the *1ˢᵗ Homily on Psalm 67* with the destiny of 'enemies' and 'sinners' in the wake of vv. 2-3, Jerome interprets Origen's idea of an unavoidable connection between the righteous and sinners more simply and directly as an indication for the preservation and repentance of sinners. Consequently, v. 2b ('Let his enemies be scattered') does not mean that the sinners should perish, but merely that they should 'flee from the face of God'.[70] And, without any apparent embarassment for v. 3 ('As smoke vanishes, let them vanish; as wax melts from before fire, so may sinners perish from before God'), Jerome again insists on the idea that the enemies should not be annihilated and perish, but rather convert and repent.[71] This may sound like a typically Origenian motive,[72] but now and then in his *Tractatus* the monk of Bethlehem proves to be even more open toward such a perspective than happens in the homilies of the Alexandrian.[73] As we shall shortly see, the remarkable passages about the salvation of the Jews, in the light of *Rom.* 11, fully conform to this attitude.

We may even catch some more echoes of Origen in the subsequent comments by Jerome, synthetic and quick as they are. The distinction between 'contemplation' (= *cantare*) and 'action' (= *psallere*) that he extrapolates from v. 5a ('Sing to God; make music to his name'), mirrors the wider elaboration on the same passage by Origen.[74] It presumably goes back to the Alexandrian,

---

[70] *Ibid.* 67, 2c: '*Et fugiant qui oderunt eum a facie eius*'. Non dixit: '*Pereant*', sed '*fugiant*', quia peccatores in conspectu Dei stare non possunt (40, 9-10).

[71] *Ibid.* 67, 3a: *non ut ad nihilum redigantur, sed ut quiescant a peccatis suis* (40, 11-2); v. 3b: sic et isti non pereant, sed deponant duritiam suam, et sic conuertantur ad paenitentiam, et saluentur (40, 13-5).

[72] As stated by Coppa in Origene-Gerolamo, *74 Omelie sul libro dei Salmi*, ed. Giovanni Coppa (Milano, 1993), 145 n. 3.

[73] See, for instance, Hieronymus, *Tractatus in Psalmos* 67, 20b: '*Prosperum iter faciet nobis Deus salutarium nostrorum*'. Securus esto, peccator, noli dubitare quod cotidie possis benedicere Deum; ecce enim dicit: '*Prosperum* [...] *Deus*'. Ergo Deus adiuuat nos, et cooperatur nobis. '*Salutarium nostrorum*'. Bene dixit pluraliter, salutarium: quod quanta peccata commisimus, tot et salutes habemus (44, 131-7).

[74] Compare Origenes, *Homiliae in Psalmum 67* II, 3-4 with Hieronymus, *Tractatus in Psalmum 67*, 5: Cantate Deo, psalmum dicite nomini eius. *Cantate, in theoria semper significat scriptura: hoc est, considerate mysteria et sensum diuinae scripturae. Psallere autem in bono*

as does the interpretation of *psallere* as pointing to the body as a 'psalter' that one should harmoniously play in all of its many chords in order to practise virtue,[75] or the idea of the voluntary death of Jesus in v. 24b ('so that your foot may be dipped in blood, the tongue of your dogs, from enemies, by him').[76] But here we have already entered *terra incognita*, where we do not have at our disposal the text of Origen's homilies anymore. Checking the few *scholia* transmitted under his name against the *Tractatus* demands much caution, as shown, for instance, by Jerome's comment on v. 14 (*Si dormiatis inter medios cleros, pennae columbae deargentatae, et posteriora dorsi eius in pallore auri*, 'If you lie down among the allotments – a dove's wings covered with silver and its back feathers with golden greenness'); according to him, the two 'allotments' (*cleri*) are the Old and the New Testament, both covered by the 'dove's wings' of the Holy Ghost and thus requesting a spiritual interpretation of their 'mysteries'.[77] Origen occasionally quotes *Ps.* 67:14, but he interprets it in a different way, without referring to the two Testaments.[78]

---

opere significat scriptura (40, 23-41, 1). On the equivalence 'to sing' = θεολογία in Origen, following *Ps.* 67:5a, see Lorenzo Perrone, 'Dire Dieu chez Origène: la démarche théologique et ses présupposés spirituels', in Bernard Pouderon and Anna Usacheva (eds), *Dire Dieu. Principes méthodologiques de l'écriture sur Dieu en patristique* (Paris, 2017), 129-57.

[75] Hieronymus, *Tractatus in Psalmum* 67, 5: *ut auditus suum opus praestet, similiter et os, et oculi, et manus, et omnia membra quasi consentiant, et ita percutiant psalterium in uirtutibus.* See Origenes, *Homiliae in Psalmum* 67 II, 4 (209, 1-211, 2).

[76] Hieronymus, *Tractatus in Psalmum* 67, 24b: '*Ex inimicis*' autem: *submissi a daemonibus negare Saluatorem et blasphemare eum. Aliter: quoniam ipse tua uoluntate uenisti et passus es, et tua uoluntate crucifixus es a Iudaeis* (45, 164-7). See *id.*, *Commentarioli in Psalmos* 67, 23-4: *Vt autem hoc totum fieret, ipsius Saluatoris uoluntas fuit* (215, 38-9); M.-J. Rondeau, *Les commentaires patristiques* (1985), 147: 'Mettre en relief la liberté et l'initiative du Christ en soulignant que ce ne sont pas les juifs qui on eu le dessus sur lui, mais que c'est parce qu'il l'a voulu et que Dieu l'a voulu qu'il a subi la passion, est tout à fait origénien'.

[77] Hieronymus, *Tractatus in Psalmos* 67, 14: '*Si dormiatis inter medios cleros*': *hoc est, si quiescatis inter nouum et uetus testamentum. Cleri dicuntur et singuli libri: hoc est Genesis, Exodus, Iudicum, Euangelia, Apostolus.* '*Pennae columbae deargentatae*'. *Inuenietis in duobus testamentis gratiam Spiritus sancti.* '*Deargentatae*': *clarum uerbum significat diuinae scripturae.* '*Et posteriora dorsi eius in pallore auri*': *hoc est, in interioribus spiritaliter mysteria intelleguntur* (42, 79-43, 86). See also *id.*, *Commentarioli in Psalmos* 67, 14: *Cum duobus credideris Testamentis, inuenies in utroque Spiritum sanctum. Et licet sit pulchritudo etiam iuxta litteram scire quae legas, tamen uis decoris omnis in sensu est. Exterior itaque uerborum ornatus in argenti nomine demonstratur: occultiora uero mysteria in reconditis auri muneribus continentur* (214, 10-5). For other references, see S. Risse, *Commentarioli* (2005), 158 n. 116.

[78] *Ps.* 67:14 is quoted by Origenes, *Commentarii in Canticum canticorum* III in Origenes, *Homilien zu Samuel I, zum Hohelied und zu den Propheten. Kommentar zum Hohelied in Rufins und Hieronymus Übersetzungen*, ed. Wilhelm Adolf Baehrens, GCS 33, Origenes Werke 8 (Leipzig, 1925), 173, 20; 224, 6; 233, 19; 234, 1; *id.*, *Fragmenta in Ezechielem*, GCS 33, 543, 27; *id.*, *Homiliae in Lucam* XXVII, in Origenes, *Die Homilien zu Lukas*, ed. Max Rauer, GCS 49, Origenes Werke 9 (Berlin, 1959), 160. As for *id.*, *Fragmenta Commentarii in Lamentationes* 83 in Origenes, *Jeremiahomilien, Klageliedkommentar, Erklärung der Samuel- und Königsbücher*, ed. Erich Klostermann, GCS 6, Origenes Werke 3 (Berlin, 1983²), 267, 7, Klostermann indicates

Moreover the excerpt attributed to him in the *Fragmenta in Psalmos* is, in fact, a *scholion* by Evagrius.[79]

The *Tractatus* on *Ps.* 74, a much shorter piece than the corresponding small homily by Origen,[80] does not seem to offer any significant elements for a comparison. Jerome is more concerned with the explanation of the title and the author, than with that of the psalm itself, limiting his exegesis to vv. 1-3. Nevertheless, he shows the influence of other commentators, since he expressly appeals to 'other' (*alii*) and 'old' (*ueteres*) interpreters. As for the title, he signals a different form of the Hebrew (*uictori*), moving closer to Eusebius, who (like Symmachus) speaks likewise of a psalm ἐπινίκιος.[81] Moreover, the discussion on context and authorship – David or Asaph? – indicates an interest in the historical nature, more akin to Eusebius' approach (if not to rabbinical exegesis).[82] Furthermore, instead of understanding spiritually the words 'Do not destroy' (*Ps.* 74, 1a: Μὴ διαφθείρῃς) in the title, as the Alexandrian immediately does, Jerome hints at a plurality of interpretations. One of these considers the words as an appeal

---

a reference to *Ps.* 54:7 ('And I said, "Who will give me wings like a dove, and I shall fly away and be at rest?"'). See further the quotation in *id.*, *Commentarii in Canticum canticorum* III, 1, 6, speaking of the eyes of the dove as the symbol of the Spirit and spiritual understanding: *Sed et si 'dormire' quis possit, hoc est collocari et requiescere 'in medio sortium' atque intellegere rationem sortium et agnoscere diuini iudicii causas, non solum 'pennae columbae', quibus in spiritalibus intellectibus uolet, promittuntur ei, sed et 'deargentatae pennae'* (cf. *Ps.* 67:14), *id est uerbi et rationis ornamento decoratae* (173). The second passage in *ibid.*, IV, 2, 22 could have inspired Jerome, although Origen refers to the Church in the middle of the two calls to Israel: *Quia autem dedit ei et pennas columbae* (cf. *Ps.* 54:7), *posteaquam 'dormiuit in medio sortium'* (cf. *Ps.* 67:14); *media enim inter duas uocationes Istrahelis ecclesia uocata est, quia primo Istrahel uocatus est, post haec ubi ille offendit et cecidit, uocata est ecclesia gentium, cum autem 'plenitudo gentium introierit', tunc iterum 'omnis Istrahel' uocatus 'saluabitur; in medio' ergo harum duarum 'sortium dormit' ecclesia; et propter hoc dedit ei 'pennas columbae deargentatas', quod significat rationabiles pennas in sancti Spiritus donis* (233-4). Hilary also has a different exegesis.

[79] Origenes, *Fragmenta in Psalmos* 67, 14, PG 12, 1508B = Evagrius, *Scholia in Psalmos* 67, 14 (10): Τοὺς κλήρους καὶ τὰς πτέρυγας οἱ μὲν εἰρήκασι Παλαιὰν καὶ Καινὴν Διαθήκην· οἱ δὲ πρᾶξιν καὶ θεωρίαν· ἄλλοι δὲ γνῶσιν σωμάτων καὶ ἀσωμάτων· ἕτεροι δὲ γνῶσιν Θεοῦ, καὶ τοῦ ἀποσταλέντος ὑπ' αὐτοῦ Χριστοῦ.

[80] Lorenzo Perrone, '*Ne corrumpas* (Sal 74, 1): l'omelia di Origene sul Salmo 74 nel codice di Monaco', in Gennaro Luongo (ed.), *Amicorum Munera: Studi in onore di Antonio V. Nazzaro* (Napoli, 2016), 99-113.

[81] Hieronymus, *Tractatus in Psalmos* 74, 1: *In hebraeo non habet 'in finem' sed habet 'uictori'. Et Septuaginta interpretes non ualde errauerunt: siquidem uictoria perfecta est* (48, 1-2); Eusebius, *Commentaria in Psalmos* 74: Οὐκοῦν περὶ ἀφθαρσίας ὁ λόγος τῆς τοῖς δικαίοις ἀποκειμένης, οἷς καὶ τὰ τῆς νίκης ἀποτεθαύρισται βραβεῖα. Διὸ καὶ ἐπινίκιος εἴρηται (PG 23, 868A). *Homilia in Psalmum* 74 does not mention the rendering of Symmachus ('ἐπινίκιος περὶ ἀφθαρίας' [Field, 219]), although Origen refers implicitly to him (*ibid.*, 1: ἀνθ' οὗ εἷς τῶν ἑρμηνευσάντων – ἀντὶ τοῦ 'εἰς τὸ τέλος μὴ διαφθείρῃς' – πεποίηκεν· 'ὑπὲρ ἀφθαρσίας' [269, 3-4]).

[82] Hieronymus, *Tractatus in Psalmos* 74, 1: *Alii dicunt, quoniam iste psalmus a Dauid compositus est, et ab Asaph cantatus est; alii autem, quoniam ipse Asaph et conposuit et cantauit* (48, 9-12).

addressed by David to a friend in order to preserve the life of Saul, and Jerome finally opts for this explanation.[83] In any case, we notice only a partial agreement with Origen on the prosopological interpretation: for the Alexandrian, until v. 2b ('We will acknowledge you, O God; we will acknowledge and call upon your name') the person speaking is a collective one, that is, the Church; from v. 2c (Διηγήσομαι τὰ θαυμάσιά σου, 'I will tell of your wondrous deeds') to the end, it is a single person, that is, Christ.[84] Did Jerome think, perhaps, of the Alexandrian when he presented this exegesis as traditional, inasmuch as Eusebius indicates 'apostles, disciples and evangelists' as the collective *prosopon*?[85] But Jerome, in contrast to Origen, extends the collective subject until v. 2c (as signalled by the plural *narrabimus* in Latin for the singular διηγήσομαι in Greek).[86] There is another important difference: Jerome understands the 'confession' by the Church in v. 2 (*Confitebimur* / Ἐξομολογησόμεθα) as a proclamation of the glory of God,[87] whereas, for Origen, the Church of the Gentiles avows its trespasses before obeying the call of the Lord.[88] Jerome probably follows the interpretation of Eusebius, who rejected the penitential value of the 'confession' of the Church by putting it in the mouth of the 'righteous', as an additional identification of the person speaking.[89]

In addition, for the *Tractatus* on *Ps*. 75 it would be excessive to consider Jerome's preaching a 'counterpoint' to Origen's homily: the monk of Bethlehem

---

[83] *Ibid.* 74, 1: *Ergo secundum Septuaginta hoc dicit: O Domine, qui me custodisti, ut non mittam manum meam super xpistum tuum Saul, usque ad finem custodi me* (48, 12-4).

[84] Origenes, *Homilia in Psalmum 74* 1: Τὸ πλῆθος μὲν γάρ φησι· 'ἐξομολογησόμεθά σοι, ὁ θεός, καὶ ἐπικαλεσόμεθα τὸ ὄνομά σου' (*Ps.* 74:2b), εἰς δὲ τὸ 'διηγήσομαι τὰ θαυμάσιά σου, ὅταν λάβω καιρόν' (*Ps.* 74:2c-3a). Τοῦτο ποιεῖ εἷς λέγων μέχρι τέλους (269, 11-3).

[85] Eusebius, *Commentaria in Psalmos*: Διὸ ἐκ προσώπου μὲν τῶν τοῦ Σωτῆρος ἡμῶν ἀποστόλων καὶ μαθητῶν καὶ εὐαγγελιστῶν ἀναφωνεῖ τό· 'ἐξομολογησόμεθά σοι, ὁ θεός, καὶ ἐπικαλεσόμεθα τὸ ὄνομά σου' (PG 23, 824D).

[86] Hieronymus, *Tractatus in Psalmos* 74, 2: *Narrabimus mirabilia tua. 'Hoc dicit ecclesia, hoc dicit multitudo credentium'. Narrabimus mirabilia tua. 'Iste uersus cum prioribus iungitur, iste autem qui sequitur ex persona Domini dicitur: sic enim interpretati sunt ueteres'* (48, 20-3).

[87] *Ibid.* 74, 2a: *'Confitebimur tibi Deus'. 'Hic 'confitebimur' non paenitentiam significat, sed gloriam. 'Et inuocabimus nomen tuum'. Nomen Dei Pater est: antea enim ignorabatur* (48, 15-6).

[88] Origenes, *Homilia in Psalmum 74* 1: ἐπεὶ οὐχ οἷόν τέ ἐστιν οὕτως 'ἐπικαλέσασθαι τὸ ὄνομα κυρίου' ὥστε τυχεῖν τοῦ 'πᾶς ὃς ἂν ἐπικαλέσηται τὸ ὄνομα κυρίου σωθήσεται' (*Joel* 3:5), ἐὰν μὴ πρότερόν τις ἀποταξάμενος τῇ ἁμαρτίᾳ ἐξομολογήσηται περὶ τῶν προημαρτημένων, διὰ τοῦτο γέγραπται· 'ἐξομολογησόμεθα καὶ ἐπικαλεσόμεθα τὸ ὄνομά σου' (270, 3-7). For further differences in the themes, see L. Perrone, '*Ne corrumpas*' (2016).

[89] Eusebius, *Commentaria in Psalmos* 74, 2: ἐκ προσώπου δὲ τῶν δικαίων τὴν καταρχὴν ποιεῖται εἰπών· 'Ἐξομολογησόμεθά σοι, ὁ Θεὸς, ἐξομολογησόμεθά σοι, καὶ ἐπικαλεσόμεθα τὸ ὄνομά σου' (*Ps.* 74:2). Μόνοις γὰρ αὐτοῖς πρέπει ἡ εὐχαριστήριος ἐξομολόγησις. [...] Ἐπειδὴ διττός ἐστιν ὁ τῆς ἐξομολογήσεως τρόπος, ἀναγκαίως δεύτερον εἴρηται ἐπὶ τοῦ παρόντος τό, "Ἐξομολογησόμεθά σοι'· τοῦ μὲν πρώτου, ὡς εἰκός, ἐφ' ἁμαρτίας τὴν ἐξομολόγησιν δηλοῦντος, τοῦ δ' ἑξῆς τὴν ἐφ' οἷς εὖ πεπόνθασιν οἱ τὸ πρῶτον ἐξομολογησάμενοι εὐχαριστίαν (PG 23, 868B-C).

goes his own way of interpretation and sets different accents.[90] For instance, in v. 7 ('At your rebuke, O God of Jacob, those mounted on horses became drowsy') he displays his biblical learning of 'bad and good horses' in the Scripture, whereas Origen is interested only in the symbolic equivalence of 'horse' = 'body'.[91] On the contrary, Jerome ignores this and does not quote, as the Alexandrian, *Ps.* 32:17a ('Unreliable is a horse for deliverance'), a verse he will refer to when commenting in a similar fashion on *Ps.* 146:10a ('To the dominance of the horse he will not be disposed').[92] Interestingly, to further emphasise the diversity between the two preachers, Jerome does not use v. 2 ('God is known in Judea; in Israel his name is great') for his polemics against Israel and Judaism. Conversely, Origen criticises the pretensions of the 'chosen people' to the land of Judah and the city of Jerusalem as the 'place of God', thus extending polemical implications to v. 3.[93]

Ps. 76 was the object of four sermons by the Alexandrian. These should be reckoned among the most beautiful of the newly discovered homilies, since they meditate on the mystery of God and his providential design through creation and redemption, discreetly hinting at the final salvation of humankind.[94] Jerome's *Tractatus* is, for the most part, rather cursory and the contacts with Origen seem, at best, to be scanty or non-existent. The available text lacks remarks on the title of the psalm, whereas the Alexandrian indicates Asaph as the author and Idithoun as its singer,[95] an explanation corresponding to what we read, on the other hand, in the *Commentarioli*.[96] Perhaps, instead of looking for echoes of Origen, it is better to focus on Jerome's particular approach, which is not devoid of interesting insights. Among other aspects, we can see that he exploits his recourse to the Hebrew to describe the condition of the sinner and his relationship with God.[97] This illustrates a distinctive accent in

---

[90] G. Coppa in Origene-Gerolamo, *74 Omelie* (1993), 158-60 tries, as usual, to use *Fragmenta in Psalmos*, but most of them are *scholia* by Evagrius.

[91] Origenes, *Homilia in Psalmum 75* 6: 'Ἀπὸ ἐπιτιμήσεώς σου, ὁ θεὸς Ἰακώβ, ἐνύσταξαν οἱ ἐπιβεβηκότες τοῖς ἵπποις'. Τροπικῶς πολλαχοῦ τῆς γραφῆς ὁ ἵππος τὸ σῶμα λέγεται (287, 8-9).

[92] *Cf.* respectively Hieronymus, *Tractatus in Psalmos* 75, 7 (51, 59-52, 84) and *ibid.* 146, 10 (334, 176-335, 200).

[93] See, for instance, Origenes, *Homilia in Psalmum 75* 2: Ἰουδαῖοι μὲν τόπον ζητείτωσαν τοῦ θεοῦ, τὴν πεπτωκυῖαν, τὴν κάτω Ἰερουσαλήμ, περὶ ἧς εἴρηκεν· 'ἰδοὺ ἀφίεται ὑμῖν ὁ οἶκος ὑμῶν' (*Matt.* 23:38) (281, 14-5).

[94] See L. Perrone, 'Scrittura e cosmo' (2017).

[95] Origenes, *Homiliae in Psalmum 76* I, 1: Ὁ μὲν γράψας τὸν ψαλμὸν ἦν ὁ Ἀσάφ, εἷς τῶν προφητῶν τυγχάνων· ᾧ δὲ ἔδωκεν αὐτὸν γράψας ἦν ὁ Ἰδιθούμ, τεταγμένος ἐπὶ τῷ ὑμνεῖν τὸν θεόν, ἵν' ἐκεῖνος λαβὼν ἀπὸ τοῦ Ἀσὰφ ἀνυμνῇ τὸν θεόν (294, 1-4).

[96] Hieronymus, *Commentarioli in Psalmos* 76, 1: *'In finem, pro Idithun'. In hebraeo 'per Idithun' habet: ut significet, non pro eo, sed per eum psalmum fuisse cantatum. Quod autem sequitur, 'Asaph psalmus', in ueteribus exemplaribus non habetur* (218, 1-4).

[97] *Id., Tractatus in Psalmos* 76, 4a: *In hebraico aliter habet: 'Memor fui Dei, et conturbatus sum'. Consideraui mansuetudinem ipsius, consideraui pietatem, consideraui immunditiam: et*

his interpretation, which at times seems to focus more on the meditation on personal faults than on the mystery of God and his mercy towards man. For instance, in v. 6 ('I considered days of old, and years of long ago I remembered and meditated') the awareness of his own sins first inspires Jerome's rethinking of the history of salvation,[98] and although his mind, then, is totally given to God with v. 7 ('at night I would commune with my heart, and I would probe my spirit'), this thinking results in questioning the fall of man and his ejection from paradise.[99] Yet, in the end, God's mercy wins over his wrath, an idea that was obviously common to the two authors.[100]

However, the diversity of Jerome's approach also emerges in v. 19 ('A voice of your thunder was in the wheel; your lightnings gave light to the world; the earth shook and was set atremble'), a passage that elicits from Origen a complex interpretation, literal as well as allegorical, on 'the thunder in the wheel'.[101] To clarify the image of the 'wheel', Jerome quotes, like Origen, *Ezek.* 1:16 ('And the aspect of the wheels was like the aspect of tharsis, and the four had one likeness, and their construction was just as if a wheel was within a wheel'), but he resorts to a different explanation. First, he sees the 'thunder' as the sound of Christ's message throughout the world. Then, he speaks of the 'two wheels' of Ezekiel as the Old and New Testament, after adding a more specific interpretation of the 'wheel' as referring to the 'inner man' or 'the saint'. At this point, at least, one might wonder whether Jerome was influenced by the *4th Homily on Ps. 76*.[102] But, once again, we note that the two authors rely on

---

uidens me ipsum immundum, uehementer conturbabar (56, 49-53); *ibid.* 76, 5: '*Anticipauerunt uigilias oculi mei*'. *In hebraeo aliter habet*: '*Prohibebam suspectum oculorum meorum, constupebam et non loquebar*' (*Ps.* 49:16). *Quod dicit, hoc est: considerans peccata mea, oculos ad caelum erigere non audebam.* '*Peccatori enim dixit Deus: Vtquid tu enarras iustitias meas? Propterea stupebam, timebam, loqui non poteram* (56, 56-61); *ibid.* 76, 11: *In hebraeo aliter habet*: '*Et dixi, inbecillitas mea*' *hoc est, quod patior, non est de crudelitate Dei, sed de peccatis meis* (58, 93-5).

[98] *Ibid.* 76, 6: '*Cogitaui dies antiquos, et annos aeternos in mente habui*'. *Quantum pro peccatis meis est, desperabam, et renuerat consolari anima mea. Coepi cogitare ab initio mundi, quando hominem fecit Deus, usque ad annum meum, ab Adam usque ad tempus meum* (57, 71-5). *Cf.* Origenes, *Homiliae in Psalmum 76* I, 9: 'Διελογισάμην ἡμέρας ἀρχαίας καὶ ἔτη αἰώνια ἐμνήσθην καὶ ἐμελέτησα' (Ps 76, 6)· ὁ βουλόμενος ὠφελεῖσθαι καὶ τὰς ἀρχαίας ἡμέρας διαλογίζεται ἀρξάμενος ἀπὸ τοῦ Ἀδάμ· τί γέγονε τῷ Ἀδάμ, τί συμβέβηκε τῷ Κάϊν, τί πέπρακται τῷ Ἐνώχ, τί ἀποβέβηκε τῷ Νῶε καί, φέρ' εἰπεῖν, ὅλας τὰς ἡμέρας τὰς ἀρχῆθεν ἐκλογιζόμενος τὸν νοῦν ἐξετάζει τῶν πραγμάτων τῶν ἀναγεραμμένων γεγονέναι ἐν προτέραις ἡμέραις (308, 9-14).

[99] Hieronymus, *Tractatus in Psalmos 76*, 8: '*Numquid in aeternum proiciet Deus?*' *Haec erat tota cogitatio mea. Deus hominem fecit de terra, et repromisit ei uitam aeternam; quomodo ergo de paradiso eiectus est, de regno Dei?* (57, 83-58, 86).

[100] *Ibid.* 10b: '*Aut continebit in ira misericordias suas?*': *Non potuit pulchrius dicere. Quam diu se teneat ut non misereatur, tamen uincit illum misericordia sua* (58, 90-2).

[101] Origenes, *Homiliae in Psalmum 76* IV, 2 (342, 19 ff.).

[102] Compare Hieronymus, *Tractatus in Psalmos 76*, 19 with Origenes, *Homiliae in Psalmum 76* IV, 3.

a set of different scriptural passages and develop their own particular motives. While Origen appeals to *Matt.* 6:5 to support his idea of the saint as 'round', that is, perfect, Jeromes introduces an ascetical perspective: like a wheel only partially touching the ground and moving forward, so the saint contents himself with few earthly goods and advances upwards to heaven.[103] Consequently, the modest similarities that one also detects in the comments to this verse confirm the general impression about this *Tractatus*: whether Jerome was acquainted with these homilies of Origen or not, he does not depend on them, either directly or indirectly.

The case of the *Tractatus* on *Ps.* 77 appears to be less negative, in spite of the fact that Jerome comments on a very short portion of this quite long psalm (only fifteen of seventy-two verses), while Origen devotes to it the longest series of his homilies on the Psalter (nine sermons!).[104] To begin with, both authors share the view of the 'mystical' character of *Ps.* 77, an idea that even prompted Jerome to introduce two 'prologues' (also as an apology for his selective treatment): after the proper preface at the beginning,[105] he has, again, a sort of hermeneutic prolegomenon before commenting on v. 9 ('Ephraim's sons, though bending and shooting their bows, were turned back on a day of war').[106] This certainly mirrors the importance the two exegetes accorded to this verse, even if their heresiological polemics reflect a different urgency and different aims.[107] In the wake of the Alexandrian – who commented on v. 9 in the

---

[103] Hieronymus, *Tractatus in Psalmos* 76, 19: *Rota modico quodam uestigio stat in terra, et non solum stat, sed quasi percurrit: non stat, sed tangit et praeterit; denique cum uoluitur, semper ad altiora conscendit. Ita et sanctus uir, quoniam in corpore est, necessitatem habet aliqua de terrenis cogitare; et quando uenerit ad uictum et uestitum et cetera huiusmodi, his contentus est tangens terram, et ad altiora festinat* (61, 185-91).

[104] Lorenzo Perrone, 'Origen's Interpretation of the Psalter Revisited: The Nine Homilies on Psalm 77(78) in the Munich Codex', *ASE* 36 (2019), 135-58.

[105] Hieronymus, *Tractatus in Psalmos* 77: *Praecipit scriptura diuina, quando ad diuitis prandium inuitati fuerimus, cum intelligentia mittamus manum nostram ad epulas* (Prov. 23:1). *Igitur et nobis diuitis prandium praepositum scripturarum est. Venimus in pratum, habet flores plurimos* [...] *si rosam colligimus, lilium relinquimus; si lilium tulerimus, uiolae nobis supersunt. Ita et in septuagesimo septimo psalmo, qui mysticus est et sacramentis plurimis inuolutus, quamcumque aspexeris litteram, flores sunt, flores diuersi, et non possumus totos eligere. Eligamus autem omne quod possumus* (64, 1-11). For the image of the 'meadow', see A. Capone, '*Folia vero in verbis sunt*' (2013), 445-6.

[106] Hieronymus, *Tractatus in Psalmos* 77, 9: *O quanta mysteria, o quanti flores. Non dico dies, sed totus mensis ad intellegentiam istius psalmi non potest sufficere. In singulis uerbis sensus sunt. Habemus et thesaurum in uasis fictilibus* (2Cor. 4:7)..., *hoc est in uerbis rusticis scripturarum* (69, 151-60).

[107] On the heresiological discourse of *Homiliae in Psalmos* see Alain Le Boulluec, 'La polémique contre les hérésies dans les *Homélies sur les Psaumes* d'Origène (*Codex Monacensis Graecus* 314)', *Adamantius* 20 (2014), 266-73; M. Simonetti, 'Leggendo le *Omelie*' (2016), 456-61. Jerome, on the one hand, evokes more directly the historical episodes of the schism and, on the other, denounces the philosophical connections of the heretics: *Dicat aliquis: Quare fecerunt uitulos aureos? Noster thesaurus repositus est in uasis fictilibus. Ecclesiastici enim rustici sunt*

magnificent *2nd Homily on Psalm 77* – Jerome also has recourse to *Hos.* 7:11 ('And Ephraim was like a dove, silly without heart') in order to interpret the 'sons of Ephraim' historically as the schismatic tribes of Israel and, allegorically, as the heretics. But he does not comment on the whole pericope of *Hos.* 7:11-8:11 in detail, as Origen did. He nevertheless explains the following verses (*Ps.* 77:10-2) according to the same interpretive key, whereas his vindication of a coherent explanation by means of an allegorical interpretation seem to echo the analogous statement of Origen dealing with the text of Hosea.[108]

Due to these parallels, we are allowed to assume that Jerome also knew the *1st Homily on Psalm 77*, in which Origen discusses the erroneous attribution of *Ps.* 77:2 ('I will open my mouth in a parable; I will utter problems from of old') to 'the prophet Isaiah' instead of Asaph in *Matt.* 13:35, according to many Gospel manuscripts. For both the Alexandrian and Jerome, the substitution of the name of the prophet was due to the ignorance of the copyists. However, Origen exploited this mistake for his polemics against those who, like the Marcionites, dared to interpolate the text of the Scripture. In turn, Jerome adds other similar cases of errors made by copyists in the text of the Gospels, rejecting, by the way, the critique by Porphyry of *Matt.* 13:35. He thus demonstrates his concern for the use of the prophetical *testimonia* in the New Testament, as we know from his commentaries on the Prophets elsewhere. Finally, Jerome and Origen agree on the change of *prosopa*: respectively, Christ (vv. 1b-2) in the initial verses and, starting with v. 3a, a collective subject, which Jerome simply identifies with the apostles.[109] The Alexandrian is, at first, less assertive than Jerome, but subsequently he too indicates the apostles as the *prosopon to legon*,[110] so that this further feature might enable us to recognise this *Tractatus* as an interesting example of a 'counterpoint' to Origen.

---

et simplices: omnes uero haeretici Aristotelici et Platonici sunt. Denique ut sciatis quoniam omnis eloquentia saecularis aurum dicitur, hoc est, quoniam lingua eorum quasi propter splendorem aurum dicitur: 'Calix aureus Babylon in manu Domini' *(Jer.* 51:7). *Videte quid dicat, Babylon confusionis. Ergo mundus iste calix aureus est. De hoc calice aureo omnes gentes propinantur* (70, 198-71, 4).

[108] Hieronymus, *Tractatus in Psalmos* 77, 9: *Dicat aliquis, nostram esse sententiam. Videamus consequentia* (71, 213-4); *ibid.* 77, 13-4: *Vim facis scripturae: simpliciter enim dicitur de populo Israhel, quando eductus est de terra Aegypti* (71, 226-7). See Origenes, *Homiliae in Psalmum* 77 II, 5: Ἀλλ' ἔστω ἡμᾶς, ὡς ὑπονοῆσαι ἄν τις ἀκούων τῶν τοιούτων διηγήσεων, βεβιάσθαι τὸ ῥητὸν τοῦτο ἀναφέροντας καὶ ἐξομαλίζοντας αὐτὸ ἐπὶ τοὺς ἀπὸ τῶν αἱρέσεων (375, 1-3).

[109] Hieronymus, *Tractatus in Psalmos* 77, 3: *'Quanta audiuimus et cognouimus eas'. Hos uersiculos 'Adtendite, populus meus, legem meam' usque in istum uersiculum 'Eloquar propositiones ab initio' ex persona Xpisti dicuntur, ipse Saluator loquitur. Iam ceteros uersiculos usque ad finem psalmi ex persona apostolorum debemus accipere* (68, 107-11).

[110] Origenes, *Homiliae in Psalmum* 76 I, 3: ἀλλά τινα λέγει τὸ πρόσωπον τὸ προφητικὸν περὶ αὐτοῦ καὶ τῶν ἀπὸ τοῦ λαοῦ ἢ ἁπλῶς πλῆθος καὶ ἐκκλησία λέγει τὰ ἑξῆς. Ταῦτα μὲν εἰς τὸ καθᾶραι τὸ λέγον πρόσωπον (356, 10-2); *ibid.*, I, 7: Καὶ ταῦτα μὲν τὰ ὑπὸ τοῦ σωτῆρος

Although well disposed to encourage such an impression, we should pay attention to the personal note which Jerome introduces just at the conclusion of this homily. Once more, it is proof of a Christian 'philo-Judaism', if we may use this notion somewhat paradoxically to characterise Jerome's more benevolent attitude toward the Jews, in spite of his anti-Judaic agenda.[111] Here, he also represents the traditional attacks against a 'Jewish' reading of the Scriptures, which, in his eyes, is merely a historical reading devoid of the Spirit of God. However, at the same time, he, along with Paul (*Rom.* 11), warns the faithful not to take for granted their being chosen in place of the Old Israel, and transforms the final prayer of the homily into a prayer for the salvation of the Jews.

Credite mihi: quotienscumque uideo synagogas, semper illud habeo in mente, quod dicitur ab apostolo, quoniam non debemus exultare super oliuam cuius fracti sunt rami, sed timere; quoniam si rami naturales praecisi sunt, quanto magis nos, qui inserti sumus de oleastro, timeamus ne fiamus sicut patres nostri [...] Ego synagogas eorum nihil aliud intellego, nisi sepulcra in deserto. Lege libros ueteres. Oremus autem Dominum, ut et ista sepulcra resurgant. Si enim filii Abrahae facti sunt lapides, filii Adam, qui mortui sunt, possunt resurgere, si uoluerit Iesus. Licet enim mortui sunt et iacent in sepulcra, etiamsi quatriduani sunt, etiam si foetent, potest eis dicere Iesus: 'Lazare, ueni foras' (John 11:43).[112]	'Believe me: every time I see a synagogue, it always comes to my mind what the Apostle said. For we should not exult over the olive tree whose branches have been broken, but we should fear. If the natural branches have been cut, how much we, who have been taken from a wild olive tree, should fear that it may happen to us what happened to our fathers [...] I regard their synagogues as sepulchres in the desert. Read the ancient books. Let's then pray to the Lord that these sepulchres may also be resurrected. In fact, if the sons of Abraham became like stones, the sons of Adam, who are dead, can be resurrected, provided that Jesus wants it. Even if they are dead and lie in the sepulchre, even if they are dead for four days, even if they stink, Jesus can tell them: "Lazarus, come out"'.

This theme is totally absent in the homilies of Origen, who does not even quote the Pauline passages on the rest of Israel and its salvation in *Rom.* 11, contrary to Jerome, as we can observe once more in the *Tractatus* on *Ps.* 80. Here, commenting on v. 16 ('The enemies of the Lord lied to him, and their season will be forever'), he wonders whether the Jews shall perish and addresses himself to God, asking: 'Why did you make promises to the fathers and do

εἰρημένα, ἀποκρίνονται <δὲ> οἱ ἀπόστολοι πρὸς αὐτὸν καὶ οἱ μαθηταὶ πάντες αὐτοῦ. Καὶ ἐκ προσώπου αὐτῶν ταῦτα λέγεται· 'ὅσα ἠκούσαμεν καὶ ἔγνωμεν αὐτά' (*Ps.* 77:3a) (364, 20-2).

[111] See, for instance, Régis Courtray, '"Que son sang retombe sur nous et sur nos enfants". L'exégèse de Matthieu 27:25 chez saint Jérôme', in Jean-Marie Auwers, Régis Burnet and Didier Luciani (eds), *L'antijudaïsme des Pères. Mythe et/ou réalité? Actes du colloque de Louvain-la-Neuve (20-22 mai 2015)* (Paris, 2017), 151-8.

[112] Hieronymus, *Tractatus in Psalmos* 77, 15 (73, 278-93).

not fulfil them for their children?' The answer comes in the quotation of *Rom.* 11:25-6: in the future, the Jews will also believe.[113] Furthermore, the extent to which Jerome was concerned with the destiny of the chosen people is also proved by the *Tractatus* on *Ps.* 105 and 108. In both cases, he extrapolates a prayer for the salvation of the Jews, since he interprets *Ps.* 105:4-5 ('Remember us, O Lord, in the good pleasure of your people; regard us in your deliverance, that we may look at the kindness of your chosen ones, that we may be glad in the gladness of your nation, that we may be commended with your heritage') as a prayer made by David on behalf of the *uetus Israel*, that he too may participate in the grace of Christ.[114] In the *Tractatus* on *Ps.* 108, it is Jesus himself who prays on the cross for the Jews and, in this way, establishes for us the model we should follow: instead of condemning the Jews, we should pray 'for our roots'![115]

4. By way of conclusion: Jerome's profile in the *Tractatus in Psalmos*

The cases that I have examined have proved that the image of the *Tractatus* as a 'counterpoint' to the preaching of Origen is only partially valid.[116] The exegesis of the Psalter by Jerome definitively avoids the accusation of being

---

[113] *Ibid.* 80, 16: *Sed isti inimici qui negaturi sunt eum, ergo perient? Ergo reliquiae non erunt? Et quomodo iurasti Abrahae, Isaac et Iacob, quoniam semen ipsorum sit quasi stellae caeli et sicut arena maris? Quare promisisti patribus et non reddis filiis? 'Inimici Domini negabunt eum'* (*Ps.* 80:16a). *Sed quid dicit? 'Et erit tempus eorum in saeculum. Cum introierit plenitudo gentium, tunc omnis Israel saluus fiet'* (*Rom.* 11:25-6). *In futuro credent, modo non crediderunt. Nunc dicam ad Iudaeos. Solent enim sibi adplaudere et dicere: 'Et erit tempus eorum in aeternum'* (*Ps.* 80:16b). *Nos dicamus: Verum est, credituri enim sunt de Iudaeis* (81, 182-91).

[114] *Ibid.* 105, 4: *propterea ergo rogo, quoniam ego prius natus sum in ueteri lege, ut inputes mihi mercedem cum nouo populo* (194, 54-6); *ibid.,* 105, 5: *Hoc est ut cum euangelio et nos habeamus partem, qui in ueteri lege facti sumus. Abraham enim pater noster uidit diem tuum, et gauisus est* (see *John* 8:56). *Videamus ergo et nos, et gaudeamus cun hereditate tua* (194, 67-70).

[115] *Ibid.* 108, 29: *Non dicit contra Iudaeos, sed pro ipsis dicit. Creator enim est et illorum et noster: non eos omnino eradicauit [...] Nos in radicem ipsorum inserti sumus, nos rami sumus, illi radix. Non debemus maledicere radicibus, sed debemus orare pro radicibus nostris. Qui inserti sumus in radicem deprecemur Dominum, ut sicuti rami salui sunt, sic et radix saluetur. Forte aliquis dicat: Tu pro Iudaeis oras, pro blasphemis? Oro Dominum pro ipsis: si enim ipse persecutorum suorum miseretur, quanto magis mei miseretur?* (220, 343-53).

[116] Hieronymus' *Tractatus in Psalmos* 80 and 81 do not modify this impression. On *Ps.* 80:7 ('He removed his back from burdens; his hands slaved at the basket') both exegeses agree on the interpretation of the baskets in Egypt and its connection with the miracle of multiplication. Presumably, Jerome has Origen's *Homiliae in Psalmum 80* I, 8 in mind, if not at hand. He stresses the mystery of the multiplication and adds a *quaestio* to emphasise the necessity of a spiritual interpretation. Origen only hints at the *quaestio*, but Jerome formulates and resolves it, after criticising the literalists: *Requiro a te, qui tantum litteram sequeris: in deserto loco non inueniuntur nisi quinque panes, et duodecim cophini quomodo inueniuntur? Si desertus erat locus, utique duodecim cophinos habere non poterat* (79, 124-5).

more or less a plagiarism of the Alexandrian. It is no longer a question of some
'spices' in the 'dough' provided by Origen, as Jean Gribomont vividly put it.
In fact, Jerome is able to introduce into the interpretation of the Psalms a
personal agenda and his own sensitivities. We could even say that, in spite of
his mostly cursory and, at first glance, simple-looking comments, the learned
biblical scholar is, to some extent, more present in the preaching of Jerome,
thanks especially to his frequent recourse to the Hebrew text, his propensity
for etymologies and the display of historical erudition nurtured by the Bible.
Moreover, the fact that Jerome does not rely on Origen alone, but now and then
has recourse to other commentators on the Psalter, is additional proof of independence. Among these interpreters, we have pointed in particular to Eusebius
of Caesarea, but we should not forget Didymus. Apart from these two Greek
authors, we are allowed to surmise on the influence of other mediators of the
eastern patristic exegesis to the Latin world, such as Hilary of Poitiers, Eusebius of Vercelli and Ambrose. Regarding this aspect, however, there is certainly
a need for further study.

The historical and personal situation in which Origen and Jerome preached
on the Psalter was deeply different. The Alexandrian was still engaged in a
battle for preserving the Christian Bible endowed with the two Testaments and
protecting the Church from doctrinal deviation through heresies, while strength-
ening the moral vigour and spiritual solidity inside the Christian communities
against the many challenges coming from outside. On the contrary, Jerome
lived in a time marked by the triumph of Christianity and yet troubled by doctrinal problems and ecclesiastical quarrels. As a response to this new context,
his exegesis of the Psalter mirrored the monastic experience in which he was
personally engaged, with its ascetic ideals and difficulties, far from the rosily
optimistic view of monasticism. Not incidentally, the awareness of the sinful
condition of man and the need for repentance in order to reconcile with God
constitute a dominating note in the texts of the monk of Bethlehem. And the
fact that he lived in the Holy Land, and was himself in touch with Jews in
everyday life, certainly contributed to the particular emphasis on their future
salvation.

The Memorisation of the Bible
among the Egyptian Clergy and Monks

Przemysław PIWOWARCZYK, Katowice, Poland

ABSTRACT

There is no doubt that the Bible constituted the very fundament of monastic and clerical life, and is omnipresent in Egyptian monastic literature. These texts give us the impression that repetition from memory, especially in the context of daily *melete*, was one of the main ways, if not the central one, for monks to have contact with the Scriptures. This paper scrutinises the evidence from late Christian Egypt to show the extent, the ways, and the limits of memorisation. First of all, however, it shows that the different authors and source corpora pay unequal attention to memorisation skills. To check the literary sources, the paper uses data obtained from documentary ostraca originating in Western Thebes, which give us the specific books and the periods in which those books were expected to be memorised. The calculations made on this basis, coupled with other pieces of information dispersed throughout various categories of sources, allow us to conclude that memorisation required written texts which were not always at hand, that the extent of the memorised Bible only rarely reached beyond the Psalter and some New Testament books, and that the omnipresence of Biblical references in the monastic literature does not necessarily reflect the average level of Biblical mastery, but rather belongs to the erudite framework of the Christian (and especially monastic) literary production.

That the Bible permeates Egyptian monastic literature is a banal fact and there is no need to discuss it any further. However, the question about the correspondence between the literature and past reality, or between *réalité narrative* and *réalité vécue*, as Ewa Wipszycka calls those two levels of the retrievable past,[1] is worth addressing, since there seems to be serious scratches on the picture of monastic versatility in the Bible. I aim to investigate only a small fraction of the problem that is the issue of the memorisation of the Scriptures,[2]

---

[1] See, for example, Ewa Wipszycka, 'The Nag Hammadi Library and the Monks: A Papyrologist's Point of View', *JJP* 30 (2000), 189. Wipszycka makes use of this distinction in many of her studies.

[2] The only wider reflection on the memorisation of the Scriptures in ancient monasticism known to me is Lorenzo Perrone, 'Scripture for a Life of Perfection. The Bible in Late Antique Monasticism: The Case of Palestine', in Lorenzo DiTommaso and Lucian Turcescu (eds), *The Reception and Interpretation of the Bible in Late Antiquity. Proceedings of the Montréal Colloquium in*

Studia Patristica CIII, 87-98.
© Peeters Publishers, 2021.

as it is commonly held that repetition from memory[3] was the main way by which monks approached the holy word. This issue could be expressed in more precise questions:

1. Do the references to memorisation have the same value in all the sources?
2. What was the extent of the memorised Bible?
3. How did the monks memorise?
4. And, finally, what were the limits of memorisation?

In my paper, I would like to touch briefly upon all of those questions. I do not limit its scope to monks only, because the source material dealing with non-monastic clergy provides very useful comparanda, and allows us to see monastic memorisation from a slightly wider perspective. We have to keep in mind, however, that virtually no sources present the point of view of the laity, so the results of my investigation are not valid for Egyptian Christians in general.

1. Source bias

Knowing the whole Bible, or extensive parts of it, by heart is a *topos* of hagiographical narratives on the great monks. However, such accounts are not evenly spread over the genres and authors, but rather appear in clusters. One of the most important and earliest sources is the *Historia Lausiaca* by Palladius. Five monks who are characterised by their knowledge of the entire Bible by heart appear in this work. According to this author, they were Ammonios, one of the Tall Brothers,[4] Marc the Ascetic from Scetis,[5] Serapion, called Sindonite,[6] Paphnutius Kephalas,[7] and the anachorite Solomon from the neighbourhood of Antinoe;[8] the Coptic *Palladiana* adds Macarius of Alexandria to the list.[9]

Honour of Charles Kannengiesser 11-13 October 2006 (Leiden, Boston, 2008), 393-417 (on memorisation, see esp. 404-5). Perrone limits his interest to Palestinian monasticism, although he refers repeatedly to the work of Palladius.

[3] The most common terms which refer to memorisation or repetition from memory are ἀποστη-θίζω (and derivations) in Greek, ⲁⲡⲟⲥⲧⲏⲑⲓⲍⲉ (verb) and ⲁⲡⲟⲥⲧⲏⲑⲟⲩⲥ (common noun) in Coptic and خَفِظَ (ḥafiẓa) in Arabic. Naturally, memorisation could also be expressed by more general terms or paraphrases. The Greek verb ἀποστηθίζω has a double meaning, denoting both learning by heart and repetition from memory. There is limited evidence for its usage; it occurs mainly in the monastic sources from Palestine: the letters of Barsanuphius and John, *Historia monachorum in Aegypto* and the *Apophthegmata* (the latter two deal with Egyptian monasticism). The Greek μελετάω and μελέτη (and Coptic ⲙⲉⲗⲉⲧⲁ) refer to recitation from memory, but not to memorisation. In Arabic, it roughly corresponds to تلا (talā).

[4] Palladius, *Historia Lausiaca* 11, 4.
[5] *Ibid.* 18, 25.
[6] *Ibid.* 37, 1.
[7] *Ibid.* 47, 3.
[8] *Ibid.* 58, 1.
[9] *Four Desert Fathers*, Macarius of Alexandria 16, trans. Tim Vivian (Crestwood, 2004), 156.

The Pachomian monks from Tabennesi also strived to master the whole Bible by heart.[10] Interestingly, Palladius does not mention this feature in his account of Didymus the Blind[11] and Evagrius.[12] To this, we may add Heron who recited Isaiah, part of Jeremiah, 15 Psalms, the "Great Psalm" (*Ps.* 118 LXX), Proverbs, Hebrews and part of Luke during the journey.[13]

The late Coptic hagiographies, mainly preserved in Arabic translation, share a predilection for the memorisation of extensive parts of the Bible as proof of sanctity. I give below the list of monks and bishops (with special focus on the bishops of Alexandria) to whom hagiographical sources ascribe the memorisation of the Bible.[14]

Serapion, a monk from Scetis[15]	The books of the Church
Elias of Bishwaw[16]	30 books
Monks from the Shenoutean congregation[17]	Jeremiah, Ezekiel
Psote, Bishop of Psoi[18]	All the books of the Scriptures
Constantin, Bishop of Syout[19]	The Prophets (Minor and Major), the Psalter, the four Gospels, the Acts, the Apostolos, the Katholikon
Pesynthius, Bishop of Coptos (Sahidic Life)[20]	Jeremiah, Ezekiel

---

[10] Palladius, *Historia Lausiaca* 32, 12.

[11] However, Palladius (*Historia Lausiaca* 4, 2) notes that 'he interpreted the Old and New Testament word by word', trans. W. Lowther Clarke, *The Lausiac History of Palladius* (New York, 1918), 52. See Socrates Scholasticus, *Historia Ecclesiastica* IV 25, 6: Οὐ μὴν ἀλλὰ καὶ τὰ θεῖα λόγια παλαιᾶς καὶ καινῆς διαθήκης οὕτως ἀκριβῶς ἐγνώκει, ὥστε πολλὰ μὲν ἐκδοῦναι βιβλία.

[12] The only reference to knowing the Scripture by heart, a reference to *melete* on the prophets, is to be found in the Coptic version. See *Four Desert Fathers*, Evagrius 24, trans. Vivian (2004), 86.

[13] Palladius, *Historia Lausiaca* 26, 3. Palladius gives only the texts Heron recited during the journey, not the full extent of his Biblical mastery.

[14] Besides the historical figures about whom we have some knowledge, the martyr St. Kolluthos was also believed to have memorised much of the Bible: *Le synaxaire arabe Jacobite (rédaction copte)*, IV, *Les mois de barmahat, barmoudah et bachons*, ed. René Basset, PO 16 (Paris, 1922), 412 [1054].

[15] *Le Synaxaire arabe jacobite (rédaction copte)*, I, *Les mois de Tout et de Babeh*, ed. René Basset, PO 1 (Paris, 1907), 345 [131].

[16] *Le Synaxaire arabe jacobite (rédaction copte)*, II, *Les mois de Hatour et de Kihak*, ed. René Basset, PO 3 (Paris, 1909), 476 [400].

[17] *Life of Shenoute* 94-5.

[18] *The Teaching of Apa Psote, the Great Bishop of Psoi*, E.A. Wallis Budge (ed.), *Miscellaneous Coptic Texts in the Dialect of Upper Egypt* (London, 1915), 148 (text), 726 (trans.).

[19] René-Georges Coquin, 'Saint Constantin, évêque d'Asyut', *Studia Orientalia Christiana Collectanea* 16 (1981), 154 (text), 157 (trans.).

[20] *The Life of Bishop Pisentius*, by John the Elder, E.A. Wallis Budge (ed. and trans.), *Coptic Apocrypha in the Dialect of Upper Egypt* (London, 1913), 78 (text), 261-2 (trans.).

Pesynthius, Bishop of Coptos (Bohairic Life)[21]	The Psalter, the Minor Prophets, John
Pesynthius, Bishop of Coptos (Arabic Life)[22]	The Psalter, Isaiah, Jeremiah, the minor prophets, 12 books, 30 books
Demetrius, Bishop of Alexandria (189-231)[23]	The books of the Church and their explanations; all the books of the Church
Hierocles, Bishop of Alexandria (231-247)[24]	Gospel, Epistles
Theophilus, Bishop of Alexandria (384-412)[25]	The books of the Church and their explanations
Cyril, Monk of Scetis and later Bishop of Alexandria (412-444)[26]	All the holy books
Andronicus, Bishop of Alexandria (616-622?)[27]	The books of the Church
Benjamin, Bishop of Alexandria[28]	The books of the Church

We can see that in this kind of literature, in the majority of cases knowing the Bible belongs to the reality of narrative and serves as an element of legitimisation. In the profile of the Alexandrian patriarch, it constitutes a topos. However, other sources present a different position. In the life of the patriarch John the Almsgiver, Leontius also refers to his biblical knowledge, apparently polemicising with some critics about putting memorisation on a pedestal:

This saintly man had also a good knowledge of the holy Scriptures, not so much an accurate knowledge of the words through learning them by heart (which is but for vainglory), but by actually practising their precepts and keeping their commandments.[29]

---

[21] *Éloge de Pisentios évêque de Keft*, in Émile Amélineau (ed. and trans.), *Étude sur le christianisme en Égypte au septième siècle* (Paris, 1887), 75, 83-4.

[22] *The Arabic Life of S. Pisentius*, ed. De Lacy Evans O'Leary, PO 22 (Paris, 1930), 330, 336, 351, 365, 452, 462 [18, 24, 39, 53, 140, 150].

[23] *Le Synaxaire* (1907), 333 [119]; *Le Synaxaire* (1909), 275 [199]. In the account of the 12th Babeh (PO 1), I accept the reading of codex B كتب الكنيسة وتفاسيرها.

[24] *Le Synaxaire* (1909), 402 [326].

[25] *Le Synaxaire* (1907), 345 [131].

[26] *Le Synaxaire arabe jacobite*, V, *Les mois de baounah, abib, mesoré et jours complémentaires*, ed. René Basset, PO 17 (Paris, 1923), 617 [1159].

[27] *Le Synaxaire arabe jacobite (rédaction copte)*, III, *Les mois de Toubeh et d'Amchir*, ed. René Basset, PO 11 (Paris, 1915), 559 [525].

[28] *Ibid.* 561 [527].

[29] Leontius Neapolitanus, *Vita Joannis Eleemosynarii episcopi Alexandrini* 18: Εἶχεν μὲν οὖν γνῶσιν καὶ τῶν θείον γραφῶν ὁ ἐν ἁγίοις, οὐκ ἐν σοφίᾳ λόγου ταύτας ὡς ἀπὸ κενοδοξίας ἀποστηθίζων, ἀλλὰ δι' αὐτῆς τῆς τῶν ἔργων πράξεως καὶ τῆς τῶν ἐντολῶν τηρήσεως (trans. Elisabeth Dawes and Norman H. Baynes).

Interestingly, memorisation of the entire Bible was not always a sign of sanctity. The only figure to whom Epiphanius of Salamis attributes this extraordinary skill was the heretic Hieracas.[30]

Conversely, *The Sayings of the Desert Fathers* do not highlight the extensive memorisation of the Scriptures. They mention the Bible only in passing, usually commenting on prayer. Macarius the Egyptian recommends repeating from memory as an occupation for the time of fasting.[31] Serapion is shown reciting the Psalter and the Apostolos by heart.[32] An elsewhere unattested saying from the so-called anachorite grotto in Faras recounts apa Hatre reciting Numbers from memory.[33] In an anonymous saying, the whole-night synaxis constitutes the Psalter, Isaiah and Jeremiah (lit. 'the two great prophets').[34] The *Sayings* not only ignore the memorisation, but sometimes we even find pieces regarding it as a threat to spiritual values, as in the *Anonymous Collection*: 'Three brothers once visited an elder at Scete. One of them asked him: "Abba, I have learnt the Old and New Testament by heart …". "You have filled the air with words", said the elder in reply to him'.[35] Disregard may even refer to the Psalter: 'We have learned the Scriptures by heart; we have perfected [our knowledge of] David, and yet we do not possess what God is looking for, that is, fear, love, and humility'.[36] In another saying, the elder who knew 14 books by heart was overcome by one *logismos*.[37]

A very interesting difference exists between the Pachomian corpus, which gives explicit commandments about learning by heart (see below), and the much more extensive Shenoutean corpus, which does not have much to say about memorisation (although it mentions *melete* many times, without going deeper into its content). In the Shenoutean corpus, there are virtually no mentions of the ways and extent of memorisation.[38] This fact could hardly be accidental, and the working hypothesis might be that the Shenoutean congregation was more book-oriented and better furnished with such books.

[30] Epiphanius, *Panarion* 67, 1, 4.
[31] Macarius the Great 3.
[32] Serapion 1. Only the extent of the scriptural prayer is given.
[33] Francis L. Griffith, 'Oxford Excavations in Nubia', *AAA* 14 (1927), 87 (n. 17).
[34] N.150 (= *Collectio Systematica* 4, 70), in *The Anonymous Sayings of the Desert Fathers. A Select Edition and Complete English Translation*, ed. and trans. John Wortley (Cambridge, 2013), 102-3.
[35] N.385 (= *Collectio Systematica* 10, 147), in *The Anonymous Sayings* (2013), 246-7 (trans. John Wortley).
[36] *Collectio systematica* 10, 135: τὰς Γραφὰς ἐμάθομεν ἀπὸ στήθους, τὸν Δαυὶδ ἐτελέσαμεν, καὶ ἃ ζητεῖ ὁ Θεὸς οὐκ ἔχομεν, τουτέστι τὸν φόβον καὶ τὴν ἀγάπην καὶ τὴν ταπείνωσιν, ed. Jean-Claude Guy, *Les apophtegmes des pères. Collection systématique, chapitres x-xvi*, SCh 474 (Paris, 2003), 102.
[37] *Collectio systematica* 10, 149.
[38] The possible exception, *De vita monachorum* 23 (published in Johannes Leipold and Walter E. Crum (eds), *Sinuthii archimandritae vita et opera omnia*, vol. 4, CSCO 73, Scriptores Coptici 5 [Parisiis, 1913], 133), in fact, belongs to *The Regulations of Horsiesius*.

2. Extent of memorisation

Antony had already exhorted his disciples to memorise from the Scriptures, but most probably he meant short directions (παραγγέλματα), as explicitly mentioned in *Eph.* 4:26, not entire books.[39] The typical repertoire committed to memory is probably reflected in the *Encomium on Theodore the Anatolian*. Theodore and Claudius, two fictive ascetics and martyrs-to-be, recited 'passages from the Scriptures which they had learnt by heart, and psalms and prayers'.[40] Psalms already had a special status for Antony. We may safely assume that many monks, indeed, knew the Psalter by heart. It was regarded as elementary preparation for anarchorites, cenobitic monks and home ascetics as well.[41] Macarius the Egyptian recommends the Gospel (all four are probably meant) and other unspecified scriptures,[42] but certainly the Psalter was too obvious to mention. Psalms belonged to the requirements demanded from Pachomian monks, as witnessed in narrative sources and rules:

Whoever enters the monastery uninstructed shall be taught first what he must observe; and when, so taught, he has consented to it all, they shall give him twenty psalms or two of the Apostle's epistles, or some other part of the Scripture.[43]

'After that they will also be given psalms [to learn] by heart; and moreover they shall also learn from the other books of holy Scriptures'.[44]

Let us be wealthy in texts learned by heart. Let him who does not memorize much memorize at least ten sections (ⲙⲉⲣⲟⲥ) along with a section of the psalter; and let him who does not recite at night recite ten psalms or five of them with a section of texts learned by heart.[45]

As for the clergy, we cannot find in the extant canon collections any which would regard memorisation of the Bible as a prerequisite for ordination. However, the issue emerges in a fictive dialogue between Cyril and two deacons (Stephen and Anthimus) regarding a standard for the clergy:

---

[39] Athanasius, *Vita Antonii* 55.

[40] *The Encomium of Theodore, Archbishop of Antioch, on Theodore the General, the Anatolian*, in E.A.W. Budge (ed. and trans.), *Miscellaneous Coptic Texts* (1915), 13 (text), 589 (trans.). Note that, in the Coptic text, there is no mention of passages from the Scriptures – because of discontinuity in the Coptic text, it seems to be an error in the edition.

[41] Mina, évêque de Pchati, *Vie d'Isaac*, ed. Elisabeth Porcher, PO 11 (Paris, 1915), 307 [9], trans. David N. Bell, in Mena of Nikiou, *The Life of Isaac of Alexandria*, Cistercian Studies Series 107 (Kalamazoo, 1988), 44.

[42] *Apophthegmata Patrum. Appendices. De abbate Macario Aegyptio* 3 (PG 65, 264A): ἀπο-στήθιζε τοῦ Εὐαγγελίου καὶ τῶν ἄλλων Γραφῶν.

[43] *Praecepta* 139 (trans. Armand Veilleux). See also *Praecepta* 49; for Epiphanius of Mount Jeme reciting from Paul, see *The Life of S. Pisentius*, De Lacy E. O'Leary (ed.) (1930), 452 [140].

[44] *Vita Pachomii* S10: ⲙ̄ⲛ̄ⲛ̄ⲥⲱⲥ ⲇⲉ ⲟⲛ ⲉⲧ ⲛⲁⲩ ⲛ̄ϩⲉⲛⲯⲁⲗⲙⲟⲥ ⲛ̄ⲁⲡⲟⲥⲧⲏⲑⲟⲟⲩⲥ ⲁⲩⲱ ⲟⲛ ⲉⲧ[ⲣⲉⲩ]ϫⲓ ⲉⲃⲟⲗ ϩⲛ̄ⲛⲕⲉ[ϫⲱ]ⲱⲙⲉ ⲛ̄ⲧⲉⲅⲣⲁ[ⲫⲏ] ⲉⲧⲟⲩⲁⲁⲃ (trans. Armand Veilleux).

[45] *Regulae Horsiesii* 16 (trans. Armand Veilleux).

Stephen: "What is a distincitve feature of an ordained cleric?"
Cyril: "When you find him full of memorised (ⲁⲡⲟⲥⲧⲏⲑⲟⲩⲥ ⳍⲛ̄ⲧⲉⲅⲣⲁⲫⲏ) Scripture and love for the poor".[46]

However, all hinged upon the local bishops. At the beginning of the 7th century, Abraham, Bishop of Hermonthis, required a deacon and presbyter to recite one gospel from memory. Aphu, Bishop of Oxyrhynchus, was much more demanding at the turn of the 4th and 5th century. From a deacon, he expected the memorisation of 25 Psalms, two letters of Paul's and one Gospel; from a presbyter, Deuteronomy, Proverbs and Isaiah as well. The author of his *Life* emphasises the fact that only a few matched this high demand.[47] We might reasonably assume that the Gospel and some Psalms might have constituted a standard for a presbyter.

3. Ways of memorisation

Thanks to Palladius, we know that there was a kind of organised system of biblical education in Tabennesi.[48] In lauras and independent hermitages, it must have relied upon the elder teaching his disciples, but our sources are completely silent about this. In the *Synaxarium*, we have an account of anba Victor teaching his disciple Youna (Jonas) to read the Scripture, but we have no idea whether it corresponded to common practices.[49]

Interestingly, even though our sources almost unanimously appreciate memorisation, they tell us next to nothing about how it used to be practised. The most developed classical method based on linking ideas of phrases to imagined or physical places in space (*topoi*, *loci*), good for the memorisation of the argument in oratory pieces, must have been of limited use for long texts learnt verbatim.[50] Nonetheless, for a hermit spending most of his life in the familiar space of his cell, loci might have been a useful tool, especially in the psalmody, but we do not know if they were known and used.[51] The other method would

---

[46] *Der Papyruscodex saec. VI-VII der Phillippsbibliothek in Cheltenham. Koptische theologische Schriften*, ed. Walter E. Crum (Strassburg, 1915), 10; trans. by myself.

[47] Ed. Francesco Rossi, *Trascrizione di tre manoscritti copte del Museo Egizio di Torino con traduzione italiana* (Torino, 1885), 21; trans. Antonella Campagnano and Tito Orlandi, *Vita di Aphu*, in *Vite di monaci copti*, Collana di testi patristici 41 (Roma, 1984), 65.

[48] Palladius, *Historia Lausiaca* 32, 12: ἀποστηθίζουσι δὲ πάσας τὰς γραφάς. Such a system was probably also present in other monasteries of the koinonia.

[49] *Le Synaxaire* (1915), 518 [484].

[50] Jocelyn P. Small, *Wax tablets of the mind. Cognitive studies of memory and literacy in classical Antiquity* (London, New York, 1997), 72-103. The most relevant description of the method are Cicero, *De oratore* 2, 357-8; *Rhetorica ad Herennium* 3, 16, 29 - 3, 19, 32; Quintilian, *Institutio oratoria* 11, 2.

[51] The exhortations by Horsiesius (with reference to *Deut.* 11:18-20) might be read in the light of such practice, but hint at the biblical dipinti as well; see *Testamentum Horsiesii* 51. For *melete*

be appending a text already committed to memory with a melody, which was also possible and probably practised in the case of the psalms.[52] Even in such cases, to begin with, the monk needed access to the text which was to be memorised.

There are two imaginable ways of learning biblical passages – by sight or by ear. Interestingly, the Greek original and the Coptic translation of *The Life of Antony*, generally assumed to be very literal, show a difference in the passage dealing with this issue:

Indeed, he paid such close attention to the reading of Scripture that nothing in the Scriptures was wasted. He remembered everything with the result that for him memory took the place of books.[53]

Indeed, he paid such close attention to what was read in church that nothing in the Scriptures escaped his notice. He kept everything in his heart, with the result that in his heart memory took the place of books.[54]

Such a change can be explained, at best, by the assumption that the Coptic translator, very well versed in Greek, deliberately adapted the passage to the historical realities of his time. The *Life* was translated into Coptic in the 7th or even the 8th century.[55] The oldest surviving manuscript is dated to 822/823.[56] Does this mean that the translator imagined that it was possible to learn the Bible from liturgical readings? That was exactly what Athanasius originally meant, as he presented Antony as an illiterate peasant, but such an interpretation is not obvious from the passage itself. It could quite well be interpreted as presenting Antony reading in private.[57] The translator strived to solve this ambiguity. But it could also mean that he was aware of the scarcity of books, and regarded book-based memorisation as virtually impossible.

---

in the cell extended beyond the Psalter, see, for instance, John Cassian, *De institutis coenobiorum* 3, 2. In the ascetic treatise by Paul of Tammah, *On the cell*, there is no clue towards practising *topoi* in *melete*.

[52] See *The Encomium of Theodore*. The shepherd Psote recites the psalms from memory and his helper-shepherd Akripitta plays a kind of musical instrument (ΟΡΓΑΝΟΝ in Coptic). The scene is fictional, but the situation must have been somehow familiar to the (probably monastic) author of the encomium.

[53] Athanasius, *Vita Antonii* (Greek) 3, 7: Καὶ γὰρ προσεῖχεν οὕτω τῇ ἀναγνώσει, ὡς μηδὲν τῶν γεγραμμένων ἀπ᾽ αὐτοῦ πίπτειν χαμαί, πάντα δὲ κατέχειν καὶ λοιπὸν αὐτῷ τὴν μνήμην ἀντὶ βιβλίων γίνεσθαι (trans. Tim Vivian and Apostolos N. Athanassakis).

[54] Athanasius, *Vita Antonii* (Coptic) 3, 7: ΚΑΙΓΑΡ ΝΕϤϮ ΝϨΤΗϤ ϨΝΟΥⲰΡϪ ΕΝΕΤΟΥⲰϢ ⲘⲘΟΟΥ ϨΝΤΕΚΚΛΗⲤΙΑ ϨⲰⲤΤΕ ΕΤⲘΤΡΕΛΑΑΥ ϨΝΝΕΤⲤΗϨ ϪΕ ΕΒΟⲗ ⲚΤΟΟΤϤ·ΝΕϤϨΑΡΕϨ ⲆΕ ΕΡΟΟΥ ΤΗΡΟΟΥ ϨΡΑΙ ΝϨΗΤϤ ϨⲰⲤΤΕ ΕΤΡΕΠΕΥⲢⲡⲘΕΕΥΕ ϢⲰⲠΕ ϨⲘⲠΕϤϨΗΤ ΕⲡⲘΑ ΝΝϪⲰⲰⲘΕ (trans. Tim Vivian).

[55] Malcolm Choat, *The Life of Antony in Egypt*, in Blake Leyerle and Robin D. Young (eds), *Ascetic Culture: Essays in Honor of Philip Rousseau* (Notre Dame, IN, 2013), 52.

[56] Pierpont Morgan Library M 579, see Leo Depuydt, *Catalogue of Coptic manuscripts in the Pierpont Morgan Library* (Leuven, 1993), 317-8 (No. 162).

[57] PGL 99, s.v. ἀνάγνωσις 1.

Apart from Antony, there is another, quite extraordinary case, that of Didymus. Hermias Sozomen relates that '[He learnt] syllables and words and the rest successively by capacity of mind and constant listening and remembering what he had caught by ear'.[58] Although memorisation of the Bible is not explicitly stated, that would have been the only way by which Didymus could have mastered it. Learning the Bible by heart demanded frequent and repeated listening to the Scriptures (συνηχὴς ἀκρόασις), but was possible only because of the personal ingenuity of Didymus' mind. Sozomen stresses that it was an extraordinary ability. Quintilian recognised this method, but considered it slow.[59]

Although it is imaginable that monks learnt the psalms during daily synaxis listening to the elders, any significant progress achieved that way beyond a couple of psalms seems very unlikely. Extensive memorisation most probably required books. Quintilian recommended learning from books piecemeal, comparing this practice to chewing the cud (*cibium remandendi*), although he considers only poetry, orations and legal writings, with no mention of narratives in prose.[60] However, our sources are reticent about this practice. Jerome advised Rusticus thus: 'Never take your hand or your eyes off your book; learn the psalms word for word'.[61] Due to the emphasis on reading skills,[62] memorisation most probably also required books in the Pachomian monasteries. There is also a piece of information given in passing in one of the Sahidic Lives of Pachomius:

ⲁϥⲁⲗⲉ ⲉ[ⲡϫⲟ]ⲓ̈ ⲙ̄ⲡϥ̄ϥⲓⲡⲉϥ [ⲡⲣ]ⲏϣ ⲛⲙ̄ⲙⲁϥ [ⲟⲩ]ⲧⲉ ⲡⲉϥϫⲱⲱⲙⲉ [ⲉ]ⲧϥ̄ϫⲓ ⲁⲡⲟⲥⲧⲏ[ⲑⲟ]ⲩⲥ ⲛ̄ϩⲏⲧϥ̄
'(Theodore) went aboard the boat and took not his cloak with him, nor his book which he had learnt by heart.[63]

4. The limits of memorisation

There are also some external factors that have to be taken into account when reassessing the source data.

a) Individual capacities. Sometimes, even in hagiography, the ability to keep extensive parts of the Bible in one's memory is portrayed as an extraordinary

---

[58] Sozomenus, *Historia ecclesiastica* 3, 15: συλλαβὰς δὲ καὶ ὀνόματα καὶ τὰ ἄλλα ἐφεξῆς καταλήψει νοῦ καὶ συνεχεῖ ἀκροάσει καὶ ἀναμνήσει τῶν ἀκοῇ θηρωμένων (trans. by myself).

[59] Quintilianus, *Institutio oratoria* 11, 2, 34.

[60] *Ibid.* 11, 2, 41.

[61] Hieronymus, *Epistula* 125, 11: *numquam de manu et oculis tuis recedat liber, psalterium discatur ad verbum* (trans. NPNF).

[62] *Praecepta* 139.

[63] *Vita Pachomii* S10 (trans. Walter Crum [modified]). In Arabic MS, ed. Émile Amélineau, *Vie de Pahkôme*, in *id.*, *Histoire de Saint Pakhôme et de ses communautés*, Annales du Musée Guimet 17 (Paris, 1889), 412: 'mais il monta dans la barque et il ne prit pas avec lui le livre dans lequel il étudiait'.

gift from God that surpasses the normal limits of the human condition.[64] Even contemporaries regarded it as an exceptional case. It is worth noting that we have very scarce evidence for the memorisation of extensive texts in classical antiquity, and even the available data only mentions Homeric poems written in verse, and thus easier to commit to memory. The ancient authors always recognised such an ability as something extraordinary.[65]

b) Education. As previously mentioned, only literate persons could memorise effectively. Although the common idea that monks were uneducated peasants *en masse* had already passed, it cannot be denied that some monks remained illiterate.[66]

c) Accessibility of books. The books were certainly kept in the church buildings, as the canons prescribe the common reading of the Scriptures in church every day at dusk.[67] Probably members of the clergy had free access to them, at least. Documentary letters bear witness to the fact, however, that there were churches where the appropriate books were lacking.[68] Furthermore, the cenobitic monasteries had libraries. But even so we should not take for granted that they possessed all the books of the Bible. The most complete catalogue we possess, ostracon IFAO 13315, lists over 70 books from 'The Monastery of Apa Elias on the Rock'. The inventory lacks some Old Testament writings.[69] Since part of an ostracon with the Biblical books is preserved intact, evidently the monks had no access to the entire Bible. Hermitages might have been almost completely devoid of books, and despite the well-recorded exchange of codices between hermitages, such a situation certainly resulted in a small amount of memorised material.

d) Time. Learning the Bible by heart had to have been extremely time-consuming. We cannot give any precise data, but some rough estimations could be given, thanks to documentary finds from Western Thebes. Pesynthius was believed to need only one day to commit a single book of a minor prophet to

---

[64] Palladius, *Historia Lausiaca* 47, 3; *Historia monachorum in Aegypto* 10, 7; R.-G. Coquin, *Saint Constantin* (1981), 154 (text), 157 (trans.); from outside Egypt, see the extraordinary case of Theodore of Sykeon in Georgius Syceota, *Vita sancti Theodori Syceotae* 13.

[65] Plinius Maior (*Naturalis Historia* 7, 24) mentions a certain Charmadas who could quote books from memory; the ability to repeat many verses after a single hearing is ascribed by Quintilian to Theodectes (*Institutio oratoria* 11, 2, 51). The prodigies brought in by the Roman authorities were, however, not their contemporaries, but belonged to the distant Greek past. On the memorisation of Homer, see Plato, *Ion*; Xenophon, *Symposium* 3, 5-6; Seneca, *Epistulae* 27, 6-7.

[66] *Historia monachorum in Aegypto* 2, 5 (Abba Hor).

[67] *Canones Hippoliti* (Arabic) 21.

[68] Walter Ewing Crum, *The Monastery of Epiphanius at Thebes. Part II: Coptic Ostraca and Papyri* (New York, 1926), No. 378; Walter Ewing Crum, Adolf Erman and Boris A. Turaieff, *Ägyptische Urkunden aus den königlichen Museen zu Berlin* (Berlin, 1904), No. 313.

[69] René-Georges Coquin, 'Le catalogue de la bibliothèque du couvent de Saint-Élie «du rocher» (ostracon IFAO 13315)', *BIFAO* 75 (1975), 223.

memory,[70] which is pure fantasy. According to a hagiographical narrative on Cyril, the monk and bishop-to-be accomplished the memorisation of all the books of the Bible in five years[71] – which proves that even a pious fantasy counts the necessary period in a significant number of years. In a dossier by Bishop Abraham of Hermonthis (from the beginning of the 6th century), we find seven pieces with commitments in which the members of the clergy take upon themselves an obligation to memorise the Bible.[72] In two cases, the exact time is given: two months, in one case for John, in another for Mark. Failure to complete this obligation effectively resulted in exclusion from the clergy (O.Crum 39). As the Sahidic Bible is a translation of the Septuagint, we may use the Greek Text, since comparable data for the Sahidic Bible is lacking. The Septuagint and the New Testament contain 761,719 words, John 15,635 words,[73] so if memorisation of the latter takes two months, the former requires almost 49 months, so four years. Of course, this is a very crude approximation that assumes the constant and cumulative increase of the memorised material and disregards all contextual factors that would hinder learning. But it makes clear that the memorisation of even a few books required years and was probably impossible for all the non-monastic members of clergy who had families and earned their living not only from the Church, as well as for the great majority of monastics who could pray ceaselessly only in the réalité narrative.

5. Conclusions

Let me now put my observations together. Their scope is much broader than the material presented in my paper allows, but I regard them as promising working hypotheses, not completely groundless, but partially verified by my ongoing studies on Theban documentary material.

1. The Bible was memorised by both monastics and non-monastic clergy, but the extent was, in most cases, limited to the Psalter (or part of it) and the Gospel(s).

---

[70] Éloge de Pisentios, ed. É. Amélineau (1887), 83.

[71] Le Synaxaire (1923), 617 [1159].

[72] Walter Ewing Crum, Coptic Ostraca from the Collections of the Egypt Exploration Fund, the Cairo Museum and Others (London, 1902), Nos. 29, 30, 31, 34, 35, 37, ad. 7. Summary and discussion in Suzana Hodak, Tonio S. Richter and Frank Steinmann, Coptica: Koptische Ostraka und Papyri, Koptische und Griechische Grabstelen aus Ägypten und Nubien, Spätantike Bauplastik, Textilien und Keramik, Katalog ägyptischer Sammlungen in Leipzig 3 (Berlin, 2013), 41.

[73] I base this calculation on statistics given by TLG for the editions Septuaginta, ed. Alfred Rahlfs (Stuttgart, 9th edition, 1935), and The Greek New Testament, ed. Kurt Aland et al. (Stuttgart, 2nd edition, 1968).

2. The learning of the Scriptures – except for the Psalter – was based on the written word, and the extent of memorised material was restricted, since access to books was limited.

3. I suggest that the overflow of biblical references in the monastic literature does not reflect the average level of scriptural mastery, but forms an erudite costume of the literary genres. Certainly, many biblical allusions and quotations passed unnoticed by both readers and listeners.

Cyrillona's New Testament Paraphrase (End of the 4th Century): An Exegetical Key for the Easter Homilies[1]

Matteo POIANI, Strasbourg, France

ABSTRACT

Cyrillona owes his theology to his most famous of predecessors, Ephrem the Syrian (307-373): we can see many links between them and even the use of quotes. Nevertheless, Cyrillona's poetry, notably compared to that of Ephrem, has a different approach to the New Testament: he rewrites it in a poetic form by inserting his own theology and emphasis. He does not speak from his own time, but as if he were really seeing the events concerning Jesus: his point of view is that of the Evangelists. Within these writings, he stresses different theological themes in order to pass from Old Testament thought to the scandal of New Testament theology. The gap between the two Testaments was still alive at that time, and Cyrillona's actions opened up a new theology through the reading and paraphrasing of the New Testament. This analysis will investigate the literal quotes from Ephrem, in order to highlight both the Ephremic tradition and the differences to it, leading to a new era of poetic experimentation. It is also worth noting comparisons found in other fathers of the Church, such as John Chrysostom and Cyril of Alexandria. Through these comparisons, we can see Cyrillona's new approach to the New Testament.

1. Ephrem the Syrian

Ephrem the Syrian[2] was born and lived in Nisibis and Edessa in the second part of the fourth century. He was ordained as a deacon and became famous for his poetic artistry. He was a theological and spiritual leader, thus creating a pattern for the generations which followed. He wrote many poems, metrical homilies, dialogues and prose works. His most important works are his

---

[1] Gratias ago Emidio Vergani, magistri Romae Pontifici Insituti Orientalis, quia monitus fecit. Gratias ago etiam David Phillips (Angliae) et Coltoni Moore (Respublicis Unitis), qui emendaverunt linguam anglicam.

[2] For an overall view, see Robert Murray, 'The Theory of Symbolism in St. Ephrem's Theology', *ParOr* 6-7 (1975-1976), 1-20; Sebastian Brock, *The Luminous Eye: the spiritual world vision of Saint Ephrem* (Kalamazoo, 1992). For further general reading, see Robert Murray, *Symbols of Church and Kingdom. A Study in Early Syriac Tradition* (London, New York, 2006²).

Studia Patristica CIII, 99-108.
© Peeters Publishers, 2021.

madrashe.³ He was very famous even when he was alive, to the point that his poems were translated into Greek⁴ and Armenian.

In the *madrashe* he usually does not tell stories, but develops arguments through symbols.⁵ This becomes a poem-prayer for the whole liturgical assembly, which the male and female choirs sang and with the responsory given by the assembly.

In *Hymn on Paradise* V, he tells how the Scripture can take him and bring him to Paradise, where he can see it as it is:

> I read the opening of this book
> and I was filled with joy,
> for its verses and lines
> spread out their arms to welcome me.⁶

Moreover, when Ephrem writes about famous stories, such as the Passion and Easter, he prefers to focus on a central theme and then widens the scope through types and symbols: the symbols always refer to other symbols, and Christ is the Lord of Symbols. For example, on the theme of the *Lamb*, Ephrem composed the *Hymn on Unleavened Bread* III. Sebastian Brock, in attempting to point out the very high standard of Ephrem's poetry, analysed the whole short hymn, highlighting the 'truly astonishing fusion of form with content'.⁷ Here, Ephrem highlights the difference between the Passover and Easter, the Jewish and the Christian feasts, emphasising the fact that in the first there is a single action, that is, the exodus of the Jews from Egypt, while in the second it is doubled, that is to say, the exodus of the gentiles from error and death in Še'ol. The theme of the two lambs, the symbolic and the real, of the Passover and Easter, of real time and of sacred time, etc. are therefore addressed and developed around a purely Easter theme. Ephrem does not narrate an event in a strictly narrative way (*i.e.* he does not follow the thread of history as it is told in the scriptures), but rather puts into dialogue the writings of the OT and the NT, bringing out salient features and different theologies.

In the same collection, the *Hymn on Unleavened Bread* XIII⁸ tells us about the 'acts of the true Lamb', from the arrest by Annas to the embalming and burial, in 32 stanzas, in 128 verses (plus the 2 of the responsory). After an invitation to the assembly to celebrate the month of Nisan (a theme dear to Ephrem),

---

³ For the extant text by Ephrem, see: S. Brock, *The Luminous Eye* (1992), 184-7 (and also the Italian version, more up to date, Sebastian Brock, *L'occhio Luminoso. La visione spirituale di sant'Efrem* [Roma, 1999], 209-13).

⁴ See Hieronymus, *De viris illustribus* 115.

⁵ See the whole work of Tanios Bou Mansour, *La pensée symbolique d'Ephrem le Syrien* (Kaslik, 1988).

⁶ Ephraem Syri, *Hymni de Paradiso* V 3.

⁷ Sebastian Brock, 'The Poetic Artistry of St. Ephrem: an Analysis of Hymni de Azymis III', *ParOr* 6-7 (1975-1976), 21-8, 23.

⁸ Ephraem Syri, *Hymni de Azymis* XIII. See Ignazio de Francesco (ed.), *Inni pasquali. Sugli azzimi, sulla crocifissione, sulla risurrezione* (Milano, 2001), 170-9.

the story of the passion begins with the second stanza, going on to Annas (2-5), returning back to Judas (6), then Herod (7), the suffering on the cross (8-10), returning to Pilate (11), the recalling of the miracle of the man born blind (12), the suffering on the cross (13) and the terror of the angels (14-15), reflections on creation (16-17), the death of Jesus and its immediate consequences (18-26), the juxtaposition of the present and eschatological future (27-29), up to the placing of Jesus in the tomb (30-32). Ephrem's reading presupposes a knowledge of the Gospel story: he, bringing to mind the central stages of that period, as well as many others, develops a trend that is not always linear, but rather typological, in order to place much – strong! – emphasis on the different situations encountered. The theological commentary is always present; it should be noted that it is a theological, but also scriptural, commentary: the 'inexhaustible fountain' is always at the core of his attention and his reflections. Ephrem seems to want to justify the scriptural text with the Scripture itself, which is like his contemporary, Theodore of Mopsuestia.[9] As the ancient Evangelists had a thousand references to the writings of the Old Testament, so also does Ephrem create a net of symbols, connecting the New Testament with itself and with the Old Testament. All of this, with the finest poetry and theology that the Syriac world had ever seen, is not a narrative of facts. At least, in these Easter Hymns there is no story to tell, but a typological vision of an account that is already known and is something that then becomes a common prayer.

2. Cyrillona

We do not know that much about Cyrillona:[10] we know that he wrote five (or six[11]) homilies, which were copied in the 6th century, together with Isaac of

---

[9] Dimitri Z. Zaharopoulos, *Theodore of Mopsuestia on the Bible: A Study of His Old Testament Exegesis* (Mahwah, NJ, 1989), 123: 'The Bible must be interpreted by the Bible'.

[10] See these four monographic works: Costantino Vona (ed.), *I carmi di Cirillona* (Roma, Paris, Tournai, New York, 1963), a monographic introduction and an Italian translation; Cyrillonas, *L'Agneau Véritable. Hymnes Cantiques Homélies*, Dominique Cerbelaud (ed.) (Paris, 1984), an introduction and a French translation; Carl Griffin, *The Works of Cyrillona* (Piscataway, NJ, 2016), a manuscript introduction, critical edition and English translation; Carl Griffin, *Cyrillona. A Critical Study and Commentary* (Piscataway, NJ, 2016), a monograph. One article on Cyrillona, by Emidio Vergani, highlights themes different to the other homilies, Emidio Vergani, '"Mondo creato" e Chiesa nella meditazione di Cirillona', in Emidio Vergani and Sabino Chialà (eds), *Le Chiese sire tra IV e VI secolo: dibattito dottrinale e ricerca spirituale. Atti del 2° Incontro sull'Oriente Cristiano di tradizione siriaca (Milano, Biblioteca Ambrosiana, 28 marzo 2003)*, Ecumenismo e Dialogo (Milano, 2005), 119-50. The three Easter homilies will be quoted only by title and verses from the critical edition by Griffin (*On the Institution of the Eucharist* = C. Griffin, *Works*, 18-70, *On the Washing of the Feet* = C. Griffin, *Works*, 72-88, *On the Pasch of Our Lord* = C. Griffin, *Works*, 90-134).

[11] For the authenticity of *On the Grain of Wheat*, see C. Griffin, *A Critical Study* (2016), 11-7. Another, and more complex, question is why there is another *soghito* before this homily; maybe the editor of the manuscript collected many homilies from different authors in only one liturgical text.

Antioch, Peter of Raqqa and others. There is only one manuscript, which is well preserved and was written in an elegant estranghelo, and is now in London, namely, BL Add. 14591. From his homilies, we can suppose that he wrote it at the end of the 4th century, around 396-397, near Edessa.

Three homilies are, above all, connected: the topic is the last supper, addressed in three different ways, and based on the Johannine story. In BL Add. 14591, the three homilies follow the order of *On the Institution of the Eucharist*, *On the Washing of the Feet* and *On the Pasch of Our Lord*. These three have much in common with the hymns and the theology of Ephrem. One of the most striking passages is 'The Lamb of the Lord / ate the lamb. / Who has ever seen / a Lamb eating a lamb?',[12] which is quoted and amplified by Cyrillona in *On the Institution of the Eucharist*, in verse 121 and following: 'The Lamb ate the lamb / and the Pasch devoured the pasch. / [...] Who has seen such as this?'

The first homily and the last share different aspects, such as their considerable length (576 verses for the first and 440 for the second; *On the Washing of the Feet* has only 152 verses) and an introduction in the Ephremic way. These two introductions are quite long and important, since they also introduce the theme theologically.[13] At the beginning of *On the Institution of the Eucharist*, we find the theme of the true lamb, which, as we have already seen, is a theme dear to Ephrem. The development that follows lasts for more than 150 verses, with an Ephremic look to it, a reflection that amplifies and connects all the various symbols. In this phase, however, Cyrillona already adds some direct discourse, which refers to events before the last supper and its preparation: the angels speak, they invite us to taste freely of the bread given by Jesus, which is freedom and light.[14] Cyrillona already introduces direct discourse in the introduction, which then remains afterwards! The whole of this ample preamble serves to prepare Jesus' discourse (*John* 13:12ss), which begins only with verse 159. In the same way, in *On the Pasch of Our Lord* there is an introduction, which, although it is shorter than that just analysed, asks important questions in the same way concerning the role of the Scripture in meditation:

> Whenever I read from the New Testament
>   new things pour out of it into me.
> Whenever I meditate upon the Gospel,
>   the Gospel of life greets me.

Then, inviting the listener[15] (not the reader!) to learn the 'power of reading', he says:

---

[12] Ephraem Syrus, *Hymni de Azymis* VI 9.
[13] See C. Griffin, *A Critical Study* (2016), 60-70, 134-5.
[14] *On the Institution of the Eucharist*, v. 41.
[15] As in the *On the Institution of the Eucharist*, v. 149: "Observe, O Hearer". It is worth noting that in the Italian translation by Vona (C. Vona, *I carmi* [1963], p. 80), there is "Tu, che

> Between sadness and joy
> the preacher must wend and go.[16]

This text is significant because it is linked in a surprising way to important passages of Cyrillona's *On the Washing of the Feet*, and also to Ephrem's *Hymns on Paradise*. Among these, in the second stanza of the first hymn we find:

> Between fear and love
> I keep myself in the middle.[17]

He says little about that which the 'desire for paradise' had led him to seek and explore. In Cyrillona, these feelings, that is, sadness and joy, while being clearly derived from Ephrem, are used as a launchpad: the next verse begins the evangelical narrative that follows the thirteenth chapter of John. 'After all the mysteries were fulfilled': the mysteries correspond to the Syriac word *rz'* which is a common term, but which in Ephrem (and, therefore, in Cyrillona) clearly indicates the symbols of God in this world. What has been written has been defined, the symbols have been completed, now only the Passion is missing: the Lord begins to speak and to gather his Twelve. Cyrillona here rewrites very different passages from chapters 12 and 13 of *John*. Continuing with the text, Cyrillona sums up part of the great discourse on love around the theme of wheat (vv. 203-286), and then deepens it again by starting with the words of Jesus (vv. 289-290) from *John* 15:1: 'I am the true vine / and the worker is my Father'. The rendering of these words does not correspond to any of the three known versions of the Gospel of John (S, P and Ḥ[18]), but to an autonomous version, or perhaps are derived from the Diatessaron; in fact, this sentence corresponds to almost everything, except for the term 'vine', which, while in the Gospel is *gpt'* ܓܦܬܐ, in Cyrillona is *krm'* ܟܪܡܐ, which is used in the other Gospels, but not in John.

In Ephrem's *Easter Hymns*, direct discourse is not present except in very rare cases. With Cyrillona, the procedure is different: it starts from the text itself, and then takes it up again, making the characters of the story talk. Ignazio de Francesco speaks of the passion according to Ephrem as a 'liturgical meditation, where individual contemplation is immediately raised to God by the whole community, and the inner rumination of the mystery immediately takes the

---

ascolti, scuotiti": here the verb *'yr* ܥܝܪ is used with the strong meaning of "stir", "shake yourself", and, in J. Payne-Smith, *A Compendious Syriac Dictionary* (Oxford, 1903), 407, you also find "to awake from the dead".

[16] *De Pascha*, vv. 17-18.

[17] Ephraem Syri, *Hymni de Paradiso* I 2.

[18] George Kiraz, *Comparative Edition of the Syriac Gospels* (Leiden, 1995), IV, 277. For a general view on Syriac New Testament, see Jean-Claude Haelewyck, *Le Nouveau Testament en syriaque*, Études Syriaques 14 (Paris, 2017).

form of choral singing'.[19] We can also transpose this definition to Cyrillona, adding drama:[20] with the presence of direct discourse, the scene certainly becomes more alive, and the most striking example is the 'song of the homily'[21] *On the Washing of the Feet*.[22]

There is no introductory part, as in the other two cases, but the story is already a summary:

> Our Lord led his Twelve
> and came to the house to wash them.
> He seated them at table as an heir
> and he rose up (and) served as a friend.[23]

In four lines, Cyrillona is able to describe the actions of all the public activities of Jesus and also his attitude: he is like a shepherd[24] who leads his flock to a quiet place where he can wash them / purify them; he is the heir and he is also their friend, and the two characteristics distinguish him for the actions they involve, that is, to make them sit (referring to the multiplication of the loaves and fish), and then to the resurrection and the service. Everything is *ex abrupto*, lightning-fast. The story is already sufficient in itself. These first moments are surprising and do not so much touch on the characters of the evangelical story, but on Cyrillona himself! He cries, hides his face, and leaves the house. Taken by the spirit (that of Ezekiel!), he begins to question the prophets in Še'ol. The dramatic action, already present in the first verses with the realistic paraphrasing narrative of the *Gospel of John*, takes different turns, introducing new characters and places in the Gospel story: the dialogue is between Cyrillona (incredulous) and the prophets (hopeful), and it seems to be an anticipation of the dialogue that will take place between Peter (incredulous and reticent) and Jesus (who asks for trust). This dialogue, quite dense and complex, already has within it a paraphrase, but it is not taken from the last chapters of John. Instead, Cyrillona takes up the prologue of the *Gospel of John*. The form it takes is of an anaphora which is repeated a number of times, and Cyrillona also uses the same form in the other two homilies. In the anaphora, a series of considerations are made about God as he is conceived by reading the Old Testament, while the references are to *Isaiah, Daniel, Ezekiel...* This whole list of statements about God ends with 'behold he is a servant': the great definitions of the Old Testament of God as fire, worthy of fear, etc., are summarised in the new

---

[19] *Inni pasquali* (2001), 65.
[20] C. Griffin, *A Critical Study* (2016), 106: '*On the Washing of the Feet* [...] reads like a short, dramatic sermon'.
[21] Bl. Add. 14591, f. 59v ܐܪܙܐܕ ܐܪܒܕ ܣܘܠܝܐܟ.
[22] There are important passages in this homily, also noted by Pier Franco Beatrice, *La lavanda dei piedi. Contributo alla storia delle antiche liturgie cristiane* (Roma, 1983), 68-70.
[23] *On the Washing of the Feet*, vv. 1-4.
[24] See C. Griffin, *A Critical Study* (2016), 107-9 for the connections with *Psalm* 23.

scandal of Jesus, since everything is summed up in becoming a servant, which is the action that Jesus performs from risen in verse 4. The connection to the flesh-servant is not entirely strange, since it has already been suggested by Ephrem, for example in *Hymn on Resurrection* I:

> From above he descended as Lord,
> And from the womb he came as servant.[25]

where Ephrem also writes about Še'ol! Furthermore, in another passage, *Hymn on Faith* XLVI, he writes: 'It is a wonder that God descended to dust!'[26] The connections with Ephrem are clear: the theology is the same for both.[27] If we also look at Greek patrology, we also find in the commentary on the Gospel of John by John Chrysostom:

> This is, "the word became flesh", and the master took on the form of the servant. [...] when you hear that "the word became flesh", do not be alarmed or disturbed. His nature did not change to flesh, since thinking this would be (indicative) of great impiety. But while continuing as he is, he took the form of a servant.[28]

Chrysostom ultimately agrees with Cyrillona: all the characteristics of God are not nullified, God remains what he is. But now we know one more thing, that he is also a servant. A very similar issue is developed by Cyril of Alexandria in his commentary on John, where he tries, more than John Chrysostom does, to explain the right relationship between the divine and human nature in Christ. He states:

> If indeed he has not truly become a man, if he has not assumed the condition of a servant, then there is really reason to be troubled, when he affirms some things that are appropriate to the servant, and one must, instead, look for everything according to what is convenient to God. If instead we firmly believe, and we have unlimited confidence that "the Word became flesh, and dwelt among us", then, when you see him speak like flesh, that is, as a man, you understand that those convenient words to man are been told to confirm the message. Indeed, it is not possible to understand differently, clearly, that the Word, being God, became man, if it had not been written that he, unmoved, suffered, and that he, sublime, said something humble.[29]

---

[25] Ephraem Syrus, *Inni pasquali* (2001), 336 (English translation is mine). In this hymn, Ephrem stresses the twofold ways with which Jesus lived, and many strophes are about the womb of Mary and the victory over death.

[26] Ephraem Syrus, *Hymni de Fide* 46, 11 (CSCO 154, 148).

[27] In *Liber Graduum* 21, 11 we can also find something similar, although there is not the direct connection of *Jn.* 1,14 with *Phil.* 2:7, *cf.* André Louf, 'Une ancienne exégèse de Phil. 2, 6 dans la Kᶜtābâ dᶜMasqātâ (Livre des Degrés)', in *Studiorum Paulinorum Congressus Internationalis Catholicus 1961*, Analecta Biblica 17-18, vol. 2 (Roma, 1963), 523-33.

[28] Jeff W. Childers (edited and translated), *The Syriac Version of John Chrysostom's Commentary on John I: Mêmrê 1-43*, CSCO 651-652 (2 vol.) (Louvain, 2013), Mêmrâ 11, 2, p. 88.

[29] Cyrillus Alexandrinus, *Commentari in Ioannem* II, IV. Other passages of the commentary of John confirm this idea of "to become flesh = to take the form of servant", such as "In fact,

Cyril clearly wants to preserve the divinity of Christ against the Antiochian views, but he does not disclaim the connection to the flesh-servant. *Jn*. 1:14 is connected to *Phil*. 2:7, but there are no concrete developments, and the state stays the same. Cyrillona, instead, adds a new piece to the puzzle, *i.e.* the last supper, and closes the circle by explaining what it means for God 'to assume the condition of a servant'.

While for Chrysostom and Cyril it is a passage of one of many comments on John, in Cyrillona it is taken as the nodal point of an Easter homily for Holy Thursday.

This first dramatic insertion by Cyrillona, complete with Cyrillona's ascent, thanks to the Spirit, departure and return home, is therefore – even in comparison with Chrysostom – a rather free transposition of the prologue of the Gospel of John, but it is, theologically, a scandal explained in order to counteract the Old Testament theology. The continuation, from verse 10 onwards, is the true paraphrase of the Gospel text of *John* 13: Cyrillona follows it step by step, as he continues in the narration of the Gospel from the point of view of those present at the Last Supper:

> After this things, in my distress, I returned
>   and straightway arrived in the house
> I saw him who was cheerful and washing them,
>   and joyful was his countenance while serving them.

Cyrillona is therefore, somehow, present at the Last Supper, and tells us not only the facts but also his and the disciples' feelings. Through the reading of the texts (as suggested by Ephrem and by passages by Cyrillona himself), the narrator-Cyrillona is also a witness who is able to move in time and space. The turning point of the washing of Judas' feet is amplified by biblical references:[30] 'the rocks emitted a voice from the walls' (v. 71), 'the terrible word from the mouth of the lambs' (v. 76), 'Great disruption when came down / the hand of our Lord over his murderer' (vv. 83-84). After this, the dialogue between Simon Peter and Jesus begins, also amplified to better express the scene and highlight other theological themes. In Jesus' reply to Simon, which is brief in the Gospel,[31] different themes are explained,

---

once, "he took the form of a slave" [*Phil*. 2:7], "he became man", and because of the union with the flesh, he did not always use, in speaking, the freedom of the authority that is appropriate to God; indeed, given the conditions, he sometimes used language that was convenient, at the same time, to God and man." (Cyrillus Alexandrinus, *Commentari in Ioannem* II, VI) and "Having become man, and taking the form of a slave, he submitted to the Law he who had made the Law, like God and Lord." (Cyrillus Alexandrinus, *Commentari in Ioannem* II, IX).

[30] C. Griffin, *A Critical Study* (2016), 116.

[31] *John* 13:7-8: 'Jesus answered: "What I do, you do not understand now; you will understand later". Peter said to him: "You will not wash my feet forever!" Jesus answered him: "If I do not wash you, you will not have part with me".

taking up the words of the Gospel with repetitions of 'If this cannot happen'; the themes of the throne are interpolated (and therefore that of eschatology, already present in vv. 41-42), that of the keys (*i.e.* the Church), that of power, of discipleship, of 'touching the body' (hence the Eucharist). We can see how Cyrillona amplifies the 'If I do not wash you, you will have no part with me' of *John* 13:8b in ten verses. Cyrillona, then, unlike other homilies, does not announce the betrayal (*John* 13:21-30), but goes directly to the great discourse on love ('full of love commanded them'), which is summed up in 18 lines (vv. 135-152). What in John is said in three very dense chapters, full of dialogue etc., for Cyrillona instead becomes a brief discourse to the disciples, who are invited to see what has happened, and then proclaim the Gospel around the world. The last four verses by Jesus are emblematic:

> I, who am your God,
>> behold, I have humbled myself, I have served you.
> This is the universal Pasch that I prepare for you,
>> and I will cheer the face of the whole world[32].

In the first verses, the relationship that exists between the disciples, Creator-creature, and the reversal that has taken place in God who, having become flesh, serves man, is made explicit. In the second couplet, there is the same pattern: first the relationship is explicated, that is, it is Jesus who prepares the Passover for all, and then the change of *John* 17:24,[33] where Jesus wants to make everyone like himself. In the canticle of the homily,[34] Cyrillona describes Jesus as *pṣyḥ* ܗ݁ܚ, that is, happy, which is the same root as Easter: Jesus, with Easter, which is what he is, wants to render us like himself.

Cyrillona moves between direct quotations, great paraphrases, dense summaries, and intertextual references. The scheme that follows is ultimately the classic one, as Brock describes it: 'there is almost always an introductory story, which gives the public (the assembly) the biblical context, and there is sometimes a brief conclusion (often in form of doxology)'. The introductory story is the first four verses, which perform the function of a summary and then the subsequent stanzas that cause all of the upheaval in Še'ol, etc. The conclusion is, instead, entrusted directly to Christ, with his words on Easter. Cyrillona, therefore, strengthens the biblical text: he inserts himself as a witness into history and the story, to be able to tell it live, but also to create new spaces of

---

[32] *On the Washing of the Feet*, vv. 149-152 (the last two verses, 151-152, are translated by myself, *contra* Griffin).

[33] *John* 17:24: 'Father, I want those you gave me to be also with me where I am, so that they may contemplate my glory, the one you gave me, because you loved me before the creation of the world'.

[34] This is the description in the manuscript before the title *On the Washing of the Feet*, see C. Griffin, *A Critical Study* (2016), 101-6. Although it would be very interesting to discuss the meaning of this heading, I cannot investigate this theme here.

dialogue, such as Še'ol, within which other passages are paraphrased and retaken from the Old Testament and from John, and which allow various insights, nuances that were internal to the community, and which Cyrillona tries, with the scandal of Jesus, to resolve, that is, 'the dust is sitting in front of its creator / and its Lord stands and washes its feet'.[35]

---

[35] *On the Washing of the Feet*, vv. 15-16.

Inappropriate Biblical Exegesis as a Source of Heresy in *Diversarum hereseon liber* by Philastrius of Brescia

Mariusz Szram, Lublin, Poland

ABSTRACT

The purpose of this article is to reflect on two issues based on the first Latin catalogue of heresies, *Diversarum hereseon liber*, written by Philastrius, Bishop of Brescia, between 380 and 388 CE. Firstly, which type of exegesis – literal or allegorical – was, according to the author, more heresogenic? Secondly, have the mistaken biblical exegesis lead, in Philastrius' view, more often to the emergence of doctrinal errors or only to damage in the spiritual life of Christians? In the opinion of Philastrius, as a supporter of the allegorical interpretation derived from the Alexandrian environment, there was a cause-and-effect relationship between remaining at the level of the literal exegesis of the biblical text and the emergence of heresy. In the case of many Old Testament texts, Philastrius considered the metaphorical explanation as the only one being in accordance with orthodoxy, most often on the basis of Christological typology. However, the main specific objection formulated in his catalogue against literalism is the lack of spiritual benefit for the reader, and not its influence on the formulation of wrong dogmatic views. According to Philastrius, literal exegesis very often inhibits the spiritual development of Christians and therefore deserves to be called heresy in the broad sense of the word. Both types of heresies presented by Philastrius are rooted in erroneous thinking about the Scriptures, as well as which his response to those views refer primarily to biblical argumentation. In this context, the Scriptures appear to be the main anchor of orthodoxy, and its correct interpretation is a basic safeguard against all heresy.

From the beginning of the 4th century, the Trinitarian and Christological heresies began to appear with great intensity. At the same time, the documentation of early Christian heterodoxy was emerging in the form of lexicon treatises discussing the more and lesser known heretical movements.[1] The author of the first Latin catalogue of heresies, *Diversarum hereseon liber*, was Bishop Philastrius

---

[1] See Epiphanius Salamiensis, *Panarion*, I, ed. Karl Holl, GCS 25 (Leipzig, 1915); II, GCS 31 (Leipzig, 1922); III, GCS 37 (Leipzig, 1933); Theodoretus Cyrensis, *Haereticarum fabularum compendium*, ed. Jacques-Paul Migne, PG 83 (Paris, 1864), 335-556; Augustinus Hipponensis, *De haeresibus*, ed. Jacques-Paul Migne, PL 42 (Paris, 1886), 21-50; Isidorus Hispalensis, *De haeresibus*, ed. Ángel Custodio Vega, PLSuppl 4 (Paris, 1970), 1815-20; Iohannes Damascenus, *De haeresibus*, ed. Bonifatius Kotter, *Die Schriften des Johannes von Damaskos IV*, Patristische Texte und Studien 22 (Berlin, 1981), 19-67.

Studia Patristica CIII, 109-118.
© Peeters Publishers, 2021.

of Brescia.[2] This work became the model for Augustine's treatise *De haeresibus*. Admittedly, Epiphanius of Salamis' *Panarion* is considered the most extensive exposition of heresies in the Patristic era (20 pre-Christian and 60 early Christian heretical groups), but Philastrius' treatise *De haeresibus*, dated between 380 and 388 CE, contains a presentation of the largest number of heterodox movements: 28 in the heart of Judaism, and 128 in early Christianity. This is by no means the result of Philastrius' superiority in knowledge or erudition over Epiphanius, doubted by Saint Augustine, who did not hold the Bishop of Brescia's education in high regard,[3] but rather the effect of Philastrius' broad understanding of the phenomenon of heresy. He often associated it not only with the doctrinal – *i.e.* dogmatic, anthropological and cosmological – errors, but also with views that could rather be classified as minor errors, not necessarily concerning doctrine, or as voices in a theological discussion that did not pose a greater threat to the identity of the Church, as well as with deviations from Christian morality or everyday Christian life practices.[4]

According to Philastrius, one important group of heresies are those views related to the misinterpretation of the Holy Scriptures, especially the books of the Old Testament. The mismatches between the interpretation of biblical texts with the spirit of the Gospel and the doctrinal teaching of the Church were, in Early Christianity, one of the obvious criteria for unorthodoxy. Epiphanius, writing his *Panarion* a few years before Philastrius, regarded erroneous exegesis as the starting point for many dogmatic heresies.[5] Similarly, Isidore of Seville, living at the beginning of the seventh century, considered the misinterpretation of biblical texts as the key element of any heresy, especially the lack of understanding of the mysteries expressed in the Scriptures, or not seeing the difference between historical truth and spiritual sense.[6]

Heresies, based on the erroneous exegesis of various Old Testament texts, were discussed in the last part of Philastrius' treatise (from chapter 128 to 156).[7] No other well-known early Christian author of the heresy catalogues has devoted a separate section to exegetical errors, nor have they provided as many examples of inappropriate interpretations of various biblical texts as Philastrius. From a historical point of view, one of the shortcomings of his catalogue is the

---

[2] I use the following edition of this work: Filastrius Brixiensis, *Diversarum hereseon liber*, ed. Frans Heylen, CCL 9 (Turnhout, 1957), 217-324.

[3] Augustinus Hipponensis, *Epistulae* 222, 2: *Neque enim putandum est aliquas ignorasse Epiphanium, quas noverat Filastrius, cum Epiphanium longe Filastrio doctiorem invenerimus.*

[4] See Mariusz Szram, '*Varii errores qui ab origine mundi emerserunt.* The Semantic Scope of the Term "Heresy" in Filastrius Brixiensis' of Brescia *Diversarum hereseon liber*', VoxP 68 (2017), 315-25.

[5] Epiphanius Salamiensis, *Panarion* 26, 6, 1 - 26, 9, 2; *ibid.* 28, 5, 1-3. See Marek Gilski, 'Epifaniusz z Salaminy i jego *Panarion*', in Epifaniusz z Salaminy, *Panarion. Herezje 1-33. Tekst grecki i polski*, ed. Marek Gilski (Kraków, 2015), 15-6.

[6] Isidorus Hispalensis, *De haeresibus liber*, Praefatio.

[7] Filastrius Brixiensis, *Diversarum hereseon liber* 128-56.

frequent manner of presenting the heretics' views without listing their names and the names of the movements they founded, as well as his discussing the erroneous exegesis of various biblical passages without indicating whether the views of one or many groups are concerned.

The purpose of my article is to reflect on two issues based on Philastrius' catalogue. Firstly, which type of exegesis – literal or allegorical – was, according to the author, more heresogenic? Secondly, have the mistaken biblical exegesis lead, in Philastrius' view, more often to the emergence of doctrinal errors or only to damage in the spiritual life of Christians? This presentation is almost exclusively of a source nature, because Philastrius' catalogue does not enjoy much interest among contemporary researchers, and the Italian translation of Gabriele Banterle from 1991 is, so far, the only translation of this work into a modern language.[8]

1. Which exegesis is more heresogenic: literal or allegorical?

The Bishop of Brescia presented his views in the vein of the majority of Latin exegetes, namely, that of an allegorical exegesis of Old Testament texts. Manlio Simonetti noted in his classic monograph devoted to the history of patristic exegesis that literal exegesis sometimes raised concerns due to its use by Gnostic movements, attempting, in this way, to denigrate the books of the Old Testament.[9] In the case of many Old Testament texts, Philastrius considered metaphorical explanation as the only one being in accordance with orthodoxy, most often on the basis of Christological typology, perceiving in Old Testament persons, events and names the announcements of Christ and the Church.[10]

In Philastrius' opinion, heresies presenting a false picture of God originated from an exaggerated literalism in the approach to biblical exegesis. One such example was the Gnostic heresy of the indefinite name, attributing to God the Creator the features of an evil god different to the good god, the Saviour. Representatives of this group literally understood the words spoken by God to the first man after sin: 'Now that the man has become like one of us in knowing good from evil, he must not be allowed to reach out his hand and pick from the tree of life too, and eat and live for ever!' (*Gen.* 3:22). On this basis, they claimed that the Lord banished Adam from paradise because of jealousy. Meanwhile, as Philastrius explained, the correct understanding of the text of

---

[8] San Filastrio di Brescia, *Delle varie eresie*, introd., trad., note e indici Gabriele Banterle, Scriptores circa Ambrosium 2 (Milano, Roma, 1991).

[9] Manlio Simonetti, *Lettera e/o allegoria. Un contributo alla storia dell'esegesi patristica*, SEA 23 (Roma, 1985), 29-30.

[10] Filastrius Brixiensis, *Diversarum hereseon liber* 128; *ibid.* 139-41.

Gen. 3:22 is as follows: God did not expel the father of humanity from paradise through jealousy, but rather, thinking of his good, he wanted to lead him
to repentance and protect him from even greater sin, and then sent Christ in
order to bestow upon man the grace of salvation and enable him to return to
paradise.[11]

The Bishop of Brescia emphasised the fact that Christological heresies also
originated in exegetical literalism. For example, the tropics, claiming that the
Word of God had turned into a body, derived this thesis from the erroneous,
literal understanding of the words of the apostle John: 'The Word became flesh
and lived among us' (*John* 1:14). The members of this grouping did not realise
that the Word was changeless and unable to change, because it was God.
Philastrius emphasised the fact that the author of the Fourth Gospel was not
talking about transforming the Word into an actual body, but about receiving
the visible element by the Son of God, so that the invisible could be seen and
known to man.[12]

In the exaggerated literal biblical exegesis Philastrius also saw the genesis
of heretical views on anthropology. He cited an example of erroneous conviction derived by unspecified heretics from the words of God: 'Let us
make man in our own image, in the likeness of ourselves' (*Gen.* 1:26). These
heretics believed that the above words testify that the human soul is the image
of God by nature, not by grace, and ascribed to it divine dignity.[13] Giving an
orthodox interpretation of the text of *Gen.* 1:26, the Bishop of Brescia referred
to the distinction between God's image and His likeness in man, widespread in
the Patristic era.[14] The soul, as the image of God in man, is a gift of grace and
was created out of nothing, while the similarity to God is achieved only through
a perfect life, consisting of doing works of faith. While the soul of every human
being was created in the image of God, its similarity to the Creator is only a
feature of saints and martyrs. Only the Son of God, who is identical to the
Father thanks to his nature, is the image of an eternal substance, born in a
proper way, and not created from nothing like men and angels.[15]

According to Philastrius, the negative image of marriage and childbearing
through bodily intercourse which was so widespread among gnosticising movements has its roots in the erroneous, literal interpretation of biblical texts, taken
out of their wider context. The Bishop of Brescia mentions rigorous heretics who,
based on the words of *Psalm* 50: 'I was conceived in iniquities; and in sins did
my mother conceive me', argued that lawful marriage ties were wickedness and

---

[11] *Ibid.* 115.
[12] *Ibid.* 70.
[13] *Ibid.* 137.
[14] See Mariusz Szram, 'Od obrazu do podobieństwa Bożego – dynamiczna koncepcja
antropologii teologicznej w II-III w. (stanowisko Ireneusza i Orygenesa)', *VoxP* 42-3 (2002), 357-
76.
[15] Filastrius Brixiensis, *Diversarum hereseon liber* 137.

a sin, forgetting other biblical texts which see marriage and childbearing positively.[16] On the other hand, Philastrius warned against the liberalist heresy of the Florians, also known as the Carpocratians or 'soldiers', because they came from a military environment. From the reproduction order (*Gen.* 1:28), they drew the absurd conclusion to encourage impure acts. They claimed that all resurrection consisted of giving birth to sons from unlawful intercourse, and in the evenings, after extinguishing the candles in the church, they had intercourse with harlots in the belief that they were obeying God's command.[17]

Philastrius considered heretical not only groups that proclaimed doctrinal errors, but also movements that practised excessive asceticism. The reason was, again, the literal interpretation of biblical texts. The first of these movements were the *excalciati*, who walked without shoes because the Lord, revealing himself to Moses, said: 'Take off your sandals, for the place where you are standing is holy ground' (see *Exod.* 3:5).[18] The second were the *passalorynchites*, or the silent, who thought that all life should be spent in silence, on the basis of a literal understanding of *Psalm* 140: 'O Lord, station a guard over my mouth and a door enclosing my lips' (*Ps.* 140:3).[19] The third movement were the *ascodrugites*, heretics from Galatia, whose behaviour evoked associations with Greek Dionysian rites. As Philastrius writes, they literally interpreted the words of the Saviour 'one must take new wineskins and pour new wine into them, not the old ones' (*Luke* 5:38), and they danced in the church around wine-filled wineskins and fell into a kind of bacchanal madness.[20]

The examples presented seem, so far, to prove that Philastrius' position on the question of the heresogenic nature of literal exegesis was one-sided and decisive. It turns out, however, that Philastrius was not entirely consistent. In several cases, he considered erroneous a departure from the letter of the biblical text. According to a belief still dominant in the Church in the much later times of Nicolas Copernicus and Galileo, the Bishop of Brescia also made the Bible an oracle in matters that were the domain of specific sciences, and described as heretical those cosmological views which did not directly undermine the articles of Christian faith, but did not agree with the descriptions found in the Bible. For instance, he discerned as heresy the belief that stars occupy a permanent place in the sky and are not taken out of hidden places, and then hidden by God Himself at certain times, as deduced in his opinion, from the words of the Book of Baruch as literally understood: '[The All-knowing ...] calls [stars], they answer: "Here we are"' (see *Bar.* 3:32-5).[21] In this case, Philastrius,

---

[16] *Ibid.* 120.
[17] *Ibid.* 57.
[18] *Ibid.* 81.
[19] *Ibid.* 76.
[20] *Ibid.* 75.
[21] *Ibid.* 133.

paradoxically, became a supporter of a view which, from the point of view of
the science, exegesis and theology of today, would be considered erroneous.
In a similar way, he questioned the view that earthquakes were caused by the
laws of nature and were not directly caused by God, as evidenced by the literally
understood biblical texts 'He looks at the earth and moves it with an earthquake'
(*Ps.* 103:32) and 'I am going to shake the heavens and the earth' (*Hag.* 2:21).[22]

2. Is incorrect biblical exegesis more often a cause of doctrinal errors or damage to the spiritual life of Christians?

Despite the abovementioned heretical views caused by inappropriate, overly
literal, biblical exegesis, we can find much more often in Philastrius' catalogue
instances of detrimental effects on the development of the human spiritual life
of Christians, but which do not lead to formal doctrinal heresy. However,
Philastrius was convinced – referring to the entire Alexandrian tradition, from
Origen forth – that spiritual benefit, variously termed *utilitas spiritalis*, *scientia
caelestis* or *scientia salutaris*,[23] is an important criterion for the orthodox exegesis of Old Testament texts. If the proposed interpretation of the biblical text
did not lead to such spiritual benefit, it was described by the Bishop of Brescia
as heretical.[24] He called the followers of literalism heretics, even if their interpretations did not clearly harm the main doctrinal truths contained in the
Church's rule of faith.[25]

The most understandable and justified is his criticism of the literal interpretation of biblical texts written in the language of allegory, and demanding a
figurative explanation because of the specific literary genre. Such texts included,
above all, the Book of the *Song of Songs*. Philastrius did not indicate, however,
whether a literal exegesis of this book led to some specific heresy. He called
those Christians employing it people who do not bring proper fruit to bear
(*infructuosi*). He criticised their literal understanding of only one verse: 'There
are sixty queens and eighty concubines, and countless girls, but my dove is the
only one' (*Cant.* 6:7). According to the Bishop of Brescia, only the spiritual
exegesis of this passage is permissible, which perceives in the above groups of
women the image of human souls of varying degrees of perfection.[26] Philastrius
thus referred to the early Christian allegorical interpretation of the well-known
fragment of Saint Matthew's parable (*Matt.* 13:8), widespread among Alexandrian circles, of a threefold type of fruit – thirty, sixty and a hundredfold – as

---

[22] *Ibid.* 102.

[23] *Ibid.* 155; 156.

[24] *Ibid.* 150. See Mariusz Szram, 'Egzegeza literalna Starego Testamentu jako źródło herezji –
stanowisko Filastriusza z Brescii', *VoxP* 67 (2017), 619-29.

[25] Filastrius Brixiensis, *Diversarum hereseon liber* 76; 81; 150; 154.

[26] *Ibid.* 150.

the image of three categories of people who deserve the highest degree of eternal reward.[27]

In Philastrius' conviction, an allegorical interpretation was also demanded in biblical texts containing prophetic visions. The Bishop of Brescia criticised the literal interpretation of animals from Ezekiel's vision (*Ezek*. 1:5 and *Rev*. 4:6-9), noting that animals were not created in God's image, are bereft of intellect and, thus, could not give praise to God. According to Philastrius, they stand for the virtues of holy men: the lion is an allegory of strength (*fortitudo*), the ox – diligence (*labor*) and the eagle – lofty thinking (*volatus sublimis*) and the pursuit of the kingdom of heaven.[28]

The Bishop of Brescia also rejected the literal understanding of the vision of the angel who purified Isaiah by touching his lips with a hot coal (*Isa*. 6:6-7). According to him, limiting oneself to a literal reading does not bring about the spiritual benefit of allegorical interpretation, which sees in this scene the bestowing of the Holy Spirit's grace (symbolised by fire), allowing for the reading of the Holy Bible (symbolised by an angel) and the announcement of the coming of Christ in his divine nature unconquered by death (symbolised by the iron with which the hot coal was taken).[29]

Another literal interpretation, described by the Bishop of Brescia as heretical, concerned the scene of the measuring of Jerusalem by an angel with a measuring line, described in the prophet Zechariah and in the psalms (see *Zech*. 2:1; *Ps*. 59:8, 107:8). According to Philastrius, the sole orthodox and spiritually beneficial explanation is the allegorical: this scene means the announcement, through an angel, of the selection of a small number of believers and morally perfect people who will be saved.[30] The Bishop of Brescia added another element of allegorical significance, of a doctrinal nature, speaking against all trinitarian errors of the 4th century, namely, that the triple force with which the measuring line was tied means – according to Philastrius – the power of the same substance of the Father, Son and Holy Spirit, which was questioned by the Arians and Macedonians. It remains to be clarified where Philastrius obtained his information about the triple tying of the line, for it does not appear in either the Hebrew Bible or the Septuagint, which he considered to be an inspired translation, or in the Vulgate.

A literal interpretation of the Mosaic Law also met with criticism from Philastrius. In his approach, the Bishop of Brescia referred to the trend initiated in the second century by the Judeo-Christian author of the *Pseudo-Barnabas'*

---

[27] See Antonio Quacquarelli, *Il triplice frutto della vita cristiana: 100, 60, 30 (Matteo 13, 8 nelle diverse interpretazioni)* (Roma, 1953); Mariusz Szram, *Duchowy sens liczb w alegorycznej egzegezie aleksandryjskiej (II-V w.)* (Lublin, 1997), 332-3, 353-5.

[28] Filastrius Brixiensis, *Diversarum hereseon liber* 139.

[29] *Ibid*. 156.

[30] *Ibid*. 153.

Letter, giving the Old Testament food regulations spiritual significance,[31] and to the position of Origen, criticising the attitude of 'corporal Jews', *i.e.* those Christian exegetes who literally interpreted the provisions of the Law of Moses.[32] Philastrius was convinced that what Moses said to the Jews in a corporeal way (*carnaliter dicta*) was revealed in a spiritual way (*spiritaliter revelata sunt*) during the time of Christ and the Church.[33] He pointed out, however, that there are heretics who ignore this course of the history of salvation. As an example, he mentions a grouping – without a specific name – which literally interprets the Jewish fasts from the fourth, fifth, seventh and tenth months, about which the Lord reminds the prophet Zacharias (see *Zech.* 8:19). According to Philastrius, reading this passage literally is of no spiritual use, but it is difficult to know what heresy it would lead to, because the initial sentences of this part of the catalogue were not preserved. Philastrius himself proposes various allegorical explanations of the four fasts, using the biblical symbolism of the number '4'. Firstly, they are an announcement of the four fasts practised in the Church in connection with the holidays of the birth, resurrection and ascension of the Lord and the Pentecost. Secondly, they can symbolise the four most important books of Moses: Genesis, Exodus, Leviticus and Numbers. Thirdly, they are the announcement of the four Gospels. Fourthly, they refer to the imitative virtues of the most important figures in the history of salvation: the faith of the patriarchs, the bravery of the prophets, the diligence of priests, and the constant struggle waged by the apostles.[34]

Another literal interpretation criticised by Philastrius is that of the Old Testament law concerning the order from Exodus (*Exod.* 22:27) in the versions of the Septuagint and Vulgate: 'You will not blaspheme the gods' (in the Hebrew versions, it is in the singular, so the whole discussion of the difficulties related to the meaning of this passage becomes groundless). The Bishop of Brescia listed – as usual, without a name – heretics who understood these words literally as a prohibition on cursing pagan gods, thus exposing themselves to the loss of salvation. In the meantime, only the figurative meaning of this command should be accepted, to which the words of the Psalm are the key (*Ps.* 82:6): 'I said: "You are gods and all are sons of the Most High"'. In the light of these words, the command from the Book of Exodus refers – according to Philastrius – not to pagan deities, but to all saints who abide by the true faith, because, through them, the word of God is preached. Such people – who are the true sons of God – should not only not be cursed, but they deserve the highest praise.[35]

---

[31] Pseudo-Barnabas, *Epistula Barnabae* 10.
[32] See Nicholas Robert Michael de Lange, *Origen and the Jews. Studies in Jewish-Christian relations in third-century Palestine* (Cambridge, 1976).
[33] Filastrius Brixiensis, *Diversarum hereseon liber* 141.
[34] *Ibid.* 149.
[35] *Ibid.* 147.

Philastrius most often criticised the literal interpretation of historical events described in the Old Testament. He remained true to Origen's principle in this matter: in the Old Testament books, God's Word often tells historical events, but not to teach the readers history.[36] As heretical, Philastrius described a literal interpretation of the wording in the Letter to the Hebrews (*Heb.* 7:3; see *Gen.* 14:17), that Melchizedek was born without a father and mother. The loss of the text of the Philastrian catalogue does not allow us to find out what this interpretation was; we can only guess that these, as usual, unspecified heretics indeed thought that Melchizedek was born in a way that ignored the laws of nature. According to Philastrius, the words about birth without a mother and father should be interpreted as learning the mystery of Christ not from the people, but from God's inspiration.[37] It is interesting that the Bishop of Brescia did not refer in his exegesis to the supernatural birth of Christ, whose type was, in the patristic literature, the priest Melchizedek and which would perfectly correspond with those heated polemics, fought in the 4th century, with those heresies which refused deity to the person of Jesus.[38]

Philastrius considered it heretical to draw literal conclusions from the text of *1Kgs.* 17:6, which tells that crows brought bread to the prophet Elijah every day and meat in the evening. According to Philastrius, Elijah despised meat and voluntarily refrained from it. If one accepts the truthfulness of the biblical account, it should be understood in such a way that the crow was devoid of reason, so it did not know what it was doing; only instinct ordered it to help the man in this way. In addition, the raven's instinctive behaviour as an unreasonable being, and yet sensitive to the needs of a man in a difficult situation, was here – as emphasised by the Bishop of Brescia – opposed to the hostile attitude of rational beings, which are the people, towards the prophet.[39]

The above examples of the literal exegesis of Old Testament texts, which do not lead directly to the emergence of doctrinal heresy, but do not bring Christians any benefits in their spiritual life, constitute the majority of the interpretations of biblical texts criticised by Philastrius in the last part of his work. Thus, it can be said that, according to the Bishop of Brescia, literal exegesis does not have to lead to doctrinal heresy, but very often it inhibits the spiritual development of Christians and, therefore, deserves to be called heresy in the broad sense of the word.

---

[36] See Henri Crouzel, 'Origène et le sens littéral dans ses *Homélies sur l'Hexateuque*', *BLE* 70 (1969), 241-63, 245: 'La Bible n'a pas en vue l'histoire, mais l'enseignement religieux et spirituel: elle n'est pas à lire comme si elle contenait des récits profanes'.

[37] Filastrius Brixiensis, *Diversarum hereseon liber* 148.

[38] See Rafał Zarzeczny, 'Melchizedek w literaturze wczesnochrześcijańskiej i gnostyckiej', *SACh SN* 9 (2009), 231.

[39] Filastrius Brixiensis, *Diversarum hereseon liber* 144.

3. Conclusions

To sum up, it should be stated that, in the opinion of Philastrius as a supporter of allegorical interpretation as derived from the Alexandrian environment, there was a cause-and-effect relationship between remaining at the level of the literal exegesis of the biblical text and the emergence of heresy. The Bishop of Brescia expressed this belief in the following statement: 'Those who do not understand the meaning of the Scriptures, remaining on the level of the letter, are in agreement with pagans, and are far from Christianity'.[40] Although Philastrius referred to the literal interpretation of the Old Testament as heresy, or referred to those who used it as heretics, the main specific objection formulated in his catalogue against literalism is the lack of spiritual benefit for the reader, and not any influence on the formulation of wrong dogmatic views.

Finally, a general remark related to the way of thinking, arguing and – hence – the methodology for presenting heresy in Philastrius' catalogue. The Bishop of Brescia's work fully reflects the thesis of the eminent Italian patrologist Manlio Simonetti, who stated years ago that the Fathers of the Church thought with the Bible.[41] The two types of heresies presented by Philastrius are rooted in erroneous thinking about the Scriptures, and his response to those views refers primarily to biblical argumentation. In this context, the Scriptures appear to be the main anchor of orthodoxy, and its correct interpretation is a basic safeguard against all heresy.

[40] *Ibid.* 147: *Non ergo intellegentes virtutem scripturarum ex littera paganitati consentiunt, et alieni a Christianitate reperiuntur.*
[41] See M. Simonetti, *Lettera e/o allegoria* (1985), 9-10.

The Resurrection of Jesus
in Jerome's *Commentary on Matthew*

Leszek MISIARCZYK, Warsaw, Poland

ABSTRACT

Jerome's *Commmentary on Matthew* was written in AD 398 at the request of Eusebius of Cremona who expected a historical interpretation of the Gospel. The author bases his interpretation on the literal and historical sense of the biblical text but, inspired by Origen, he also deepens his interpretation using the allegorical method. In his interpretation of the resurrection of Jesus as described in the Gospel of Matthew, Jerome gives us many historical and geographical details about Palestine and Judaism from the first century. The resurrection of Jesus is, for him, proof of his divinity and the truth of the Gospels. When finding apparent contradictions between the Synoptic Gospels, Jerome tries to explain them in order to save the infallibility of the sacred text.

1. Introduction

Eusebius of Cremona, one of Jerome's companions in Bethlehem, when returning to Italy in AD 398 asked him to prepare a short and literal commentary on the Gospel of Matthew. We know the circumstances of the Commentary on the Gospel of Saint Matthew from the Letters of Jerome, mainly from the letters *Ad Lucinium Baeticum*,[1] *Ad Evangelum presbyterum*[2] and also from the *Preface* of the *Commentary* itself. He mentions that, for a long time, he was seriously ill and it was only during Lent that he began to feel better and gain strength. The improvement in his health meant that he began to write this very *Commentary*. Even if too much intellectual effort resulted in the deterioration of his health, he did not quit writing the *Commentary*, but it became increasingly difficult. In the *Preface* to this work, he noted that he had worked very quickly and had written the entire *Commentary* probably within two weeks in 398, shortly before Easter.[3] The fact that the text was written so quickly explains its

---

[1] Hieronymus, *Epistula* 71, 5.

[2] *Id., Epistula* 73, 10.

[3] See Émile Bonnard, *Introduction*, in Saint Jérome, *Commentaire sur S. Mattheu*, I, SCh 242 (Paris, 1977), 11-3; Thomas Scheck, *Introduction*, in St. Jerome, *Commentary on Matthew* (Washington, DC, 2008), 15-6. In the Preface to Matthew, Jerome complains: 'But with Easter now imminent and the winds blowing, you are forcing me to dictate this work in two weeks, so that at one time the stenographers are taking notes, at another the sheets are to be written, at

very synthetic nature. In fact, in the *Commentary* we find many short sentences, sometimes shorter than the biblical text being commented on. It also happens that one or more verses are omitted entirely, and others are simply discussed briefly and, even then, not very accurately. But, as an exegete, Jerome is very well prepared to comment on every biblical text. He does not start discussing a difficult topic in a biblical text unless he has previously established the best version of that same text. Thanks to his knowledge of the Hebrew text of the Old Testament, he refers to it, *e.g.* by commenting on *Matt.* 2:23.[4] Jerome also assumes the truth and complete lack of any error in the Holy Scriptures, contrary to Celsus or Julian, who accused the evangelists of lies. Although he saw the differences between the accounts of the individual evangelists and tried to explain them, he never doubted that the holy text is free from error. He once defended this fundamental harmony of the evangelists by referring to the Hebrew text of the Old Testament; another time, in *Matt.* 2:5, he noted an inaccurate quote from the prophet Micah and blamed the copyists for it. Commenting on *Matt.* 1:16, he noted that Matthew presents Joseph as the son of Jacob, but Luke as the son of Eli, and explains this by the law of levirate.[5] Similarly, in the case of the Transfiguration which, according to Matthew, took place six days after Peter's confession, but eight days according to Luke, it was because Luke added the days of confession and transfiguration;[6] and that the different times of visiting the grave of Jesus by the women is proof that they came many times and went away.[7]

Although for Jerome the spiritual sense of the biblical text is the most important, nevertheless, as he himself states in the Preface to the *Commentary on Matthew*, at the request of Eusebius of Cremona he wishes to give him a historical commentary (*historicam interpretationem*).[8] Therefore, he took great care of the geographical and historical accuracy of the events presented in the Gospel of Matthew. Not only did he learn the works of Eusebius (*Church History*, *Chronicle* and *Onomasticon*), but he himself personally visited many places in Palestine, explaining their origin and meaning. According to Jerome, ignoring history leads to errors because the spiritual and mystical sense of the Gospel text must be based on its historical sense.[9] Thanks to his own knowledge, he corrects many geographical and historical errors present in the

---

yet another corrections are being made, in order to complete it in the given time – and this especially when you are well aware that I have been so ill for the last three months that I am hardly now beginning to walk about, and could not possibly balance the immensity of the task against the brevity of time' (*ibid.*, 57).

[4] See George Bardy, 'Jérôme et ses maîtres hébreux', *RBen* 46 (1934), 145-64.

[5] See Adam Kamesar, *Jerome, Greek Scholarship, and the Hebrew Bible* (Oxford, 1993), 111-25.

[6] Hieronymus, *Commentarius in Evangelium Matthaei* 19, 1.

[7] *Ibid.* 28, 1.

[8] *Ibid.* Praefatio.

[9] See David Brown, *Vir Trilingus: A Study in the Biblical Exegesis of Saint Jerome* (Kampen, 1992), 145-68.

comments of his predecessors, such as Origen. Jerome was also well aware of
the Judaism of the era and introduces many explanations into the *Commentary*.
Since he assumes that the Gospel of Matthew was written for converted Jews,
the evangelist did not explain Jewish customs. Thus, in order to better understand the teachings of Jesus, Jerome sometimes recalls a law or some Jewish
tradition.[10] In the Preface, however, he adds, 'I have sometimes thrown in a
few of the flowers of the spiritual interpretation, while I reserve the perfect
work for a future day'.[11] In seeking a deeper spiritual sense, Jerome was
inspired by his master Origen, whose *Commentary on Matthew* and *Homily* he
had read.[12] However, he perceives allegory in two ways: on the one hand, as a
search for a deeper spiritual meaning of the biblical text; on the other, he is
still aware that it is impossible to completely explain the mystery.[13]

In the Preface, Jerome mentions comments on the Gospel of Matthew written
by his predecessors, such as Theophilus of Antioch, Hippolytus Martyr, Theodore
from Heraclea, Apollinaris, Didymus, and Hilary, but immediately adds that
'neglecting the authority of ancient writers, since I have no opportunity of reading or following them, I have confined myself to the brief exposition and translation of the narrative which you particularly requested'. The most visible influence
of Origen is both in the search for the spiritual meaning of the biblical text, as
well as the recalling of the same subjects. Thus, he emphasises the goodness of
God, as did Origen against the Gnostics. Jesus Christ is a teacher and pedagogue
who is the only one who knows the Father fully and is able to reveal Him,[14] and
that the Church is the depository of his teaching. Jerome frequently expresses his
admiration for Origen, even if he disagrees with some of his interpretations.[15]

As for the structure of the *Commentary*, it is based on the structure of the
Gospel according to Saint Matthew. The work is divided into four parts: the first
part (chapters 1, 1-10, 42), the second part (chapters 11, 2-16, 9), the third part
(chapters 16, 13-22, 37) and the fourth part (chapters 22, 41-28, 20). The last part
can be divided into two sections: the passion and death of Jesus (ch. 26-27) and
His resurrection (ch. 28). In this essay, I will concentrate my analysis only on the
resurrection of Jesus, trying to pick up on what is most important in Jerome's
interpretation of *Matt.* 28:1-20. The Gospel's text will be quoted in the Latin
version used by Jerome, according to the critical edition of *Sources Chrétiennes*.[16]

---

[10] See Andrew Souter, 'Greek and Hebrew Words in Jerome's Commentary on St. Matthew's
Gospel', *HTR* 28 (1935), 1-4; *id.*, 'Notes on Incidental Gospel Quotations in Jerome's Commentary
on St. Matthew's Gospel', *JTS* 42 (1941), 12-8.

[11] Hieronymus, *Commentarius in Evangelium Matthaei*, Prefatio.

[12] *Ibid.* Praefatio.

[13] *Ibid.* 6, 26; 15, 15.

[14] *Ibid.* 7, 29; 11, 27.

[15] See Elisabeth Clark, *The Origenist Controversy: The Cultural Contruction of an Early
Christian Debate* (Princeton, 1992).

[16] Saint Jérome, *Commentaire sur S. Mattheu*, ed. Émile Bonnard, II, SCh 259 (Paris, 1977),
308-19.

2. The Resurrection of Jesus (*Matt.* 28:1-20)

Vespere autem sabbati, quae lucescit in prima sabbati, venit Maria Magdalenae et altera Maria videre sepulchrum (Matt. 28:1).[17]

Jerome was perfectly aware that, in the various Gospels, we have different statements on the time when the women arrived at the grave of Jesus, but, nevertheless, he defends the truthfulness of the gospel message. In fact, in the Gospel of Matthew we find this statement: 'after the Sabbath, and towards dawn on the first day of the week'; in *Mark* 16:1: 'when the Sabbath was over'; in *Luke* 24:1: 'on the first day of the week'; and in *John* 20:1: 'It was very early on the first day of the week and still dark'. Jerome himself quotes the Latin version of the text: *vespere autem sabbati, quae lucescit in primam sabbati.* According to him, the different times of the day when the women visited Jesus' grave are not evidence of a lie, as the *impii* accuse, but a sign of zealous fulfillment of the obligation to visit the grave. The women often departed from the grave and returned, not allowing themselves to move away from it for a long time. We do not know whom he meant by *impii*, we can only guess that they could have been Jews or pagans who used these apparent contradictions between the Gospels to completely undermine its historicity. Jerome rejects such an accusation and indicates that the women often go away and return (*dum crebro abeunt ac recurrunt*), hence the impression that, according to the individual Gospels, they come to the grave at different times of the day. However, this only means that the individual Evangelists described not the same visit to the grave, but subsequent ones. Secondly, according to Jerome, the women did so because they did not even want to move away from the grave for even a short while and leave it uncared for (*non patiuntur a sepulchro Domini diu abesse vel longius*). Perhaps they were afraid that some of Jesus' enemies would come and defile it. In any case, Jerome's interpretation, that the women did not want to leave the empty grave unattended for a moment, is very interesting.

Et ecce terrae motus factus est magnus; angelus enim Domini descendit de caelo, et accedens reuoluit lapidem, et sedebat super eum; erat autem aspectus eius sicut fulgur, et vestimentum eius sicut nix (Matt. 28:2-3).[18]

Commenting on verses 2-3, Jerome focuses on two things: demonstrating that Jesus is both the Son of God and Man and that He has two natures, divine and human (*iuxta utramque naturam, divinitatis et carnis*), which are the signs of His greatness and humility; and he also emphasises the presence of angels at the occasions of major events in His life. Thus, the great earthquake and the

---

[17] *Ibid.* 308.
[18] *Ibid.*

descent of the angel from Heaven prove that Christ, although a man who was crucified, buried and enclosed in a grave with a boulder (*qui crucifixus est, qui sepultus est, qui clausus tumulo, quem lapis oppositus cohibet*), nevertheless, is the Son of God (*ostendunt Filium Dei*) as shown by external signs such as the darkened sun (*sol fugiens*), the engulfing of the darkness (*tenebrae ingruentes*), the earthquake (*terra commota*), the torn curtain (*velum scissum*), the cracking of the rocks (*saxa dirupta*), the dead being resurrected (*mortui suscitati*) and the angels' service (*angelorum ministeria*). In a further part of his *Commentary*, Jerome lists events related to the life of Jesus in which angels take part: Gabriel comes to Mary (*Ad Mariam Gabriel venit*), an angel talks to Joseph (*cum Joseph Angelus loquitur*), an angel announces to the shepherds (*idem pastoribus nuntiat*), a chorus of angels is later heard singing "Glory to God" (*angelorum postea auditur chorus dicentium: Gloria in excelsis Deo*), Christ is tempted in the wilderness and then the angels tend to him (*tentatur in solitudine, et post victoriam statim serviunt angeli*). Now an angel comes, the guardian of the tomb of the Lord, and in a shining robe indicates the glory of the triumphant (*Nunc quoque Angelus venit custos sepulcri Dominici, et in vestitu candido signat gloriam triumphantis*). When Christ ascends to heaven, we can see two angels on the Mount of Olives promising the apostles the second coming of the Lord (*Nec non ascendente ad caelos Domino, duo angeli in Oliveti monte cernuntur, pollicentes apostolis secundum Salvatoris adventum*). Thus, just as the passion, death, and burial are signs of the human nature of Christ, so all extraordinary signs, especially the presence of angels, are proof of His deity. Jerome emphasises the deity of Jesus Christ in the context of the polemics with Arianism in the 4th century which, as we know, was, at that time, undermining it.

Prae timore autem eius exterriti sunt custodes et facti sunt uelut mortui; respondensque angelus dixit mulieribus: Nolite timere vos; scio enim quod Iesum qui crucifixus est quaeritis (Matt. 28:4-5).[19]

Jerome emphasises the fact that the guards were so dumbfounded and shaken by fear of Him that they lay as if dead (*Custodes, timore perterriti instar mortuorum stupefacti iacent*). However, the angel did not comfort them at all, but the women who came to the grave: You need not be afraid (*et tamen angelos non illos, sed mulieres consolatur. Nolite timere vos*). The others – let them be afraid, let fear remain in those in whom disbelief persists (*Illi, inquit, timeant: in his perseveret pavor, in quibus permanet incredulitas*). The angel does not comfort those who do not believe in Jesus, leaves them to themselves and lets them continue to be afraid. Instead, since 'you are looking for Jesus crucified, hear that he has risen and fulfilled His promises' (*Caeterum vos Iesum quaeritis crucifixum, audite quod resurrexit et promissa perfecerit*). Jerome emphasises

---

[19] *Ibid.* 310.

not only the fact of the resurrection of Jesus, but also that, in this way, he fulfilled his promises when he announced his resurrection.

Venite et videte ubi positus erat [...] et cito euntes dicite discipulis eius quia surrexit et ecce praecedit vos in Galilaeam ibi eum videbitis; ecce praedixi vobis (Matt. 28:6-7).[20]

According to Jerome, the angel showing the empty tomb to the women wants to tell them: believe an empty grave if you don't believe my words (*Ut si meis verbis non creditis, vacuo credatis sepulcro*). Secondly, the angel recommends that the women go quickly, and tell His disciples, 'He has risen from the dead and now he is going ahead of you to Galilee; that is where you will see him. Look! I have told you'. In this way, the women who went to the sepulchre of Jesus became the first apostles of His resurrection. Thirdly, he explains the term 'Galilee' as a pagan swamp (*volutabrum gentium*), where earlier there was error and deceptiveness (*ubi ante error erat et lubricum*) and where Christ did not step with a strong and stable foot (*et firmo ac stabili pede vestigium non ponebat*). Jerome defines the Galilee of the Gentiles as a swamp, an area where pagans dominated by erroneous polytheism, without faith in the one God. Although Christ, during his earthly life, lived in Galilee and stayed there many times, according to Jerome he was never at home there. Now, after his resurrection, he wants to meet his disciples there, as an announcement of the future conversion of the pagan world.

Et exierunt cito de monumento cum timore et gaudio magno currentes nuntiare discipulis eius (Matt. 28:8).[21]

Jerome emphasises that fact that the women's minds have a double feeling: fear and joy (*Duplex mentes mulierum tenebat affectus, timor et gaudii*). The fear arose under the influence of the greatness of the miracle of the resurrection (*alter de miraculi magnitudine*), the joy from longing for the Risen One (*alter ex desiderio resurgentis*), because he is alive and will be seen again. According to Jerome, both of these feelings stimulated the women (*et tamen uterque femineum concitabat gradum*) to go to the apostles, so that, through them, as official witnesses, the germ of faith could grow (*ut per illos fidei seminarium spargeretur*).

Et ecce Iesus occurrit illis dicens: Avete (Matt. 28:9).[22]

In his *Commentary*, Jerome emphasises the meeting of the women with the risen Lord and refers to a curse on Eve. At first, the Stridonian shows that those

---

[20] *Ibid.*
[21] *Ibid.* 312.
[22] *Ibid.*

women who sought the Saviour and hurried with the Good News about his rising from the dead merited the first meeting with the Lord (*Quae sic quaerebant, quae ita currebant, merebantur obvium habere Dominum resurgentem et primum audire: Avete*). Seeking the Lord and then, after discovering the empty grave, running to announce the joyful news of the Lord's resurrection to the Apostles, are efforts which the Lord rewarded by appearing personally to the women. Secondly, adds Jerome, through this meeting with the Lord a curse was lifted, that which had rested on Eve because of her disobedience in Paradise (*ut maledictum Evae mulieris in mulieribus subverteretur*). However, it is not explained exactly what this curse-lifting would consist of. If, as we remember from the Book of Genesis, the curse of Eve after committing original sin consisted of giving birth to children in pain, and giving her heart to a man who was to dominate her, it would not seem that the meeting with the risen Christ changed anything.

Illae autem accesserunt et tenuerunt pedes eius et adoraverunt eum (*Matt.* 28:9).

According to Jerome, the women come and embrace Jesus' feet because they worshipped Him (*Istae accedunt et teneant pedes eius, quia adoraverunt eum*). The writer from Stridon then refers to the attitude of Mary in *John* 20:17, who was looking for the living Jesus among the dead because she did not know that the Son of God had already risen (*Illa quae quaerebat viventem cum mortuis, et nesciebat adhuc Filium Dei surrexisse*); she rightly hears the words that she should not touch Jesus because he has not yet ascended to the Father (*merito audit: Ne tangeas me, nondum enim ascendi ad Patrem meum*). The women, according to the Gospel of Matthew, cannot touch Jesus, but only come and embrace His feet, for He has not yet ascended to the Father.

Tunc ait illis Iesus: Nolite timere (*Matt.* 28:10).[23]

Jerome emphasises the fact that, in both the Old and the New Testament, whenever there is a divine revelation, people first experience fear (*Et in veteri et in novo Testamento, hoc semper observandum est: quod quando angustior aliqua apparuerit visio, primum timor pellitur*). All of this is done so that the silent soul can hear the words spoken (*mente placata, possint quae dicuntur audiri*). That is why Jesus says to the women 'Do not be afraid', and they are able to hear His messsage.

Ite nuntiate fratribus meis ut eant in Galileam, ibi me videbunt (*Matt.* 28:10).

Although the Gospel text clearly suggests that it concerns the Apostles, Jerome sees the second part of verse 10 as referring to the Gentiles. The brothers are those

[23] *Ibid.*

about whom *Ps.* 21(22):23 says: 'I shall proclaim your name to my brothers', that is, to those who no longer see the Saviour in Judea, but among many nations.

Et congregati cum senioribus, consilio accepto, pecuniam copiosam dederunt militibus, dicentes: Dicite quia discipuli eius nocte venerunt, et furati sunt eum nobis dormientibus; et si hoc auditum fuerit a praeside, nos suadebimus ei, et securos vos faciemus (Matt. 28:12-4).[24]

Jerome, in his commentary on this verse, raises the issue of paying for telling a lie. At the very beginning, he writes that those guards who knew about the miracle were hastily returning to the city to announce to the high priests what they had seen, what events had occurred before their very eyes (*Custodes miraculum cognoscebant: ad urbem conciti redeunt, nuntiant principibus sacerdotum quae viderant, quae facta conspexerint*). The high priests and elders, who should have turned to repentance and sought the risen Jesus (*Illi qui debuerant converti ad poenitentiam, et Iesum quaerere resurgentem*), persevere in their malice (*perseverant in malitia*) and the money that was given for temple use (*et pecunia quae ad usus templi data fuerant*) they use to pay for lies (*verterunt in redemptionem mendacii*), just as previously they had given 30 silver pieces to Judas (*sicut antea triginta argenteos dederant Iudae proditori*). As the chief priests and elders of the people had used money from the Temple of Jerusalem to pay for the betrayal of Judas, so now they give money from the treasury of the temple to the soldiers for lying. Jerome ends his commentary on this verse by saying that all who abuse the temple contributions or the money collected for the Church in other matters in order to fulfill their will (*Omnes igitur qui stipe templi et his quae conferuntur ad usus Ecclesiae abutuntur in aliis rebus, quibus suam expleant voluntatem*) are similar to those scribes and priests paying for lying and the blood of the Saviour (*similes sunt scribarum et sacerdotum redimentium mendacium et Salvatoris sanguinem*). He applies this verse to the very real situation of the Church in his time.

Undecim autem discipuli abierunt in Galileam, in montem ubi constituerat illis Iesus (Matt. 28:16).[25]

Jerome notes that, after his resurrection, Jesus is seen on the mountain in Galilee and his disciples worship Him there (*Post resurrectionem Jesus in monte Galilaeae conspiciuntur, ibique adoratur*). Although some are doubtful, their doubt increases our faith (*licet quidam dubitent, et dubitatio eorum nostram augeat fidem*). In what sense? As in the case of doubting Thomas (*John* 20:27), Jesus appears to him more openly, and shows him His side wounded by the

---

[24] *Ibid.* 314.
[25] *Ibid.*

spear and His hands pierced by the nails (*Tunc manifestius ostenditur Thomae et latus lancea vulneratum, et manus fixas demonstrat clavis*). Had it not been for Thomas's disbelief, Christ would not have appeared more clearly to everyone, showing his pierced hands and side. Thus, the disbelief of the disciples was helpful, according to Jerome, to increase the faith of subsequent generations of Christians.

Accedens Iesus locutus est eis, dicens: Data est mihi omnis potestas in caelo et in terra (Matt. 28:18).[26]

Commenting on this verse, Jerome states that power was given to he who had been crucified, buried in a grave and risen again (*Illi potestas data est, qui paulo ante crucifixus, qui sepultus in tumulto, qui mortuus iacuerat, qui postea resurrexit*). This power was given to Christ in Heaven and on Earth, that the one who had previously reigned with God in Heaven would also reign on Earth through the faith of the believers (*In coelo autem et in terra potestas data est, ut qui ante regnabat in coelo, per fidem credentium regnet in terris*). The theme of Christ's reign on Earth, thanks to the faith of his disciples, is undoubtedly the most interesting point of his explanation.

Euntes ergo docete omnes gentes baptizantes eos in nomine Patris et Filii et Spiritus Sancti (Matt. 28:19).[27]

Jerome notes that Christ's command is that the Apostles first teach all nations (*Primum docent omnes gentes*), and then baptise those instructed nations (*deinde docetas intingunt aqua*). According to our exegete, the body cannot receive the sacrament of baptism if the soul has not previously accepted the truth of faith (*Non enim potest fieri ut corpus baptismi recipiat sacramentum, nisi ante anima fidei susceperit veritatem*). Therefore, instruction must precede baptism. And they are baptised in the name of the Father and of the Son and of the Holy Spirit, that those whose divinity one would have one generosity, and one God is the name of the Holy Trinity (*Baptizantur autem in nomine Patris et Filii, et Spiritus Sancti, ut quorum una est divinitas, una sit largitio; nomenque Trinitatis unus Deus est*).

Docentes eos servare omnia quaecumque mandavi vobis (Matt. 28:20).[28]

Jerome emphasises the order. Christ commanded the Apostles to first teach all nations (*Iussit apostolis ut primum docerent universas gentes*), then to baptise

---

[26] *Ibid.* 316.
[27] *Ibid.*
[28] *Ibid.*

them in the sacrament of faith (*deinde fidei intingerent sacramento*), and, after faith and baptism, to teach them what should be preserved (*et post fidem ac baptisma, quae essent observanda praeciperent*). However, so that readers do not think that this is something trivial and small that they are being ordered to keep, he adds: everything I have commanded you, that those who believe and will be baptised in the name of the Holy Trinity may still do everything that has been ordered (*Ac ne putemus levia esse quae iussa sunt et pauca, addidit: Omnia quaecumque mandavi vobis. Ut quicumque crediderint qui in Trinitate fuerint baptizati, omnia faciant quae praecepta sunt*).

Et ecce ego vobiscum sum omnibus diebus usque ad consummationem saeculi (*Matt.* 28:20).[29]

According to Jerome, Christ promises that he will be with his disciples until the end of the world, and shows that they will always win and he will never abandon the believers (*Qui usque ad consummationem saeculi cum discipulis se futurum esse promittit et illos ostendit semper esse victuros, et se numquam a credentibus recessurum*). Christ, promising his presence until the end of the world, knows well the day when he will be with the Apostles after His second coming (*Qui autem usque ad consummationem mundi sui praesentiam pollicetur, non ignorat eam diem in qua se scit futurum cum apostolis*). Jerome clearly emphasises the fact that Christ, announcing that he would remain with his disciples until the end of the world as the Son of God, knew exactly the day the world ends.

3. Conclusion

Jerome, explaining ch. 28 of the Gospel of Matthew, used either the literal method of interpretation or the allegorical one. Some of his interpretations seem quite interesting, insightful and very deep spiritually. Others are less so, but he tried to explain the most difficult verses of this chapter and to apply its message to the historical context of a Christian's life in the 4th century. The principle of his exegesis is the truthfulness of the Gospels, so he tries to explain the apparent contradictions in a way which would not undermine this principle. Thus, we find, for example, the fact that the women came to the tomb of Jesus at different times according to the Synoptic Gospels. Jerome explains this in a very simple way: the women came to the tomb of Jesus many times and at different times, and so it is understandable that the Evangelists noted only some of them.

---

[29] *Ibid.*

Biblical *Tannin/tannim* in St. Jerome's Translation and Interpretation

Krzysztof MORTA, Wrocław, Polska

ABSTRACT

This article is dedicated to the Hebrew term *Tannin*, which appears in the Bible and signifies a monster, giant serpent, sea snake. Ancient translations – the Septuagint, Symmachus, Aquila and Theodotion – combined it with another Hebrew word, *tannim* (appearing in the Bible only in the plural form). This probably happened due to the similarity between these forms. St. Jerome does not distinguish between these words either. In those places where they appear, he consistently translates them using the Latin word *draco*, the meaning of which is so broad that it encompasses both a mythical, giant serpentine monster and a typical snake found in the wild. However, in some problematic places, where such an identification would have aroused controversy, he decided on introducing different equivalents more fitting to the context. There are two such places: in the *Book of Lamentations* (4:3), where he used the equivalent of Lamiae, and in the *Book of Isaiah* (13:22), where he translated *tannim* as 'Sirens'. Jerome's view of *Tannin/tannim* as equivalents shows us that, although he drew from his Greek predecessors, he does not follow them uncritically, and decides to choose his own interpretational propositions and solutions. As we can see from the examples discussed, he makes these distinctions by taking into consideration the imagery, symbolism and a whole range of associations. He tries his best to choose more familiar, ancient Greco-Roman names for culturally remote and incomprehensible Hebrew terms.

The world of beasts and monstrous creatures is present in many belief-systems and has been reflected and described in the cosmology of many cultures and civilisations. The origins of this world reach back so far into the past that we can speak of a long oral tradition even before its appearance in written sources. Even in the Bible we can find some echoes of those stories, for instance in the appearance of the names of the seven monsters. Although they have been largely de-mythicised since then, they used to embody the forces of chaos, of evil. In fact, they incarnated the elements that evoked fear and anxiety due to their range, untameable nature and might. If we want to look for the biblical genesis of their appearance in the holy scriptures, we should go back to the mythology of the Canaanites, and also of their neighbouring peoples, with whom the ancient Israelites stayed in contact. Those mythological depictions enabled the Bible's authors to use more expressions and partly recognisable images that illustrated more clearly their new message. They were the perfect material to show in a dramatic, easily conceivable way the struggle between good and evil, between the forces of harmony and destruction.

A comparison of these images with other ancient literary works, including those in Ugaritic, allows us to abstract those creatures that appear most commonly in texts referring to the beginnings of the world, *i.e.* to the original, primordial cosmology: Tannin, Nahash, Rahab, Leviathan, Behemoth, Yam, Tehom. In this article, we will take a closer look at the monster called Tannin (תַּנִּין). We will focus in particular on St. Jerome's translation, rendition and interpretation of this term.

Tannin, which appears for the first time in the *Book of Genesis* (1:21), had already caused many difficulties in ancient translations. Its identification was difficult, but the fact that in the Hebrew text of the Bible there appears a similar name, *tannim* (תַּנִּים), made the situation even more complex. It is the plural form of the singular *tan* (תַּן)[1] which is not mentioned in the Bible. This form referred to a rather demonical creature and appears in different contexts to Tannin. Today, this distinction is respected as a general rule and the name *tannim* is translated as Jackals.[2] However, even as late as the 17th century dictionaries of the Hebrew language, due to the similarities between the forms, still used one entry for *Tannin*, treating *tannim* as its alternative transcription. For several centuries, scholars had regarded the two forms as one Hebrew term, but with different interpretative possibilities, and so they adapted them to specific contexts.

This occurs, for example, in Christian Stock's (1672-1733) Hebrew-Latin dictionary[3] and also in *Janua Hebraeae linguae Veteris Testamenti*.[4] In his monumental work *Hierozoicon*,[5] Samuel Bochart (1599-1667), the great researcher, polyglot and specialist in Semitic languages, also did not introduce any distinction between *Tannin* and *tannim*. Nonetheless, soon after that Johann Simonis

---

[1] More misunderstandings were caused by the distorted plural form in *Ezek.* 29:3; 32:2, which is *tannim* written in a way that suggests it comes from *tan*. See also *Ps.* 44:20, where a more sensible correction from *tannim* to *Tannin* should be made.

[2] Gerhard Lisowsky, *Konkordanz zum Hebräischen Alten Testament* (Stuttgart, 1981), 1524; Martin Hagen, *Realia Biblica. Geographica, naturalia, archeologica* (Paris, 1914), 385.

[3] *Christiani Stockii Clavis linguae sanctae Veteris Testamenti*, Ienae Apud Joh. Felicem Bielckium MDCCXXVII, 1191 (*Tannin – draco, cetus, balaena, serpens, crocodilus*).

[4] *Janua Hebraeae linguae Veteris Testamenti* [...] *accessit una cum grammatica Lexicon Hebraeo-Chaldaicum accurante M. Christiano Reineccio*, Lipsiae Sump. Haered. Lanckisianorum anno 1733. For example, in the explanation to *Isa.* 13:22 the form *Tannin* appears (instead of the *tannim* present in the Hebrew text), translated as *draco*.

[5] Samuel Bochart, *Hierozoicon, Sive Bipartitum Opus De Animalibus S. Scripturae: Cujus Pars Prior Libris IV. De Animalibus in Genere, & de Quadrupedibus Viviparis & Oviparis: Pars Posterior Libris VI. De Avibus, Serpentibus, Insectis, Aquaticis, & Fabulosis Animalibus agit. Cum Indice Septuplici, editio quarta, apud Lugduni Batavorum* (Lugdunum: apud Cornelium Boutesteyn et Samuelem Luchtmans, 1712), 728-40.

from Halle (1698-1768) recognised this terminological division in his Hebrew-Latin dictionary.[6] Throughout the centuries, the Hebrew Bible translators have struggled with the correct understanding of these mixed, misinterpreted and indistinguishable terms.

What, then, is Tannin? Let us start with the fact that it is mentioned fourteen times in the Bible, including five times in its plural form *Tanninim*.[7] Contemporary researchers derive this name from the root *tnn*,[8] which means 'to stretch', 'to be long'. Other alternatives offer the roots *tnh*[9] or *jtn*.[10] Yet this does not change the meaning. It should be emphasised, though, that a similar name also appears in other languages, *e.g.* in Egyptian and Ugaritic. We find it in Arabic, too, but in this case it could be derived from Hebrew. It is associated with a sea monster,[11] a serpent, a dragon.

The term must have evolved in the Hebrew Bible, since it appears as a mighty sea creature in the *Book of Genesis* (*Gen.* 1:23). It is synonymously juxtaposed with the sea beasts Rahab and Yam. In turn, in the story of Moses's staff becoming[12] *Tannin*, it is reduced to a snake (*Exod.* 7:10-2).

As has been mentioned above, to this already ambiguous depiction of Tannin have been added images attributed to *tannim*. They accompany the descriptions of desertic and desolated places. Translators of the Septuagint viewed those creatures as the same, usually referring to them as *drakontes*. This Greek term, however, is also ambiguous in its own language. If we look into the ancient literature, it is easily noted that the name was given to both mythical beasts and actual or 'real' snakes, meaning many different creatures. It was applied to different species from the natural world, *e.g.* snakes and lizards. It was used for enormous African[13] or Asian snakes that were several metres long, and for regular, common snakes and small lizards (*draco volans*).

[6] Johann Simonis, *Lexicon manuale Hebraicum et Chaldaicum, secensuit, emendavit,* auxit Io. Godofr. Eichhorn, Halae, Typis et Impensis curti Haered. MDCCXCIII, 1755 (*tan - canis ferus*), 1756 (*Tannin - draco, serpens magnus, crocodilus*).

[7] G. Lisowsky, *Konkordanz* (1981), 1524.

[8] Julius Fürst, *Hebräisches und chaldäisches Schul-Wörterbuch über das Alte Testament* (Leipzig, 1897), 637.

[9] Eduard König, *Hebräisches und aramäisches Wörterbuch zum alten Testament mit Einschaltung und Analyse aller schwer erkennbaren Formen, Deutung der Eigennamen sowie der massoretischen Randbemerkungen und einem deutsch-hebräischen Wortregister* (Leipzig, 1936), 549.

[10] Pirmin Hugger, *Jahwe meine Zuflucht. Gestalt und Theologie des 91. Psalms*, Münster-schwarzacher Studien 13 (Münsterschwarzach, 1971), 253, footnote 176.

[11] On prebiblical relics, see Godfrey Rolles Driver, 'Mythical Monsters in the Old Testament', in *Studi orientalistici in onore di Giorgio Levi della Vida*, v. I (Roma, 1956), 234-49.

[12] Nonetheless, Christian Brüning reckons that Tannin is synonymous with Nahash and Leviathan. See Ch. Brüning, '"Lobet den Herrn, ihr Seeungeheuer und all ihr Tiefen!". Seeungeheuer in der Bibel', *ZAW* 110/2 (1998), 250-5, 251.

[13] For instance, a python of several metres was brought to Ptolemy II Philadelphus's court in Alexandria, where the Septuagint was composed. See Liliane Bodson, 'A Python (Python sebae

On the other hand, mythical monsters with a serpentine nature are also found under the name *drakon*. The ancient writers were usually in agreement that this term must have been derived from the verb δέρκομαι, which means 'to see', 'to look at', 'to gaze on'.[14] In modern etymological dictionaries, we can also find an explanation that δράκων has this name because it incessantly kept watch.[15] Thus, the name would have resulted from the observation of nature, and would refer to the snakes' lack of eyelids. Probably this very feature of those reptiles made the *drakon* a very frequent guardian of treasure.[16]

The ancient δράκων did not physically resemble the dragon hybrids we know from mediaeval legends and stories. We can reconstruct its appearance based on Greek and Roman literature, as well as on its depictions in ancient art. Put simply, we could say that it was a serpent of gigantic size. Sometimes, it had more than one head, just like the Hydra, or, in some versions, the Ladon. Some images show it with bird-like wings. Moreover, δράκων was often equipped with sharp teeth and its body was covered with scales. However, its most important attributes were a beard and a comb on its head.[17] We could say that those features distinguished the mythical *drakontes* from normal, typical snakes.

Beards appeared on dragon imagery as early as the 7th century BC.[18] We can see beards on the dragons growing out of Medusa's head, on the dragon at the end of Typhon's tail, on Ladon, on the serpents accompanying Cerberus, on the Colchian dragon, and on Python. But it is not only the literary sources that indicate that dragons had beards. It had already been mentioned by a Hellenistic author, Nicander of Colophon, and later by Lucius Flavius Philostratus and Claudius Aelianus.[19] As for the dragon comb,[20] it appears in these animals' imagery as early as the 4th century BC and it usually serves as a type of balance to the beard. In literary sources, it was already mentioned by Euripides, and later on by Aelianus and Nonnus.[21] It seems natural, then, that the Alexandrian translators of the Bible used the Greek word *drakon* in lieu of the Hebrew terms *Tannin/tannim*. They were not, however, strictly consistent in their

---

Gmelin) for the King. The Third Century BC Herpetological Expedition to Aithiopia (Diodorus of Sicily 3, 36-37)', *Museum Heveticum* 60 (2003), 22-38.

[14] Robert Maltby, *A Lexicon of Ancient Latin Etymologies* (Leeds, 1991), 196.

[15] Robert Beekes and Lucien van Beek, *Etymological Dictionary of Greek* (Leiden, Boston, 2010), 3521.

[16] Macrobius, *Saturnalia* I 20, 1-4.

[17] See *e.g.* Aelianus, *De natura animalium* 11, 26: ἔχει γοῦν ὁ μὲν δράκων ὁ ἄρρην τὸν λόφον καὶ τὴν ὑπήνην.

[18] Daniel Ogden, *Drakōn: Dragon Myth and Serpent Cult in the Greek and Roman Worlds* (Oxford, New York, 2013), 155.

[19] *Ibid.* 155-61.

[20] A satisfying clarification as to what the possession of a beard by dragons could mean has not yet been found, despite long scholarly debate. Aelianus, *e.g.* in his *On the Nature of Animals*, gives an easy explanation. He believes that a beard indicates a dragon's masculine gender.

[21] D. Ogden, *Drakōn: Dragon Myth* (2013), 155-61.

rendering, and so, in many places, instead of the abovementioned Hebrew terms, they used other creatures' names: Sirens (*Isa.* 34:13), ostriches (*Jer.* 10:22), or hedgehogs (*Isa.* 13:22).

We should also mention the marine counterpart of *drakon*, that is, *ketos*. The term κῆτος was used by the ancient Greeks to define different sea beasts with a snake-like nature, and so this name is commonly translated as a sea snake.[22] Daniel Ogden shows the similarities between this creature and a dragon. The κῆτος had a snake's body, a beard and fiery eyes. The same heroes who busied themselves with killing sea snakes also specialised in slaying land dragons.[23]

St. Jerome, looking for Latin equivalents for Hebrew terms in his translation work on *hebraica veritas*, does not distinguish between *Tannin* and *tannim*. Nor does the Septuagint. The Stridon-born translator believed these two terms to be synonyms concerning the very same creature, and this is why, in a great many places where those Hebrew terms are found, he uses the name *draco*, equating it with the Greek *drakon*.

And so, in St. Jerome's rendition, we can find *draco* in lieu of the Hebrew original:

Tannin (*Ps.* 91:13; *Isa.* 27:1; 51:9; 51:34; *Ezek.* 29:3; 32:2; *Neh.* 2:13), *Tanninim* (plural) (*Exod.* 7:12; *Deut.* 32:33; *Ps.* 74:13; 148:7),

as well as, where some desert creatures are mentioned:

tannim (*Job* 30:29; *Ps.* 44:20; *Isa.* 34:13; 35:7; 43:20; *Jer.* 9:10, 10:22; 14:6; 49:33; 51:37; *Mic.* 1:8; *Mal.* 1:3).

Whereas, in a few places, St. Jerome uses other names, more related, however, to serpentine nature:

coluber (*Exod.* 7:9-10),
and *cetus* (*Gen.* 1:21; *Job* 7:12).[24]

If we take the choice of the *Tannin/tannim* equivalents into consideration, Jerome's translation is quite firmly consistent. In that regard, it differs not only from the Septuagint, but also from other second-century AD versions (by Symmachus, Aquila of Sinope and Theodotion). This fact should be further emphasised, as we know that St. Jerome based his identification of biblical background elements on these very translations.

As has already been mentioned, the meaning of *draco* in the Greco-Roman world is rather broad (from mythical creatures, to dragons, to common snakes).

---

[22] *Ibid.* 116.

[23] *Ibid.* 117-8.

[24] See Hieronymus, *Commentarii in Esaiam*, ed. Mark Adriaen, CCL 73 (Turnhout, 1963), 34: *Unde Hebraei autumant Leviathan habitare sub terra et in aethere: Thannim vero in mari, quae Iudaica fabula est.*

Nonetheless, they all have a common feature: their serpentine nature. These different conceptions can also be seen in St. Jerome's translation, where, depending on the contexts, they can be understood differently. Thus, an analysis of individual references in the Bible and their comparison to the commentaries makes it possible to identify which type of *draco* St. Jerome had in mind.

Without a doubt, the *Psalms* mention a snake-like monster (*Ps.* 74:13; 148:7). We can find out what Jerome's image of these creatures was in his *Commentary on Isaiah* 13:22: *dracones magnos interpretabimur, qui cristati sunt et volantes.*[25] What we have here is a description alluding to ancient ideas that St. Jerome could have come across when reading his favourite Roman writers. For instance, Ovid in his *Metamorphoses* provides us with the description of a crested dragon with fearsome teeth:

Pervigilem superest herbis sopire draconem,
qui crista linguisque tribus praesignis et uncis
dentibus horrendus custos erat arboris aureae.[26]

Admittedly, *draco* appears in the passage about Moses's staff changing into a snake. But Jerome also uses a synonym (*Exod.* 7:9-10) and introduces the word *coluber* (a general name for a snake). This allows us to understand that the fragment speaks of a serpentine monster, and not of an actual snake. *Nota bene*, in the Septuagint *drakon* appears in this whole story in lieu of the Hebrew *tannin*.

The *dracones* in the Prophets (Isaiah, Jeremiah, Micah and Malachi), for that matter, are not of monstrous size and so are devoid of dragon-like features. They are still dangerous serpents, but with more natural features, and they can still be incarnated by demons. The *dracones* in the Prophets are present in some specific places: devoid of water, desertic, as well as the ruins of destroyed cities, *e.g.* in Babylon. Thus, they appear in different environments than *Tanninim*.

St. Jerome uses his knowledge of nature to help him interpret the more difficult fragments, *e.g.* about asses that suck in the air like *dracones* (Hebrew *Tannim*): *et onagri steterunt in rupibus traxerunt ventum quasi dracones defecerunt oculi eorum quia non erat herba* (*Jer.* 14:6). 'And wild asses were standing on the rocks and drawing in wind like snakes. Their eyes were weakened for there was no grass'.

Jerome understands this rather problematic passage literally, that wild asses suck in air like snakes through their nostrils (we understand that here *dracones* are simply small, real reptiles). He draws here from the ancient knowledge he had from school or from Greek commentaries on the Bible. In his own *Commentary on Jeremiah* he writes:

Et onagri steterunt in rupibus, traxerunt ventum quasi dracones, defecerunt oculi eorum, quia non erat herba sive faenum. Grandis sterilitas, quando et cervae in agro pariunt et

---

[25] *Ibid.* CCL 73, 166.
[26] Ovidius, *Metamorphoses* 7, 150-3.

relinquunt fetus suos, quia non sit herba vel faenum, ut, quae odore narium serpentes extrahunt de cavernis et venenata interficiunt animantia, cibo gratiae non utantur.[27]

Such information, gathered from ancient scholarly works,[28] helped Jerome to explain, as far as contemporary knowledge allowed, the strange piece about the wailing or weeping of a snake. It also proves his exegetical ingenuity. Being consistent in his choice of *Tannin/tannim* equivalents as *dracones*, St. Jerome obtained some rather peculiar information in Micah about snakes uttering mournful sounds: *Super hoc plangam et ululabo vadam spoliatus et nudus faciam planctum velut draconum et luctum quasi strutionum* (*Mic.* 1:8). 'Therefore I will weep and moan, I will walk barefoot and naked, I will wail like snakes and lament like ostriches':

Quomodo enim dracones terribili sibilo personant, iuxta historias eorum, qui dephysicis conscripserunt, eo tempore quo vincuntur ab elephantis.[29]

In this commentary, Jerome asks himself: in what possible way could snakes utter such a terrible hiss? And he answers: according to the accounts of those who have written about nature, they will, at the very moment that they are being defeated by elephants.[30]

Such an example, where a snake's hiss is not an ominous sound, but a mourning whine, is, for the ancients, the story of a *draco*'s fight against an elephant and, eventually, the crushing of the reptile by the collapsing elephant. This very moment, and the presumed sound uttered by the *draco* dying under the weight of the elephant, was supposed to be *planctum draconis*.

There are, however, two places in the Bible where St. Jerome diverges from his consistency in translating the Hebrew *Tannin/tannim*. In *Lamentations* 4:3, where we can find the depiction of a terrible famine in Jerusalem, we have the meaningful simile of the *tannim* breast-feeding their young. Nonetheless, in this passage Jerome forwent their identification with *dracones*: *Sed et lamiae nudaverunt mammam lactaverunt catulos suos* ('Even lamiae exposed their breasts, nursing their young'). The character of this description, where some creatures were breast-feeding their young, together with logic, did not allow their equivalents to be snakes. No ancient knowledge, no Greek or Roman sources, would give here any basis for introducing the term *draco*. Therefore, Jerome introduced Lamiae[31] – demons in the form of women – as the equivalent of *tannim*. What he got is a vivid comparison that, in a graphic way, underlines the extent of the tragedy.

---

[27] Hieronymus, *In Hieremiam prophetam libri VI*, ed. Siegfried Reiter, CCL 74 (Turnhout, 1960), 138.

[28] See *Plinius Senior, Naturalis Historia* VIII 118: *et his cum serpente pugna: vestigant cavernas nariumque spiritu extrahunt renitentes.*

[29] Hieronymus, *Commentarii in Michaeam*, ed. M. Adriaen, CCL 76 (Turnhout, 1969), 427.

[30] See Plinius Senior, *Naturalis Historia* VIII 34.

[31] Pierre Grimal, *Dictionnaire de la mythologie grecque et romaine* (Paris, 1951), 330.

More thought-provoking is the second case where St. Jerome did not introduce the term dragon substituting *Tannin/tannim*, but, instead, he used the Siren
equivalent. This occurs in the *Book of Isaiah* 13:22, in a passage concerning
the description of the destroyed Babylon and the demonic beasts dwelling in
its ruins. Among them, in Jerome's version, we find the Sirens: *et responde-
bunt ibi ululae in aedibus eius et sirenae in delubris voluptatis*. It seems that
the determinant factor for Jerome to introduce the Sirens here was the context
caused by the literal rendition of the Hebrew phrase בְּהֵיכְלֵי עֹנֶג, which the
Stridon-born scholar translated directly as 'in the temples of pleasure".

This Homeric image – of the Sirens as hybrid creatures luring victims with
their sweet song – had, over time, evolved towards more sexual references and
associations.[32] Sirens started not so much to lure with their song, or enchant
with their sweet voice, but to seduce with their sensual bodily charms.[33] They
evolved from birds with only a woman's head, to more and more human-like
creatures, losing their feathers to uncover more of their female bodies. Finally,
only their wings and legs with bird's talons are left from their image, and
the Sirens are defined as *puellae*.[34] We can clearly see this in the attempts by
the Roman grammarians at rationalising the myth. In his commentary on the
Aeneid, Maurus Servius Honoratus (4th/5th century AD), writes about the Sirens
as follows:

*Sirenes secundum fabulam tres, parte virgines fuerunt, parte volucres, Acheloi fluminis
et Calliopes musae filiae. Harum una voce, altera tibiis, alia lyra canebat. Et primo
juxta Pelorum, post in Capreis insulis habita verunt. Quae inlectos cantu in naufragia
deducebant. Secundum vero veritatem meretrices fuerunt, quae, transeuntes quoniam
deducebant ad egestatem, his fictae sunt inferre naufragia.*[35]

This linking of the Sirens with sensual delights, or maybe even with lustful-
ness, would also be reflected in the Church Fathers' writings. St. Ambrose in
particular recalls them many times in the context of *voluptas*.[36] For Ambrose,
the Sirens – enticing young women, as he sees them – embody overwhelming
lust, taking away the steadiness and clarity of perception from one's mind. The
Sirens symbolise the sweet temptations of this world, behind which the real
danger lurks (this one, in turn, symbolised by reefs): *Quid sibi vult puellarum*

---

[32] In the Homeric version there is no sexual aspect. The Sirens lure their victims mainly by
their ability to foresee the future: ἴδμεν δ' ὅσσα γένηται ἐπὶ χθονὶ πουλυβοτείρῃ (Homerus,
Odyssea 12, 204-5).

[33] Although, according to some myths, the Sirens lost their beauty by Aphrodite's hand, for
they had 'despised the pleasures of love', later on their association with sensual delights became
quite strong. See P. Grimal, *Dictionnaire de la mythologie* (1951), 330.

[34] See Ambrosius Mediolanensis, *Expositio Evangelii secundum Lucam* 4, 3.

[35] Maurus Servius Honoratus, *In Vergilii Aeneidos Libros* 5, 864.

[36] James N. Adams, *Seksualizmy łacińskie*, trans. Joanna Janik (Kraków, 2013), 264. The term
voluptas has mostly sexual connotations. See *P. Ovidi Nasonis Amorum Libri Tres*, ed. Paul Brandt
(Leipzig, 1911).

figura, nisi eviratae voluptatis illecebra, quae constantiam captae mentis effeminet?[37]

Jerome's translation *in delubris voluptatis* ('in the temples of pleasure') allowed him, in a, we could say, natural way, to leave the Sirens in this very place as an equivalent for the Hebrew term *tannim*. The phrase *in delubris voluptatis* juxtaposed with the Sirens gives a more suitable connection than other identifications – even more so, since St. Jerome used the term *voluptas* in this sexual context many times in his other writings.[38] The effect of such a translation is a clear message: the Sirens, with their sexual connotations, find their dwelling place in the abandoned temples of pleasure.

Perhaps an additional influence on St. Jerome's location of the Sirens here (following the Greek second-century AD translations) was his usage of a snake equivalent in an earlier passage: *sed requiescent ibi bestiae et replebuntur domus eorum draconibus et habitabunt ibi struthiones et pilosi saltabunt ibi* (*Isa.* 13:21). St. Jerome, in Book VI of his *Commentary on Isaiah*, speaks clearly about how the earlier Greek translations rendered the Hebrew name used in the plural form *ochim* אֹחִים (*hapax legomenon*) which appears in this verse. This account also gives us a clear hint as to which translations the scholar referred to in his work.[39]

Et implebuntur domus eorum, hoc est Babyloniorum, iuxta LXX et Theodotionem ἤχου, id est, sonitu et clamoribus; **iuxta Aquilam, typhonibus, quos nos in dracones vertimus;** *iuxta Symmachum oiim, quod verbum in Hebraico continetur.*[40]

---

[37] Ambrosius Mediolanensis, *Expositio Evangelii secundum Lucam* 4, 3.

[38] See also Jerome's translation *Gen.* 18:12: *quae risit occulte dicens postquam consenui et dominus meus vetulus est voluptati operam dabo.* See Hieronymus, *Epistula* 69, 9: *Didicimus quales esse debeamus: discamus quales non esse debeant Sacerdotes. Vinolentia scurrarum est, et comessatorum: venterque meroaestuans, cito despumat in libidines. In vino luxuria, in luxuria voluptas, in voluptate impudicitia est. Qui luxuriatur, vivens mortuus est: ergo quiinebriatur, et mortuus et sepultus est. Noc ad unius horae ebrietatem nudat femora sua, quae per sexcentos annos sobrietatecontexerat. Lot per temulentiam, nesciens libidini miscet incestum: et quem Sodoma non vicerat, vina vicerunt.* In letter 70, in relation to the *Book of Deuteronomy* 21:2, Jerome mentions *voluptas* – delight, together with the denounced idolatry: *Legerat in Deuteromonio Domini voce praeceptum, mulieris captivae radendum caput, supercilia, omnes pilos, et ungues corporis amputandos, et sic eam habendam in coniugio. Quid ergo mirum, si et ego sapientiam saecularem propter eloquii venustatem, et membrorum pulchritudinem, de ancilla atque captiva Israelitidem facere cupio? et si quidquid in ea mortuum est, idololatriae, voluptatis, erroris, libidinum, vel praecidio, vel rado: et mixtus purissimo corpori vernaculos ex ea genero Domino Sabaoth?* (Hieronymus, *Epistula* 70, 2).

[39] In the first commentary on the ten visions of Isaiah against foreign nations (*Isa.* 13:1-23:18, that eventually appeared in Book V of the *Commentary on Isaiah*), that he wrote in 397 AD at the request of Amabilis, a Pannonian bishop, there is no clear indication whose translation influenced him to introduce the *dracones* equivalent: *Et replebuntur, inquit, domus, ut nos diximus, draconibus: ut Aquila transtulit, typhonibus, ut Symmachus ohim, ipsum verbum Hebraicum exprimens: LXX vero et Theodotio clamores, vel sonitus interpretati sunt* (Hieronymus, *Commentarii in Esaiam*, CCL 73, 165-6).

[40] *Ibid.* 234.

From this information, we can clearly see that St. Jerome followed Aquila in his choice of the equivalent. In Aquila's work, he found the name *typhones* in this place. Thus, the Stridon-born scholar diverged from the Septuagint translations and Theodotion, who translated this word as a sound (supposedly, Symmachus only transcribed the Hebrew name). St. Jerome followed here maybe not the translation itself, but rather Aquila's suggestion, because the Typhons posed some interpretational problems. The term referred to Typhon, but this mythological serpentine beast[41] appeared only in the singular form, and its name was a proper noun. Typhon had already been mentioned by Hesiod in his poem *Works and Days*. In his description, the creature had a hundred dragon heads growing out of its shoulders. Nonnus, in turn, in his *Dionysiaca* makes those snake-like features even more pronounced. His Typhon has serpentine hair,[42] snake-like feet[43] and snakes growing out from the shoulders.[44] In addition, a Roman mythographer, Gaius Julius Hyginus, indicates the snake-dragon-like traits: *Typhonem immani magnitudine, specieque portentosa, cui centum capita draconum ex umeris enata erant*.[45] On the basis of the information included in the *Commentary on Isaiah*, we could say that St. Jerome, in Aquila's work, read about the case of *typhonon*. This strange plural form probably made him decide on substituting this term with a more general and, at the same time, less mythological name: snakes (*dracones*).

The truth is, however, that Aquila had not introduced typhons as an equivalent for the Hebrew *ochim* אֹחִים. Similar to the Septuagint translators and to Theodotion, he wrote about voices, sounds (*phonon*)[46] filling the houses. Most likely, St. Jerome did not decipher this piece clearly. He probably took the article *ton* next to *phonon* (τῶν φώνων) as *tyfonon* (τυφώνων) and, because of this mistake, he introduced snakes into this part of the description of the ruined Babylon.

Therefore, having the *dracones* equivalent, in the following verse, to the next identification, he left the Sirens in lieu of the *tannim*, following the coincidental versions of Aquila, Symmachus and Theodotion. This is due to context, and to the influence of the phrase 'temples of pleasure' – inasmuch as snakes in temples of pleasure would have been something rather strange, or at least incomprehensible.

To sum up, we might say that an analysis of the Hebrew word *Tannin/tannim* in terms of its equivalents in St. Jerome's translation allows us, to some extent, to take a closer look at his interpretational work itself. The Stridon-born scholar

---

[41] D. Ogden, *Drakōn: Dragon Myth* (2013), 72.
[42] Nonnos, *Dionysiaca* I 173.
[43] *Ibid.* II 143.
[44] *Ibid.* I 187.
[45] Gaius Iulius Hyginus, *Fabulae* 152, 1, 1.
[46] See *Origenis Hexaplorum quae supersunt*, ed. Frederick Field (Oxonii, 1875), II, 455, note 28.

did not offer his own answers as to the identification of biblical background elements. He depended on earlier solutions provided by the Greek translators of the Septuagint, and especially by Aquila, Symmachus and Theodotion. He did not, however, take their renditions automatically, but selectively, applying a certain conceptual rotation. What he tried to do was provide a translation understandable to the reader of his times. Combining the Hebrew term *Tannin* (giant serpentine beast, sea snake, dragon) with the word *tannim* (unspecified creatures dwelling in desertic areas), St. Jerome followed the earlier solutions of his predecessors. Nonetheless, unlike those Greek translations, his equivalents in that matter are distinguished by their strict consistency. We could even say that Jerome aimed at some type of regularity or normalisation in that regard. The terms *Tannin/tannim* he translated by the use of the Latin word *draco*, the meaning of which was so broad that it contained both a mythical, giant serpentine monster and an average snake found in the wild. However, in some problematic places, where such an identification would have aroused controversy, he decided on introducing different equivalents, more fitting to the context. St. Jerome's equivalent translation for *Tannin/tannim* shows us a translator deliberately striving – while having regard for the imagery, symbolism and a whole range of associations connected to the term(s) – to choose names from Greco-Roman antiquity for culturally remote and incomprehensible Hebrew terms.

The Song of Deborah as Interpreted by Pseudo-Jerome

Magdalena JÓŹWIAK, Wrocław, Poland

ABSTRACT

This article concerns *Commentarius in Canticum Debborae* (*cf.* PL 23, 1321-8), ascribed by J.P. Migne to St. Jerome of Stridon. Having presented the results of the latest studies on *Deborah's Song* (*cf. Judg.* 5:1-31) and having signalled the problems of taking the *Song* to the LXX and Vulgate based on the example of *Judges* 5:7b, I try to show, on the basis of evidence found in *Commentarius in Canticum Debborae*, as well as on the general knowledge about Jerome, that the Stridonian is not the author of this work and that its author remains anonymous. We may aptly call him Pseudo-Jerome. In the final subsection of this article, I present selected exegetic questions from Pseudo-Jerome's commentaries with respect to the protagonists of *Judges* 5:1-31 (Barak, Deborah, Jael). In my opinion, *Commentarius in Canticum Debborae* is worth recommending not so much because of its extensive and detailed exegetic explanations, but because its value is undoubtedly interesting for researchers dealing with Ancient translations of the Bible. Furthermore, it is extremely interesting when the version presented by Pseudo-Jerome differs from that provided by St. Jerome of Stridon in the Vulgate, which I illustrate based on the example of a fragment from *Genesis* 49:14-5.

Deborah is one of few women praised with a song in the Old Testament. The woman who interests us appears in *The Book of Judges*; it is Deborah, the wife of Lapidoth, who deserved such a special mention. Her name has been commemorated in the songs of Israel with golden print. She was one of the group of so-called "seers" (Hebr. *rō'eh*), which had existed in Israel from the very beginning of its existence. Deborah was regarded as a prophetess (Hebr. *nᵉbî'āh*) by the entire Israelite nation. She is ranked among such heroes as Gideon, Samson and Jephthah, none of whom are called prophets in the Bible.

In this article, I shall discuss the interpretation of one of the oldest songs written down in the Old Testament (*cf. Judg.* 5:1-31) made by Pseudo-Jerome. This subject would seem to be interesting, since the language (Hebrew) of *Judges* 5 is difficult, and hence it is worth seeking an answer to the question of how the author of the Vulgate coped with the translation of the Hebrew text of *Judges* 5 into Latin, and how Pseudo-Jerome explains *The Song of Deborah* in the context of *Judges* 4, which describes the death of Sisera, to which the prophetess Deborah contributed by the order of God. It is also worth noting that

Studia Patristica CIII, 141-153.
© Peeters Publishers, 2021.

the commentary under discussion has never been the subject of a detailed study, hence, when preparing the article, I proceeded into a certain *terra incognita*.

1. *Deborah's Song*. Introductory issues

The name of Deborah is mentioned in the Bible nine times[1] – leaving out her "namesakes", namely Rebecca's nurse (*cf. Gen.* 35:8) and Tobias' grandmother (*Tob.* 1:8) – and, at that, exclusively in *The Book of Judges*. Jewish tradition has interpreted the name of Deborah rather negatively. The Babylonian Talmud recounts that 'Rav Naḥman said: Haughtiness is not befitting a woman. And a proof to this [*sic*] is that there were two haughty women, whose names were identical to the names of loathsome creatures. One, Deborah, was called a hornet, as her Hebrew name, Devorah, means "hornet"; and one, Huldah, was called "a marten", as her name is the Hebrew term for that creature. From where is it known that they were haughty? With regard to Deborah, the hornet, it is written: "And she sent and called Barak" (*Judges* 4:6), but she herself did not go to him. And with regard to Huldah, the marten, it is written: "Say to the man that sent you to me" (*2Kgs* 22:15), but she did not say: Say to the king'.[2]

Origen explains Deborah's name somewhat differently. He maintains that the name means "bee" (Gr. *mélissa*).[3]

In the Old Testament, we find numerous verbs associated with the root d-b-r, which enable us to get to know the entire gamut of meanings of that stem. The basic meaning of the base d-b-r is the act of speaking, telling something, expressing something, though not infrequently this stem also denotes the act of governing, ruling, managing.[4]

Deborah's Song is usually regarded as one of the oldest, if not the oldest, text of the Hebrew Bible. This opinion has been shared by researchers for decades.[5] Numerous exegetes date *Judges* 5 to the same period, more or less,

---

[1] The name appears in the biblical text in two different versions. Seven times it is the form of *plene scriptum* (*cf. Judg.* 4:4.5.9.10; 5:1.7.12), and twice the defective one (*cf. Judg.* 4:14 and 5:15).

[2] *Cf. Megillah* 14b:10, http://www.sefaria.org/Megillah.14b?lang=bi [access 04.12.2019].

[3] In his *Fifth Homily on Judges*, Origen finds that the name 'Deborah' means 'bee' or 'speech', *cf.* Origenes, *In librum Iudicum homiliae* 5. The Hebrew Bible mentions a bee four times (*Deut.* 1:44; *Judg.* 14:8; *Isa.* 7:18; *Ps.* 118:12). Two others contained in LXX should be added to those texts (*Prov.* 6:8 and *Sir.* 11:3). In each case, "bee" was used as an image in a comparison, and all examples concern a negative aspect.

[4] *Cf.* Benjamin Davidson, *The Analitical Hebrew and Chaldee Lexicon* (London, 1974), 144-5, 739.

[5] *Cf.* William F. Albright, 'Earliest Forms of Hebrew Verse', *JPOS* 2 (1922), 69-86; *id.*, 'The Song of Deborah in the Light of Archaeology', *BASOR* 62 (1936), 26-31; Charles F. Burney, *The Book of Judges* (London, 1920), 158-71; Peter C. Craigie, 'The Song of Deborah and the

when the military campaign the song refers to took place. Therefore, it would be the period of activity of the judges corresponding with Iron Age I. However, there are others who do not agree with this opinion.[6] For instance, Johannes C. de Moor is convinced that *Deborah's Song* must not be dated earlier than *ca.* 1100 BC. He provides an argument of an archaeological nature as the most convincing proof of this thesis.[7]

The majority of earlier commentators believed that *Deborah's Song* constitutes a homogenous and autonomous composition. This opinion was a fundamental research assumption for many of them. At the end of the 19th century, Heinrich Ewald expressed the belief that *Judges* 5 was a compilation of several independent fragments.[8] This statement also found its advocates in our century.[9] In response to such a position, some scholars began to defend the traditional unity of the text of *Judges* 5.[10]

The song has the form of a paean to Divine intervention. It is composed of 106 stanzas, of which one half are unclear in one respect or the other. Only 7 out of the 31 verses do not pose interpretational problems (vv. 12, 19, 20, 24, 28, 30, 31). It is one of the most obscure poetic works. The meaning of many words used therein is unknown; furthermore, the grammatical structures give rise to many doubts.[11] One of the Italian scholars studying the Hebrew of the work believes that the language of the *Song* is earlier than the classical Hebrew of the 8th century, but without a doubt later than the one we know from the Gezer calendar which dates to the 10th century BC.[12]

So far, nobody has managed to reconcile the diverse opinions and positions of scholars on this subject (the dating of the song, its composition or structure).

Epic of Tukulti-Ninurta', *JBL* 88 (1969), 253-65; Charles Echols, *Tell Me, O Muse: The Song of Deborah (Judges 5) in the Light of Heroic Poetry* (New York, 2008), 44-61; Hans P. Müller, 'Der Aufbau des Deboraliedes', *VT* 16 (1966), 446-59.

[6] *Cf.* Michael Waltisberg, 'Zum Alter der Sprache des Deboraliedes Ri 5', *ZAH* 12 (1999), 218-32.

[7] *Cf.* Johannes C. de Moor, 'The Twelve Tribes in the Song of Deborah', *VT* 43/4 (1993), 489.

[8] *Cf.* Heinrich Ewald, *The History of Israel* (London, 1869) II, 350-54.

[9] *Cf.* for instance Peter R. Ackroyd, 'The Composition of the Song of Deborah', *VT* 2 (1952), 160-2; Joseph Blenkinsopp, 'Ballad Style and Psalm Style in the Song of Deborah: A Discussion', *Biblica* 42 (1961), 61-76; Artur Weiser, 'Das Deboralied: Eine gattungs- und traditionsgeschichtliche Studie', *ZAW* 71 (1959), 67-97.

[10] *Cf.* Michael D. Coogan, 'A Structural and Literary Analysis of the Song of Deborah', *CBQ* 40 (1978), 143-66; Gillis Gerleman, 'The Song of Deborah in the Light of Stylistics', *VT* 1 (1951), 168-80; Alexander Globe, 'The Literary Structure and Unity of the Song of Deborah', *JBL* 93 (1974), 493-512; Mark A. Vincent, 'The Song of Deborah: A Structural and Literary Consideration', *JSOT* 91 (2000), 63-82.

[11] For more on this subject in the context of the Greek translation of the Hebrew version of *Judges* 5, *cf.* Nathan LaMontagne, *The Song of Deborah in the Septuagint* (Tübingen, 2019), 76-89.

[12] *Cf.* Giovanni Garbini, 'The Phonetic Shift of Sibilants in Northwestern Semitic in the First Millennium B.C.', *JNSL* 1 (1971), 32-8.

Their authors have failed to confront other opinions in a comprehensive manner. Usually, they just focus on a single aspect of the problem.[13]

In 2011, Serge Frolov successfully carried out a comprehensive study of the internal parameters of *Judges* 5:2-31.[14] Against the prevailing opinion of contemporary exegetes, he found that the *Song* did not originate in Iron Age I, and most probably never functioned as an autonomous piece. Frolov sees it as an integral part of the deuteronomistic works, and dates it to a time between 700 and 450 BC.[15]

Without going into a discussion as to the legitimacy of the research results presented, we may accept an opinion which would be agreed with by a majority of scholars: the origins of *The Song of Deborah* date back to after 1100 BC, and it gained its final form not earlier than in 700 BC. Thus, the campaign against the Canaanites described in the *Song* is the historically earliest event whose poetic version, or at least a considerable part, is chronologically closest to the event itself.

2. St. Jerome's problems with the translation of *Judges* 5 into Latin. A selected passage

As I have already mentioned, the Hebrew language of *Judges* 5 constitutes a great challenge for researchers analysing that text, since only 7 out of the 31 verses do not pose any interpretational problems. I would like to illustrate the problem with an example of a verse, namely the second part of verse 7.

In the Hebrew Bible, *Judges* 5:7b reads as follows:

'Ad *šaqqamtî* Dᵉḇôrāh, *šaqqamtî* 'ēm bᵉyiśrā'ēl.

In the Masoretic text, a certain problem is encountered in this phrase. It seems that Deborah is the subject, while the verb (*qámtî*) is used twice in the first person singular of the *Qal* conjugation, *perfectum* tense of the verb *qām* ('to rise'). Therefore, this verse should be translated as: "I, Deborah, arose, etc."

This form is explained as follows. Perhaps we are dealing here with an archaic form of the second person singular feminine, which assumes the elided vowel 'i' (the same form is found in *Jer.* 31:21).[16] Such an explanation would

---

[13] For example, syntax (*cf.* Jan A. Soggin, *Judges: A Commentary* [Philadelphia, 1981], 80-1), or a socio-historical perspective (*cf.* Ulrike Bechmann, *Das Deboralied zwischen Geschichte und Fiktion. Eine exegetische Untersuchung zu Richter 5* [St. Ottilien, 1989], 198-213).

[14] *Cf.* Serge Frolov, 'How Old is the Song of Deborah?', *JSOT* 36/2 (2011), 163-84.

[15] *Cf. id.*, 'How Old is the Song of Deborah?' (2011), 163.183.

[16] *Cf.* Robert H. O'Connell, *The Rhetoric of the Book of Judges* (Leiden, New York, Köln, 1996), 383-4.

make us translate this verse as a call addressed to Deborah: "until you rise, Deborah, until you rise a mother in Israel".

And now, let us refer to the ancient translations. The chief problem presented by the Greek text is that it has undergone many revisions and recensions.[17] Nathan LaMontagne, who wrote a monograph entitled *The Song of Deborah in the Septuagint* (Tübingen, 2019), 15-6 notes:

'A number of writers began examining the Greek text of Judges prior to the nineteenth century. Their work has been eclipsed by more recent work. David E. Montalvo[18] makes a brief assessment of their contribution to the problems of the text, but these early commentators accepted uncritically that there must be a single original Greek. This view was called into question however by Paul A. de Lagarde in his work on the LXX. In it, he set the framework of a theory that has held sway for many years, namely the Urseptuaginta – the idea that all of the LXX stems originally from a single source translation.[19] In his examination of Judges, however, P.A. de Lagarde was forced to admit that the wide differences in the A and B texts might very well indicate separate translations. [...] In the text assembled by Alfred Rahlfs the A text and the B text are printed one above the other, each having their own apparatus'.[20]

In turn, Emanuel Tov specifies:

One may nevertheless speak of a common opinion, namely that the A text is closer to the original translation than the B text, and that the B text probably incorporates an early revision of the original translation. This view has recently been supported by the investigation of. D. Barthelemy who included the B text in the *kaige* – Theodotion [...].[21]

Returning to the verse which is the object of our interest: in *Judges* 5:7b, the translators of the Septuagint corrected the Hebrew form of *qámtî* to the third person singular:

LXX (A): *Heōs hoû **eksanéstē** Debbōra, hóti **anéstē** mḗtēr en tō Israēl.*

LXX (B): *Heōs hoû **anastē** Debbōra, heōs hoû **anastē** mḗtēr en Israēl.*

And now, a question does arise: did the translators of the LXX have at their disposal a different version of the Hebrew text of *Judges* than that edited by the Masoretes? Or, perhaps, they simply changed the predicate to the third person singular in order to harmonise the text? It is hard to give an unequivocal answer to this question, since we do not have the necessary source material, namely the *Vorlage* LXX of the text of *Judges* 5, while scholars have spared

---

[17] *Cf. id., The Rhetoric* (1996), 369-73.

[18] *Cf.* David E. Montalvo, *The Texts of A and B in the Book of Judges* (Ph.D. diss., The Dropsie College, 1977), 34-43.

[19] *Cf.* Paul Anton de Lagarde, *Septuaginta Studien* (Göttingen, 1892), 71-2.

[20] *Cf.* Alfred Rahlfs (ed.), *Septuaginta. Id est Vetus Testamentum graece iuxta LXX interpretes* (Stuttgart, 1935) I, 405-95.

[21] Emanuel Tov, 'The Textual History of the Song of Deborah in the A Text of the LXX', *VT* 28 (1978), 224.

no effort in an attempt to resolve the above questions and provide various explanations.[22]

In turn, the Vulgate version of *Judges* 5:7b reads: *Donec **surgeret** Debbora, **surgeret** mater in Israël.*

St. Jerome, like the translators of the LXX, used the verb in the third person singular so as to make the text of *Judges* 5:7b understandable. Jerome's knowledge of the Hebrew language[23] is, in this case, limited to the regular conjugation of the verb *qām* in the *perfectum* tense in the *Qal* conjugation, although – as he himself testifies in *Letter* 125[24] – he had learned Hebrew from a Jew. There are 24 such problematic verses in *Judges* 5 out of 31! I used this example merely to illustrate the problem.

---

[22] As regards small differences between the Greek translation and the Hebrew text of *Judges* in the Masoretic version, it can be mostly explained by the transmission of the text through an Aramaic speaking cursive writing scribe of the 5th century BC, a theory totally in agreement with what is already known or presumed about the *Vorlage* of the Septuagint. Simply put, the translator engaged in practices such as replacing words he did not know with words that were similar, as though that were a legitimate substitution. Wherever greater deviations from the Masoretic text occur in the Greek version of *Judges*, it is more difficult to explain. The selected bibliographic items presenting solutions for those issues are as follows: Angel Saenz-Badillos, 'Tradicion griega y texto hebreo del Canto de Debora', *Sefarad* 33 (1973), 245-57; Albert V. Billen, 'The Hexaplaric Element in the LXX Version of Judges', *JTS* 43 (1942), 12-9; Barnabas Lindars, 'Some Septuagint Readings in Judges', *JTS* 22 (1971), 1-14; Joseph Schreiner, *Septuaginta-Massora des Buches der Richter*, AnBib 7 (Roma, 1957); Alexander Sperber, 'The Problems of the Septuagint Recensions', *JBL* 54 (1935), 74-81; E. Tov, 'The Textual History' (1978), 224-32.

[23] Among the host of opinions and views of researchers concerning St. Jerome's knowledge of the Hebrew language, a pretty peculiar position is presented by Pierre Nautin who claims that St. Jerome did not know even a single word in Hebrew! *Cf.* P. Nautin, *Hieronymus*, TRE 15 (1986), 310. Contrary to the opinion of Nautin denying St. Jerome knowledge of Hebrew, Adam Kamesar, in his study concerning *Quaestiones Hebraicae in Genesim*, appreciates and praises the author of the Vulgate for having introduced a new methodological approach to the translated text, and for paying more attention to the philological issues and problems than his Greek predecessors (*cf. Studies in Jerome's "Quaestiones Hebraice in Genesim" : The Work as Seen in the Context of Greek Scholarship* [Ph.D. Diss., Oxford University, 1987], 96, 115, 120, 129). In turn, Pierre Jay stresses that the good point of St. Jerome is that, in his studies of the biblical text, he dared reach for the Hebrew original and Jewish exegesis, which makes him more prominent than his predecessors (*cf. L'exégèse de saint Jérôme d'après son "Commentaire sur Isaïe"* [Paris, 1985], 39). Moreover, the critical studies carried out by Eitan Burstein confirm that Jerome read and understood the Hebrew Bible, *cf.* 'La compétence de Jérôme en hébreu. Explication de certaines erreurs', *REAug* 21 (1975), 12.

[24] Hieronymus, *Epistula* 125, 12: *Dum essem iuvenis, et solitudinis me deserta vallarent, incentiva vitiorum ardoremque naturae ferre non poteram, quem cum crebris ieiuniis frangerem, mens tamen cogitationibus aestuabat. Ad quam edomandam, cuidam fratri, qui ex Hebraeis crediderat, me in disciplinam dedi, ut post Quintiliani acumina, Ciceronis fluvios, gravitatemque Frontonis, et lenitatem Plinii, alphabetum discerem, et stridentia anhelantiaque verba meditarer. Quid ibi laboris insumpserim, quid sustinuerim difficultatis, quoties desperaverim, quotiesque cessaverim, et contentione discendi rursus inceperim, testis est conscientia, tam mea qui passus sum, quam eorum qui mecum duxerunt vitam. Et gratias ago Domino, quod de amaro semine litterarum, dulces fructus carpo.*

3. The Authorship of *Commentarius in Canticum Debborae*

In my opinion, the question of the authorship of the discussed work seems to be problematic, although in *Patrologia Latina* Jacques Paul Migne ascribes this comment to St. Jerome.[25] In this subsection, I shall try to show, on the basis of presumptions found in the text itself, as well as of general knowledge about Jerome, that the author of the Vulgate is not the author of the *Commentary on the Song of Deborah*, and its author remains anonymous. My arguments are as follows:

In the lists of writings penned by St. Jerome, scholars do not include *Commentarius in Canticum Debborae* as a text which would have been authored by the Stridonian.[26] Obviously, this is not the crowning argument, but merely an indication of sorts. More important are the arguments stemming from the very text of the *Commentary*, namely:

First, in his biblical commentaries Jerome tried to provide the etymology of almost each and every proper name that could be derived from Hebrew. This avocation of Jerome to explain etymology bore fruit in the publication of the trilogy comprised of *Liber interpretationis hebraicorum nominum*,[27] *Liber de situ et nominibus locorum hebraicorum*[28] and *Liber quaestionum hebraicarum in Genesim*.[29] This trilogy may seem to be a technical and dry summary, but it actually, in large measure, consolidated St. Jerome's reputation as erudite. The Church Father wished to provide the West with an *instrumentarium* consisting of an etymological dictionary of the proper names found in the Bible, a biblical geographical lexicon and a critical analysis of difficult passages in *The Book of Genesis*. The fascination with the etymology of names was strengthened by the conviction that the proper names used in the Bible have a hidden meaning, as maintained by St. Augustine in *De doctrina christiana*.[30] However, there are very few such considerations in *Commentarius in Canticum Debborae*. The author of the commentary does not even give the etymology of the name of the central character of the story, that is Deborah, although he believes that she speaks in the name of God (*Debbora in persona Dei loquitur*[31])!

---

[25] *Cf.* PL 23, 1321-8.

[26] *Cf.* for example John N.D. Kelly, *Hieronim. Życie, pisma, spory* (Warszawa, 2003), 461-2.

[27] *Cf.* Hieronymus, *Liber interpretationis hebraicorum nominum*, PL 23, 771-858. For a translation of and elaboration on this commentary by Jerome *cf.* Magdalena Jóźwiak, *"Kwestie hebrajskie w Księdze Rodzaju" św. Hieronima. Przekład i komentarz* (Wrocław, 2010); Adam Kamesar, *Jerome, Greek Scholarship and the Hebrew Bible. A study of the "Quaestiones Hebraice in Genesim"* (Oxford, 1993).

[28] *Cf.* Hieronymus, *Liber de situ et nominibus locorum hebraicorum*, PL 23, 859-928.

[29] *Cf.* Hieronymus, *Liber quaestionum hebraicarum in Genesim* 23, 935-1010.

[30] Augustinus Hipponensis, *De doctrina christiana* 2, 38.

[31] Pseudo-Hieronymus, *Commentarius in Canticum Debborae*, PL 23, 1324B.

On the other hand, in the work entitled *Liber de nominibus hebraicorum*, St. Jerome devotes an entire chapter to explaining the etymology of the proper names occurring in the *Book of Judges* (*De libro iudicum*).[32] For example, he explains the name of Deborah as *apis sive eloquentia*[33] – ('bee' or 'eloquence'). In turn, Jael, who kills Sisera, in the opinion of the Stridonian means *cerva vel conjugium cervale sive incipiens* ('female deer' or 'deer couple' or 'incipient').[34] In this fashion, Jerome explains the etymology of each name occurring in *The Book of Judges*. Hence, in my opinion, the failure to provide at least the etymology of the main characters (Deborah and Jael) in *Commentarius in Canticum Debborae* is an argument to reject the authorship of Jerome, who liked boasting of his knowledge of Hebrew in his works.

Secondly, when commenting on a given fragment of the Bible the Stridonian frequently indicates which translations he has used. He notes whether he has used the translation of the Septuagint, or else he refers to the translations by Aquila, Symmachus or Theodotion. Meanwhile, the author of *Commentarius in Canticum Debborae* never precisely says what version he has used, apart from general remarks such as: *notandum quod in Hebraeo* (PL 23, 1324B; PL 23, 1325B), *in Hebraeo dicitur* (PL 23, 1325B), *in Hebraeo non legitur, sed Latinus interpres sensus gratia hoc addidit* (PL 23, 1326A), *in Hebraeo legitur* (PL 23, 1326A; PL 23, 1328B). Apart from this, it is also very important that not once does a notation in the Hebrew alphabet occur in the commentary, and all references to the Hebrew versions of the text are represented exclusively in italics.

Thirdly, when commenting on *Judg.* 5:11, the author of *Commentarius in Canticum Debborae* refers to *Gen.* 49:14-5, where in the Vulgate version the word *asinus* ('ass') is used. And then the commentator explains: *Et quod iidem doctores asini nuncupentur, monstratur ex libro Genesis, ubi sequitur: «Issachar asinus fortis accubans inter terminos»* […].[35]

In turn, St. Jerome wrote a commentary to *The Book of Genesis*, and in this passage refers to the Hebrew version of the text according to which Issachar is a 'bony ass', not a 'strong ass'. In *Quaestiones Hebraicae in Genesim* in 49:14-5, the author of the Vulgate notes: *In Hebraeo ita scriptum est: «Issachar asinus osseus, recumbens inter terminos»* […].[36]

---

[32] *Cf.* Hieronymus, *Liber de nominibus hebraicorum*, PL 23, 809-12.

[33] *Ibid.* PL 23, 777.

[34] *Ibid.* PL 23, 810.

[35] Pseudo-Hieronymus, *Commentarius in Canticum Debborae*, PL 23, 1325A. The author of *Commentarius in Canticum Debborae* calls Issachar a 'strong ass', which he understands as a metaphor for the scribes (*doctores*) because of the force of the Law and the care of it which they exercise: *Asinus in Libro Geneseos fortis dicitur, propter fortitudinem legis, eo quod in humero legem portaret, et caeteris tribubus tributum, id est doctrinam legis impenderet.*

[36] Hieronymus, *Quaestiones Hebraicae in Genesim*, PL 23, 1006C. Jerome calls Issachar a 'bony ass', because he had to work in the field as hard as an ass. He then adds that the Hebrews

Those different Latin versions of the Hebrew text of *Gen.* 49:14-5 constitute one of the arguments that the Stridonian is not the author of *Commentarius in Canticum Debborae*. All the more so, since in *Quaestiones Hebraicae in Genesim* Jerome repeatedly refers to various versions of the text.[37] Therefore, one does wonder why, in the case of the commentary to *Gen.* 49:14-5, he would not do so? Especially since the version presented by the author of the Vulgate in *Quaestiones Hebraicae in Genesim* is consistent with the Masoretic version of the text, according to which Issachar is called a 'bony ass' (Hebr. *hămōr gārem*).

Fourthly, another argument excluding Jerome's authorship may be the fact that, in his works, Jerome liked invoking quotations from classical authors, thus showing off his erudition,[38] while *Commentarius in Canticum Debborae* does not contain a single such quotation, apart from the references to the Bible. Since the memorable works of the Ancient writers constituted an integral part of the education of an Ancient intellectual, making references to knowledge of those writings was both a literary convention and proof of scholarship.

Summing up this subsection, in my opinion Jerome of Stridon is not the author of *Commentarius in Canticum Debborae*, and the commentator remains unknown to us. We may thus call him Pseudo-Jerome.

4. Pseudo-Jerome's exegesis of *Judges* 5

When commenting on *Judges* 5, the author mostly uses the text of the Vulgate, which he contrasts with the available Hebrew versions of the text translated by earlier commentators into Latin. It does not seem that Pseudo-Jerome knew Hebrew, or that he had access to several variants of the original text.

In his analysis of *Deborah's Song*, Pseudo-Jerome, to a large degree, follows a dual track, supplementing verbatim understanding with supra-literal interpretations. Like St. Jerome, the author of *Commentarius in Canticum Debborae* enhances the literal sense, which forms a kind of a foundation on which the edifice of allegories can be raised.[39] The breadth of Pseudo-Jerome's sight, and

---

explain that, through this metaphor, the biblical author showed that by deliberating on the Holy Scripture day and night he became involved in his studies very conscientiously, and that is why all the tribes serve him and bring him gifts as merits a wise man: *Asinum autem osseum vocat, et humerum ad portandum deditum, quia in labore terrae, et vehendis ad mare oneribus, quae in suis finibus nascebantur, plurimum laboraret, regibus quoque tributa comportans. Aiunt Hebraei, per metaphoram significari, quod Scripturas sanctas die ac nocte meditans, studium suum dederit ad laborandum, et ideo ei omnes tribus serviant, quasi magistro dona portantes* (ibid. PL 23, 1007A).

[37] *Cf.* M. Jóźwiak, *Kwestie hebrajskie* (2010), 38-9, 41-2, 49, 66-7, 78-9, 83, 86-7, 89-90, 94, 101-2, 109-10, 115, 117, 128-9.

[38] *Cf. ead.*, "*Komentarz do historii Hioba*" *Filipa Prezbitera* (Wrocław, 2015), 57.

[39] Hieronymus, *Commentarius in Zachariam, Prologus: Historiae Hebraeorum tropologiam nostrorum miscui, ut aedificarem super petram et non super arenam* (PL 25, 1418B).

the fact that he does not limit himself to a single interpretation, testifies to the extraordinary openness of the author's mind, especially if we take into account that, in his time, a specific intellectual conflict prevailed in this respect. On the one hand, the Alexandrine school limited the understanding of the Holy Scripture exclusively to the level of allegory, whereas, on the other, the Antiochian school recognised only a literal interpretation.

In the patristic literature, the Bible was the point of reference for reflection. The Church Fathers and Christian writers 'thought' the Holy Scripture; hence numerous and valuable exegetic commentaries were written. All of their writings were based on the Holy Writ, which constituted the foundation for the doctrine of the Church. Hence, it is not surprising that one of the characteristic traits of *Commentarius in Canticum Debborae* is the fact that, wherever there is such a possibility, the commentator makes references to various fragments of the Bible as he tries to explain the Bible in its own light. For instance, explaining *Judges* 5:20: *De caelo dimicatum est contra eos*, Pseudo-Jerome notes:

Quia in quadraginta millibus Israel clypeus et hasta inveniri non poterat, idcirco Dominus de coelo lapidibus grandinis, et igne dimicavit pro eis contra hostes suos. Sicut est et illud in libro Josue: «Stellae manentes in ordine suo, et cursu adversum Sisaram pugnaverunt» (Jos. 10:11). Stellae Angeli intelliguntur, qui de coelo contra Sisaram pugnaverunt.[40]

Let us now have a look at the protagonists of the story analysed, based on Pseudo-Jerome's commentary: Barak, Deborah and Jael.

BARAK

Reference to Barak, the son of Abinoam from Kedesh in Naphtali, the commander of the Israelite army, appears in the first verse of the commentary. As I have already noted earlier, the author of *Commentarius in Canticum Debborae* does not provide too many etymologies for proper names, although he does so in the case of the name "Barak". Following the Jewish interpretation or more the earlier commentators of *The Book of Judges*, Pseudo-Jerome notes that Barak is Deborah's husband, and Lappidoth[41] is his second name. He explains Barak as *fulmen* ('lightning'), and Lappidoth as *fulgur* ('flame'). The commentator then goes on to explain that the man was called 'flame', since, before

---

[40] Pseudo-Hieronymus, *Commentarius in Canticum Debborae*, PL 23, 1327C. Translation: 'There wasn't a shield or spear to be seen among 40,000 soldiers of Israel (*cf. Judg.* 5:8), and that is why the Lord from heaven fought for those, [hurling] hailstones and fire against their enemies. It was so written in the Book of Joshua: "The stars remaining in order and in their movement fought against Sisera" (*Josh.* 10:11). The stars should be understood as angels who fought against Sisera from heaven' (by M. Jóźwiak).

[41] Hebr. *lappîḏôṯ* is derived from the noun *lappîḏ*, which means 'flambeau' or 'flame', as well as 'lamp in a temple' or 'God's glory' (*cf.* B. Davidson, *The Analytical Hebrew* [1974], 446).

Israel took revenge on the Canaanites, he had shone among the peoples like a 'flame', obviously because of his virtuous acts. Later on, Israel took revenge on the Canaanites, and hence he came to be called 'lightning', that is, he who strikes dead:

Barac vir Debborae prophetidis fuisse traditur. Ipse etiam Baracin praecedentibus Lapidoth vocatur. Lapidoth enim interpretatur «fulgur», Barac quoque «fulmen». «Fulgur», idcirco, quia antequam ulcisceretur Israel de Chananaeis, quasi «fulgur» splendebat in populo, meritis scilicet et praerogativis operum: postquam vero ultus est Israel de Chananaeis, «fulmen», id est, percutiens vocatus est.[42]

Deborah

The first verses of *Commentarius in Canticum Debborae* provide information that Deborah was a married woman (*Barac vir Debborae prophetidis fuisse traditur*).[43] In order to assess this information critically, reference should be made to *Judg.* 4:4, where the author starts his narration by enumerating the "titles" of the main heroine of the story. One of the titles he ascribes to her is: 'the wife of Lappidoth' (Hebr. *'ēšet lappîdôt*). The Hebrew word *lappîd*, as has been shown above, may mean 'flaming torch', and in the plural it is *lappîdôt*. Therefore, the phrase *'ēšet lappîdôt* might not necessarily denote the "wife of Lappidoth", but "woman of torches". Numerous syntagmas of this type may be found in the Hebrew Bible (*e.g. Prov.* 9:13; 11:16; *Ruth* 3:11). Apart from this, in the narration of *Judg.* 4 and *Deborah's Song* Lappidoth does not play any special role. Neither is he known from other pages of the Hebrew Bible. Therefore, it may be conjectured that the information contained in *Judg.* 4:4 is not about Deborah's husband, but rather is indicative of the extraordinary features of the protagonist. That is why, when Deborah is called *'ēšet lappîdôt*, she is simply "a woman of torches", namely, she is characterised by a special brightness of the mind or has some other special abilities in fulfilling the will of Yahweh.

In the case of the name of Deborah, who is the main protagonist, since it is she who calls Barak to fight, the commentator does not provide its etymology. Commenting on *Judg.* 5:9-10: *Cor meum diligit principes Israël*, Pseudo-Jerome merely notes that it is God Himself who speaks through Deborah, that is, he emphasises her prophetic function. In this passage, the author of the commentary notes that this verse does not read that she loves "leaders" (*principes*), but rather "doctors" (*doctores*).[44] As a prophetess, Deborah speaks *in persona*

---

[42] Pseudo-Hieronymus, *Commentarius in Canticum Debborae*, PL 23, 1321D; 1322D-1323A.

[43] *Ibid.* PL 23, 1321D.

[44] The author of *Commentarius in Canticum Debborae* is, in this place, mistaken, because in the Masoretic text of *Judg.* 5:9 there is the *participium activum* of the *Qal* conjugation from the Hebrew stem h-q-q ("forge", "carve", "set", "decide"), which may be literally translated as "those who set the law", that is, the leaders.

Dei: *Notandum quod in Hebraeo, non «principes», sed «doctores» legitur. Hoc Debbora in persona Dei loquitur, quod Deus diligat doctores legi Dei studentes.*[45]

JAEL

The biblical author of *Judges* 5 mentions Jael in verse 6, hence the first reference to this heroine occurs in Pseudo-Jerome's commentary to this verse: *In diebus Samgar filii Anath, in diebus Jahel quieverunt semitae, et qui ingrediebantur per eas, ambulaverunt per calles devios.* The commentator notes that Jael is the wife of Heber the Kenite (*cf. Judg.* 4:17), and emphasises her vital role in that story, namely, that Jael killed Sisera, the commander of the Canaanite army (*Et quod Jahel ante Debboram fecisse dicitur, eo quod Jahel uxor Aber Cinaei Sisaram interfecerit*), who, in his flight after the lost battle with the Israelites, hid in her tent.[46]

Then, explaining *Judges* 5:24: *Benedicta inter mulieres Jahel uxor Haber Cinaei*, Pseudo-Jerome places Jael in the ranks of Old Testament women from *The Book of Genesis*: Sarah, Rebecca, Rachel and Leah. He then adds that Jael should be praised for her actions, and she did so wisely and prudently when she gave Sisera milk, although he asked her for water. The commentator also informs us that Jael did not serve wine to Sisera, since there was no such custom in the house of Rekab (*cf. Jer.* 35:14):

Inter mulieres, scilicet Saram, Rebeccam, Rachel, Liam, et caeteras ferme mulieres. [...] Et redditur causa cur benedicatur, quia scilicet sapienter et prudenter fecerit, eo quod «petenti aquam, lac dederit». Idcirco lac dedit, ut hostis fugiens sibi fidem potiorem accommodaret. Et si quaeritur cur non vinum dederit, respondendum est quia domus Rechab vinum non bibunt, sicut habes in Jeremia propheta.[47]

5. Conclusion

It is my belief that *Commentarius in Canticum Debborae*, ascribed by J.P. Migne in the 23rd volume of *Patrologia Latina* to St. Jerome, is not of his authorship, which I have tried to substantiate with relevant arguments in the course of my deliberations.

Evaluating the usefulness of Pseudo-Jerome's commentary in the exegesis of *Deborah's Song*, I have found that, when choosing any fragment of *Judges* 5

---

[45] Pseudo-Hieronymus, *Commentarius in Canticum Debborae*, PL 23, 1324B.

[46] *Ibid.* PL 23, 1323B-C: *Quod vero interponitur paulo superius, «in diebus Jahel», intelligendum est, quia interempto Sisara a Jahel, apertae sunt viae, et absque ullo timore ibant in domum Domini, qui antea per calles devios illuc gradiebantur. Et quod Jahel ante Debboram fecisse dicitur, eo quod Jahel uxor Aber Cinaei Sisaram interfecerit.*

[47] *Ibid.* PL 23, 1328C.

to be explained, the authors always used the translation of the Vulgate. Pseudo-Jerome interprets *Deborah's Song* literally and allegorically. He studies the Bible in the Bible's light, adorning his commentary with biblical quotations. Alas, in his commentary he devotes little space to the etymology of proper names (he does not even provide the etymology of the name of Deborah, although she is the main character of the story). He makes no attempt to search for the concealed meanings of numbers, although *e.g.* a number occurs in *Judg.* 5:8, nor refers to the symbolism of the animal realm, although an ass appears in *Judg.* 5:10.

In my opinion, *Commentarius in Canticum Debborae* is to be recommended not so much because of its extensive and detailed exegetic explanations, but for its value for researchers dealing with Ancient translations of the Bible, since Pseudo-Jerome in many places states that a given verse is different in the Hebrew text (he obviously copied those suggestions from earlier commentators) than in the Latin versions. And it is extremely interesting when the version presented by Pseudo-Jerome differs from that provided by St. Jerome of Stridon in the Vulgate, which I illustrated with the example of the fragment from *Genesis* 49:14-5.

Graeca Veritas:
Saint Augustine's Historical and Theological Rationale for the Septuagint as Authoritative Scripture

Colton Moore, Minneapolis, USA

ABSTRACT

This essay attempts to uncover the historical and theological assumptions that under-girded Saint Augustine's conviction that the Septuagint is authoritative Scripture. After surveying several key church fathers' understanding of the Septuagint's historical incep-tion and authoritative nature, we find that the majority of the fathers simply took for granted the historicity of the Septuagint's divinely inspired inception. Though many of the fathers vary in the details of their renditions of this inception, their accounts can be traced back to *The Letter of Aristeas* (*ca.* 250-300 BC). Like the fathers, Augustine also assumes the historicity of the Septuagint's divinely inspired inception. However, his words stand out because he applies divine inspiration not only to the Septuagint, but also to the Hebrew Scriptures. Specifically regarding the Septuagint, he argues for its authority on historical and theological premises: (1) the Septuagint, being in the Greek language, spread the divine Scriptures to the gentiles and emended the Hebrew Scrip-tures, before Christ's advent, by adding prophetic words about the historical incarnation of Christ; (2) since the apostles approved of the Septuagint, as testified by their use of it in the New Testament, the Septuagint is divinely authoritative; and (3) since the testimony and authority of the Septuagint is handed down by the Catholic Church (*peritiores ecclesias*), therefore the Septuagint is authoritative Scripture.

1. Introduction

The majority of the early church before the 5th century AD attributed the first Greek translation of the Hebrew Bible to either seventy or seventy-two Jewish translators (hence, the name 'Septuagint'),[1] which comes from a tra-dition that goes back at least to *The Letter of Aristeas* (*ca.* 250-300 BC).[2]

---

[1] In this essay, 'Septuagint' should be understood loosely to refer the Greek Old Testament in general, sometimes referring to only the Pentateuch, and other times referring to the entire Greek Old Testament. In the account given by *The Letter of Aristeas*, the translation endeavor consisted of only the Pentateuch.

[2] For the potential dates of the composition of Aristeas, see Benjamin G. Wright, *The Letter of Aristeas: "Aristeas to Philocrates" or "On the Translation of the Law of the Jews"* (Berlin, 2015), 21-30.

Studia Patristica CIII, 155-164.
© Peeters Publishers, 2021.

However, John A. Lee has recently made a notable case for only five translators.[3] For Lee and others, Aristeas was a mere fable, albeit a fable that was
not without some historical facts, that later promulgated Jewish and Christian
agendas.[4] And so, Lee, pondering the reasoning behind why so many in the
early church would even believe in 'the Seventy' (or 'Seventy-Two'), writes
'It could of course be that people "believed" [the Septuagint] was done by
72 translators, "but why would they"?'[5] Why would they believe in seventy
or seventy-two translators if modern historical and linguistic research says
otherwise? Even more, why would they believe that these translators were
'inspired' by God? Indeed, why would many in the early church believe that
seventy (or seventy-two) Jewish elders,[6] as if orchestrated purposefully (οἱονεὶ
κατὰ πρόθεσίν τινα τοῦ τοιούτου γεγενημένου), worked together (συναγόμενοι τὸ προκείμενον ἐπετέλουν)[7] to produce an authoritative, and therefore
unalterable translation?[8] 'Why would they?' That is the question of this essay.
This is a simple question, yet a very important question given the mass witness
in the early Church.

We first see statements of divine intervention in the Septuagint translation
within the works of Philo.[9] We also see later statements of divine intervention
within the documents of first-century Palestinian rabbinical Judaism.[10] We then
see the church fathers simply taking for granted this 'miracle translation' as an
actual historical event. Were the church fathers so naïve to simply accept without question the 'story' of the Septuagint's origin? Or worse, knowing (or at
least suspecting) the miracle translation to be a hoax, did the fathers simply use
this miracle tradition to bolster their own personal theological propaganda?
Given the early church's general ill-feelings toward Judaism, did they not

---

[3] John A. Lee, *The Greek of the Pentateuch* (Oxford, 2018), 202-8.

[4] Abraham Wasserstein and David J. Wasserstein, *Legend of the Septuagint: From Classical Antiquity to Today* (Cambridge, 2006), X.15.25.49-50; Benjamin G. Wright, 'The Letter of Aristeas and the Question of Septuagint Origins Redux', *JAJ* 2/3 (2011), 304-26.

[5] J.A. Lee, *The Greek of the Pentateuch* (2018), 271.

[6] Pseudo-Aristeas, *Epistula ad Philocratem* 46-50.

[7] J.A. Lee, *The Greek of the Pentateuch* (2018), 307.

[8] *Ibid.* 310.

[9] Philo Alexandrinus, *De vita Mosis* 2, 37: καθίσαντες δ᾽ ἐν ἀποκρύφῳ καὶ μηδενὸς παρόντος [...] καθάπερ ἐνθουσιῶντες προεφήτευον οὐκ ἄλλα ἄλλοι, τὰ δ᾽ αὐτὰ πάντες ὀνόματα
καὶ ῥήματα, ὥσπερ ὑποβολέως ἑκάστοις ἀοράτως ἐνηχοῦντος. Philo even attributes divine
intervention to the efforts of the king who chose the seventy-two: ὁ δ᾽ οἷα εἰκὸς ἡσθεὶς καὶ
νομίσας οὐκ ἄνευ θείας ἐπιφροσύνης περὶ τὸ τοιοῦτον ἔργον ἐσπουδακέναι τὸν βασιλέα
(*ibid.* 2, 32).

[10] For example, the Babalonian Talmud (Megilla 9 a-b) records that Ptolemy, placing the
seventy-two elders in separate houses, told the elders to translate for him the Law of Moses
(ואמר להם כתבו לי תורת משה רבכם נתן). God then placed wisdom into the hearts of all the translators, thus causing all their translations to perfectly align with one another (נתן הקב״ה בלב כל אחד
ואחד עצה והסכימו כולן לדעת אחת וכתבו לו). See rabbinical documents printed in A. Wasserstein
and D.J. Wasserstein, *Legend of the Septuagint* (2006), 55-83.

realize this 'story' handed down 'by Jews' might have been tampered with, and therefore not to be completely trusted?

As we will see below, many of the church fathers took for granted the historicity of the story of God's intervention during the translation event. The question at hand is *why* they accepted such a story. This question is even more important in light of the pervading skepticism in modern scholarship regarding the historical veracity of *Aristeas* and its contents. Rather than providing a case for or against the historical veracity of the contents of *Aristeas*, and rather than providing a case for or against the Septuagint as Holy Christian Scripture, this paper will (1) attempt to contextualize Augustine's justification of an authoritative Septuagint by showing that the majority of the church fathers simply believed that God 'in history' inspired the Greek Old Testament, and (2) highlight Saint Augustine's particular rationale for an inspired Septuagint translation. Augustine, similar to some of the fathers that preceded him, takes for granted the historicity of the 'miracle translation.' He also understands the Septuagint to be a God-breathed translation because (1) it, being translated 'before' Christ's incarnation, both prepared the gentiles to receive salvation, and (2) it was used by the apostles and *omnes peritiores ecclesias.*

2. The Septuagint in the Early Church

As mentioned above, Augustine wasn't the only early Christian to believe in the miracle translation. In this section, I will briefly overview several of the fathers in order to provide an initial answer, though space and time restricts us from a more thorough presentation. Within the fathers, there are many divergences from the original 'legend' of the Septuagint's origin as we see it in *Aristeas*. Instead of exposing these divergences, my focus will simply remain on why they believed what they asserted about the legend, regardless of whether their words lay more or less in accord with *Aristeas*. What we find is that most fathers simply believed the miracle translation to be nothing less than historical fact.

Justin Martyr (*ca.* 100-165 AD). In several places throughout his writings, Justin assumes the historicity of the Septuagint's origin taking place in the court of Ptolemy.[11] In his *Dialogue with Trypho*, in order to stake further his case against Trypho the Jew, he asserts that the seventy Jewish elders who translated the Septuagint are indeed *Trypho's* 'seventy elders that were with Ptolemy the king of the Egyptians'.[12] That Justin asserted these elders come from Trypho's Jewish heritage implies that he believed in the historicity of the Seventy's translation.

---

[11] Iustinus Martyr, *Apologia I* 1, 31; *Dialogus cum Tryphone Iudaeo* 68, 7; 71; 84, 3.
[12] *Id., Dialogus cum Tryphone Iudaeo* 68, 7; see also 84, 3.

Irenaeus (*ca.* 130-200 AD). Irenaeus writes that the seventy elders translated separately under King Ptolemy,[13] and because 'the one and the same Spirit of God, who proclaimed by the prophets what and of what sort of advent the Lord should [appear]', the Seventy translated with perfect fidelity.[14] Irenaeus takes for granted the historicity of the translation during Ptolemy's reign and adds yet another layer of reasoning for the translation: since the Spirit-filled apostles relied upon the Spirit-produced translation,[15] the translation is divine, authoritative prophecy. Augustine will make the same argument later.

Clement of Alexandria (*ca.* 150-215 AD). Like Irenaeus, Clement of Alexandria includes divine activity in his historical account.[16] For Clement, the translation was God's will in order that the Greek-speaking world might receive Israel's Scriptures. Regarding the translators themselves, Clement seems to assert that the 'seventy elders' translated separately.[17] His undergirding assumption is that this God-produced translation is rooted in history, and that since God has already produced prophecy in the Scriptures, it isn't surprising that he has also produced this new Greek prophetic translation.[18]

Eusebius of Caesarea (*ca.* 263-339 AD). In his *Praeparatio evangelica*, Eusebius of Caesarea also takes for granted the historicity of what we find in *The Letter of Aristeas*.[19] What seems to undergird his rationale for trusting this historical account is a theological conviction understood retrospectively in light of the incarnation of Jesus Christ (τοῦ σωτῆρος).[20] God anticipated in his foreknowledge (προλαβὼν το μέλλον ὡς ἂν θεὸς τῇ προγνώσει) that Jesus would come as the savior of all men and therefore caused the translators to translate with impeccable precision (ἀκριβές) for the gentiles' participation in the knowledge of God (θεογνωσίας).[21]

---

[13] Irenaeus Lugdunensis, *Adversus haereses* III 21, 2.

[14] *Ibid.* III 21, 4: *Unus enim et idem Spiritus Dei, qui in prophetis quidem praeconavit quis et qualis esset adventus Domini, in Senioribus autem interpretatus est bene quae bene prophetata fuerant.*

[15] *Ibid.* III 21, 3-4.

[16] See Clemens Alexandrinus, *Stromata* I 22. Interestingly, he also explicitly states that *both* the Law and Prophets were translated, even though tradition records that only the Law was translated (Pseudo-Aristeas, *Epistula ad Philocratem* 309; Philo Alexandrinus, *De vita Mosis* 2, 38).

[17] Clemens Alexandrinus, *Stromata* I 22: ἑκάστου δὲ ἐν μέρει κατ᾽ἰδίαν ἑκάστην ἑρμηνεύσαντος προφητείαν συνέπνευσαν αἱ πᾶσαι ἑρμηνεῖαι συναντιβληθεῖσαι καὶ τὰς διανοίας καὶ τὰς λέξεις. θεοῦ γὰρ ἦν βούλημα μεμελετημένον εἰς Ἑλληνικὰς ἀκοάς.

[18] *Ibid.*: οὐ δὴ ξένον ἐπιπνοίᾳ θεοῦ τοῦ τὴν προφητείαν δεδωκότος καὶ τὴν ἑρμηνείαν οἱονεὶ Ἑλληνινὴν προφητείαν ἐνεργεῖσθαι.

[19] Eusebius Caesariensis, *Praeparatio evangelica* 8, 1-9.

[20] See also Theodorus Mopsuestenus, *Commentarius in Sophoniam* 1, 4-6: ὧν την τε ἑρμηνείαν καὶ τὴν ἔκδοσιν καὶ οἱ μακάριοι ἀπόστολοι δεξάμενοι φαίνονται προδήλως, οἱ καὶ τοῖς ἀπὸ ἐθνῶν πεπιστευκόσιν οὐδ᾽ ὅλως προσέχοσι πρότερον τοῖς τῆς Παλαιᾶς Διαθήκης, παρέδωκεν τὰς θείας Γραφάς ἐπὶ τῆς Ἑλλήνων κειμένας γλύπττης κατὰ τὴν τῶν Ἑβδομήκοντα ἑρμηνείαν.

[21] See Eusebius Caesariensis, *Praeparatio evangelica* 8, 1-15. See also Pseudo-Aristeas, *Epistula ad Philocratem* 32: τὴν ἑρμηνείαν ἀκριβές.

Hilary of Poitiers (*ca.* 310-368 AD). Hilary of Poitiers attributes perfect authority to the seventy translators.[22] As such, to disagree with them is an unsafe endeavor that would compromise simple rationality.[23] The seventy's translation was *ante* [...] *corporalem domini*[24] and *ante passionem domini*,[25] which proves Hilary's belief in the historicity of the miraculous translation. Furthermore, the seventy elders translated *per Moysen quoque doctrina secretiore perfecti*.[26] And so, Hilary advocates for the Septuagint because (1) the seventy elders translated *ante* the incarnation and sufferings of Christ and (2) because they inserted secret, more mature teachings of Moses into the Hebrew Scriptures.[27]

Cyril of Jerusalem (*ca.* 315-386 AD). Cyril also took the miracle translation as an historical event. And like Clement of Alexandria,[28] he concludes that the translators all translated the Law and the Prophets unanimously, despite being separated from one another in chambers.[29] The translator's words were not a human invention (εὑρεσιλογία, *verborum inventio*) or a κατασκευὴ σοφισμάτων ἀνθρωπίνων. Rather, 'from the Holy Spirit', ἡ τῶν ἁγίῳ πνεύματι λαληθεισῶν θείων γραφῶν ἑρμηνεία συνετελεῖτο.[30]

Saint Jerome (*ca.* 347-420 AD). Of all the church fathers, Saint Jerome stands out. Jerome strictly held to a *hebraica veritas* and refused to accept the premise that the translators were prophets, asserting a distinction between prophet and translator.[31] He believed the Hebrew alone was inspired by the Holy Spirit;[32] the Septuagint is merely a translation of men, subject to infallibility. However, Jerome did not totally abandon the Septuagint; he sought to

---

[22] Hilarius Pictaviensis, *Tractatus super psalmos* 2, 3: *Sed perfecta horum septuaginta interpretum auctoritas manet. Primum, quod ante aduentum corporalem domini transtulerunt.*

[23] *Ibid.* 118, 6: *Sed nobis neque tutum est translationem septuaginta interpretum transgredi, et sane ratio et sensus dictorum ita admonet.*

[24] *Ibid.* 2, 3.

[25] *Ibid.* 59, 1.

[26] *Ibid.* 2, 3: *quod ipsi illi principes doctoresque synagogae et praeter scientiam legis per Moysen quoque doctrina secretiore perfecti non potuerunt inprobabiles esse arbitri interpretandi, qui certissimi et grauissimi errant auctores docendi.* See Adam Kamesar, 'Hilary of Poiters, Judeo-Christianity, and the Origins of the LXX: A Translation of *Tractus Super Psalmos* 2, 23 with Introduction and Commentary', *VC* 59 (2005), 264-85, 264-9.

[27] See Iohannes Chrysostomus, *In Matthaeum homiliae* 5, 2: ἑβδομήκοντα πρὸ ἑκατὸν ἢ καὶ πλειόνων ἐτῶν τῆς τοῦ Χριστοῦ παρουσίας ἐπὶ τοῦτο ἐλθόντες καὶ τοσοῦτοι ὄντες. See also Irenaeus Lugdunensis, *Adversus haereses* III 21, 1, 3.

[28] Clemens Alexandrinus, *Stromata* I 22.

[29] Cyrillus Hierosolymitanus, *Catecheses* 4, 34.

[30] *Ibid.* 4, 34, 5-6.

[31] Hieronymus, *Prologus in Pentateuchum*: *Et nescio quis primus auctor septuaginta cellulas Alexandriae mendacio suo extruxerit, quibus divisi eadem scriptitarint, cum Aristeas eiusdem Ptolemei* ὑπερασπιστὴς, *et multo post tempore Iosephus nihil tale retulerint, sed in una basilica congregatos, contulisse scribant, non prophetasse. Aliud est enim vatem, aliud est esse interpretem. Ibi Spiritus ventura praedicat: hic eruditio et verborum copia, ea, quae intelligit transfert.*

[32] *Id., Prologus in Pentateuchum; Apologia adversus libros Rufini* 2, 25.

purify the Hebrew text by utilizing the Septuagint and the 'Jewish' *recentiores*, Origen's Hexapla, and other Jewish rabbinical documents.[33] Jerome calls the translators 'the Seventy'[34] and even implies the historical reliability of the Jewish accounts found in *Aristeas* and Josephus.[35] Yet, he asserts that the legend of the translators translating separately in individual cells is a *mendacium*.[36] Though Jerome generally acknowledges the historicity of the translation event, he rejects a divinely inspired Septuagint because of his commitment to a *hebraica veritas* and his trust in Josephus's and *Aristeas*'s account, both of which, according to Jerome, say nothing about a divinely inspired translation.

As we have seen, many of the church fathers took for granted the historical veracity of the Septuagint story, and most, with the exception of Jerome, maintained a divinely inspired translation. As quickly as we have surveyed these fathers, we now briefly investigate Saint Augustine, whose approach to the Greek Old Testament stands out among the rest.

3. *Graeca Veritas*: Saint Augustine's Theological Rationale for the Septuagint as Christian Scripture

If Jerome held to a strict *hebraica veritas*, Augustine maintained what we can call a *hebraica graecaque veritas*. Augustine believed both the Hebrew and Greek Old Testaments contained equal divine authority. And so, 'how' and 'why' did he arrive at this conclusion? But more specific to our purposes in this paper, 'how' and 'why' did he arrive at a *graeca veritas*?[37]

Augustine records an account of the translation near to what we find in *Aristeas*,[38] though with slight deviations.[39] Augustine even considers reliable the testimonies of those who speak of each translator *singuli cellis etiam singuli separati*.[40] That is, as we will see below, those who carry the story of the miraculous translation account are trustworthy sources of history. Throughout

---

[33] See A. Kamesar, *Jerome, Greek Scholarship, and the Hebrew Bible: A Study of the Quaestiones Hebraicae in Genesim* (Oxford, 1993), 4-40.

[34] Hieronymus, *Prologus in Pentateuchum*; *Apologia adversus libros Rufini* 2, 24.25.33-5.

[35] *Id.*, *Prologus in Pentateuchum*; *id.*, *Apologia adversus libros Rufini* 2, 25. See Iosephus Flavius, *Antiquitates Iudaicae* 12, 1-118.

[36] See Hieronymus, *Prologus in Pentateuchum*.

[37] As far as I am aware, Augustine never wrote this phrase.

[38] Augustinus Hipponensis, *De Civitate Dei* 18, 42.

[39] *E.g.* Augustine includes the translators being in separate locations, whereas Aristeas wrote that they undertook (ἐπετέλουν) their work καθ᾽ ἑκάστην εἰς τὸν τόπον [...] συναγόμενοι τὸ προκείμενον (Pseudo-Aristeas, *Epistula ad Philocratem* 307).

[40] Augustinus Hipponensis, *De doctrina Christiana* II 15, 22, 54: *qui si, ut fertur multique non indigni fide praedicant, singuili cellis etiam singulis separati cum interpretati essent, nihil in alicuius eorum codice inventum est quod non isdem verbis eodemque verborum ordine inveniretur in ceteris.*

his writings, we read of the one Holy Spirit inspiring the individual transla-tors.[41] The Holy Spirit brought their individual translations into perfect unity.[42] Furthermore, like Irenaeus and Clement of Alexandria but contra Jerome, Augustine esteems these translators to be prophets.[43] And as prophets, their unanimous translation has perfect divine authority[44] – especially since it bears the apostolic stamp of approval as seen in the New Testament.

Augustine can make this assertion of a divinely inspired Septuagint 'only if' he first accepts the historical reliability of the seventy(-two) elders being phys-ically separate from one another while they translated.[45] This fundamental assumption not only shapes his approach to the text of the Old Testament, but also his Old Testament exegesis, since the Septuagint, as a *divinae dispensa-tioni*,[46] at times amends and clarifies meaning in the Hebrew text.[47]

As an historical event, Augustine reinterprets the 'miracle translation' in light of three major theological premises: (1) 'the arrival of the Word of God, Jesus Christ'; (2) 'the apostles' approval of the Septuagint as testified in Scrip-ture'; and (3) 'the testimony and authority of the catholic church'. Augustine's argument for the Septuagint stands upon these three pillars, so to speak. And yet, neither of these three are independent of themselves. The only way Augus-tine can speak of Christ's advent (#1) is through the authority and testimony of the apostles and the church (#2 and #3). The only way Augustine can follow

---

[41] *Id.*, *Ennarrationes in Psalmos* 87, 10; *De Civitate Dei* 18, 43; *De doctrina Christiana* IV 7, 15, 48; *Epistula* 28, 2.

[42] *Id.*, *De doctrina Christiana* II 15, 22; *Ennarrationes in Psalmos* 87, 10: *verum Septuaginta interpretes, quorum auctoritas tana est, ut non immerito propter mirabilem consonantiam divino Spiritu interpretati esse credantur.*

[43] *Id.*, *De Civitate Dei* 15, 14: *Non enim est illa diversitas putata mendositas; nec ego ullo modo putandam existimo: sed ubi non est scriptoris error, aliquid eos divino Spiritu, ubi sensus esset consentaneus veritati et praedicans veritatem, non interpretantium munere, sed prophetantium libertate aliter dicere voluisse credendum est.*

[44] *Ibid.* 18, 42: *Et ideo tam mirabile Dei munus acceperant, ut illarum Scripturarum non tamquam humanarum, sed, sicut erant, tamquam divnarum etiam isto modo commendaretur auctori-tas, credituris quandoque gentibus profutura, quod iam videmus effectum.*

[45] *Ibid.*: *Traditur sane tam mirabilem ac stupendum planeque divinum in eorum verbis fuisse consensum, ut, cum ad hoc opus separatim singuli sederint [...] in nullo verbo, quod idem sig-nificaret et tantumdem valeret, vel in verborum ordine alter ab altero discreparet; sed tamquam unus esset interpres, ita quod omnes interpretati sunt unum erat; quaniam re vera Spiritus erat unus in omnibus.*

[46] *Id.*, *De doctrina Christiana* II 15, 22, 55: *Quam ob rem, etiamsi aliquid aliter in hebraeis exemplaribus invenitur quam isti posuerunt, cedendum esse arbitror 'divinae dispensationi', quae per eos facta es.*

[47] *Id.*, *Ennarrationes in Psalmos* 135, 3: *Quod quidem in hebraeo dicitur ['Dii Gentium dae-monia'] non ita esse scriptum; sed: 'Dii Gentium simulacra'. Quod si verum est, multo magis credendi sunt Septuaginta divino Spiritu interpretati, quo Spiritu et illa dicta sunt quae in hebraeis litteris sunt. Eodem namque operante Spiritu, etiam hoc dici oportuit quod dictum est: 'Dii Gentium daemonia': ut intellegeremus sic etiam in hebraeo positum: Dii Gentium simulacra; ut daemonia potius quae sunt in simulacris, significarentur.*

the apostle's use of the Septuagint (#2) is by reading and affirming the apostles' New Testament writings in which they utilize the Septuagint to prove Christ from the Old Testament (#1). And finally, the only way Augustine can rely on apostolic and church authority (#3) is because Christ physically appeared in the flesh (#1), appointed his apostles, and established his church through whom his Spirit now operates with authority.

First, Augustine retrospectively interprets the translation event in light of Christ's advent. Like Eusebius,[48] Augustine believed the Spirit-inspired Septuagint anticipated and prepared the way for the ingathering of the Gentiles not only by making the Scriptures available to the Greek-speaking world,[49] but also by adding prophetic, pre-incarnation, emendations to the Hebrew Scriptures.[50] Therefore, we see the fact of Christ's advent and mission to the gentiles influencing Augustine's argument for an inspired, prophetic, and authoritative Septuagint.

Nestled tightly within this first aspect of Augustine's argument for an authoritative Septuagint is his claim to merely follow the apostles' use of the Old Testament (which is an argument that modern Christians today, particularly Protestants, must wrestle with). Since the apostles who composed the Holy Scripture quoted their Old Testament citations from both Greek and Hebrew, Augustine sees no problem following in their 'footsteps' because both the Hebrew and Greek *utraque una atque divina est*.[51] In one of Augustine's letters, Augustine asks Jerome why he has not based several passages of his Latin Old Testament on the Septuagint, since the Septuagint *Neque enim parvum pondus habet illa quae sic meruit diffamari, et qua usos Apostolos*.[52] In other words, since the apostles utilized the Septuagint, and since there is a wide attestation of its use in the church, the Septuagint should receive an authoritative status when considering Bible translation.

Finally, the last aspect of Augustine's theological rationale for a *graeca veritas* stems from his understanding of ecclesial authority. Generally speaking, Augustine relies exclusively on church authority to confirm the Scripture's canon[53] and doctrine.[54] Yet, for Augustine the church does not have 'absolute' authority; her authority is always a derivative of God's authority. That is, God

---

[48] Eusebius Caesariensis, *Praeparatio evangelica* 8, 1-9.

[49] Augustinus Hipponensis, *De doctrina Christiana* II 15, 22, 55. See also *ibid.* II 6, 7, 9, where Augustine mentions various other translations in *varias interpretum linguas* that spread the message of salvation to the gentiles.

[50] *Id., De Civitate Dei* 15, 14; 18, 33.

[51] *Ibid.* 18, 44: *Unde etiam ego pro meo modulo vestigia sequens Apostolorum, quia et ipsi ex utrisque, id est, ex hebraeis et ex Septuaginta, testimonia prophetica posuerunt, utraque auctoritate utendum putavi, quoniam utraque una atque divina est.*

[52] *Id., Epistula* 71, 6. In another letter to Jerome, he writes that the Septuagint is of *gravissima auctoritas* (*ibid.* 28, 2).

[53] *Id., De doctrina Christiana* II 15, 22; *Contra Faustum* 33, 6; 11, 3.

[54] *Id., Contra Faustum* 18, 7; *Quaestiones Evangeliorum* 1, 38.

himself grants the church her apostolic authority to establish the canon of Scripture and orthodox doctrine. Augustine affirms this in several of his writings,[55] but he expresses this quite clearly in *Quaestionum evangelicarum libri II*: *Dominus de auctoritate Ecclesiae docet Gentes*.[56]

Knowing Augustine's general conviction of church authority sheds light on his words regarding the miraculous translation of the Septuagint in both *De Doctrina Christiana* and *De Civitate Dei*:

> To correct any Latin manuscripts Greek ones should be used: among these, as far as the Old Testament is concerned, the authority of the Septuagint is supreme. Its seventy writers are now claimed *in all the more informed churches* (*omnes peritiores ecclesias*) to have performed their task of translation with such strong guidance from the Holy Spirit that this great number of men spoke with but a single voice. If, *as is generally held* (*fertur*), and indeed asserted by many *who are not unworthy of belief*, each one of these wrote his translation alone in an individual cell and nothing was found in anyone's version which was not found.[57]

> '*It is said* (*traditur*) that the agreement in their words was so marvelous, so amazing, as to be plainly divine in origin. For, though each of them sat in a separate place while engaged on the work [...] they did not differ from one another in a single word, not even by a synonym conveying the same meaning, and there was no discrepancy even in the order of their words. There was such unity in their translations that it was as if there had been only one translator; for, truly, the one Spirit was present in them all (*vera Spiritus erat unus in omnibus*). And they received so wondrous a gift of God precisely so that, by means of it, the authority of those Scriptures might be commended not as humans, but as divine, to the Gentiles, who were to come to believe in Christ: a purpose which, as we see, has now been accomplished'.[58]

Though Augustine does not explicitly make known the sources from which he takes these accounts,[59] it's important to note that in these two recordings of the translation event, Augustine is relying on previous church witnesses. Given that (1) the majority of the early church before Augustine gave an account of the translation similar to the two accounts he gives here; (2) Augustine understood the church as the locus wherein Holy Scripture is established and affirmed; and (3) Augustine here in *De Doctrina Christiana* has just referred to the 'more informed churches',[60] I think we can safely infer that in these two

---

[55] See *id.*, *De doctrina Christiana* II 15, 22; *Contra Faustum* 33, 6; 11, 3; 18, 7; *Quaestiones Evangeliorum* 1, 38.

[56] *Id.*, *Quaestiones Evangeliorum* 2, 2. See *id.*, *Contra Faustum* 18, 7: *non aliam Legem, nec alios Prophetas, quam eos quos catholica tenet auctoritas, non venit solvere, sed adimplere*.

[57] *Id.*, *De doctrina Christiana* II 15, 22, 53-54 (emphasis mine). English translation taken from Augustine, *De Doctrina Christiana*, ed. and trans. R.P.H. Green (Oxford, 1995).

[58] *Id.*, *De Civitate Dei* 18, 42. English translation taken from Augustine, *The City of God against the Pagans*, ed. and trans. Robert W. Dyson (Cambridge, 1998).

[59] Note the passives *fertur* and *traditur* which hide the actual, historical subjects of these verbs.

[60] Augustinus, *De doctrina Christiana* II 15, 22, 53.

texts Augustine likely refers to these 'more informed churches' as the sources from which he received the historical account of the translation event. If this is correct, then for Augustine there is no question: because God works *de auctoritate Ecclesiae*, therefore what the 'more informed churches' have handed down contains no small authority. And what these churches have handed down is a conviction in a *graeca veritas*.

4. Conclusion

I began this essay by inquiring into why so many church fathers would believe in a divinely-guided translation if, indeed, the miraculous story of the translation is merely a 'story', as most modern scholars assume. We looked briefly at the rationales that lay behind several early church figures, and we concluded that the majority of the early church (aside from Jerome) simply *believed* in the historicity of the miracle translation. This is no different for Saint Augustine, who reinterprets the translation event through (1) 'the historical arrival of the Word of God, Jesus Christ'; (2) 'the apostles' approval of the Septuagint, testified in the New Testament'; and (3) 'the testimony and authority handed down by the catholic church'. And through this theological reinterpretation of history, Augustine affirms the reliability of what we can call a *graeca veritas Vetus Testamentum* – or more specifically, a *hebraica graecaque Vetus Testamentum*.

The Symbolism of Biblical Birds in the Letters of Paulinus of Nola

Marcin WYSOCKI, Lublin, Poland

ABSTRACT

Paulinus of Nola, in his correspondence, drew abundantly from the texts of the Holy Scriptures, recalling, among other things, the birds present in the Bible. Properly interpreted, they served Paulinus primarily to show the path of Christian conversion and life, and pointed to the behaviours and attitudes of Christians, of which Paulinus some demanded, but also some he condemned. Finally, they symbolically described people and their features, and also referred to God. Paulinus did not make a deep interpretation of individual birds and their features, but focused on the most important features, in his opinion, that were important in his pastoral and literary influence. This article presents the birds that Paulinus uses as the symbols in his letters (eagle, raven, dove, pelican, owl, sparrow) and their interpretation.

Paulinus of Nola (354-431) is known primarily as the person who gave up senatorial dignities and earthly riches to settle in the monastery he founded at the tomb of St. Felix in Nola near Naples, and to live there first as a monk and then as a bishop, giving up his social and political life and his practising of pagan poetry. In return, he decided to honour the Martyr with a poem once a year and to exchange letters with the leading figures of the Christian life of his time, as well as with ordinary people seeking spiritual advice. In his poems and letters, which are the legacy of the period after his conversion, Paulinus appears as a master of the word, which he first proved by writing pagan poems, the excellence of which was confirmed by his teacher and friend Ausonius.[1] One of the determinants of this mastery is the biblical interpretations that are included in his works – certainly not as deep theologically as that by other exegetes of that time – but, above all, the excellence of their literary form and their fullness of both Christian and practical wisdom, focusing on pastoral help and the development of spiritual life.[2] Certainly, Paulinus drew on this attitude

---

[1] See Ausonius, *Ep.* 20-5; Paulinus Nolensis, *Carmen* 10-1. *Cf.* Roger P.H. Green, 'The Correspondance of Ausonius', *AC* 49 (1980), 191-211; Andrea Ruggiero and Domenico Sorrentino, *Dalle muse a Cristo: Storia di una conversione. Brani di Meropio Ponzio Paolino e Decimo Magno Ausonio* (Nola, 1984); Giovanni Santaniello, 'Il dramma della conversione nel dibattito tra Paolino e Ausonio', *ID* 14 (2001), 205-31.

[2] About the biblical exegesis by Paulinus see: Serafino Prete, *Motivi ascetici e letterari in Paolino di Nola*, Strenae Nolanae 1 (Napoli, 1987); Giovanni Rizza, 'Imitazione biblica ed influenza

Studia Patristica CIII, 165-173.

from his own life and daily experience, and one of these was the experience
of living in the countryside. In interpreting the Bible, he repeatedly referred
to nature, and from it he took examples and ways of explaining the biblical
texts. Therefore, by raising issues related to the Bible in the correspondence of
St. Paulinus, it is worth looking at how he uses the world of nature in his interpretations and in the spiritual directions based on the examples of the birds that
appear in the Bible and which he recalls in his letters,[3] all the more so, because
this is a topic that has not yet been brought up in the study of the works of
Paulinus of Nola.

1. Nature as an example

It could be said that Paulinus is perfectly aware of the usefulness of the
world of nature in his interpretations and in spiritual advice. He often points
out the importance of looking at spiritual life from the perspective of the countryside and nature, as, for instance, in letter 5 (to Severus), in which he recalls
the beginnings of his spiritual life:

Finally, when I seemed to obtain rest from lying scandal and from wanderings,
unbusied by public affairs and far from the din of the marketplace, I enjoyed the leisure

retorica nell'opera di Paolino di Nola', *MSLCA* 1 (1947), 153-64; Sandro Leanza, *Aspetti esegetici
dell'opera di Paolino di Nola*, in *Atti del Convegno. XXXI Cinquantenario della morte di San
Paolino di Nola* (Roma, 1983), 67-91; Gaetano Di Palma, 'Paolino di fronte alla Bibbia', in Luigi
Longobardo and Domenico Sorrentino (eds), *Mia sola arte è la fede* (Napoli, 2000), 151-66;
Elizabeth A. Clark, 'Reading Asceticism: Exegetical Strategies in the Early Christian Rhetoric of
Renunciation', *BI* 5 (1997), 82-105.

[3] Unfortunately, there is no extensive literature on the birds in the Bible and their symbolic
meaning, as well as there not being a large number of studies on the symbolism of birds in the
early Christian writers. Most often than not, information about the symbolic significance of birds
can be found in encyclopaedias or other collections on biblical animals or general studies. See
Robert M. Grant, *Early Christians and Animals* (London, New York, 1999); David S. Wallace-
Hadrill, *The Greek Patristic View of Nature* (New York, Manchester, 1968); Francis Klingender,
Evelyn Antal and John P. Harthan (eds), *Animals in Art and Thought to the End of the Middle
Ages* (Cambridge, 1971); Gillian Clark, 'The Fathers and the Animals: The Rule of Rome', in
Andrew Linzey and Dorothy Yamamoto (eds), *Animals on the Agenda: Questions about Animals
for Theology and Ethics* (London, 1998), 67-79; Gordon L. Campbell (ed.), *The Oxford Hand-
book of Animals in Classical Thought and Life* (Oxford, 2014) esp. chapter 21: Ingvild Sælid
Gilhus, 'Animals in Late Antiquity and Early Christianity'. Among the literature on the subject,
it is worth mentioning the following publications: Godfrey R. Driver, 'Birds in the Old Testament: I. Birds in Law', *PEQ* 87/1 (1955), 5-20; *id.*, 'Birds in the Old Testament: II. Birds in
Life', *PEQ* 87/2 (1955), 129-40; *id.*, 'Once Again: Birds in the Bible', *PEQ* 90/1 (1958), 56-8;
Alice Parmelee, *All the Birds of the Bible: Their Stories, Identification and Meaning* (New York,
1959); Debbie Blue, *Consider the Birds: A Provocative Guide to Birds of the Bible* (Nashville,
TN, 2013); Peter Altmann, *Banned Birds. The Birds of Leviticus 11 and Deuteronomy 14* (Tübingen,
2019).

of country life and my religious duties, surrounded by pleasant peace in my withdrawn household.[4]

Therefore, Paulinus' stay in the countryside was a time of peace, during which he could take up service for the Church and develop his own spiritual life. This is the starting point for our reflection on the interpretation of the importance of animals in Paulinus' correspondence. It shows the roots of Paulinus' interpretation – his personal experience of nature and country life. However, Paulinus does not base it only on this, but points to the second important foundation of his interpretations – the will of God Himself, who wants to instruct people via rural examples:

Wisdom in fact teaches all the country lore that can be applied to the schooling of the soul, when It directs Its disciples to the ant and the bee, both country creatures [...]. Again, how much has the Lord taught us in the Gospel by rustic similes![5]

The Creator deliberately planned all creatures and gave them to man so that they would show His splendour and, through them, He would instruct man about how to achieve salvation.[6] And man's task is to discover this plan of salvation by interpreting the meaning of these creatures that were given by God, and which were given as the symbols and images of spiritual realities. Therefore, Paulinus not only referred to his own rural experiences, but he also sought from others the meaning of those creatures mentioned in the Holy Scriptures in order to draw spiritual teachings from them and pass them on to others.[7]

Paulinus devotes a lot of attention in his letters to birds,[8] as they often appear on the Scripture's pages, but they have, for Paulinus, one very important feature above all, which is appropriate to recall when talking about spiritual life – they soar on their wings towards the highest, to heaven, to God. Therefore, for him, all birds are primarily a symbol of "the troubled pauper, who is the repentant man reduced to poverty of hope by some sin".[9] However, thanks to their wings, as he states in the song for Licentius, anyone can fly to the stars, to God.[10] According to Paulinus, the virtues are these wings that lift man up[11] and allow

---

[4] Paulinus Nolensis, *Epistula* 5, 4 [hereafter: *Ep.*]. The English translation of the letters I quote from: *Letters of St. Paulinus of Nola*, trans. Patric G. Walsh, vol. 1-2, Ancient Christian Writers 35-36 (New York, 1966-1967).

[5] *Ep.* 39, 2.

[6] See *Ep.* 43, 7.

[7] See *Ep.* 46, 3.

[8] The aim of Paulinus' correspondence is primarily pastoral, which is why his interpretations, as well as that of bird symbolism, are not as extensive and deep as, for example, the interpretations of Augustine, who is also one of Paulinus' correspondents. *Cf.* Marek Cieśluk, 'Symbolika ptaków w „Enarrationes in Psalmos" świętego Augustyna' [= 'Symbolism of the Birds in the "Enarrationes in Psalmos" by Saint Augustine'], *VoxP* 52/1 (2008), 87-98.

[9] *Ep.* 40, 6.

[10] See *Carmen ad Licentium* 86 (*Ep.* 8, 5).

[11] See *Ep.* 40, 6.

him to fly above earthly nature.[12] Following the example of the birds, we should beware of descending during flight towards the ground, towards the lowlands. On Earth, there are ambushes awaiting us – the temptations of this world – and only people armed with faith and enlightened by the truth can avoid them and fly upwards.[13]

2. The Birds and their meaning

The Eagle – Aquila. For Paulinus, the eagle is primarily a symbol of rebirth and recovery, of the renewal of youth.[14] Paulinus bases this on the texts of the prophet Isaiah (*Isa.* 40:31) and the Book of Psalms (*Ps.* 102:5). One example of this is Paulinus himself, who, although he had retired and closed himself off from his worldly life, nevertheless wanted his life to be renewed – after his conversion, and having being released from an old man's weakness and putting on a new man created according to God's image.[15] This renewal is about freeing oneself from the weaknesses of an old man, who lives in the world, and putting on a new man who is a man of God.[16] New strength, like that of an eagle, can only be obtained through trust in the Lord.[17] The eagle's strength can also be obtained from God by being in the service of others, such as being a messenger.[18] Parents who raise their offspring and feed them with the food of God's wisdom are also compared to the eagle and are an example of a righteous life, but they also teach us how to destroy the hostility of the body to the spirit.[19] Interestingly, this royal bird, which appears in many interpretations and works by many other Church Fathers with whom Paulinus exchanged letters or knew personally,[20] was not fully used and interpreted by him.

The Dove – Columba. The dove is another bird referred to by Paulinus in his letters. He evokes the texts from the Book of Genesis (*Gen.* 8:11) and *Psalm* 54.

---

[12] See *Ep.* 40, 9.

[13] See *ibid.*

[14] In this way, Paulinus recalls false opinions about eagles, which in ancient times were based on false observations of nature and which are the source of legends, *e.g.* about testing eagles' chicks or about the regaining of youth by eagles. *Cf.* Dorothea Forstner, *Świat symboliki chrześcijańskiej*, trans. from German (Warszawa, 1990), 240-1; *Physiologus latinus* (Versio B) VIII; Bogdan Czyżewski, 'Alegoryczna interpretacja właściwości ptaków według „Fizjologa"' [= 'Allegorical Interpretation of the Features of Birds according to „Physiologus"'], in Maciej Olczyk and Paweł Podeszwa (eds), *Credidimus caritati* (Gniezno, 2010), 39-52.

[15] See *Ep.* 40, 6.

[16] See *ibid.*

[17] See *Ep.* 5, 18.

[18] See *Ep.* 21, 5.

[19] See *Ep.* 44, 5. *Cf.* Forstner, *Świat* (1990), 241.

[20] *Cf.* Augustinus, *Enarrationes in Psalmos* 102, 9n; Ambrosius, *Sermo* 47, 7; *id., De sacramentis* IV 2, 7.

Thus, the dove is the bird that brings the branch of peace to Noah's Ark and is therefore an image of the Holy Spirit which works not only for one family, but for the whole of the human race.[21] The dove is also for Paulinus a symbol of the returning man who is to not only serve the monk in delivering the letters and in the daily needs,[22] but also to fulfil the service of mercy towards those waiting for the letter to be delivered from that monk.[23] Sometimes, Paulinus allegorically asks for dove's wings for himself in order to fly and to be with friends or people important to him.[24] One must have the wings of dove to fly far away from the din of the world.[25]

The Raven – Corax/corvus. This bird has a double meaning in Paulinus' letters. He himself states in one of his letters that "that bird is found symbolising now sin and now grace".[26] This is reflected in the two names by which it is described. The term *corax* is once used to denote the raven and once the term *corvus* is used.[27] According to Paulinus, the first term means a night bird that brings death, punishes the wicked and vile[28] and refers to the raven that was released from Noah's Ark and did not return (*cf. Gen.* 8:6).[29] The second term refers to the raven belonging to the day and which fed the prophet Elijah (*cf.* 1*Kgs.* 17:4-6),[30] and whose chicks call the name of the Lord.[31] Such a raven can be someone helpful, sent by the Lord, helping monks who devote themselves to prayer and to God's daily service.[32] The black colour of the raven can also have two meanings: it can signify the saints[33] and indicate the dignity and beauty of the colour black,[34] and at other times it can mean the wickedness and the blackness / darkness that embraces people.[35]

The Pelican – Pelicanum. The pelican has an even deeper meaning in the correspondence of Paulinus,[36] about which, similarly to the information given about a craven, he presents a lot of information obtained from experts and people who saw these birds in their natural environment. Paulinus quotes the

---

[21] See *Ep.* 49, 10.
[22] See *Ep.* 26, 1.
[23] See *Ep.* 37, 1.
[24] See *Ep.* 38, 9.
[25] See *Ep.* 26, 1.
[26] *Ep.* 23, 29.
[27] See *Ep.* 23, 28.
[28] See *Ep.* 23, 29.
[29] See *Ep.* 23, 28.
[30] See *ibid.*
[31] See *Ep.* 23, 29.
[32] See *Ep.* 26, 1.
[33] See *Ep.* 23, 28.29.
[34] See *Ep.* 23, 29.
[35] See *ibid.*
[36] See Antoni Swoboda, 'Egzegeza alegoryczna Pisma Św. w Listach Paulina z Noli' [= 'Allegorical Exegesis of the Holy Scripture in the Letters of Paulinus of Nola'], *VoxP* 32-33 (1997), 261-8, 266-7.

words of the Book of Psalms (*Ps.* 101) about the pelican in the wilderness and expresses regret that he is not like it.[37] Paulinus begins the allegorical interpretation of the pelican by presenting the facts:

I have been told by a holy man, one most learned and dear to me whose wide knowledge has been won by travel as well as reading, that the pelican is a bird commonly found in Egypt or in neighbouring regions. It wanders in the wilderness close to the Nile, and feeds on snakes after battering them into submission.[38]

On this basis, Paulinus goes further in order to show the symbolic meaning of the bird. The pelican is a distressed poor man – a penitent[39] who

is beggared of the wealth of grace; in mindfully aware of his sad faults, he mourns the loss of his glory; his pitiable troubles make him woebegone; groaning, he strives to recover the life of his soul from the death of his flesh, and by expenditure of prayers and lamentation he solicitously and tearfully seeks the approval which will heal the wound to his salvation.[40]

Paulinus emphasises the accuracy of describing such a man as an "Egyptian or nocturnal bird",[41] and then he explains the name:

For to lament and to confess his sins he seeks solitary retirement from the general congregation of the church, and sadly shuts himself inside the prison of his cell, departing in flight from this world that he may remain in the loneliness of lamentation.[42]

Therefore, starting from the definition presented, Paulinus focuses on the distance and loneliness of the bird in order to show the state of the sinner. Then he takes into consideration the motif of a fight, noting that the pelican "fights to conquer, and if defeated it dies; but if it wins it both escapes death and gains sustenance",[43] and thus he refers again to the sinner who "strives to grapple with the longings of the flesh, and fight it out against his sins which must be worn down in spiritual conflict".[44] The pelican fights with snakes, and the sinner and penitent "emulates the snake-hating bird by warring on the devil himself and on the princes of darkness, by laying assault to sins and the thoughts of the flesh".[45] In this way, Paulinus shows the penitent's spiritual struggle, which aims to overcome his sins, and its purpose is to defeat his enemies and to gain life, to win the prize of life. A penitent, if he wins this fight, becomes

[37] See *Ep.* 40, 6.
[38] *Ibid.*
[39] See Giovanni Santaniello, 'La spiritualità di Paolino di Nola: Il cammino ascetico e mistico del convertito', *ID* 10 (1995), 205-38.
[40] *Ep.* 40, 7.
[41] *Ibid.*
[42] *Ibid.*
[43] *Ep.* 40, 6.
[44] *Ep.* 40, 7.
[45] *Ibid.*

"victorious over sin and the devil".[46] Such a victory is possible thanks to the help of God, who allows us to walk on snakes. Referring to himself as an example of a pelican, although this can also be said of all the monks who occupied a special place in the Nolian's theology, Paulinus asks his correspondents to pray for him so that he may live like a pelican, off the beaten path, in the wilderness, and that he may kill snakes until his inner man is cleansed of the darkness and is shining with virtue.[47]

The Owl – Noctua. In this same way, Paulinus goes on to interpret another bird that appears on the pages of the Bible and in which he sees the next stages of spiritual development and conversion. After eradicating the devil and Satan, as the pelican does, and thus after the cleansing of the soul, man is to become "like a night raven in the house" (*Ps.* 101:7). Interestingly, Paulinus, referring once more to the learned man, corrects the biblical text here and states that instead of "night raven", the name "night owl" should be used:

But my friend claimed that correct form of the other bird is not 'nycticorax' but 'nycticora'. His argument for this seemed sound enough, for he said that the bird mentioned in that passage of Scripture is what we call the night owl, because it whistles by night from hidden places, and in flight it can see even in that pitch-darkness which causes all living creatures to grope. So it is called 'nycticora' more accurately than 'nycticorax', for 'nycticorax' means 'night raven', whereas 'nycticora' means "having night vision", being derived from kórê, the Greek for the pupil of the eye. Now obviously the night owl has no connexion with the raven; moreover, as I have said, it is certain that like some other night birds it sees better in the dark and is blind in the light, and that during the day it endures darkness and obtains light from the night.[48]

Thus, after eradicating Satan, man is to become like "a night owl in the house", that is, in the Lord's house, when "the inward man may direct the sharp gaze of a purified mind amidst the darkness of this world".[49] This is possible, according to Paulinus, when, in man, that which is of the earth, that is, the body, is in harmony with the soul. Paulinus, therefore, strives to reconcile the bodily with the spiritual, but he gives the superiority and leadership role to the spiritual, when "the flesh denies its earthly nature and joins the soul in concord and spiritual feeling"[50] like the owl, which, with "the light" of its eyes, penetrates the darkness of the night in which Paulinus sees the darkness of this world.[51] This state is, for Paulinus, the goal of spiritual development.

---

[46] *Ibid.*
[47] See *ibid.*
[48] *Ep.* 40, 6.
[49] *Ep.* 40, 7.
[50] *Ibid.*
[51] See *Ep.* 40, 8.

The Sparrow – Passer. Paulinus' letters also include the sparrow,[52] which, although it may seem to be the smallest of all the birds discussed here, is, however, a unique and special creature for the Nolian. Paulinus, first of all recalling the words of the Book of Psalms: "like a lonely sparrow on the roof" (*Ps.* 101:8), sees in these words a remoteness from worldly matters, an avoidance of the desire for earthly things and the ascension to Christ who is in the highest.[53] A man raised to the highest on the wings of virtue becomes like a sparrow who is on the roof.[54] It is a symbol of the soul, which avoids earthly temptations, ambushes and dangers, and, thanks to faith and truth, rises upwards, towards God.[55] Such a sparrow is the man who has gone through all the stages of spiritual development symbolised by all of the birds presented above – from destroying one's enemies like a pelican, through eyes which sees in the darkness of this world like an owl's – to the very end, when one's "feet shall be established upon the heights of perfected virtue, and by prayerful vigils and meditation on God's law",[56] and such a man becomes "as a sparrow all alone on the housetop" (*Ps.* 101:8). Such a man achieves harmony of the body and soul with the will of God, he becomes one – the sparrow, in Paulinus' thought, becomes the symbol of the perfect man who, fully united in himself and with God, lives at God's altar.[57] Paulinus, however, goes further in exploring the symbolism of this seemingly ordinary bird. He recalls the words of the Gospel of Matthew about two sparrows, one of which does not fall to the ground (*Matt.* 10:29).[58] That which falls, according to Paulinus, is "the highest Sparrow" (*passer hic summus*), *i.e.* the only Son of God who flies high, looks at the humble believers, and whose fall to earth, made while in the body, was death on the cross, after which He rose again from the earth through the Resurrection. In Paulinus' interpretation, this fall was, at the same time, an elevation, and therefore this "highest Sparrow" is Wisdom that shows all those who seek Him a way to himself and invites them to the highest, to His abode, which is the cross. Paulinus emphasises the freedom of will of "the highest Sparrow" and, at the same time, total subordination to the will of the Father.[59] In Paulinus' theological thought, mentioned above, Christ – the highest Sparrow – via His "fall" to the earth, that is, the Incarnation, and his rising to the highest, that

---

[52] See Swoboda, 'Egzegeza alegoryczna' (1997), 267.

[53] See *Ep.* 40, 9.

[54] See *Ep.* 40, 6.

[55] See *Ep.* 40, 9.

[56] *Ep.* 40, 8.

[57] See *ibid.*

[58] Paulinus used the version of the Holy Bible, in which it is written, as in the Vulgate, of one sparrow that does not fall to the earth, while modern translations say rather that none falls to earth without the will of the Father.

[59] See Luigi Padovese, 'Considerazioni sulla dottrina cristologica e soteriologica di Paolino di Nola', in Gennaro Luongo (ed.), *Anchora Vitae. Atti del II Convegno Paoliniano nel XVI Centenario del Ritiro di Paolino a Nola* (Napoli, Roma, 1998), 209-24.

is on the cross, restored the harmony and peace between that which is carnal and that which is spiritual, and he gave an example of the path that every believer should follow.[60] According to Paulinus, only by following this Sparrow and imitating those who preached the Good News will we be allowed to become the second sparrow that has not fallen, but which, as a perfect man, can be in the highest where the highest Sparrow resides, where there is a place for every sparrow, that is, every man who makes the effort to fly upwards.[61] However, even when staying in the highest, on the roof, that is, above earthly nature, everyone must beware of descending to lower places, where ambushes and "evil-spirited fowlers" lurk, who try to seduce people with the temptations of the world, and the only way to save oneself is to fly up to the highest places like a sparrow (cf. Ps. 10:2).[62]

3. Conclusion

As can be seen, even from the above considerations, Paulinus of Nola in his letters abundantly drew on the texts of the Holy Scripture, recalling, among other things, the birds found in the Bible. Properly interpreted, they served Paulinus primarily to show the path of Christian conversion and life and pointed to the behaviour and attitudes of Christians, which Paulinus demanded from them, but which he also he condemned. Finally, they symbolically described people and their features and also referred to God. Paulinus did not make a deep interpretation of any individual birds and their features, but focused on the most important features, in his opinion, that were important in his pastoral and literary influences.

---

[60] See Tadeusz Kołosowski, 'Natura i sens tajemnicy wcielenia Chrystusa oraz jej wpływ na życie moralno-duchowe człowieka w świetle korespondencji św. Paulina z Noli' [= 'The Nature and Significance of the Mystery of Incarnation of Christ and its Influence on the Moral and Spiritual Life of Man in the Correspondence of St. Paulinus of Nola'], VoxP 38-39 (2000), 281-91.

[61] See Ep. 40, 8.

[62] See Ep. 40, 9.

John Chrysostom's Teaching about the Holy Bible and the Necessity of Reading it Daily

Eirini Artemi, Athens, Greece

ABSTRACT

For John Chrysostom, the Holy Bible is not only a historical book or a book which should be used for pedagogical reasons. It is the word of God: 'All Scripture is inspired by God' (2*Tim.* 3:16; Ioannes Chrysostomus, *In epistulam II ad Timotheum homiliae* 9), and for this reason Christians should not enclose the texts of the Holy in books, but have an obligation to engrave them upon their hearts. The Holy Scriptures, given by the inspiration of God, are of themselves sufficient for the discovery of truth. The Scriptures show people the way to salvation. This was given by God to the people, in order to help the people communicate with God. Direct communication between God and the people was lost after the original sin of Adam and Eve. For this reason, Chrysostom advises his congregation: 'I also always entreat you, and do not cease entreating you, not only to pay attention here to what I say, but also when you are at home, to persevere continually in reading the divine Scriptures' (Ioannes Chrysostomus, *De Lazaro conciones* 3). In this paper, we are going to present how the Bible should be read and why there is the necessity of continually reading it. Does Chrysostom accept the divine origin of the Holy Scripture? Which method does he use for the interpretation of the Bible? Does the reading of the Bible refer only to monks? Is the Scripture alone the final Authority, or should it be read with the texts of the Church Fathers? Is the Bible the only way for our salvation, or should we combine the reading of the Bible with our participation in the Holy Sacraments and Holy Divine Mass?

1. John Chrysostom and the use of the Bible in his works

John Chrysostom is one of the most articulate and influential preachers of the early Christian church. The golden-mouthed Church father deals with the interpretation of the Scripture because he supports the idea that theology should be based on the Bible. The latter doesn't tell lies 'For the Scripture by no means speaks falsely',[1] so the theology will be orthodox and there will be no inclination towards any heresy.[2]

His writings are some of the most perfect expositions on the books of the Bible, with great emphasis on the books of Genesis, the Psalms, the prophet

---

[1] Iohannes Chrysostomus, *De statuis* 2, PG 49, 44.
[2] *Id., In Iohannem homiliae* 43, PG 57, 291-3.

Studia Patristica CIII, 175-182.
© Peeters Publishers, 2021.

Isaiah, the gospels of Matthew and John, the Acts of the Apostles and the
epistles of Saint Paul.[3] Moreover, his exegetical works on the Book of Acts are
the only surviving commentary on the book from the first thousand years of
Christianity.[4]

In his writings and in their interpretation, John uses the books of the Bible;
he tries to find the depth of the divine truth which is hidden in the biblical
words. The words of the Scripture are not always self-explanatory. If he wants
to understand the real meanings of the words, Chrysostom realises that this can
only happen with the illumination of the Holy Spirit.[5] Thus, the Holy Spirit had
a major role in inspiring the writing of the Bible.[6] 'Generally, the biblical interpretation is not merely an art of understanding written and historical facts, but
a pure "theological" and "existential" case. It is not simply an interpretative
method, but energy, a movement of the healthy mind to the knowledge and
oversight of the beings, ultimately referring to the ultimate knowledge, the truth
of real and personal God'.[7]

John uses the Bible in his texts and interprets them in order to deepen their
meaning and to express the dogmatic and moral theology of the two Testaments.
For the interpretation of the Scripture's text, he uses the very rare allegorical
method of the Alexandrian School,[8] but he mainly employs the historical-literary[9] method of interpretation which he adopted from his professor, Diodorus
Tarsus, the dominant figure of the Antioch school. Of course, he does not trust
the historical-literary method at all. For him, the basic presupposition for the
interpretation of the Scriptures is the faith, orthodox teaching, prayers and piety
of a Christian in his daily life.[10] Of course, the most important thing is the grace

---

[3] Mary Fairchild, 'John Chrysostom, the Golden-Tongued Preacher. The Greatest Preacher of
the Early Church' (3 September 2019), https://www.learnreligions.com/john-chrysostom-4764128
[accessed 05/09/2019].

[4] *Ibid.*

[5] Iohannes Chrysostomus, *In Epistulam ad Galatas commentarius* 1, PG 61, 629.

[6] *Ibid.*, PG 61, 624; *id.*, *In Acta Apostolorum homiliae* 19, PG 60, 156.

[7] Eirini Artemi, 'The School of Alexandria and the use of allegorical method by Origen of
Alexandria', *Mirabilia Ars* 8/1 (2018), 1-15, 4.

[8] *Ibid.* 5: 'The aim of this exegesis was to discover everywhere the spiritual sense underlying
the written word of the Scripture. Allegory reveals the obscure meaning within the ostensive report
of a text without any references to any historical realities. Allegory thinks every word of the
Scriptures as a shell, which includes the inner kernel of a moral and superior spiritual truth. The
reader should open this shell and to look for the real true meaning of every story, parable, word'.

[9] The characteristic features are: attention to the revision of the text, a close adherence to the
plain, natural meaning according to the use of language and the state of the writer, and justice for
the human factor. See Allain Le Boulluec, 'L'École d'Alexandrie. De quelques aventures d'un
concept historiographique', in *Alexandrina. Hellénisme, judaïsme et christianisme à Alexandrie.
Mélanges offerts à C. Mondésert* (Paris, 1987), 403-17.

[10] Iohannes Chrysostomus, *In Iohannem homiliae* 21, PG 59, 127; *Homiliae in Genesim* 15,
PG 53, 321-2; *In Epistulam ad Hebraeos homiliae* 8, PG 63, 74; *In Epistulam ad Galatas commentarius* 1, PG 61, 629.

of the Holy Spirit and His illumination for anyone who studies the Scriptures.[11] After all, the Holy Spirit inspired the writers of the biblical books to reveal the divine economy in human history.[12] Furthermore, the use of the Scripture in Chrysostom's writings shows the generosity of God towards the people in order for them to live virtuously and to ethically improve their lives. In order to achieve this goal, Chrysostom emphasis 'making ourselves like God as much as possible for us'.[13]

2. The Holy Scripture is inspired by God

The Holy Scripture was written by men divinely inspired, and is God's revelation of Himself to man. John Chrysostom supports the idea that the Old and the New Testaments are equal parts of the Holy Scripture,[14] sisters which have the same father.[15] Their bond has to do with their unity for the same purpose, which is to make people better and to show them the way to be saved from sin.[16] Moreover, the whole Scripture is a testimony to Christ, who is Himself the centre of the divine revelation in the history of human race.[17] Chrysostom parallels this unity of the two covenants with the unity of the parts of any being:

But the harmony between them [...] But if there were any hostility in their statements, neither would the sects, who maintain the contrary part, have received all, but only so much as seemed to harmonize with themselves; nor would those, which have parted off a portion, be utterly refuted by that portion; so that the very fragments cannot be hid, but declare aloud their connection with the whole body. And like as if you should take any part from the side of an animal, even in that part you would find all the things out of which the whole is composed – nerves and veins, bones, arteries, and blood, and a sample, as one might say, of the whole lump – so likewise with regard to the Scriptures.[18]

In the Old Testament the New is concealed, in the New the Old is revealed, so their whole is blasphemous and undoubted for Christians. The Old Testament realities point to the events of the New Covenant. Thus, through the Bible, Chrysostom

---

[11] *Id.*, *In Acta Apostolorum homiliae* 19, PG 60, 156.

[12] *Id.*, *In epistulam ad Hebraeos homiliae* 17, PG 63, 74; *De incomprehensibili Dei natura homiliae* 3, 5, PG 48, 720-1.

[13] *Id.*, *In Psalmum 134*, PG 55, 398; *In Matthaeum homiliae* 52, PG 58, 523.

[14] Jason Soroski, 'What Does "Bible" Mean and How Did it Get That Name?' (1 February 2019), https://www.biblestudytools.com/bible-study/explore-the-bible/what-does-bible-mean.html [accessed 15/09/2019]: 'Chrysostom first refers to the Old and New Testament together as τά βιβλία (the books)'. B.F. Westcott says: '"There are many sacred writings, yet there is but one Book; there are four Evangelists, yet their histories form but one Gospel" they all conspire to one end, and move by one way'.

[15] Pseudo-Ioannes Chrysostomus, *In illud: Exiit edictum*, PG 50, 796.

[16] Ioannes Chrysostomus, *Synopsis scripturae sacrae*, PG 56, 313.

[17] *Id.*, *In Epistulam ad Romanos homiliae* 1, PG 60, 397. See *Rom.* 1:20.

[18] *Id.*, *In Matthaeum homiliae* 1, PG 57, 18.

analyses his perception of divine adaptability as a constitutive and basic principle of the entire economy of the salvation of man and his reunification with his Creator.[19] The Bible is considered the first and most important of the sources of Christian faith. It is inspired by God, and contains the supernatural revelation of the Triune God as almighty, good, omniscient and omnipotent. The whole Scripture analyses and presents the Lord's plan for the salvation of mankind.[20]

John Chrysostom stresses the fact that all of the Scripture is God-breathed and God-inspired, and is useful for teaching, criticising mistakes, correcting and training oneself in the righteousness of Christ.[21] The Bible is not magical literature, but divinely inspired human literature. God inspired the devout writers of the Scripture to reveal His truth, the only truth to the people. All of the words in the Holy Bible have come directly to the people from God the Father through the Holy Spirit. It is the perfect treasury of divine instruction.[22] Chrysostom understands the Word of God as being the most important and greatest deed of His condescension (συγκατάβασις) to the human race, in order for man to have the opportunity to praise God along with the angels.[23] The term condescension (συγκατάβασις) here means that the language and the Bible is not proportionate to the nature of God, but to the finite limits of human nature, of the human mind.

Although the authors of the books of the Bible wrote under the guidance, inspiration, and illumination of the Holy Spirit (see *2Pet.* 1:20),[24] divine inspiration did not reject and erase the personality of the Scripture's authors, but rather heightened them. Through these sacred texts, God reveals His plan for the objective salvation of all human beings through the incarnation of the second Person of the Triune God. Christ is the Messiah, the Logos incarnate. All the texts of the Bible underline this truth and, for this reason, Christ advised the people to 'search the Scriptures'[25] in order to deepen the true sense of the Bible.[26] When people, such as Abraham, Moses and Noah, were near God, they could speak to God directly without any written text. The same happened with the apostles. With the number of Christians increasing every day, there was the necessity to write down some things of the life, miracles and teaching of Christ, in order for Christians to keep the teachings of Christ and the Apostles unchanged.[27]

---

[19]   *Id., In Epistulam ad Romanos homiliae* 1, PG 60, 397-9.
[20]   *Id., In Epistulam I ad Corinthios homiliae* 33, PG 61, 283-4.
[21]   *Id., De Lazaro et divite* 3, PG 48, 993.
[22]   *Id., In Epistulam II ad Timotheum homiliae* 9, PG 62, 649. See *2Tim.* 3:16.
[23]   Iohannes Chrysostomus, *In Osiam seu de seraphinis homiliae*, PG 56, 97-140.
[24]   *Id., In Mattheum homiliae* 1, PG 57, 15: 'By whom Matthew also, being filled with the Spirit, wrote, what he did write: Matthew the Publican, for I am not ashamed to name him by his trade, neither him nor the others. For this in a very special way indicates both the grace of the Spirit, and their virtue'. See *id., Adversus Iudaeos orationes* 7, PG 48, 1041; *In Iohannem homiliae* 1, PG 59, 26.
[25]   *Id., In Genesim homiliae* 37, PG 53, 341. See *John* 5:39.
[26]   Iohannes Chrysostomus, *In Genesim homiliae* 37, PG 53, 341-2.
[27]   *Id., In Matthaeum homiliae* 1, PG 57, 13.

The Bishop of Constantinople supported the idea that the divine roots of the Holy Scripture are revealed in its power and the immense wealth of ideas which are concealed in its expressions.[28] Knowledge of the Bible is the only royal path to the divine knowledge of God. Moreover, the divine writings of the Old and New Testaments, including the divine teaching about God and his plan for the salvation of all humans, have had such a widespread effect, in comparison with the teachings of the philosophers. The teachings of the Bible are eternal and that of philosophers temporary.[29] For this reason, John Chrysostom argues that the Old and the New Testaments have been the gift of the revelation of God Himself, and express the aim of the reformation of mankind by God Himself.[30] Therefore, all of the Scripture is totally true and trustworthy. It shows the principles and measures by which God will judge us, and therefore is, and will be and will remain the centre of Christianity until the end of the world. The writers of the books of the Bible do not speak by their own will, but with God's grace.[31]

To sum up, Chrysostom stresses the fact that the divinely-inspired Scripture is a unique book and cannot be compared to anything else. For this reason, he characterises the Bible as a 'spiritual meadow'[32] whose flowers are always in bloom,[33] an 'earthly paradise',[34] a 'place full of precious stones',[35] a 'healing medicine',[36] a 'gate for the entrance into paradise'.[37] By these – and other – characterisations of the Bible, Chrysostom lyrically shows the importance of the Holy Bible in the life of any Christian who wants to continue in the true faith; he should resort only to the Holy Scriptures which are the only real nourishment of the soul.[38] Both Testaments have as their aim the salvation of mankind in order to be reunited with God. But the New Testament reveals the perfect redemption of man, his renaissance through the incarnation, the passion,

---

[28] *Id., In Genesim homiliae* 37, PG 53, 342.

[29] *Id., In Iohannem homiliae* 59, PG 59, 321-2.

[30] *Id., In Matthaeum homiliae* 1, PG 57, 15.

[31] *Id., In Psalmum 145*, PG 55, 520.

[32] *Id., In Genesim homiliae* 3, PG 53, 32.

[33] *Id., De capto Eutropio* 1, PG 52, 395-7, trans. William R.W. Stephens, http://www. document acatholicaomnia.eu/03d/0345-0407,_Iohannes_Chrysostomus,_In_Eutropim_[Schaff],_ EN.pdf, 309: 'Delectable indeed are the meadow, and the garden, but far more delectable the study of the divine writings. For there indeed are flowers which fade, but here are thoughts which abide in full bloom; there is the breeze of the zephyr, but here the breath of the Spirit: there is the hedge of thorns, but here is the guarding providence of God; there is the song of cicadæ, but here the melody of the prophets: there is the pleasure which comes from sight, but here the profit which comes from study. The garden is confined to one place, but the Scriptures are in all parts of the world; the garden is subject to the necessities of the seasons, but the Scriptures are rich in foliage, and laden with fruit alike in winter and in summer'.

[34] Ioannes Chrysostomus, *In Genesim homiliae* 3, PG 53, 32; *De capto Eutropio* 1, PG 52, 395-7.

[35] *Ibid.*

[36] *Id., In Genesim homiliae* 29, PG 53, 261.

[37] *Id., In Psalmum 150*, PG 55, 496; *Interpretatio in Isaiam prophetam* 5, PG 56, 59.

[38] *Id., Interpretatio in Isaiam prophetam* 4, PG 56, 56.

the crucifixion and the resurrection of Christ.[39] John Chrysostom, through his comments on both Covenants, presents the Old Testament with the same characteristics as those of the New.

3. The necessity of reading the Bible daily by Christians

The Bible is the very Word of God and clarifies the creation of man, his sin and the exile from Paradise, the hope of the incarnation of the Son of God, Christ's teaching and the salvation of mankind. In the Bible, besides the beginning of the world we learn how it will end, and how we should live in the meantime according to Christian virtues. Reading the Scriptures is the armour of security against any sins. Ignorance of the Scripture is a great cliff and a deep abyss; to know nothing of the divine laws is a great betrayal of salvation.[40] This is responsible for the birth of heresies, has introduced sinful ways of life full of passions, and has put down the things above.[41] All of these can be avoided if we read the Scriptures every day. Therefore, it is impossible for anyone to depart without benefit, if he attentively and continually reads the Holy Bible.[42]

Chrysostom does not cease entreating his listeners. He advises them not only to pay attention to his preaching, but also, when they are at home, to persevere in continually reading the divine Scriptures. If someone does not read the Bible, he should use no excuse such as:

I cannot leave the courthouse, I administer the business of the city, I practice a craft, I have a wife, I am raising children, I am in charge of a household, I am a man of the world; reading the Scriptures is not for me, but for those who have been set apart, who have settled on the mountaintops, who keep this way of life continuously.[43]

After all, ignorance of the Scriptures is a great betrayal of salvation. It harms Christians.[44] Instead of having the advantage of a remedy, Christians are led to their death. It is the same with medicine. If someone doesn't follow the instructions for taking medicine, they can die instead of recovering and living healthily.[45]

The reading of the Scriptures should not be as superficial as the reading of an actual book, because the reader does not penetrate beneath the surface meaning

---

[39] *Id., Synopsis scripturae sacrae*, PG 56, 313.

[40] *Id., In Epistulam II ad Timotheum homiliae* 9, PG 62, 649. See *2Tim*. 3:15.

[41] *Id., In Epistulam ad Romanos homiliae* 1, PG 60, 391.

[42] *Ibid.*

[43] *Id., De Lazaro et divite* 3, PG 48, 991-3, trans. Catherine P. Roth: John Chrysostom, *On Wealth and Poverty* (Crestwood, NY, 1984), 58-60.

[44] *Hos.* 4:6: 'My people are destroyed for lack of knowledge; because you have rejected knowledge, I reject you from being a priest to me. And since you have forgotten the law of your God, I also will forget your children'.

[45] Iohannes Chrysostomus, *De Lazaro et divite* 3, PG 48, 993; *In Acta Apostolorum homiliae* 29, PG 60, 213-20; *ibid.*, 34, PG 60, 245-51.

of the text. A simple, surface reading is bound to be a false reading, because everything in the Scriptures has a great significance and the slightest meaning of any word can contain a hidden treasure.[46] On this, John Chrysostom argues:

there is nothing superfluous, nothing added at random in the Scriptures [...] but there are some even so low-minded, and empty, and unworthy of Heaven, as not to think that names only, but whole books of the Bible are of no use, as Leviticus, Joshua, and more besides. And in this way, many of the simple-minded ones have been in favour of rejecting the Old Testament, and, advancing in this way which results from this evil habit of the mind, have likewise pruned away many parts of the New Testament also. [...] But if any be a lover of wisdom, and a friend to spiritual entertainments, let him be told that even the things which seem to be unimportant in Scripture are not placed there at random and to no purpose, and that even the old laws have much to benefit us. For it says: All these things are examples and are written for our instruction.[47]

In every text of the Bible, the reader can find something for his family, how to bring up his children, how to banish his disappointment and sadness,[48] how to struggle with his passions[49] and, generally, for every problem in his daily life there is a solution. Moreover, if we want to gain the greatest benefit from the reading of biblical texts, we should not read them alone, but with other people and with the help of a capable interpreter.[50] In this way, we will arrive safe at the port of the biblical meaning without fear of being drowned in waves of heresies.

Of course, Christians should read the biblical texts every day, but they must, as a presupposition, request the enlightenment of God in order to deepen the meaning of the Bible and to understand the text of these God-breathed books of the Scripture. This is profane in the prayer before the gospel in the Orthodox Liturgy of St. John Chrysostom, which begins:

'Illumine our hearts, O Master, Who loves mankind, with the pure light of Thy divine knowledge, and open the eyes of our mind to the understanding of Thy gospel teachings; implant in us also the fear of Thy blessed commandments, that trampling down all lusts of the flesh, we may enter upon a spiritual way of life'.[51]

4. Conclusions

John Chrysostom has a great love for the Scripture, which is the result of the cooperation between God and man. God revealed His being and His aim of

---

[46] *Id., In illud: Paulus vocatus* 1-6, PG 51, 143-53.

[47] *Id., In Epistulam ad Romanos homiliae* 31, PG 60, 667-8. See *1Cor.* 10:11.

[48] *Id., De utilitate lectionis Scripturarum*, PG 51, 90.

[49] *Ibid.*, PG 51, 89; *De capto Eutropio* 1, PG 52, 397; *In Epistulam ad Romanos homiliae* 29, PG 60, 654.

[50] *Id., In Genesim homiliae* 15, PG 53, 119.

[51] *Divine Liturgy of St. John Chrysostom*, In Service Books of the Orthodox Church 1 (South Canaan, 2017), 15.

man's salvation through the Bible. The two Testaments constitute the Holy Scripture and they are as united as the organs of the human body. One cannot exist without the other. The Old Testament is the foundation and the New Testament is based on that foundation, with further revelations from God and the fulfillment of the prophesies. The Old Testament reveals the hidden truths about the Triune God, the incarnation of the Logos and the establishment of the Christian Church, whilst the New Testament uncovers these truths through the holy divine economy of the incarnate Christ, of His passions, His death and resurrection, and the establishment of the historic Christian Church after the Pentecost. Both Testaments are Christ-centred.

The method of Chrysostom's biblical interpretation is more historic-literal than typological and allegorical. Najeeb George Awad observes: 'Chrysostom does not seek to offer intellectual analysis or sophisticated theorization. He attempts instead to create a relationship between the ordinary people – who have no time to spend studying due to life duties – and the writers of the Testaments'.[52]

It is necessary that the reading of the Bible be performed every day, and there is no excuse for neglect in or dereliction of this task by Christians, because the benefits for any one reader are many. Therein, he can find answers for most of his daily problems. Moreover, he will be taught ways to behave towards his wife or to bring up his children, to love and forgive other people. Of course, the reading of the Scripture should be done by two or more people and not by a Christian on his own. The reason for this is that the understanding of the hidden meanings of the biblical texts needs an orthodox interpretation, which can be found in the majority of the Church Fathers.

It is important to be known this: both as Christians and, generally, as human beings:

we have a continuous need for the full armor of the Scriptures [...] There are many things [...] which besiege our souls: we need the divine medicines to heal the wounds which we have received and to protect us from those which we have not yet received but will receive. We must thoroughly quench the darts of the devil and beat them off by continual reading of the divine Scriptures. For it is not possible, not possible for anyone to be saved without continually taking advantage of spiritual reading.[53]

Thus, reading the Scriptures is a great means of security against sin. If we want to succeed our likeness to God in the eternity, we should take our medicine against sin as they are found in the Scriptures.

---

[52] Najeeb George Awad, 'The influence of John Chrysostom's hermeneutics on John Calvin's exegetical approach to Paul's Epistle to the Romans', *SJT* 63/4 (2010), 414-36, 414.

[53] Iohannes Chrysostomus, *De Lazaro et divite* 3, PG 48, 993, trans. C.P. Roth, *On Wealth and Poverty* (1984), 560.

Joy, Truth, and the Search for God in St. Augustine's *Confessions* X

Samuel PELL, Washington, DC, USA

ABSTRACT

In Book X of the *Confessions*, Augustine attempts an answer to the paradox of inquiry, first formulated by Plato in his dialogue *Meno*. Augustine reframes the question to consider how one can ground a successful search for God when one has never encountered God. He dispenses with Platonic theories of recollection by considering how finite memories of joy and truth can help orient him towards God, who is the ultimate source of joy and truth. He nevertheless maintains that certain false joys lead away from God, and that people with perverse wills often blind themselves to this fact. This paper will examine how Augustine defends the notion that finite memories of joy and truth provide an adequate answer to Meno's paradox, while still preserving his skepticism towards temporal joys and finite truths.

1. Introduction

The *Confessions* is an account of Augustine's search for truth and happiness, terminating in his conversion to Latin Christianity. In recounting the story of his restless quest, Augustine also wrestles with a philosophical paradox related to the possibility of searching for anything. This paradox, first presented in Plato's dialogue *Meno*, asks how one can successfully search for something of which one has no knowledge. Gareth Matthews breaks Meno's paradox into two parts: 1) a *targeting problem*, which asks how we can know to search for something we have never experienced, and 2) a *recognition problem*, which asks how we can know we have found something if we do not have any prior knowledge of it.[1] In his paper, 'The Paradox of Inquiry in Augustine's *Confessions*', Scott MacDonald argues that any successful resolution to the paradox must satisfy what he calls the 'qualified knowledge constraint on searching': namely, that, 'if it is possible to come to know an object by searching for it, it must be that one already knows in some way or to some extent the object one is searching for'.[2] MacDonald goes on

---

[1] Gareth Matthews, 'Augustine on the Mind's Search for Itself', *Faith and Philosophy* 20/4 (2003), 415-29.
[2] Scott MacDonald, 'The Paradox of Inquiry in Augustine's "Confessions"', *Metaphilosophy* 39/1 (2008), 22-36, 22.

Studia Patristica CIII, 183-194.

to show how Augustine ultimately resolves this problem by considering how God can dwell in his memory. By MacDonald's interpretation, Augustine discovers that he has memories of joy and truth in his mind which serve as finite 'tokens' of God, who is joy and truth itself. In this paper, I will argue that this model based on 'tokens' essentially works, though MacDonald's presentation does not account for the cases of concupiscence and self-deception. To account for these cases, I will show how even ephemeral joys can solve the recognition problem, and how memories of truth can resolve the targeting problem by eliciting a search for higher forms of truth. As we will see, Augustine's resolution to Meno's paradox is at once philosophically satisfying and psychologically penetrating.

2. The Constraints of Augustine's Search

Augustine's resolution to the paradox of inquiry occurs in Book X, in the context of a larger discussion of memory. Augustine thinks he must somehow have a memory of God in order to seek and find him successfully. This is a reformulation of Meno's paradox, but to understand the formulation, we must understand how Augustine conceives of thought and memory. MacDonald provides a good summary:

Augustine adopts what we might think of as an act/object model of thought: to think a thought is to have before the eye of one's mind, so to speak, the object of one's thought. Memory is the 'place' in us [...] where the objects of our thought are stored, or reside, or can be encountered.[3]

With this understanding of memory, Augustine develops what MacDonald calls an 'in-mind constraint' on searching for something: 'if one is to find an object by searching, it must be that one has the object in mind'.[4] Augustine gives the example of a lost coin to illustrate this point. Someone who loses a coin must know what the coin looks like (*i.e.* have its appearance in their memory) in order to search for it and find it successfully.[5] In a more mysterious way, if we forget someone's name, we cannot successfully recall it again unless the name we have forgotten is somehow stored in the recesses of our memory.[6] By extension, Augustine argues that we must have some notion of God in our memory to seek and find him successfully.

However, this raises some problems. If God is already in our memory before we search for him, why is it necessary to seek him out? If God dwells

---

[3] S. MacDonald, 'Paradox of Inquiry' (2008), 28.
[4] *Ibid.* 29.
[5] See Augustinus Hipponensis, *Confessiones* X 18, 27. We use: *The Confessions of Augustine: An Electronic Edition*, ed. James J. O'Donnell (Oxford, 1992). Retrieved online from http://www.stoa.org/hippo/ on 18 October 2019.
[6] See Augustinus Hipponensis, *Confessiones* X 19, 28.

in everyone's memory, why do some people not believe in him? These questions all point to another constraint on searching, which I will formalize as the 'similarity/dissimilarity constraint':

If one is to search for object O on the basis of prior knowledge P, O and P must be a) similar enough that one can recognize O on the basis of P, but b) dissimilar enough that one cannot be said to have O simply because one has P.

In this way, we must have some prior knowledge that enables us to search for God, but this prior knowledge must be different enough from actual knowledge of God to account for the empirical facts that we still must search for him, and that not everyone finds him even with this prior knowledge.

3. The Search for God as a Search for the Happy Life

Augustine addresses these difficulties by considering his search for God as a search for the happy life:

How do I seek you, Lord? For when I seek you, my God, I seek a happy life. I seek you, that my soul may live. For my body lives on account of my soul, and my soul lives on account of you [...] Is it not the happy life that everyone wants? Can it be that anyone does not want it?[7]

According to MacDonald, Augustine believes he can make this substitution because he understands eternal life with God to be the ultimate happy life. In MacDonald's words, 'the search for the happy life and the search for God are the same search; they are coterminous'.[8] Moreover, by substituting the happy life for God, Augustine is framing his investigation in such a way so as to satisfy the similarity/dissimilarity constraint: what memory does everyone have prior to encountering God that allows them to search for him successfully?

By understanding the search for God as a search for the happy life, Augustine has broadened his reflections beyond his experience as a Christian. However, the search for the happy life is subject to the same in-mind constraint on searching as the search for God:

Where have they known it, that they would want it? Where have they seen it, that they would love it? [...] I wonder whether the happy life is in the memory. For we would not love it unless we knew it'.[9]

---

[7] Augustinus Hipponensis, *Confessiones* X 20, 29: *quomodo ergo te quaero, domine? cum enim te, deum meum, quaero, vitam beatam quaero. quaeram te ut vivat anima mea. vivit enim corpus meum de anima mea et vivit anima mea de te. quomodo ergo quaero vitam beatam [...] nonne ipsa est beata vita quam omnes volunt, et omnino qui nolit nemo est?*

[8] S. MacDonald, 'Paradox of Inquiry' (2008), 30.

[9] Augustinus Hipponensis, *Confessiones* X 20, 29: *ubi noverunt eam, quod sic volunt eam? ubi viderunt, ut amarent eam? [...] quaero utrum in memoria sit beata vita. neque enim amaremus eam nisi nossemus.*

Augustine's argument relies on an act/object model of volition, much like the model of thought described above. If a desire is not to be empty, it must be for some object, and this object must be known in the memory. Augustine's question is what sort of knowledge can reasonably ground our desire for the happy life.

Augustine rules out the possibility that the happy life is known by immediate intellectual apprehension, in the manner of a mathematical concept. This would violate the similarity/dissimilarity constraint:

Surely it is not in the way we remember numbers? No, for the one who has numbers in his knowledge [*notitia*], does not still desire to attain to anything, but truly we have the happy life in our knowledge [*notitia*], and this is why we love it and still desire to attain it, so that we can be happy.[10]

There is no gap between our understanding of a mathematical concept and our experience of the reality it represents: our memory of the number 'three' causes our minds to grasp fully the content of the idea. If our memory of the happy life works this way, however, we could attain happiness simply by think-ing about it – or at least we could know precisely what it is we are seeking, when we desire happiness. But this is not the way we discover the happy life: we desire happiness before we become happy, and in some sense before we even understand what would make us happy. Augustine's task is to identify the sort of memory that we have prior to achieving a happy life, which can allow us to target a successful search for it.

4. Joy as a Token of the Happy Life

Augustine then considers whether we can seek the happy life by means of a memory of joy. By joy, he does not mean the affective experience itself, but some kind of intellectual memory of the experience. Unlike the memory of a mathematical concept, he can know what joy is without simultaneously experiencing it:

I experienced [joy] in my soul when I was happy, and some knowledge [*notitia*] of it clung to my memory, with the result that I could remember it, sometimes with regret, sometimes with desire, in accord with the diversity of things in which I remember rejoicing.[11]

---

[10] Augustinus Hipponensis, *Confessiones* X 21, 30: *numquid sicut meminimus numeros? non. hos enim qui habet in notitia, non adhuc quaerit adipisci, vitam vero beatam habemus in notitia ideoque amamus et tamen adhuc adipisci eam volumus, ut beati simus.*

[11] Augustinus Hipponensis, *Confessiones* X 21, 30: *expertus sum in animo meo quando laetatus sum, et adhaesit eius notitia memoriae meae, ut id reminisci valeam, aliquando cum aspernatione, aliquando cum desiderio, pro earum rerum diversitate de quibus me gavisum esse memini.*

We can remember a former joy and simultaneously experience another emotion, such as longing or regret. Augustine uses this observation to argue that the memory and the experience of joy satisfy the similarity/dissimilarity constraint. A memory of a former joy can guide us to seek out joyful experiences, by reminding us what circumstances brought us joy in the past.

The question, then, is how these joyful experiences relate to the happy life. In the following passage, Augustine speaks as if the happy life is nothing other than experiencing joy:

> Even if one pursues it this way, and another pursues it that way, there is nevertheless one thing which all are striving to attain, namely to experience joy. And because joy is something which no one is able to say is outside of their experience, we can discover joy in our memory and thus understand joy to be signified when we hear the phrase "happy life".[12]

In commenting on this passage, MacDonald thinks that Augustine's assertion requires some nuance. 'Augustine cannot mean simply that people take the expressions "joy" and "happy life" to be synonymous, or even that those expressions, while not synonymous, refer precisely to the same thing'.[13] This is because everyone has experienced joy, but not everyone has experienced the happy life. By MacDonald's understanding, Augustine believes the ultimate happy life is only fully realizable after death, with God in heaven.

To make Augustine's account work, joy and the happy life must somehow be related so as to resolve the similarity/dissimilarity constraint. MacDonald suggests that one could resolve this problem by thinking of joy as 'a kind of taste or token of [the happy life] ... in the sense that a ring might be given as a token of one's love'.[14] In the same way that a man gives a woman an engagement ring as a pledge of future love, God gives humans joy as a pledge of future glory. Even though the joys we experience in this life are not the same thing as heavenly bliss, our memories of joy are sufficient to help us target a search that culminates in heaven.

The psychological realism of this account is appealing: everyone knows what it means to seek joy, and we all do it instinctively. By MacDonald's 'token' model, this universal desire for joy can ground a successful search for authentic happiness. As MacDonald says, '[t]he theoretically powerful thing about this model is that it ... move[s] beyond the models based narrowly on recollection suggested to [Augustine] by his Platonist heritage'.[15] Augustine does not

---

[12] Augustinus Hipponensis, *Confessiones* X 21, 31: *quod etsi alius hinc, alius illinc adsequitur, unum est tamen quo pervenire omnes nituntur, ut gaudeant. quae quoniam res est quam se expertum non esse nemo potest dicere, propterea reperta in memoria recognoscitur quando beatae vitae nomen auditur.*

[13] S. MacDonald, 'Paradox of Inquiry' (2008), 33.

[14] *Ibid.* 33.

[15] *Ibid.* 34.

need to posit a realm of the forms or a pre-existent soul in order to describe a search for happiness; he can answer Meno's paradox simply by appealing to psychological introspection. We seek happiness because we seek joy (the targeting problem), and we will know we are living a happy life because it brings us joy (the recognition problem).

Nevertheless, MacDonald's interpretation contains a significant vulnerability. Experiencing joy may be a necessary condition for a happy life, but it is not sufficient. Augustine would be the first to admit that people spend their lives chasing after joys that do not bring happiness: 'our heart is restless until it rests in thee', he famously says at the beginning of the *Confessions*.[16] Since many joyful experiences are grounded in what Augustine would call concupiscence, joy alone cannot account for the inner restlessness that is only fulfilled in God. If we hope to preserve the token model in light of Augustine's larger body of thought, we must find some way of addressing this issue.

5. True *vs.* False Joys: The Recognition Problem

MacDonald thinks Augustine can adequately address this issue if he distinguishes 'between *true* and *false* joys or, perhaps better, between true and false sources of the experience of joy'.[17] According to MacDonald, the token model can be preserved if we simply restrict our understanding of a token to cases of true joy. Augustine does indeed distinguish between true and false joys, but he does so in a way that still poses difficulties for MacDonald's account:

Far be it, Lord, far be it from the heart of your servant making confession to you, far be it that I consider myself happy, whatever be the joy in which I rejoice. For there is a joy which is not given to the wicked, but to those who seek you by grace, whose joy is you yourself. And this is the happy life: to rejoice before you, about you, because of you: this is the happy life and there is no other. Those who think that it is some other thing, follow some other joy and not the true one. Their will, however, is not averted from some sort of image of joy.[18]

Here, Augustine suggests that the only joys that count as tokens of the happy life are joys experienced in the presence of God, concerning God, and caused

---

[16] Augustinus Hipponensis, *Confessiones* I 1, 1: *inquietum est cor nostrum donec requiescat in te.*

[17] S. MacDonald, 'Paradox of Inquiry' (2008), 34.

[18] Augustinus Hipponensis, *Confessiones* X 22, 32: *absit, domine, absit a corde servi tui qui confitetur tibi, absit ut, quocumque gaudio gaudeam, beatum me putem. est enim gaudium quod non datur impiis, sed eis qui te gratis colunt, quorum gaudium tu ipse es. et ipsa est beata vita, gaudere ad te, de te, propter te: ipsa est et non est altera. qui autem aliam putant esse, aliud sectantur gaudium neque ipsum verum. ab aliqua tamen imagine gaudii voluntas eorum non avertitur.*

by God: one might say, spiritual joy. It is true that spiritual joy can answer Meno's paradox for a believing Christian. Assuming heaven to be an uninterrupted experience of spiritual joy, a Christian can long for the eternal bliss of the afterlife on the basis of her contemplative experiences in this life.

If we accept Augustine's distinction, however, it is unclear how the token model can work for a nonbeliever. Until a nonbeliever has an experience of joy grounded in God, she can neither target a search for happiness that culminates in God, nor can she recognize God when she finds him. If the token model can explain how a nonbeliever targets a successful search for God, we must concede some validity to temporal, earthly joy – the sort of experience anyone can have in their memory.

Augustine seems to make such a move at the end of the passage quoted above, where he says that the will of an irreligious person 'is not averted from some sort of image of joy'.[19] Though Augustine does not develop this point further, he appears to think that temporal joys can be 'images' or 'tokens' of spiritual joy, in the same way that spiritual joy is a token of heavenly bliss. By this reading, memories of temporal joys can serve as a type of 'second-tier token' of God. They allow one to see spiritual joy as a kind of fulfillment of ordinary human joy, and not a *sui generis* experience disconnected from all other joys.

Perhaps we can illustrate this point by extending the example of a lover's ring. Let us imagine that a woman receives a ring from a man and is overjoyed, convinced she has found true love. Now let us suppose the man proves fickle and ends up leaving her. She still remembers how she felt when the man gave her the ring, and she knows that a man who truly loves her will make her feel the same way. Similarly, a joyful experience that proves to be false can still help us recognize what the real thing must look like. To Augustine, all forms of joy are false in comparison to God, but these false sources of joy still serve as tokens that can help us recognize God when we find him.

6. Settling for Mere Images of Joy

Although memories of temporal pleasures provide a hypothetical resolution to the recognition problem, it is difficult to see how they can help solve the targeting problem. Many people never migrate beyond earthly pleasures to their supposed fulfillment in spiritual joy, so it is unclear how memories of these pleasures can propel anyone closer to true happiness. Augustine expresses the issue in the following way: 'It is not therefore certain that everyone wants to be happy, because whoever does not want to find joy in you, who are the only

---

[19] Augustinus Hipponensis, *Confessiones* X 22, 32: *ab aliqua tamen imagine gaudii voluntas eorum non avertitur.*

happy life, certainly does not desire a happy life'.[20] Why should we presume that a memory of a temporal pleasure can help someone search for anything beyond that pleasure? I may enjoy the taste of beer, for instance. When I remember this taste, I desire to buy myself a drink. An inebriated tavern guest may indeed claim that beer provides a glimpse of heaven, but even so, it is difficult to see how this glimpse allows him to target a search for heaven. In fact, a love of drinking can inhibit true happiness, leading to addiction and dependency.

This problem is not restricted to harmful and addictive substances. Every 'second-tier token' of true joy falls short of authentic happiness, but is similar enough that it can act as a deceptive imitation. This is an unfortunate corollary of the similarity/dissimilarity constraint. If the prior knowledge P by which I search for object O allows me to recognize O when I encounter O, I might also be deceived into thinking that I have O simply because I have P. Perhaps we can better grasp this problem if we consider a person who keeps returning to an unfaithful lover. She ignores the infidelity by focusing on whatever 'tokens of joy' her relationship shares in common with a healthy one: perhaps her partner placates her with flowers or a flattering compliment. We want to say that such a person still desires to be happy, even as she clings to a relationship that perpetuates her long-term misery. For this to be true, however, she must long for happiness by some token other than the false joys that blind her to the toxic nature of the situation.

In the following passage, Augustine suggests that he needs a memory in addition to joy to explain the search for the happy life:

Or perhaps everyone does desire [a happy life], but because the flesh lusts against the spirit and the spirit lusts against the flesh, so that they do not do what they will, they fall into whatever they have the strength to do and settle in that, because the thing for which they have not the strength, their will is not strong enough to give them the strength.[21]

Memories of joy can help us recognize authentic happiness, because an authentic happy life will bring us joy. However, these memories can also enable one to settle into a life of concupiscence that falls short of true happiness. Memories of joy, then, are not sufficient to solve the targeting problem. If we are to resolve Meno's paradox, the in-mind constraint requires that we find some memory other than joy by which one can ground a successful search for a happy life.

---

[20] Augustinus Hipponensis, *Confessiones* X 23, 33: *non ergo certum est quod omnes esse beati volunt, quoniam qui non de te gaudere volunt, quae sola vita beata est, non utique beatam vitam volunt.*

[21] Augustinus Hipponensis, Confessiones X 23, 33: *an omnes hoc volunt, sed quoniam caro concupiscit adversus spiritum et spiritus adversus carnem, ut non faciant quod volunt, cadunt in id quod valent eoque contenti sunt, quia illud quod non valent, non tantum volunt quantum sat est ut valeant?*

7. The Desire for Truth

If MacDonald's token model is correct, this second memory must also be a kind of token of God: it must be something everyone has experienced, which nevertheless helps them seek out something they have not experienced. Mac-Donald does indeed believe another such token exists, though he does not seem to think the targeting problem necessitates it. MacDonald discovers this second token in the following passage, when Augustine is considering the desire not to be deceived:

I have encountered many people who want to deceive others, but no one who wants to be deceived. When has anyone known the happy life, unless they have also known truth? For they also love the happy life, when they do not want to be deceived. And when they love the happy life, which is nothing other than rejoicing in the truth, in every way they also love truth. They would not love the truth unless they had some notion [*notitia*] of it in their memory.[22]

MacDonald understands this passage as an 'argument based on truth' as 'isomorphic with the [argument] based on joy'.[23] Everyone has a desire not to be deceived, says Augustine, and this desire is grounded in some memory of the joy that comes from knowing the truth. MacDonald argues that a memory of 'the sort of truth of which everyone has some cognizance' can serve as a 'token [...] of God, who is [...] truth itself'.[24] MacDonald, however, does not go into any detail about what this memory of truth consists of, or how it might solve the targeting problem.

In the following passage, Augustine breaks the memory of truth into two distinct parts. As we will see, only one of these parts is capable of solving the targeting problem:

Truth, everywhere you preside over all who seek counsel of you, and at the same time you respond to all, even though they are seeking your counsel on different matters. You respond clearly, but not all hear you clearly. Your best servant is not the one who thinks that he hears from you whatever he desires, but rather the one who takes care to desire whatever he hears from you.[25]

---

[22] Augustinus Hipponensis, *Confessiones* X 23, 33: *multos expertus sum qui vellent fallere, qui autem falli, neminem. ubi ergo noverunt hanc vitam beatam, nisi ubi noverunt etiam veritatem? amant enim et ipsam, quia falli nolunt. Et cum amant beatam vitam, quod non est aliud quam de veritate gaudium, utique amant etiam veritatem, nec amarent nisi esset aliqua notitia eius in memoria eorum.*

[23] S. MacDonald, 'Paradox of Inquiry' (2008), 35-6.

[24] *Ibid.* 36.

[25] Augustinus Hipponensis, *Confessiones* X 26, 37: *veritas, ubique praesides omnibus consulentibus te simulque respondes omnibus etiam diversa consulentibus. liquide tu respondes, sed non liquide omnes audiunt. optimus minister tuus est qui non magis intuetur hoc a te audire quod ipse voluerit, sed potius hoc velle quod a te audierit.*

In the last sentence, Augustine describes two types of people. For the first sort, the memory of truth is nothing more than a memory of the feeling one has when one is in the right. They desire this feeling in conjunction with false joys, with the result that they christen their ephemeral pursuits with the false label of truth. They take pleasure in their false joys, but they also delude themselves into thinking that they are rejoicing in the truth.[26] The second sort of people take care to desire the truth for its own sake.[27] The purity of their intention allows them, with time, to acquire a set of true beliefs. These true beliefs introduce forward movement to the search for happiness, such that one can propel oneself from false sources of joy into more authentic ones.

We can illustrate this point by returning to our previous example: a person who contents herself with an unfaithful lover must engage in a sort of self-deception. Perhaps she tells herself that her lover is truly a good man, and that her friends just can't see the good in him. At a certain point, however, she has to acknowledge that she is deceiving herself. She must admit to herself what sort of a man he is, as painful as such an admission can be. She can come to make this admission through a desire not to be deceived, which is grounded in a memory of rejoicing in the truth.

In this way, Augustine has identified three distinct memories which can help target a search for the happy life: memories of joyful experiences, memories of true beliefs, and a memory of the joy found in acquiring true beliefs. These three memories can interact in such a way that they provide the means to seek after and rejoice in the truth, but they can also counteract one another, allowing one to settle in empty pleasures.

---

[26] In *Confessiones* X 23, 34, Augustine gives a more extended account of such people: 'Although they love the happy life, which is nothing else but rejoicing in the truth, nevertheless they love the truth in such a way that, whenever they love something else, they desire this thing to be the truth, and because they do not wish to be deceived, they do not want to be convinced that they are wrong. Therefore, because of this thing which they love as if it were true, they hate the truth. They love it when it enlightens [*luceat*] them but hate it when it contradicts them'. [*cum ametur beata vita, quae non est nisi gaudium de veritate, nisi quia sic amatur veritas ut, quicumque aliud amant, hoc quod amant velint esse veritatem, et quia falli nollent, nolunt convinci quod falsi sint? itaque propter eam rem oderunt veritatem, quam pro veritate amant. amant eam lucentem, oderunt eam redarguentem*].

[27] The astute reader will wonder what sort of memory can ground a desire for truth 'for its own sake'. Desiring the truth in this way implies some sort of awareness of universal, unbounded truth beyond the finite truths one searches for. Augustine is aware of this implication, I think, and he seems to allude to it when he describes finite truths as 'counsels' which we 'hear' from the Divine Truth of God. In *Confessiones* VII 27, 23, he argues that a preference for the immutable over the mutable requires some sort of subliminal knowledge of the absolute immutability of God, and I think he would make the same argument to prove that the person who desires the truth 'for its own sake' has some sort of subconscious awareness of the absolute truth of God. The precise nature of this subconscious awareness, however, is unclear, and I hope to address it in another paper. For an extended treatment of Augustine's argument on immutability in *Confessiones* VII 27, 23, see Stephen Menn, *Descartes and Augustine* (1998), 266-7.

8. The Memory of Truth is Perfected in God

So far, Augustine has shown how a desire for truth can propel one from less authentic sources of joy to more authentic ones. He still needs to show how one can target a search for God from a desire to rejoice in true beliefs. Augustine first explains why true beliefs, on their own, are not sufficient for living a happy life:

Why, therefore, do they not rejoice in that [memory of truth]? Why are they not happy? Because they are (1) rather distracted by other things, which make them more miserable than that [memory of truth] makes them happy, which (2) they remember only dimly.[28]

This account identifies two reasons why a person with a memory of truth is not necessarily living a happy life. The first reason is based on the weakness of her will and attention: the false joys which serve as tokens of true happiness can also distract one from contemplating the truth. The second reason suggests some defect in the memory of truth itself: it is only a dim recollection of ultimate truth.

Based on these two reasons, Augustine identifies two ways that the memory of truth is perfected with God in heaven. These two ways show how the deficiencies of our memory of truth can help us long for (and therefore target a search for) the ultimate truth of God:

However, even if someone is wretched, he prefers to rejoice in true things over false things. He will therefore be happy, if (1) he rejoices solely in that truth by which all things are true, (2) with no distraction interfering from it.[29]

The joy elicited by our 'dim' contemplation of ultimate truths, Augustine argues, is inferior to the joy of contemplating the ultimate truth of God, 'through which all things are true'.[30] Religious and philosophical contemplation both

---

[28] Augustinus Hipponensis, *Confessiones* X 23, 33: *cur ergo non de illa gaudent? cur non beati sunt? quia fortius occupantur in aliis, quae potius eos faciunt miseros quam illud beatos, quod tenuiter meminerunt.*

[29] Augustinus Hipponensis, *Confessiones* X 23, 33-4: *tamen etiam sic, dum miser est, veris mavult gaudere quam falsis. beatus ergo erit, si nulla interpellante molestia de ipsa, per quam vera sunt omnia, sola veritate gaudebit.*

[30] This locution casts God in the Neoplatonic conception of *Nous*. Stephen Menn provides a good summary of this notion: 'Wisdom is a virtue, a virtue which, for Plato, exists eternally by itself, separate from the souls which become wise by participating in it; and this [wisdom] is *Nous*. We might render the word, a bit archaically, by "Reason" with a capital R. The *Nous* that is the universal source of order to the sensible world is not the rationality immanent in human souls (or even in the word-soul), nor is it the objective rationality exhibited especially by the heavenly bodies, but the separate Reason that souls (and, in a different way, bodies) must participate in, in order to become wise and rational and orderly' (S. Menn, *Descartes and Augustine* [1998], 88). This summary gives us some insight into how Augustine thinks our knowledge of truth can be expanded to include *Nous*: the finite truths we all possess have *Nous* as their transcendent cause, and we can contemplate *Nous* directly by focusing our attention on this cause.

allow us some vision of ultimate truth,[31] but we are constantly distracted from this vision by the concerns of our earthly life. Because of these distractions, we come to desire heaven as a state of eternal contemplation. In this way, the desire to rejoice in the truth provides a forward movement from finite truth to ultimate truth to the eternal contemplation of ultimate truth. A desire to rejoice in the truth can solve the targeting problem in a way the desire for joy, taken by itself, cannot.

9. Conclusion

MacDonald argues that Augustine resolves Meno's paradox by appealing to joy and truth as tokens of God:

The joy and truth that each of us has encountered are sufficient to permit us to target a search for God and recognize God should we find God, without requiring us previously to have encountered God.[32]

MacDonald does not spell out exactly what kind of joy and what kind of truth can serve as tokens of God, or how the tokens relate to each other. In this paper, I have described two distinct forms of joy: spiritual joys and temporal pleasures, which both serve as different sorts of tokens of God. Spiritual joys stir up our desire to spend eternity with God, but they are at least recognizably similar to temporal pleasures. We must have some memory of truth if we are to prefer lasting spiritual joy over ephemeral pleasures, but this memory of truth can take different forms. If we simply remember the joy that comes from being in the right, we can desire the truth in such a way that we rationalize our false pleasures. Our memories of specific finite truths, however, can cause us to transcend these ephemeral pursuits. When we discover God as the ultimate source of truth, we bear a memory of our contemplative encounter that causes us to desire to spend eternity beholding him. Our memories of joy and truth, then, can cooperate in different ways to propel us forward in our search for God.

---

[31] For the point on prayer, see Augustine's description of his vision at Ostia at *Confessiones* IX 10, 25. Augustine describes a similar contemplative experience prior to his conversion, while reading the Platonist books in *Confessiones* VII 17, 23. This suggests that a vision of ultimate truth can be attained by a non-Christian philosopher, albeit in an imperfect way.

[32] S. MacDonald, 'Paradox of Inquiry' (2008), 36.

Isidore of Seville's Treatise *De ortu et obitu patrum*: Biblical Salvation History 'in a Short Tale'

Tatiana KRYNICKA, Gdańsk, Poland

ABSTRACT

Isidore's work *On the Lifes and Deathes of the Fathers* contains biographies of out-standing biblical figures from Adam to Titus. The Sevillian describes the ancestry (*ortus*), virtues and achievements (*vita*), circumstances of the death and the burial of the heroes (*obitus*), among which we find patriarchs, judges, kings, prophets, the Lord's apostles and disciples. Isidore composes laudatory descriptions pervaded by an exceptional concentration of thought and emotion, colourful and rich in detail, but, at the same time, imbued with a sententional conciseness. The composition of the analysed treatise's individual descriptions is studied in this article.

Isidore of Seville (*ca*. 560-636 AD) entered into the history of European culture, above all, as the author of *Etymologies* (*Etymologiae*) – the first medieval encyclopedia, which contains the summary of the knowledge of the ancient scientists, who were interested both in the world of nature and in all spheres of human activity.[1] In the twenty books and eight thousand entries of this monumental work,[2] and which was the book most frequently copied, commented on, cited – in brief, the most willingly read – after the Bible of the Latin Middle Ages,[3] we find data about the structure of the sentence and of the human organism, about literary genres and species of animals and plants, about drosophilas, called by Latin drunkard flies (*bibiones*),[4] as well as about the mysteries of the Holy Trinity.

The Sevillian strongly affirms that *Ignorantia mater errorum est, ignorantia vitiorum nutrix. Peccatum magis per ignorantia praevalet*.[5] Bearing in mind

---

[1] Ernst Robert Curtius calls *Etymologiae* 'the fundamental book of the Middle Ages'. See E.R. Curtius, *Literatura europejska i łacińskie średniowiecze* (Kraków, 1998), 28.

[2] Manuel Cecilio Díaz y Díaz, 'Introducción general a San Isidoro de Sevilla', in San Isidoro de Sevilla, *Etimologías*, ed. José Oroz Reta, BAC 433 (Madrid, 1982) I, 1-257, 189.

[3] Jacques Fontaine, 'Introduction', in Isidore de Séville, *Traité de la Nature*, ed. J. Fontaine (Bordeaux, 1960), 1-162, 19.

[4] Tatiana Krynicka, 'Pomysłowe mrówki, zawzięte mole i muszki pijaczki: owady w XII księdze *Etymologii* Izydora z Sewilli', in *Owady, robaki, insekty: referaty pokonferencyjne. Materiały z sesji z cyklu 'Bestiarium'* (Gdańsk, 2013), 31-7, via: https://docplayer.pl/5318251-Owady-robaki--insekty-referaty-pokonferencyjne.html [access 15 XI 2019].

[5] Isidorus Hispalensis, *Synonyma* II 65, 700-1.

Studia Patristica CIII, 195-203.
© Peeters Publishers, 2021.

that a pastor of the Church is obliged not only to look after the beauty of the liturgy and the development of monastic life, to convene synods, to counsel sovereigns and support the poor, but also to take care of the spiritual and intellectual formation of the believers, he wrote a lot of works aimed at the education of the reader. Among his numerous writings, we find treatises on theological issues (doctrinal, exegectical, litugical) and on mundane subjects (grammatical, historical, life and physical sciences). Most of them were composed after 602 AD, when Isidore was elected Bishop of Hispalis.[6] The great Sevillian was able to combine various duties related to exercising the functions of this office with composing so many works, because, in writing them, he shared with his readers information acquired in his youth. He had spent his young years in the shadow of his great elder brother,[7] the Sevillian Bishop Leander, at school (monastic and cathedral),[8] at church and at the library.[9] It should be noted that in all of the centres mentioned of Isidore's education, the Holy Scripture played a crucial role. The Bible's words became material for learning to read;[10] it was meditated on during prayer; it led to a union with God;[11] it was discussed; it guided one into the arcana of faith;[12] it commented on and widened the view of the world and of the text that transmits the picture of this same world.[13] The Sevillian's writings served as a compendia of theology, grammar, natural sicences, providing information and fair entertainment, and were even used as manuals for Latin and Greek.[14] Beyond that, they introduced the reader to the text of the Holy Scripture.[15]

Isidore's writing *On the Lifes and Deathes of the Fathers* is a small work[16] (twenty-seven columns in Jacques-Paul Migne's edition[17]). It contains eighty-five

---

[6] José Carlos Martín-Iglesias, *Isidoro de Sevilla († 636): obra y memoria*, via: https://fil.ug.edu.pl/sites/default/files/_nodes/strona-filologiczny/73250/files/martin-iglesias_isidoro_de_sevilla.pdf [access 15 XI 2019], 1-3.

[7] J. Fontaine, *Isidore de Séville. Genèse et originalité de la culture hispanique au temps des Wisigoths* (Turnhout, 2001), 101.

[8] *Id.*, *Isidore de Séville et la culture classique dans l'Espagne wisigothique*, I (Paris, 1959-83), 7-8; Pierre Riché, *Edukacja i kultura w Europie Zachodniej (VI-VIII w.)* (Warszawa, 1995), 307-38.

[9] J. Fontaine, *Isidore de Séville et la culture* (1959), 8; M.C. Díaz y Díaz, 'Introducción' (1982), 182-3.

[10] P. Riché, *Edukacja* (1995), 127.

[11] Isidorus Hispalensis, *Sententiae* III 8-12.

[12] *Ibid.* III 14; P. Riché, *Edukacja* (1995), 120-30.

[13] Henri-Irénée Marrou, *Historia wychowania w starożytności* (Warszawa, 1969), 437-8.

[14] T. Krynicka, 'Literacki charakter botanicznej wiedzy Izydora z Sewilli: *Etymologie*, księga XVII', *SCN* 9 (2010), 23-36, 23.

[15] María Adelaida Andrés Sanz, 'Bibliothecam compilavit: La Bible d'Isidore de Séville', *Connaissance des Pères de l'Église* 142 (2016), 37-50, 42-4; Anna Ledzińska, *Gramatyka wobec sztuk wyzwolonych w pismach Izydora z Sewilli. Origo et fundamentum liberalium litterarum* (Kraków, 2014), 56-7, 71-2, 86-9; T. Krynicka, *Izydor z Sewilli* (Kraków, 2007), 35-6.

[16] I quote, translate and analyse the text using the following edition: Isidoro de Sevilla, *De ortu et obitu patrum. Vida y muerte de los santos*, ed. César Chaparro Gómez (Paris, 1985).

[17] Isidorus Hispalensis, *De ortu et obitu patrum*, PL 83, 129-56.

biographies of outstanding biblical figures, from the forefather Adam to Titus, the disciple of Saint Paul.[18] Explaining what the treatise offered to readers, and what the purpose of its composition is, Isidore writes in the preface:

Quorundam sanctorum nobillisimorumque virorum ortus vel gesta cum genealogiis suis in hoc libello indita sunt; dignitas quoque et mors eorum atque sepultura sententiali brevitate notata. Qua, quamvis omnia nota sint qui per amplitudinem Scripturarum percurrunt, facilius tamen ad memoriam redeunt, dum brevi sermone leguntur.[19]

According to what has been announced in the titles[20] and in the quoted introduction, the author describes the ancestry (*ortus*), virtues and achievements (*vita*) and circumstances surrounding the death and burial of the heroes (*obitus*), among which we find patriarchs, judges, kings, prophets, the Lord's apostles and pupils. His descriptions tend to praise the heroes through demonstrating them as persons worthy of being imitated. Isidore strives not only to consolidate and complete his readers' knowledge of the Holy Scripture, but to show them how to live their everyday lives just as the famous biblical heroes did, serving God and trusting Him. In order to achieve these goals, he composes laudatory descriptions pervaded by an exceptional sense of thought and emotion; colourful, but, at the same time, succinct, imbued, as the Sevillian himself says, with a sentential conciseness. It is precisely the composition of the analysed treatise's individual descriptions that is studied in this article.

The Sevillian achieves the aforementioned conciseness by resorting to certain syntactic solutions. His compound (usually complex) sentences are predominantly coordinate, less frequently subordinate, and, due to this, close to the spoken language with its vivid, unforced and unaffected tone. The asyndeton that speeds up the pace of the phrases is quite frequent, although not regular. The following fragments are examples:

Namque avem misit, redeuntem sustenuit, sed perfida fraude corvi decipitur, merito columbae gestantis ore ramum paciferum educitur. Reseratisque foribus arcae, bestias cunctaque animantia per septem dies abire permittens, ipse postmodum egressus cum liberis, Deum conlaudat et laetus victimas immolat; cuius arcam veteres sedisse testantur in Armeniam super montes Ararath.[21]

Ruben primitivus filius Israhel, aetate fratribus maior sed posteritatis numero minor; paternum torum polluit atque ordinem primogenitae dignitatis amisit.[22]

---

[18] T. Krynicka, *Izydor* (2007), 36-8.

[19] Isidorus Hispalensis, *De ortu et obitu patrum*, Praefatio.

[20] In the manuscripts, the treatise has different titles: *Isidori Hispalensis Episcopi Vita vel obitus sanctorum qui in Domino praecesserunt*; *Incipit ortus, vita vel obitus sanctorum patrum, qui in scripturarum laudibus efferuntur*; *De ortu et obitu patrum*.

[21] Isidorus Hispalensis, *De ortu et obitu patrum* IV 2.

[22] *Ibid.* XII.

Single sentences are often semantically enriched by constructions that are substituted for (1) subordinate substantive clauses (*accusativus cum infinitivo*) or (2) subordinate clauses describing circumstances (time, condition, cause, concession) relative to the action of the main sentence; gramatically and semantically, they are independent of the latter (*ablativus absolutus*). Beyond this, Isidore frequently deploys (3) participles as predicates (so called *participia coniuncta*) instead of *verba finita*. Their use leads to the replacement of subordinate clauses of circumstances (time, condition, cause, concession) by adverbial clauses. The latter transmits information in a more economical way, because it serves in its entirety – as if it were just one adverb – to modify the verb of the main clause.[23] It is worth pointing out that in some biblical heroes' descriptions, Isidore uses only *participia coniuncta* (4). The following fragments illustrate this:

1.
Hunc esse aiunt Hebraei Sem primogenitum Noe, triavum Abrahae.[24]
Hunc Hebraei adserunt non fuisse de genere Esau, sed de Nachor fratris Abraham discendisse stirpe et fuisse eum temporibus patriarcharum.[25]
Tradunt Hebraei hunc esse filium viduae, quem a mortuis resuscitavit Helias.[26]

2.
Amissaque immortalitate in pulverem [...] post cursum annorum nongentorum triginta rediit.[27]
Emensisque centum quadraginta et septem annis, naturae reddidit obitum.[28]
Exactisque aetatis centum decem annis [...] diem ultimum clausit.[29]

3.
Hic Abraham revertentem post victoriam benedixit.[30]
Iaddo, in Samaria natus; hic est qui ad Hieroboam immolantem vitulis missus in sermone Domini venit eumque arguit immolantem. Hunc ad propria revertentem leo in via strangulavit.[31]

4.
Levi, sacerdotalis auctor originis, cum tribu Iuda permixtione generis iunctus sed in Israhel totus divisus; carens propriae sortis funiculum et habitans in universis sceptris fratrum.[32]

---

[23] Hubert Wolanin, *Gramatyka opisowa klasycznej łaciny w ujęciu strukturalnym* (Kraków, 2012), 456-7, 779-90.
[24] Isidorus Hispalensis, *De ortu et obitu patrum* V 1.
[25] *Ibid.* XXIV 3.
[26] *Ibid.* XLV 2.
[27] *Ibid.* I.
[28] *Ibid.* VIII.
[29] *Ibid.* X.
[30] *Ibid.* V.
[31] *Ibid.* LV.
[32] *Ibid.* XIV.

Dan, cuius ex germine Samson, sceptrum tenens Israhel, fortis nazareus et triumphator in hostibus, obsidens in morem serpentis Philistinorum semitas et equitatum eius ut regulus spiritu oris sui depopulans.[33]
Aser, divitiis insignis, replens deliciis principes.[34]

It is worth noting that the very syntactic constructions applied by Isidore help him to draw the recipient's attention to the theological content and to create the intended atmosphere of laudation. For example, when describing Abraham's extraordinary virtues he uses consecutive clauses. They are introduced by the subordinate conjunction *ut* and, in the main clauses, accompanied by the correlative words *eo* and *adeo* that indicate the high extent or intensity of the presented person's quality or activity. This construction sounds solemn and evokes in the recipient's mind a feeling of admiration, thus creating an additional praising effect:

Abraham fuit eo summus, ut Trinitatem in typo videret et unitatem in mysterio veneraret; eo fidelis, ut in promisso germine contra spem naturae Deo crederet; adeo iustus atque devotus, ut indulgentiam unici pignoris divinitati non praeponeret, sed incunctanter praecepti parens religiosus parricida gladio dexteram armaret.[35]

Furthermore, Isidore constantly bears in mind that the analysed text is meant to be read aloud, and therefore its recipient is primarily a listener, not a reader. This is why he tends to begin the successive segments of presentations by repeating the same relative or demonstrative pronouns. Let us observe that the latter not only organises the text by signalising the commencement of a new segment, but also enriches the story with a certain dose of fitting emphasis. Moreover, they not only point out the subject, but also, in a certain sense, bring him closer to the recipients, as they replace his exotic Hebrew name. The following examples clarify these observations:

(1) *Isaac filius Abrahae [...] qui excludentes non armis sed patientia vicit, qui poenitentes cum bonitate recepit; qui per timorem Dei eo usque detulit honorem parenti, ut ad aram sponte sacrificandus accederet atque in figura Christi mortem non recusaret.*[36]

(2) *Iacob filius Isaac [...] Hic tamen, postquam primogeniti benedictionem praeripuit, matri oboedivit et fraternae iracundiae patienter cessit, patriamque et parentes relinquens, exsul effectus servitutem longam sustenuit; laborem famis et frigoris pertulit, servivit socero, ut pastor mercenarius pavit gregem, expectans non de divisione sed de gregis lucro mercedem. Hic autem Domino conluctatus praevaluit, hic facie ad faciem Deum vidit, hic famis inopia pulsus cum praeclara progenie ingressus est Aegyptum.*[37]

[33] *Ibid.* XVII.
[34] *Ibid.* XIX.
[35] *Ibid.* VI 2.
[36] *Ibid.* VII.
[37] *Ibid.* VIII.

However, more often, while tending to provide conciseness of expression, the Sevillian employs nominal phrases. In the analysed text, we find numerous grammatical constructions in which several elements (normally two nouns, a noun and an adjective, a noun and a pronoun, a noun and a prepositional phrase) are placed side by side, in apposition to each other. One of them, called the head or the nucleus of the nominal phrase, determines the syntactic category of the phrase, and rules the other, the so-called dependent. As the latter serves to modify the head noun, it is also called a modifier (or an adnominal). Describing the head in different ways, the adnominal thus fulfills the function of an attribute. It agrees with the nucleus in case, and generally tends to agree with it in gender and number, whenever this is possible. Therefore, both nouns remain in the connection of agreement, the closest of all possible grammatic connections. Similarly when it comes to the reference, as they have, or represent, together, the same designation, the described head noun and the modifier describing it are strictly united. Therefore, the whole nominal phrase can be replaced by one pronoun, for example *Adam protoplastus*[38] can be substituted by *is* (= *Adam*).

The reader's impression of dealing with a highly concentrated text is additionally strengthened by the fact that, in Isidore's treatise, adnominals conspicuously frequently constitute the nuclei of further nominal syntactic groups, either simple (consisting of one described and one describing element) or composed (consisting of one described and more than one describing elements). The single elements of the abovementioned words' clusters are also connected between themselves by an attributive tie. This can be strict, when the modifier is constituted by an adjective, a possessive pronoun, a participle, or semistrict, when it connects two nouns being in apposition to each other or a noun followed by a prepositional phrase. Regardless of the type of the words' clusters, the syntactic relationships occuring between its elements unite them into a new semantic unity.[39] The series of syntactic groups formed as a result of that stringing together of subsequent words as described above serve to modify the first head noun and can be reduced to same.[40] For example, the abovementioned *Adam* can replace *protoplastus et colonus paradisi, princeps generis et delicti, ad imaginem Dei factus, universitatis praelatus*;[41] *eius* (= *maris*) can replace *maris magni, is* (= *possessor*) can replace *possessor maris magni et litorum, in eis* (= *in urbibus*) can replace *in cunctis urbibus Sidonum, is* (= *dominus*) can replace *dominus in cunctis urbibus Sidonum* and, finally, *is* (= *Zabulon*) can be substituted for all of them: *Zabulon possessor maris magni et litorum et dominus in*

---

[38] *Ibid.* I 1.

[39] Michał Kaczmarkowski, *Nominalne grupy syntaktyczne łaciny okresu klasycznego* (Lublin, 1985), 53-6.

[40] *Ibid.* 42.

[41] Isidorus Hispalensis, *De ortu et obitu patrum* I 1.

cunctis urbibus Sidonum.[42] As a result, a sentence in which there are numerous nominal phrases seems to be extremely tightly welded together.

In line with Isidore's intentions, separate modifiers should evoke – like keywords – the whole stories from the described person's life, as well as make the reader visualise the details. Furthermore, the modifiers enrich the text with an abundance of allusions, stimulate the recipient's memory and imagination, empathy and senses. Connected to the prevailing head noun and to each other, the modifiers create an extremely dense network of semantic connections. Due to this, the image of the hero being described comes into being in the recipient's mind. This image is coherent, although multifaceted. It can be compared to a multiple portrait, composed of numerous modifiers, which, like single shots, focus on various features and deeds of the figure portrayed, seen somehow from a new point of view. Every new shot is different to the previous one, but firmly embedded in the whole picture. Isidore's description of Abel, which proves these conclusions, is set out below.[43]

 1 *Abel*
 2 *filius Adam*
 3 *et pastor ovium,*
 4 *in vita innocens,*
 5 *in morte patiens,*
 6 *post mortem non silens,*
 7 *in martyrio primus,*
 8 *in oboedientia summus,*
 9 *in sacrificiis Dei placens,*
10 *in meritis fratri displicens;*
              11 *quem*
12 *Cain*
13 *impius*
14 *et parricida novus,*
15 *ira stimulante invidiae,*
              16 *innocuum*
17 *ferro nondum sanguine maculato prostravit,*
18 *quum adhuc innocens ferrum cruoris humanum facinus non haberet.*[44]

In the description of Abel we can distinguish three parts. In the first (1.-10.), Isidore presents mankind's first martyr in the manner of those icon painters who tend to show the whole terrestrial life and posthumous deeds of the saint on one canvas. When describing Abel's destiny from the moment of his birth (2.) till his postmortem miracle (6.), he employs nine nominal groups, all of

---

[42] *Ibid.* XV.

[43] The division into segments and their numeration comes from the author of the article, and are meant to serve in the carrying out of the analysis of the quoted text.

[44] Isidorus Hispalensis, *De ortu et obitu patrum* II.

which modify the noun *Abel* (Noun) and depend on it. They follow the subsequent patterns:

1. Noun 2. noun + noun
[Noun] 3. noun + noun
[Noun] 4. prepositional phrase + adjective
[Noun] 5. prepositional phrase + participle
[Noun] 6. prepositional phrase + participle
[Noun] 7. prepositional phrase + ordinal number
[Noun] 8. prepositional phrase + adjective
[Noun] 9. prepositional phrase + noun + participle
[Noun] 10. prepositional phrase + noun + participle

It must be noted that the 4.-8. and 9.-10. sections are built on the basis of parallelism. Some of their elements are repeated (such as the preposition *in* which opens all the sections except 6.; the nouns *morte* and *mortem* that are placed as the second of three elements in sections 5.-6.), while others are made up of words with the same endings (*innocens – patiens, Dei – fratri*, 4.-5., 9.-10.). This leads to internal rhymes that ensure consistency and the chanting tone of the text, as well as facilitating its reception and contributing to its coherence. For the sake of the latter purpose, the Sevillian links seven of the nine nominal groups asyndetically (with the exception of 2. and 3.). Let us observe that, due to the use of antithesis, he introduces a strong contradictory tension between the elements connected by homoioteleutons: *primus – summus, placens – displicens* (7.-8., 9.-10.), as well as between the similarly sounding and identically placed *in vita – in morte* (4.-5.).

The second part (11.-17.) consists of one relative clause and is dedicated to the circumstances of the hero's death. It begins with the relative pronoun *quem*, which refers to Abel and thus introduces the entire content of the first part into the second one, enriching the latter's message and, at the same time, binding both of them firmly together. The Sevillian names the murderer (the subject of clause 12.) and briefly characterises him (two attributes connected with *et*, consists of an adjective and a nominal group (noun + adjective), 13.-14.). Then, he explains the cause of Cain's crime (*ablativus absolutus* and an adjective which modifies the noun that constitutes it, together with a present active participle; the construction replaces a subordinate reason clause, 15.) and, once again, underlines the martyr's innocence (11.-16., the emphasis placed on these two words is enhanced by the similarity of their endings (*quem innocuum*) and by the insertion of eight words (seven full words and one conjunction) between them (12.-15.). Furthermore, he speaks about the way of killing Abel, deploying the first in the analysed fragment *verbum finitum* and quoting Ovid's summary of Pythagoras' doctrine[45] to describe the murder weapon (17.).

---

[45] Publius Ovidius Naso, *Metamorphoses*, XV 60-478, esp. 107: *maculatum sanguine ferrum.*

The latter becomes the subject of the last, third part of the description. It consists of a subordinate reason clause introduced by *quum causale* (18.). According to the Sevillian, Cain killed his brother not with an animal's jaw-bone, as was often imagined in later epochs,[46] but with a tool of iron (*ferrum*). César Chaparro Gómez suggests that, by using this word, Isidore follows Prudentius[47] and means an indispensable tool to a farmer who tilled soil (*cf. Gen.* 4:2), namely a hoe (*sarculus*).[48] However, taking into consideration the abovementioned Ovidian reminiscence, it may be assumed that the Sevillian is speaking about an iron weapon (a sword – *gladius*, a spear – *hasta*, a metal-tipped pole – *trudis*)[49] that could be used to kill a living creature. Isidore also draws the reader's attention to *ferrum* at the level of sound. As a true master of all kinds of alliteration, he makes this the key-noun of the analysed description of sound in *facinus*; *cruoris*, *haberet*; *quum* and *humanum* (18.). It should be pointed out that when Isidore devotes a whole sentence to the murderer's tool, he does not act haphazardly nor follows a whim by breaking the principle of conciseness. He consciously stresses the integrity of *ferrum*, which, before Cain's crime, was as immaculate as the first martyr, Abel, himself: both of them appear in the Sevillian's treatise accompanied by the same attribute *innocens* (17.). In this way, the tool's description expresses the erudite bishop's longing for a world in which there is no cruelty nor bloodshed, reminding us that it is human sin that pollutes God's creation, as well as – or, perhaps, primarily – serving to characterise the presented hero. Isidore makes the reader aware that Abel was the most innocent of all human beings and suggests that, by killing his brother, Cain destroyed the whole of creature's guiltlessness. All of this, the Sevillian transmits in just two lines of the cited edition of the text.

In the preface to the analysed treatise quoted above, Isidore underlines the fact that he is going to present the scriptural heroes in a laconic way: *sententiali brevitate* (with a sententional conciseness), *brevi sermone* (in a short tale). As a matter of fact, his readers may come to the conclusion that, against the background of the rich tradition of ancient biography, *De ortu et obitu patrum* is distinguished due to its author's admirable skill of encapsulating extraordinary rich and various content in very few words. The treatise, once again, proves the Sevillian to be not only a great teacher and tutor for generations of European readers, but also a master of Latin prose.

---

[46] Christopher Scheirer, 'The Slaying of Abel in Apocryphal Tradition', in *Medieval Studies Research Blog: Meet Us At the Crossroads of Everything*, via: https://sites.nd.edu/manuscript-studies/2015/04/09/the-slaying-of-abel-in-apocryphal-tradition/ [access 17/11/2019]; Alphons Augustinus Barb, 'Cain's Murder-Weapon and Samson' Jawbone of an Ass', *Journal of the Warburg and Courtauld Institutes* 35 (1972), 386-9.

[47] C. Chaparro Gómez, *De ortu* (1985), 113.

[48] Prudentius, *Hamartigenia*, Praefatio 14-21.

[49] Isidorus Hispalensis, *Etymologiae* XVIII 6-7.

Oriental Exegesis
Based on the Example of the Argumentation Used in
The Disputation of Sergius the Stylite Against a Jew

Jan W. Żelazny, Cracow, Poland

ABSTRACT

This article focuses on the versions of a Biblical text and its adaptation for a discussion with a Jew. It would seem that the text which was treated in such a specific way constituted the author's own exegesis, which manifests itself not so much in comments, but rather in the paraphrasing and the choosing of consecutive fragments adapted for the discussion. It is not about forgery or misuse, but more about the form of narration, which, at the same time, clarifies the text and places it in the context of the whole Bible and the faith of Sergius. The textual changes are dictated by hermeneutical principles, in which both the truth about the Word and a typological approach towards scriptural data come to the forefront. The absence of some translations of the Bible and the reference to testimonies give us a better understanding of both the man conducting the dialogue and the environment in which he lived.

It is difficult to discuss the entire oriental exegesis in only one presentation. I therefore refer the reader to the – still – only study on this issue, in the form of the lectures recorded by Sabino Chialà at Studium Biblicum Franciscanum in Jerusalem, published under the title *La perla dai molti riflessi*.[1] One of the characteristic elements of this exegesis is the approach to the text of the Holy Bible, the multiplicity of versions and the specific exegesis which consists of a biblical story in which the interpretation is introduced through additions and omissions; in other words, in which the biblical text is paraphrased, and the manner of this paraphrase constitutes its exegesis. In this presentation, based on the work analysed, I want to address the exegesis in respect to this.

The analysed text dates from the 8th century and is preserved in one manuscript. It was published along with an English translation in 1973 by CSCO in volumes 152 and 153 of the *Scriptores Syri* series.[2]

---

[1] Sabino Chiala, *La perla dai molti riflessi* (Magnano, 2014). See Sebastian Brock, *The Bible in the Syriac tradition* (Kottayam, 1988), 54-61.

[2] *The disputation of Sergius the Stylite against a Jew*, ed. A.P. Hayman, CSCO 338, 339 tr. (Louvain, 1973).

The heading contains the following information: *The letter of Blessed Sergius the Stylite of Gousit, which was composed by him against a Jew who contended that God has no son, and (that) God has not begotten.*[3] To this day, it has not been established whether the text is purely literary or whether it is a record of an actual debate that took place between the monk and a Jew. Both interlocutors are actually unknown to us. Summing up the disputation, Hayman comes to the conclusion that the treatise is a literary transformation of a real debate, supplemented with some passages quoting longer biblical texts in a form known from similar apologetic literature preserved from that time. This is important for our considerations regarding the text of the Holy Bible used in the treatise, as it is not known to what extent specific versions were widely known.

1. Syrian translations of the Bible available in the eighth century

During this period, several versions of the biblical text were used in the circle of Oriental Christians. The origin of the Old Testament translation was different from the origin of the translation of the New Testament.[4] The Hebrew Bible was initially translated from the original language and the oldest one, *i.e.* the Vetus Syra, probably dates back to the early 2nd/early 3rd century AD,[5] although the Vetus Syra itself was created over many years and there is no one single author or single creation environment. It is the work of Jewish communities, perhaps from around Edessa and Nisibis, a work that was adopted by Syrian Christians.

In the fifth century, before the split in the Oriental Church into a Syriac Orthodox Church and an Oriental Church, the entire Bible was revised, and in this form the text of the Holy Scriptures was adopted for liturgical use in both communities. We know this text as the Peshitta.

In the years 614-616 in Alexandria, Bishop Paul of Tella translated the Old Testament from the Septuagint. This is a Greek translation. The work of Paul of Tella, known as Syro-Hexapla, was not intended for liturgical use, although in some Syriac Orthodox Churches it is still used today during some services. It was known to a wider audience, not only in Syriac Orthodox Churches, and enjoyed a certain recognition, as evidenced by the fact that Patriarch Timothy I copied it at the turn of the eighth and ninth centuries. We have many manuscripts of this translation, although they do not contain a complete Bible translation, since all fragments of the Pentateuch or Historical Books have not been completely preserved.[6]

---

[3] *The disputation of Sergius the Stylite against a Jew*, tr. A.P. Hayman, CSCO 339 (Louvain, 1973), 1.

[4] Sebastian Brock, *The Bible in the Syriac Tradition* (Kottayam, 1988), 13-6.

[5] *Ibid.*, 13.

[6] *Ibid.*, 23-4.

In the circle of the Syriac Orthodox Church, the Philoxenian version of the Bible was also created, named after Philoxenus of Mabbug (†523), who, according to many researchers, wrote it.[7] Fragments of this text have been preserved. At the same time, a version by Thomas of Harkleia was created. Another attempt was made by Jacob of Edessa (†708), based on both the Septuagint and the Peshitta. It should be remembered that the latter translations were not very popular, especially among Oriental Christians.[8]

In addition to those texts prepared for liturgical use, there were also manuscripts whose purpose was different. Apart from the text of the entire books, there were thematic excerpts, including the so-called *Testimonia*. They were widespread, both during the polemic with the Jews, which took place in this Church up until modern times, as well as during the period of violent Christological disputes, which divided, and still divide, Oriental communities. For the needs of argumentation, key fragments of biblical texts, according to the antagonists, were prepared, along with comments.

2. Versions of the biblical text used in *The Disputation*

The quotes and paraphrases of the Bible present in *The Disputation* can be divided into four basic groups.[9] According to the publisher of the text, 130 quotes (the majority) out of about 300 come from the Peshitta. A few of them are so long that they are unlikely to be memorised quotes, but were rather copied.

The next group consists of fragments probably from the so-called testimony texts, *i.e.* extracts from the Old Testament which were popular among the first Christians, showing announcements of newly testamentary events, and created for the purpose of polemics with Jews. Sometimes these texts are given just as they are quoted in the New Testament, while others are adapted to the New Testament in order to allow both Jesus and His mission to be shown as the fulfillment of the Law and the Prophets.

Some references are clearly memorised quotes. The differences between these and the Peshitta can be explained in many ways. There may be a mistake by the quoter, which is very likely in a real debate. Some differences may have been introduced by subsequent copyists. Finally, and this is probably the most interesting interpretation, some of them resulted from the exegetical method adopted by Sergius, in which the narrative of the text and its minor changes constituted a form of interpretation.

Four references, or allusions within them, refer to the Vetus Syra, the oldest translation of the Bible into Aramaic.

---

[7] *Ibid.*, 24, 30-2.

[8] *Ibid.*, 32.

[9] See Allison Peter Hayman, 'Introduction', in *The disputation of Sergius the Stylite against a Jew*, tr. A.P. Hayman, CSCO 339 (Louvain, 1973), 7*-9*.

We are interested in the presence of so many versions of the biblical text in one work. This does not seem to be by accident. What factors testify to this and how can it be explained?

3. The unity of the text and its interpretation in *The Disputation of Sergius the Stylite*

In the Judeo-Christian tradition, as Daniélou writes,[10] the text and its interpretation are intertwined. In the Semite's mind, the reader is an active element of the interpretation and the concept of objectivity known to us cannot apply. A literal reading in our sense gives way to what can be called the spiritual sense of the text, or its immediate application. The changes present in the text of *The Disputation*, such as the introduction of the future tense ('will come together') instead of the present perfect tense ('have come together') in *Ps.* 47:10, which permits the interpretation of the text as a prophecy regarding the future, allow the text to be Christianised.

Such changes are not an attempt to falsify the text, but to interpret and explain other passages. The New Testament writers acted in a similar manner and, as the analysed text shows, this tradition continued. Since almost 25% of the cited fragments are given as they were remembered, and they are a paraphrase of the text, we are dealing with a certain method of text exegesis.

Sometimes the interference is important, because it changes the meaning of the entire Bible. This is the case, for example, when Sergius, quoting Isaiah's prophecy (*Isa.* 48:16),[11] adds *His Word*. In this way, the text takes on Trinitarian overtones. Since, according to the Stylite, in the Bible God speaks in the unity of the Divine Persons from the very first verses, the wording about the Two (God and His Spirit) is supplemented with the Son. In this way, the textual differences show us not so much competitive variants of the text, as the possibilities of its interpretation.

Much more interesting, as Hayman points out, are the differences in the biblical text used in *The Disputation*, differences which are found in other anti-Judaic treatises. The publisher quotes six such citations present in *The Disputation* by Sergius, which offer a version of the text which is not consistent with the Peshitta, the Septuagint or the Masoretic text, and which are present in another work from those times, namely, *The Discussion of St. Sylvester with Jews at Rome.*[12] In his opinion, this testifies to the existence of the

---

[10] *Cf.* Jean Daniélou, *Études d'exégèse judéo-chrétienne*, Théologie Historique 5 (Paris, 1966).

[11] 'And now the Lord God has sent me, and his Spirit' in the text of Sergius is transformed into 'So now God sends me with His Word and His Spirit'. See *The disputation of Sergius the Stylite against a Jew* II, 5, CSCO 338, 5; CSCO 339, 6-7.

[12] See Zacharias Rhetor, *Historia Ecclesiastica*, ed. E.W. Brooks, CSCO 5, Scriptores Syri 5 (Paris, 1903-1905), 69-93.

aforementioned collection of biblical testimonies, in which this, and not another version of the inspired text, had been preserved, and which was used in debates with Jews.

4. The multiplicity of texts in exegesis

Sergius refers to some books of the Bible more than once. However, the versions he uses change. It seems that each time he is guided not so much by the principle that the end justifies the means, but by the conviction that the multitude of variants indicates different interpretative possibilities, opening further dimensions to the reader and listener of the Word, and indicating the meaning hidden in the text. The explanation of the Scripture is not simple, but complex. Moreover, his way of exegesis, which has a lot in common with diaspora Judaism, consists of paraphrasing the text, of creating collections of biblical quotes that combine fragments from various books of the Holy Bible. Not all of them meet today's rules of proving the exegesis of a text, but at that time they were accepted by both parties. In any case, although there is no sign in the text itself that Sergius the Stylite managed to convince his interlocutor, there is no objection from the one who is debating with him about the method of biblical proof. The debater did not agree with the conclusions of the quoted passages, rejected the arguments regarding the distinctions proposed by the Stylite (the prohibition of touching the bodies of dead people concerns the dead in the sense of the dead in sin, the prohibition of making images does not apply to symbols, etc.), but he did not question the biblical quotes appearing as confirmation, or the manner of linking them.

The preserved text is a testimony to how much the Bible and its study were at the centre of the Church's life. Also noteworthy is the knowledge of the Bible by Sergius the Stylite, and its use in the course of debate.

Another issue is the prevalence of the text known as the Peshitta. Most of the material collected in *The Disputation* comes from this. The other version, the Vetus Syra, is represented in a rudimentary way and, as far as the Philoxenian version, Thomas of Harchel's text and the Syro-Hexapla, created in the Syriac Orthodox environment, are concerned, there is no evidence that they were known. It is puzzling that, in the eighth century, testimonies containing old biblical texts and the Agrafa were present. Their content, along with the liturgical Peshitta, is the basis of the argumentation in the debate with the Jew.

Another issue is the use of various passages as a way of conducting exegesis, which, referring to the text and interpreting it typologically, remains deeply Semitic in its origin. Importantly, Sergius allows for the complexity of the inspired text.

PRINTED ON PERMANENT PAPER • IMPRIME SUR PAPIER PERMANENT • GEDRUKT OP DUURZAAM PAPIER - ISO 9706

N.V. PEETERS S.A., WAROTSTRAAT 50, B-3020 HERENT